After the end

Manchester University Press

After the end

Cold War culture and
apocalyptic imaginations in
the twenty-first century

David L. Pike

MANCHESTER UNIVERSITY PRESS

Copyright © David L. Pike 2024

The right of David L. Pike to be identified as the author of this work has been asserted in accordance with the Copyright, Designs and Patents Act 1988.

Published by Manchester University Press
Oxford Road, Manchester, M13 9PL
www.manchesteruniversitypress.co.uk

British Library Cataloguing-in-Publication Data
A catalogue record for this book is available from the British Library

ISBN   978 1 5261 7404 8   hardback

First published 2024

The publisher has no responsibility for the persistence or accuracy of URLs for any external or third-party internet websites referred to in this book, and does not guarantee that any content on such websites is, or will remain, accurate or appropriate.

Typeset
by New Best-set Typesetters Ltd

For my parents

Contents

List of figures and plates	*page* viii
Preface	xix
Acknowledgments	xxiii
List of abbreviations	xxviii
Introduction: After the imminent apocalypse: the bunker fantasy since the Cold War	1
1 The fantasy of 1980s survivalism since the Reagan years	22
2 *Survivance* in fictions of survivalism since the Reagan years	50
3 The hedgehog, the tortoise, and the world: Switzerland, Albania, and the global bunker fantasy	90
4 Life in the ontological bunker: Cold War continuance, appropriation, and repurposing from America to Taiwan	137
5 Writing from the epistemological bunker: fictions of postnuclear apocalypse	191
6 Wall and tunnel: security, containment, and subversion	224
Conclusion: Biosecurity, siloing, and the legacies of a shelter society	273
Select Bibliography	294
Index	310

List of figures and plates

Figures

P.1 Neville (Will Smith) and his dog Samantha on their way to an East Village video store in a postapocalyptic Manhattan shot on location in 2006–07. Video frame grab from *I Am Legend*. Dir. Francis Lawrence. Dist. Warner Bros. Pictures, 2007. *page* xx

I.1 Sartaj Singh (Saif Ali Khan) negotiating with the bunker in Mumbai in *Sacred Games*, ep. 1.1. Netflix, 2019. 13

I.2 'Every golden age must be preceded by an apocalypse': the multilingual fantasy of '*pralay, qayamat*, apocalypse' in *Sacred Games*, ep. 2.8. Netflix, 2019. 13

I.3 Waiting for the end of the world: the deserted streets of Melbourne, Australia, at the end of the slow death of the world from nuclear war in the north. Video frame grab from *On the Beach*. Dir. Stanley Kramer. Dist. United Artists, 1959. 16

1.1 From Stewart Brand's pages in the first *Whole Earth Catalog* on Drop City: 'a rural vacant lot full of elegant funky domes and ditto people.' Brand, *Whole Earth Catalog: Access to Tools* (San Rafael, CA: Point Foundation, 1998 [1968]), 15. Permission of the author. 28

1.2 Cresson Kearny's cheery DIY update of family survivalism in the backyard shelter: 'This family completed their Protection Factor 200 (PF 200) fallout shelter, a Door-Covered Trench Shelter with 2 feet of earth on its roof, 34 hours after receiving the building instructions at their home.' Kearny, *Nuclear War Survival Skills* (1979). Updated and expanded 1987 edition. Cave Junction, Oregon: Oregon Institute of

List of figures and plates ix

Science and Medicine, 2004. np. Copyright © 1986 by Cresson H. Kearny. 32

1.3 Early 1960s paternalism alive and well in the 1980s: 'Two non-athletic college girls who completed a 4-person Pole-Covered Trench Shelter in 35 ½ hours, despite tree roots.' Kearny, *Nuclear War Survival Skills*, np. Copyright © 1986 by Cresson H. Kearny. 32

1.4 An easy chair softens the long wait for the end: the managing partner of the group shelter built in the late 1980s by followers of Elizabeth Clare Prophet's Church Universal and Triumphant. *Charlie Hull's Shelter, Emigrant, Montana, 2003.* Photo by Richard Ross. Permission of the artist. 37

1.5 Survivalists out of their natural element: the countercultural family in a culture clash with the twenty-first century. The younger children's costumes heighten both the alien and the retro context – especially the gas mask. Video frame grab from *Captain Fantastic*. Dir. Matt Ross. Dist. Bleecker Street, 2016. 38

1.6 Self-proclaimed survivalist Doug Huffman demonstrates one of the many camouflaged 'spider holes' scattered across his rural California compound. Video frame grab from *Doomsday Preppers*, season 1, ep. 7. National Geographic Channel. Originally aired 13 March 2012. 43

1.7 Collective survivalism, Canadian style. Retired scientist Bruce Beach and two grandchildren set to work on improvements to 'Ark 2.' Video frame grab from *Doomsday Preppers* season 1, ep. 8. National Geographic Channel. Originally aired 27 March 2012. 45

2.1 The modern family, masked, prepped, and trapped in Curtis LaForche's rudimentary backyard shelter. Video frame grab from *Take Shelter*. Wr. and dir. Jeff Nichols. Sony Picture Classics, 2011. 57

2.2 The ambiguous status of Howard Stambler's (John Goodman) bunker: the room Michelle (Mary Elizabeth Winstead) is handcuffed to at night, and her imagination of the fallout shelter. Video frame grab from *10 Cloverfield Lane*. Dir. Dan Trachtenberg. Paramount Pictures, 2016. 61

2.3 The ambiguous status of Howard Stambler's bunker: the common space and his imagination of the fallout shelter.

| | Video frame grab from *10 Cloverfield Lane*. Dir. Dan Trachtenberg. Paramount Pictures, 2016. | 61 |

2.4 Empowered by the ambiguous bunker: the hazmat suit that Michelle believes is necessary for her to survive aboveground, made from a book in Stambler's shelter library. Video frame grab from *10 Cloverfield Lane*. Dir. Dan Trachtenberg. Paramount Pictures, 2016. 62

2.5 Cyndee Pokorny (Sara Chase) in the ontological BunCo: the challenges of emerging from the bunker. Video frame grab from 'Kimmy and the Trolley Problem!' *Unbreakable Kimmy Schmidt*, season 3, ep. 12. Netflix, 19 May 2017. 67

2.6 'It's all still here.' Cyndee (left) and Kimmy Schmidt (Elle Kemper, right) experience the wonder and the horror of emerging from bunker captivity. Video frame grab from the opening credit sequence to *Unbreakable Kimmy Schmidt*. Netflix, 2015–19. 68

2.7 Revisionary patriotism and shelter as trap: playacting war as seduction or as rape, depending on the decade and the perspective. Louis (Peter Frechette) and Sharon (Maureen Teefy) sing 'Let's Do It for Our Country' in a backyard fallout shelter. Video frame grab from *Grease 2*. Dir. Patricia Birch. Dist. Paramount Pictures, 1982. 69

2.8 Revisionary patriotism and shelter as trap: the father (Ed McMahon) of teen werewolf Tony (Adam Arkin) seeks refuge in the icons of his vanishing world: Joseph McCarthy, a hunting rifle, and a well-stocked fallout shelter. He will soon die from the architecture of his time when the rifle shot aimed at his son ricochets around the Quonset hut. Video frame grab from *Full Moon High*. Wr. and dir. Larry Cohen. Dist. Filmways Pictures, 1981. 70

2.9 It takes one to know one: Cold War huckster Lawrence Woolsey (John Goodman) shows what the sheltering craze was really made of in Joe Dante's homage to atomic spectacle and blinkered politics. Video frame grab from *Matinee*. Dist. Universal Pictures, 1993. 72

2.10 The galactic housewife (Sissy Spacek) shopping in her husband's bunkered vision of a 1962 stuck in time. Video frame grab from *Blast from the Past*. Dir. Hugh Wilson. Dist. New Line Cinema, 1999. 74

List of figures and plates xi

2.11 1962 appropriated for the coming twenty-first century:
the final incarnation of the lot above the bunker
renovates its concept as a retro-futurist diner. Video
frame grab from *Blast from the Past*. Dir. Hugh Wilson.
Dist. New Line Cinema, 1999. 76

2.12 The impending end to the Cold War promise of endless
plenty in Grandma's pantry. Video frame grab from
Shelf Life. Dir. Paul Bartel. Dist. Northern Arts
Entertainment, 1994. 77

2.13 The concluding surprise of emergence into an unknown
but essentially comic and open future. Video frame grab
from *Shelf Life*. Dir. Paul Bartel. Dist. Northern Arts
Entertainment, 1994. 78

2.14 Survivance and nuclear tourism: the unintended irony of
an atomic ruin as World Heritage Site. 'Genbaku Dome
(Atomic Bomb Dome) with World Heritage Site plaque
in foreground. Hiroshima Peace Memorial Park, 26 Oct.
2010.' Judy Bellah / Alamy Stock Photo. 84

3.1 Map showing artillery placements on Kinmen and Little
Kinmen Islands. Information panel, Mount Lion
Artillery Front, Kinmen Island. Photo by author, 2012. 95

3.2 Map showing artillery placements on Kinmen and Little
Kinmen Islands. Kinmen is at the convergence of the
lines from Taiwan, demarcated from the mainland by a
gray line. Information panel, Mount Lion Artillery
Front, Kinmen Island. Photo by author, 2012. 96

3.3 So near, but only birds, bullets, and propaganda can
travel between Kinmen and the mainland. Video frame
grab from *Paradise in Service / Jun Zhong Le Yuan*. Dir.
Doze Niu. Hontu Productions / Atom Cinema, 2014. 98

3.4 Exterior bunker linked to tunnels beneath Qongling
Village, Kinmen. Photo by author, 2012. 98

3.5 'Combat village' tunnel excavated beneath their homes
by the inhabitants of Qongling Village, Kinmen. The
villagers now provide tours of the homemade
fortifications. Photo by author, 2012. 99

3.6 'La Suisse Vigilante,' popularly known as *Le Hérisson*
('The Hedgehog'), the Swiss Army Pavilion at the
National Exposition in Lausanne, 1964. ETH-Bibliothek
Zürich, Bildarchiv / Fotograf: Comet Photo AG (Zürich)
/ Com_BC25-004-016 / CC BY-SA 4.0. http://
doi.org/10.3932/ethz-a-000264830. 107

xii *List of figures and plates*

3.7 The 'proud owner' shows off his state-of-the-art shelter. 'Near Andelfingen, Switzerland, 2003.' Photo by Richard Ross. Permission of the artist. 108

3.8 'Keep your eyes open. You may see something': an entrance to the *gruyère* hidden in plain sight on public land not far from Saint-Maurice, Valais, Switzerland. Photo by author, 2011. 118

3.9 And they will also see you … Not long after taking these photos, the author was informed by a passerby that photos were not allowed. Close-up of entrance to tunnel deep into the mountain, informing of the presence of closed-circuit surveillance. Photo by author, 2011. 119

3.10 'Bunkerizing' everyday life in Hoxha's Albania. Video frame grab from *Kolonel Bunker*. Dir. Kujtim Çashku, 1996. 127

3.11 The foreboding entrance in the showpiece kitchen to the basement concealing a deep-level nuclear bunker in the modernist home in Seoul, South Korea, at the center of the action in Bong Joon-ho's 2019 film *Parasite*. Video frame grab. 134

4.1 The antinuclear bunker displaced to the periphery of Mumbai, India. Video frame grab from *Sacred Games*, ep. 1.1. Netflix, 2019. 149

4.2 Sedan Crater, at 1,280 feet in diameter and 330 feet at its deepest, the largest of the hundreds of subsidence craters in Yucca Flat, created in 1962 by 'Operation Plowshare' to 'develop peaceful uses for nuclear weapons.' *Sedan Crater, Northern Part of Yucca Flat, Looking Southeast, Banded Mountains in the Distance, Nevada Test Site, 1996.* Photo by Emmet Gowin. Permission of the artist. 153

4.3 The dead-end spur leading to Mountain View, the 'impossible' American town in the middle of Siberia. Kyle Higgins (wr.) and Stephen Mooney (art), *The Dead Hand* #1 (Portland, OR: April 2018), 25. Permission of the artists. 156

4.4 The retro-contemporary exterior and static interior of the Soviet 'dead hand' facility Mountain View was created to guard. Higgins and Mooney, *The Dead Hand* #4 (Portland, OR: July 2018), 24. Permission of the artists. 157

List of figures and plates xiii

4.5   The ever-popular photo op of post–Cold War irony: a road sign for the Kelvedon Hatch Secret Nuclear Bunker, Brentwood, Essex, England, 5 Nov. 2011. Rick Strange / Alamy Stock Photo.   160

4.6   The communications room in the decommissioned Congressional fallout shelter, complete with explanatory panel, in the Greenbrier resort, White Sulphur Springs, West Virginia, Dec. 2012. Ian Patrick / Alamy Stock Photo.   161

4.7   The hidden face of nuclear tourism during the Cold War: 'Atomic Tour' bus. Video frame grab from *Hiroshima mon amour*. Wr. Marguerite Duras, dir. Alain Resnais. Dist. Pathé Films, 1959.   163

4.8   Nuclear tourists make their way to the Atomic Bomb Dome in the center background. Video frame grab from *Hiroshima mon amour*. Wr. Marguerite Duras, dir. Alain Resnais. Dist. Pathé Films, 1959.   163

4.9   Dwelling in a postapocalyptic landscape: one of the inhabitants who decided to return to their home in the Exclusion Zone. 'Woman living in the Chernobyl zone, Ukraine, monday Februrary [sic] 14th 2011.' Xavier Durand / Alamy Stock Photo.   166

4.10 The 'New Safe Confinement' that covers Reactor Number 4 in the radioactive heart of the Chornobyl Exclusion Zone, viewed through the new growth of a once urban region, 20 Sept. 2016. Konrad Zelazowski, agefotostock / Alamy Stock Photo.   167

4.11 High-tech conversion in a low-tech space. Jugon tunnel, formerly an underground hospital for Republic of China forces on Little Kinmen Island; now the Lieyu/Kinmen National Park Visitors Center. Photo by author, 2012.   169

4.12 A knifemaker converts spent shells from the PRC into kitchen implements in the Kinmen studio of Maestro Wu. Photo by author, 2012.   170

4.13 Marketing the vices of Tunnel 88: display window in the subterranean shop of the Matsu Distillery, in its present location on Nangan Island since 1970. Photo by author, 2012.   171

4.14 Tourists in Jhaishan Tunnel, Kinmen Island, where it opens to the sea. Photo by author, 2012.   171

4.15 The forbidding entrance to Felsenhotel La Claustra, Airolo, Switzerland. © La Claustra and BMI Invest Est.   173

xiv *List of figures and plates*

4.16 A banquet room inside the Felsenhotel La Claustra, Airolo Switzerland. © La Claustra and BMI Invest Est.   174

4.17 The separate entrance to the 292 m² space in the former air-raid shelter beneath the Haus der Kunst, Munich. The basement bunker was converted for exhibition in 2011 in collaboration with the Goetz Collection. Photo by author, 2011.   184

4.18 Bunker art on a Normandy beach, displaced in space and time by JR and Agnès Varda. Video frame grab from *Visages Villages* (*Faces Places*). Dir. Varda and JR. Dist. Le Pacte, 2017.   186

4.19 The bunker returned to its 'underground' identity. '"The Trendy Griboyedov Club," St. Petersburg, Russia, 2003.' Photo by Richard Ross. Permission of the artist.   187

5.1 Studying the wonders of the past, preserved in a pristine front-yard bunker. Video frame grab from *The Road*. Dir. John Hillcoat. Dist. Dimension Films, 2009.   192

5.2 Trying to look away from the wrong stuff of the bunker fantasy in the dark basement of a former plantation. Video frame grab from *The Road*. Dir. John Hillcoat. Dist. Dimension Films, 2009.   192

5.3 Leaving the bunker in a radical rejection of futurity and modernity as dictated by Brazil's military government. Video frame grab from *Abrigo Nuclear*. Sc. & dir. Roberto Pires. Dist. EMBRAFILME, 1981.   196

5.4 Worshipping the bomb: mutant priests reveal their 'true selves' to their thermonuclear god in *Beneath the Planet of the Apes*. Dir. Ted Post, sc. Paul Dehn. Dist. 20th Century Fox, 1970. Video frame grab.   215

5.5 Excavating for the distant future: the Onkalo spent nuclear fuel repository, Finland. Video frame grab from *Into Eternity: A Film for the Future*. Dir. Michael Madsen. Dist. Films Transit International, 2010.   220

6.1 Lovers separated by the grim reality of a separation wall: the original incarnation of the Berlin Wall, as reimagined in the 2001 German historical drama *Der Tunnel*. Dir. Roland Suso Richter. Video frame grab.   227

6.2 The tunnel as ideological spectacle: a cameraman films the construction of an escape tunnel funded in 1962 by NBC in violation of international law in a 2001 recreation of a Cold War media frenzy. Video frame grab from *Der Tunnel*. Dir. Roland Suso Richter.   230

List of figures and plates

6.3 The tunnel as ideological spectacle: a 2001 studio recreation of a 1962 facsimile of the Berlin Wall on a Berlin film set for the Hollywood docudrama *Tunnel 28* (1962, dir. Robert Siodmak). Video frame grab from *Der Tunnel*. Dir. Roland Suso Richter.   231

6.4 The physical manifestation of an ontological wall. *Route 60, Beit Jala, Bethlehem area, Israel-Palestine, 2011*. Josef Koudelka. © Josef Koudelka/Magnum Photos.   236

6.5 The practical and the ideological functions of tunneling: frames from Joe Sacco, 'The Underground War in Gaza.' *New York Times Magazine* (6 July 2003), 27.   239

6.6 The Gaza tunnel as photo op: 'U.S. Senator Lindsey Graham inspects a recently found cross-border Hamas tunnel during a visit to the Israel-Gaza border area March 10, 2019 in Golan, Israel.' US State Department / Alamy Stock Photo.   241

6.7 The Gaza tunnel as lifeline: 'Palestinian smugglers bring a goat to the Gaza Strip through an underground smuggling tunnel between Egypt and the Palestinian territory. Rafah, Palestine – 29.10.08.' WENN Rights Ltd / Alamy Stock Photo.   242

6.8 'CTRL+ALT+DELETE': the epistemological wall made material. 'Graffiti on the Separation Wall, Ramallah, Palestine, 5 November 2008.' STEVE WHYTE / Alamy Stock Photo.   244

6.9 An epistemological hole in the wall. Banksy's wall painting with additional graffiti, Bethlehem, 2008. Dimitry Bobroff / Alamy Stock Photo.   245

6.10 Still standing in 2018: blasting a virtual tunnel in the Wall, paired with signs pointing to the commercial side of Banksy's Bethlehem endeavor. 'Graffiti at Palestine-Israel border wall in Bethlehem, Palestine, West Bank, 15 April 2018.' Idris Ahmed / Alamy Stock Photo.   245

6.11 Another kind of hole in the wall. *Crusader map mural, Kalia Junction, Dead Sea area, ISRAEL- PALESTINE, 2009*. Josef Koudelka. © Josef Koudelka/Magnum Photos.   247

6.12 A hand through the Wall: 'Agua Prieta, Sonora, Mexico – Painting on the U.S.-Mexico border fence, 13 Oct. 2016.' Jim West / Alamy Stock Photo.   249

6.13 A hand through the Wall: 'Nogales, Arizona USA and Nogales, Sonora Mexico – 11 November 2017 – A hand

xvi | *List of figures and plates*

reaches through the border fence as rallies were held on both sides of the fence calling for more open immigration. The events were organized by the School of the Americas Watch, a group of religious and community activists.' Jim West / Alamy Stock Photo.   250

6.14 Part of the mostly straight-line border that runs from the Pacific coast to El Paso, Texas. Video frame grab from *Best of Luck with the Wall*. Josh Begley, 2016. https:// vimeo.com/189015526.   254

6.15 Part of the border that follows the Rio Grande to the Gulf of Mexico. Video frame grab from *Best of Luck with the Wall*. Josh Begley, 2016. https:// vimeo.com/189015526.   255

6.16 Iconography of *la bestia*: Sayra and her family on their dark way from San Pedro Sula, Honduras to the US border in *Sin Nombre*. Dir. Corey Fukiyama. Dist. Focus Features / Universal, 2009. Video frame grab.   258

6.17 Iconography of *la bestia*. Oscar riding *la bestia* from San Pedro Sula to the US border through the brightly colored world of *Barrier*. Wr. Brian K. Vaughan, art Marcos Martín, colors Muntsa Vicente. Issue #1, Dec. 2015. Permission of the artists.   258

6.18 A women's sanctuary in a phantasmagoric border setting in the revenge fantasy, *Coyotes*. Wr. Sean Lewis, illust. Caitlin Yarsky. Portland, OR: Image Comics. Issue #8 (Nov. 2018.), p. 26. Permission of the artists.   263

6.19 The view from across the border of JR's gentle giant. San Diego, California, 7 Sept. 2017. ZUMA Press, Inc. / Alamy Live News.   268

6.20 The view from behind the scenes. San Diego, California, 7 Sept. 2017. ZUMA Press, Inc. / Alamy Live News.   269

6.21 'The American Dream': ontologically bunkered in a *maquiladora* in Tijuana while laboring virtually in southern California. Video frame grab from *Sleep Dealer*. Dir. Alex Rivera. Dist. Maya Entertainment, 2008.   271

6.22 Imagining the end of the wall at a future border that looks a lot like today's. Video frame grab from *Sleep Dealer*. Dir. Alex Rivera. Dist. Maya Entertainment, 2008.   272

C.1 Symbolic rewilding in the DMZ: 'Fence with barbed wire in green nature, trees and bushes with painted deer

List of figures and plates xvii

on the fence along the DMZ, the third tunnel, South
Korea, at Korean Demilitarized Zone, 8 Sept. 2017.'
Loes Kieboom / Alamy Stock Photo. 284
C.2 Zealandia excludes unwanted invasive species and warns
off the canine invaders who remain welcome. 'Poison
sign on Predator exclusion fence at Zealandia eco
attraction park Wellington, New Zealand, 3 Feb. 2015.'
Tom Uhlman / Alamy Stock Photo. 286

Plates

1 *Qander zjarri* or 'single fire' bunkers, colloquially known as 'tortoises,' in the mountain landscape of southeastern Albania. *Line of Bunkers, Edge of Ersekë, Albania, 2011.* Photo by Wayne Barrar. Permission of the artist.
2 *Pike zjarri* or 'fire point' bunkers, colloquially known as 'oranges.' *Bunker (slipping seaward), Durrës beach, Albania, 2011.* Photo by Wayne Barrar. Permission of the artist.
3 Large-scale bunker in the mountains outside Tirana. *Covered ammunition bunker, near Fushë-Krujë, Albania, 2011.* Photo by Wayne Barrar. Permission of the artist.
4 Practical sheltering in a disused large bunker. *Sheep in abandoned bunker, near Tirana, Albania, 2011.* Photo by Wayne Barrar. Permission of the artist.
5 A concrete mushroom gutted for raw materials and left overturned on the shore of Lake Ohrid. *Toppled bunker (near Macedonian border), Lake Ohrid, Albania, 2011.* Photo by Wayne Barrar. Permission of the artist.
6 Adaptive reuse on the Adriatic coast. *Seawall made from broken bunkers/swimmers, Durrës, Albania, 2011.* Photo by Wayne Barrar. Permission of the artist.
7 Beach colors on a bunker converted for seaside tourism. *Painted bunker restaurant, Durrës beach, Albania, 2011.* Photo by Wayne Barrar. Permission of the artist.
8 A surviving bunker guards a remote mountain pass at the southeast border with Greece. *Roof of bunker, road to Elbasan, Albania, 2011.* Photo by Wayne Barrar. Permission of the artist.
9 Looking south. *Bunker Converted to a Bar, Bilisht, Albania, 2011.* Photo by Wayne Barrar. Permission of the artist.
10 Misplaced from their origins: bunker and Audi. *Front Yard Bunker / Car, Durrës, Albania, 2011.* Photo by Wayne Barrar. Permission of the artist.

xviii *List of figures and plates*

11 At home in the bunker form. *Building over bunker (restaurant), Durrës beach Albania, 2011.* Photo by Wayne Barrar. Permission of the artist.

12 The iconography of apocalypse in an everyday scene of biosecurity. *Rotenone pesticide application to Whitby Lake (removal of invasive fish), Porirua (NZ) 2007.* Photo by Wayne Barrar. Permission of the artist.

13 Imagining what it feels like to be an invasive species targeted for extinction. *Binned invasive koi at Koi Carp Classic (bowfishing event), Waikato (NZ) 2007.* Photo by Wayne Barrar. Permission of the artist.

14 The ambiguity of the laboratory setting: site for preservation or for elimination of the species pictured? *Biotron growth chamber, Bio-protection Research Centre, Lincoln (NZ) 2007.* Photo by Wayne Barrar. Permission of the artist.

15 The Santa Monica Wonderwall physically manifests the simultaneously massive and tenuous grip of future LA on the 'real' world. Frame from *Private Eye #6.* Story Brian K. Vaughan, art Marcos Martín, colors Muntsa Vicente. Panel Syndicate, 2015. P. 15. Permission of the artists.

16 The Wonderwall breached. Frame from *Private Eye #10.* Story Brian K. Vaughan, art Marcos Martín, colors Muntsa Vicente. Panel Syndicate, 2015. P. 125. Permission of the artists.

Preface

Unbreakable!
They alive, dammit!
It's a miracle
Unbreakable!
They alive, dammit!
But females are strong as hell
That's gonna be uhhh you know uhhhh fascinating transition
Dammit!

The Gregory Brothers and Mike Britt, Title credits sequence to
  Unbreakable Kimmy Schmidt (2015–20)

One spring day around the middle of the first decade of the twenty-first century, I was walking with my preschool-aged daughter down 5th Avenue on our way to a playground in lower Manhattan. Something was amiss. There were burned-out cars parked along both curbs of this enclave of wealth. Debris scattered the sidewalks and long weeds were growing along the curb. The so-called Gold Coast had been transformed overnight into a postapocalyptic urban wasteland (Figure P.1). When we rounded the corner of the arch at Washington Square Park, the mystery was explained: workers were loading wrecked cars onto a tractor-trailer and collecting the artfully placed foliage and garbage for transport back to a Brooklyn warehouse. We were walking through an on-site set for the production of the 2007 movie *I Am Legend*. The movie's protagonist, Neville (Will Smith), lives in a bunkered townhouse on the north end of Washington Square and the second unit had been shooting exteriors to be cut into an action sequence. Tourists were snapping pictures and muttering about the parlous state of the city. My daughter was transfixed by the vehicles and the weeds. As for myself, I had long been immersed in Cold War fantasies of the destruction of New York. And I had experienced on 9/11 what the apocalyptic destruction of the city I lived in might look and feel like. But what entranced me here was the fantasy that it could also be restored just as quickly.

Figure P.1 Neville (Will Smith) and his dog Samantha on their way to an East Village video store in a postapocalyptic Manhattan shot on location for *I Am Legend*.

That vexed double consciousness is characteristic of what I call the bunker fantasy in the twenty-first century. Following the ten years it took for the end of the Cold War to sink in, the twenty-first-century world began living a curiously double life in relation to the nuclear condition it had both survived the end of and never in any way truly escaped. Like television's bunker-hostage survivor Kimmy Schmidt, we are all alive, dammit, unbreakable survivors of forty years of insanity; and like Kimmy Schmidt, we continue to relive those years over and over in our postapocalyptic lives. The twenty-first century is imbued with the afterlives of the Cold War exactly in the way it is imbued with proliferating forms of the postapocalyptic. We live in a world constantly authorizing itself to make itself anew but always unbreakably bound with the past from which it can only imagine breaking away through cataclysmic disaster. This book is about those afterlives and the often unrecognized or unacknowledged cultural work they perform around us, every day and all the time.

When I first conceived the bunker fantasy project after reading Cormac McCarthy's novel *The Road* while researching something completely different in London in 2006, the part of the project that eventually became my book *Cold War Space and Culture in the 1960s and 1980s: The Bunkered Decades* (2021) was meant to be just a couple of brief chapters before I got to what had first pulled me in: Cold War culture since the Cold War. But during the course of research and writing, I discovered just how little contemporary scholarship had really engaged with what seemed important and relevant to me about the texts and ideas around the years 1962 and 1983. I finally acknowledged to myself that what I had thought of as the prelude to the book I had planned to write was in fact its own project. I reconceived that book around two nested historical sections framed by a conclusion in the present day, and published it first, as a prequel to this one, the book I had always planned to write. It's just that I had to write *The Bunkered Decades* first in order to create the space in which this one, hopefully, would make sense.

This book's conclusion is the only part that wasn't in the original conception. That's because it reckons with the changes undergone by the bunker fantasy over the fifteen eventful years between the conception and the completion of the overall project. I thought – and still most of the time believe – that the most enduring and impactful of these changes was the development of the public understanding of climate change from a looming threat of global warming not so different in its imaginary from the always-impending-but-never-arriving nuclear holocaust to today's here-already-and-inevitably-getting-worse, full-blown crisis. And yet, even though the cultural work it does seems ever more profoundly misplaced from its origins, most of our public discourse somehow still has not found an imaginary better suited to the climate crisis than the one we inherited from the Cold War.

Then in 2020, as I was preparing *The Bunkered Decades* for publication and finishing writing *After the End*, there came the global pandemic, which somehow brought to horribly banal fruition another form of bunkered thinking: the previous decade's obsession with zombie apocalypse. I had in fact used George Romero's ground-breaking and long-running horror movie series to punctuate the earlier book, from *Night of the Living Dead* (1968) at the tail end of the first bunkered decade to *Day of the Dead* (1985) in the middle of the second. I was sure that, with this update, I had caught up with the world again.

No such luck: current events again gave new meaning to the book's core argument, this time making it far too real. While I write this preface in 2023, war continues to rage in Ukraine, with nuclear power plants held hostage and nuclear arsenals a looming threat for an autocrat backed in a corner. The Cold War may have ended, but the nuclear age it inaugurated and gave cultural form to remains stubbornly with us today. The security imaginary – still to me the bunker fantasy's dominant legacy – remains fundamentally unaltered from the form it inherited from the 1980s even as its scope seems to broaden all the time, with no lessening in sight.

And just as the racial justice movement of 2020 and the anti-immigration policies of the 2016 Trump presidency stressed borders, divisions, policing, and exclusion, so reactions to climate crisis and the pandemic were consumed as much by concerns over climate refugees and disease spreaders as with mitigating climate change and collective responses to COVID-19. As in the

American focus on individual sheltering and government bunkers, so the American – and often the global – imaginary continues to revert to bunkering as both initial response and best practice. Why this continues and how else we might imagine the various global crises facing the twenty-first century are the paired questions addressed in the pages that follow.

Acknowledgments

Because this book began in the same project as *Cold War Space and Culture in 1960s and 1980s America*, gratitude and debts frequently overlap. So a lot is repeated from that book's Acknowledgments. We start with the infrastructure. I am grateful to the American University College of Arts & Sciences Dean's Office, and especially former Dean Peter Starr, for many years' support of my travel and research, and for underwriting the cost of images and permissions when fair use did not apply. The American University Library Interlibrary Loan office must at times have thought from my requests that I was cracked (*The Coming of the Rats*? … *The Survivalist #8: The End Is Coming*?) but never blinked in procuring hard-to-find pulp for my scholarly consumption. The New York Public Library's generous MaRLI program granted me invaluable access to the circulating libraries and research spaces of the NYPL Main Branch, New York University, and Columbia University. The staff of the NYU library, where I most frequently exercised my MaRLI privileges, was unfailingly helpful. And during a sabbatical year, the now-retired Jay Barksdale granted me access to the charmed confines of the NYPL's Wertheim Study, my principal opportunity for full-time concentration during the many years of work on this project.

Over the years, Chris Lewis (now retired), Sean Casey, and the rest of the team at the AU Library's Media Services have been essential to this project: buying or borrowing media as needed, and Sean in particular with key assistance in pulling together the final selection of frame grabs. Thanks to Princess Pratt, Cheyenne Dawson, and the rest of the team at Alamy; Nickie Osborne at Hal Leonard (once my request finally reached her); Anh at Aperture; Clarisse Bourgeois, Ruth Hoffmann, and Michael D. Shulman at Magnum Photos; Dave Lloyd at the Center for Cartoon Studies' Schulz Library; Daniel Hoffmann and Rainer Geissmann at Uniq Hotels; Tim Noakes and Fred Turner at Stanford University; Dirk Wood at Image Comics, and anyone else who actually took the time or made the effort to answer my emails and help me out: what a difference it makes to correspond with thoughtful and helpful human beings. (In contrast,

xxiv *Acknowledgments*

hard feelings indeed go out to A24, DC, Universal, and Alfred Publishing, and to whomever (hopefully not The Boss) makes decisions regarding the Springsteen catalog; if you see unexplained absences where lyrics or images obviously *should* be but aren't – now you know why. Have a listen or a look in the obvious places online and then return to the book. Apologies in advance for these gaps.) On the other hand, very special thanks to writer Stewart Brand, photographer Emmet Gowin, writer Kyle Higgins, writer Sean Lewis, musician David Lowery, artist Marcos Martín, artist Stephen Mooney, photographer Richard Ross, artist and journalist Joe Sacco, musicians James Saad and Sue Saad, writer Bryan K. Vaughan, artist Muntsa Vicente, and artist Caitlin Yarsky for gracious responses to digital cold-calling from a stranger about the at times distant past. I'm grateful to Thaer Husien for permission to quote from his fabulous SFF novel-in-progress 'Beside the Sickle Moon.' More power to independent artists, musicians, and writers and their extraordinary work!

At Manchester University Press, I'm grateful to editorial director Emma Brennan for her initial faith in the project and enthusiasm for its interdisciplinary approach; to editorial co-ordinator Paul Clarke for seeing it through the review process and into production; and to the two anonymous reviewers of the manuscript. The production team was thorough, flexible, and professional, especially production manager David Appleyard and superlative copy-editor and indexer Rachel Goodyear.

When you're researching an imaginary, everything you read and everybody you meet is a potential source; thank you to every one of them, whether they knew they were contributing or not. If I've somehow left you out, I'm sorry; please let me know! I owe especial thanks to Maura Donohue for the serendipitous gift of Richard Ross's *Waiting for the End of the World*, scored with an eagle eye as a remainder in a local bookstore, and to the Swiss bunker enthusiast who initially told me I was breaking the law, then invited me to his home, offered me lunch and pamphlets, and ended up running me in his car many miles down the road to visit a local mine (perhaps it's just as well he wouldn't write down his name for me). Nothing is more precious than invaluable leads that arrive out of nowhere. Also precious was the generosity of Kujtim Çashku and his Marubi Film & Multimedia School in Tirana and especially my wife's former student Altiona Stefanllari in New York, Altiona's brother Genti Josifi in Korçë, and her cousin Alban Thimo in Tirana. Thanks to Peter Geoghegan for sharing his expertise on the Balkans, and to Chris Raines and her friend Caroline for sharing their photos of beach bunkers near Berat. Ting-chi Wang, founder of Local Methodology on Kinmen Island, generously shared with me from her capacious knowledge of the history and current situation there. On

Acknowledgments xxv

Matsu, thanks to the couple running the Dayspring Hotel and their daughter in New Zealand who helped translate for us long-distance while chatting about Jane Austen. Thanks also to the welcoming staff at the Matsu National Scenic Area Administration: As Altiona reassured us before we left for Albania, 'People outside US actually help for free!!!'

And even, at times, Altiona, inside as well: Thanks to George Veni, Maria Perez, and Robert Hoke for sharing their expertise on caves. I'm grateful to Dan Zak for his conversation about current nuclear culture and his advocacy of *Testament* as a key film of the 1980s. To Sue Boecker for sharing with me some of the background to her song 'Radioactive Dreams.' To Matt Coolidge of the Center for Land Use Interpretation (CLUI) and Wayne Barrar for their expert company on a tour of the Packard Campus of the Library of Congress; to Gregory Lukow, Chief of the Motion Picture, Broadcasting & Recorded Sound Division of the Library of Congress, Packard Campus, for organizing the tour; and to Library of Congress veteran Arlene Balkansky for setting it up. To Matt, Wayne, Bruce Robbins, Rosalind Williams, Lindsey Green-Simms, Daniel Esser, Maxwell Uphaus, Michael Ravenscroft, and Despina Kakoudaki for their participation in the 2011 Colloquium, The Ground beneath Our Feet: Building, Living, and Thinking Underground. To anyone I've omitted who over the years shared a Cold War memory, experience, or space with me: thank you, and heartfelt apologies. Inevitably, I could not include every story or space and, if I got anything wrong, obviously that's on me.

Thanks to all of the friends, colleagues, and institutions that have hosted me over the years of this book: to Sasha Colby at Simon Fraser University; to Deirdre D'Albertis at Bard College; to Michael Thurstone and Smith College's Kahn Liberal Arts Institute; to Rachel Falconer and the welcoming faculty at the University of Lausanne; to Sukhdev Sandhu at NYU for opening my eyes to Nigel Kneale; to Sarah Pike and the Humanities Center at California State University, Chico, multiple times; in New Zealand, to the department of Fine Arts at Massey University, the Auckland Branch of the New Zealand Institute of Architects, Kathy Waghorn at the University of Auckland, Lynn Freeman at Radio New Zealand, everyone at the Dunedin School of Art, and Lynda Cullen and Aaron Kreisler at the Dunedin Public Art Gallery for their tri-city hospitality; to Michael Northcott, Devin Zuber, Steve Paulson, Sarah Pike, Bron Taylor, and Amanda Nichols for their conversation and scholarship on mountains and sacred landscapes at and around the 2017 International Society for the Study of Religion, Nature and Culture conference; to Bruce O'Neill, Kevin O'Neill, Alaina M. Lemon, Andrea Ballestero, and Maria Perez for their conversation and scholarship on subterranean ethnography at the 2015 American Anthropological Association and ever since. For their

xxvi *Acknowledgments*

conversation and scholarship on literature, technology, and infrastructure over the years: Martin Collins, Bruce Robbins, Michael Rubenstein, David Trotter, Rosalind Williams, and the Society for the History of Technology (SHOT). And for their unfailing support of my research over several decades now: David Damrosch, Deborah Nord, Michael Levenson, and Andreas Huyssen.

Thank you to all of my current and former colleagues at American University and especially in the Department of Literature for their friendship, support, and ideas. Special thanks to Cindy Bair van Dam, Kirstie Dorr, Erik Dussere, Daniel Esser, Stephanie Grant, Lindsey Green-Simms, Thaer Husien, Despina Kakoudaki, Sara Clarke Kaplan, David Keplinger, Jeffrey Middents, Glenn Moomau, Malini Ranganathan, Alejandro Hirsch Saed, Kathleen Smith, Sarah Trembath, David Vazquez, Linda Voris, Lily Wong, and Lacey Wootton for sources, stories, advice, support, and inspiration. Mark Stein read the manuscript in full, providing insight and suggestions, as always. And for their invaluable support of my scholarship, thank you to these esteemed administrators and colleagues: Keith Leonard, Jonathan Loesberg, Richard Sha, Kim Blankenship, Peter Starr, Max Paul Friedman, Linda Aldoory, Monica Jackson, Mary Clark, Phyllis Perez, Dan Myers, and Scott Bass. To David Keplinger for taking over as chair during the research semester I needed finally to wrap up a full draft. To Jeffrey Middents for serving as Summer Chair, and to Jeff and Kate Wilson for stepping in as Interim Co-Chairs so I could take a sabbatical in the middle of my term and in the middle of a pandemic.

I'm grateful to so many inspiring students over my decades of teaching. But I want to single out the students (some of them now colleagues) in my 2013 MA seminar 'The Bunker Fantasy' for their patience and willingness to pretend *Underworld* could be read in three weeks while also taking other classes, for their engagement, conversation, and scholarly and creative writing on this unexpected topic, and for their ongoing ideas since that year: Mina Anderson, Jessie Atkins, Patrick Bradley, Will Byrne, Bryan Freeland, Melanie Germond, Claire Handscombe, Chelsea Horne, Angela Kwak, Hanna Mangold, Emily Prince, Kate Quinn, Nada Serhan, Devin Symons, Jeremy Wade, and Christine Weidner. What an amazing group: you stretched and tested my thinking on this topic in so many ways.

To Wayne, for many years of collaboration and conversation, and so many stunning photographs. To Kerry Hines, for her patient tolerance, perfect company, brilliant poetry, and generosity with beautiful stamps.

And, most of all, to Ana and Emilia, for keeping me company from Albania to Taiwan to Colombia to our New York home. Emilia, thank you for being willing always to go everywhere and explore everything. Ana, thank you for always still being there even when you couldn't join us.

Acknowledgments xxvii

Portions of Chapters 3 and 4 have been adapted and revised from 'The Bunkerization of Albania,' *Cabinet* 50 (2013); 'Cold War Reduction: The Principle of the Swiss Bunker Fantasy,' *Space and Culture* 20.1 (2017); 'Defensible Spaces: The Underground Cities of Kinmen and Matsu,' in *Global Undergrounds: Exploring Cities Within*, ed. Paul Dobraszczyk, Carlos López Galviz, and Bradley L. Garrett (London: Reaktion, 2016); and 'Of Parasites and Their Hosts: Bong Joon-ho's *Gisaengchung* (2019),' *Bright Lights Film Journal* (27 Nov. 2019). Portions of Chapter 5 have been adapted and revised from 'Future Slums: Problems of Urban Space in Science Fiction Cinema,' *The Apollonian* 5 (2018); and of Chapter 6 from 'Wall and Tunnel: The Spatial Metaphorics of Cold War Berlin.' *New German Critique* 110 (2010).

'Radioactive Dreams,' lyrics by Sue Saad, music by Sue Saad, Tony Riparetti, and Steve LaGassick. Used by permission.

'Good Guys & Bad Guys,' words and music by Victor Krummenacher / Greg Lisher / David Lowery / Chris Molla / Chris Pedersen / Jonathan Segel. Used by permission.

'Mother.' Words and Music by Roger Waters. Copyright © 1979 Roger Waters Music Overseas Ltd. All Rights Administered by BMG Rights Management (US) LLC. All Rights Reserved. Used by Permission. Reprinted by Permission of Hal Leonard LLC.

'Survivalist.' Words and Music by Trent Reznor. Copyright © 2007 Leaving Hope Music Inc. and Arlovol Music. All Rights for Leaving Hope Music Inc. Administered Worldwide by Kobalt Songs Music Publishing. All Rights for Arlovol Music Administered by Penny Farthing Music c/o Concord Music Publishing. All Rights Reserved. Used by Permission. Reprinted by Permission of Hal Leonard LLC.

All translations are by the author unless otherwise noted.

All emphases and italics are in the original, unless otherwise noted.

List of abbreviations

AI – artificial intelligence
CBP – US Customs and Border Protection
CIA – Central Intelligence Agency
GDR – German Democratic Republic
GGW – Great Green Wall
MAD – mutually assured destruction
NAFTA – North American Free Trade Agreement
PRC – People's Republic of China
PTSD – post-traumatic stress disorder
RECA – Radiation Exposure Compensation Act
ROC – Republic of China
RTV – reality television
SFF – science fiction/fantasy
SIS – British Secret Intelligence Service
USMCA – United States–Mexico–Canada Agreement
YA – young adult

Introduction
After the imminent apocalypse: the bunker fantasy since the Cold War

[For this epigraph, please read the lyrics of or listen to the first verse and chorus of the referenced song]

Serge Gainsbourg, 'Rock around the Bunker' (1975)

In January 1975, iconoclastic French chanteur Serge Gainsbourg released the album *Rock around the Bunker*, his hermetic revision of postwar history according to early American rock 'n' roll. The Paris-born son of Jewish Ukrainian parents who had survived the Second World War with false papers in the Vichy-controlled city of Limoges, Gainsbourg opened the album with 'Nazi Rock' and closed side two with the title song followed by 'SS in Uruguay.' The compositions alternate Gainsbourg's trademark heavy-breathing talk-singing in French with female backup singers chanting the English choruses of the songs' titles, anchored by the now-retro 'new' sound Bill Haley & the Comets had inaugurated in their 1955 single 'Rock around the Clock.' The concept album's implicit argument was that the Nazi history with which its lyrics are concerned continued to make sense in 1975 only as filtered through the lens of Cold War America. Opening with the sound effect of exploding bombs, 'Rock around the Bunker' is simultaneously an irreverent account of the last days of Adolf Hitler and Eva Braun locked down in Berlin and a vision of the end of the world proper to the nuclear condition that had followed the war around the world, from France to Uruguay. It is unsurprising, then, that when the Milanese cabaret singer Giangilberto Monti released *Maledette canzoni* (2006; Accursed Songs), a tribute to his favorite French singers, the only song from Gainsbourg's album he chose to cover was 'Rock around the Bunker.' Come the early twenty-first century, the Hitler imaginary had been bunkered out of sight; however, nuclear war remained a potent postapocalyptic fantasy. And the international sound of rock 'n' roll had migrated easily to Italy, even as Gainsbourg's non-English lyrics still did require translation into Monti's native tongue. As Gainsbourg had already intimated in 1975, the bunker fantasy of late 1950s and early 1960s Cold War America continued to afford displaced opportunities for meaning-making the world over.

I coined the term 'bunker fantasy' to encompass the capacious and contradictory imaginary surrounding the nuclear condition and the spaces associated with it in a world in which nuclear weapons and nuclear power exist, and the ways in which that condition colors how we now conceive differently of the pre-1945 past, the present in which we live, and the futures we imagine. The bunker fantasy is at once a realistic nightmare about the end of the world and an imaginative tool using apocalypse to prompt thinking about alternate pasts and speculative futures in which the world would not only survive but even, perhaps, prosper. It's realistic in that the condition of a nuclear-armed world is one that can be ended cataclysmically at any moment. It's bunkered in that the dominant mode of imagining an end that could not be experienced directly was through forms of literal and figurative sheltering. It's fantasy in that the moment of apocalypse tends to exist primarily in order to clear the ground for imagining the world differently.

Some brief clarification of terms: I use the pronouns 'we' and 'you' to express the assumed collectivity of this social imaginary, simultaneously inclusive, coercive, and polarizing. I mean 'fantasy' to describe the range of representations and associations that imagine an event never yet experienced and impossible to experience as such; 'bunker fantasy' to describe the ways in which bunkered spaces figure this imaginary; and 'bunker' in the broad sense to encompass a variety of related spaces literally or figuratively fortified and subterranean. These spaces include the bunker as a type of hardened military fortification ranging in size from single-occupancy pillboxes to missile silos to sprawling government facilities, usually but not necessarily partially or wholly underground. They include physical shelters in a variety of forms, including basement and backyard fallout shelters; purpose-built private and public supershelters; dedicated fallout shelters in public and private buildings; and caves, mines, and other natural and manmade subterranea converted either permanently or temporarily into shelters. They include other spaces ranging from bodies to homes to urban areas to communities to states, regions, and nations to entire worlds when treated or imagined *as* bunkered: that is, fortified, isolated, and protected from the world around them, and equipped with controlled ingress and egress. These spaces may be identified as bunkered solely in terms of their inhabitants' will and ability to make them such by means of weapons or signage or verbal cues; they may be walled, moated, domed, or otherwise surrounded by barriers more or less permeable. I mean 'bunker fantasy' to refer to the real and imagined energies mobilized by these various forms of bunkering. Reading the ways and degree to which these bunkered spaces dominate narratives related to the nuclear condition provides essential information regarding the meanings of a particular fantasy and the uses of the bunker fantasy more generally, both during and since the Cold War.

After the End: Cold War Culture and Apocalyptic Imaginations in the Twenty-First Century treats the legacies of the bunker fantasy in the post–Cold War world, continuous with and derived from the four decades it encompassed but in the distorted, variable, and unpredictable ways typical of the global circulation of locally generated ideas and spaces. It argues that, although not always recognized as such, the bunker fantasy continues to dominate any imagination of the relationship between present and future bridged by a cataclysm, even as the formatively nuclear ground of that fantasy often recedes from consciousness. This book builds on and continues from the arguments of *Cold War Space and Culture in the 1960s and 1980s: The Bunkered Decades.*[1] The first section of the introduction ('The bunker fantasy, then and now') rehearses the key concepts and claims of that book and explains how I use them to analyze the ways Cold War culture has permeated the twenty-first century. The second section ('The bunker fantasy, here and there') lays out the theoretical and practical grounds for the global focus of the current book and other ways in which the bunker fantasies of the twenty-first century differ from those of the years around 1962 and 1983, and the meanings accrued by the ideas of the past misplaced in the fulcrum of the neoliberal, explicitly globalized and digitized present day. The final section provides an overview of the book's six chapters on the bunker fantasy as they have circulated the globe since the Cold War.

The bunker fantasy, then and now

In her 1984 novel *Clay's Ark*, Afrofuturist writer Octavia Butler imagined a dystopian 2021 where walled enclaves shelter privileged families while armed gangs roam the 'sewers,' or unprotected spaces in between. On the road home to the Palos Verdes Enclave, Blake Maslin and his two daughters are waylaid and kidnapped by a strange pair of men who, rather than doing the expected – raping, robbing, and killing them – take them up the mountains to their own kind of enclave, a cluster of primitive homes isolated both in space and in time. From this enclave of primitivism will eventually issue an alien plague that will infect and transform the world. Butler narrates the initial reaction from the perspective of the kidnapped father:

> The girl was sixteen, naïve, and sheltered. Like most enclave parents, Blake had done all he could to re-create the safe world of perhaps sixty years past for his children. Enclaves were islands surrounded by vast, crowded, vulnerable residential areas through which ran sewers of utter lawlessness connecting

1 David L. Pike, *Cold War Space and Culture in the 1960s and 1980s: The Bunkered Decades* (New York: Oxford University Press, 2021).

cesspools – economic ghettos that regularly chewed their inhabitants up and spat the pieces into surrounding communities. The girls knew about such things only superficially.[2]

The radically unequal future of Butler's 2021 is divided between walled suburbs modeled on nostalgia for the world around 1962 and surroundings generated by the ghetto imaginary that was prevalent around the book's composition in the early 1980s. So much of the imaginary of the twenty-first century turns out, in fact, to have followed the temporal patterning Butler identified in *Clay's Ark*. In the event, like many persons of color before and since, Butler found that bunkering had perhaps even less to offer marginalized Americans than the ghetto did. *Clay's Ark* uses the starting point of the bunker fantasy to imagine a mutated and transformed future whose ambiguous quality is evident from the fact that Asa Elias Doyle, aka Eli, the astronaut whose will to survive drives him knowingly to bring the alien virus to earth that will infect the planet, is also a Black man who is the most sympathetic and compassionate character the novel has to offer us.

As form, as image, and as physical space, the bunker dominated Cold War culture; since 1989 it has continued to dominate the ways much of the world, and especially the global North, responds to and processes everything we inherited from that war, and the ways we think about shelter, security, boundaries, and difference. But we seldom attend to the affective meanings mobilized by these forms, images, and spaces, to our profound ambivalence toward them, and to the ways they contain our deepest fears entangled with our strongest desires. On the one hand, as Josephine Rowe wondered in 2019, revisiting Nevil Shute's slow-burn apocalypse of a bestseller *On the Beach* (1957, film 1959), 'Has there been, in the interim, a time so similarly propelled by dread?'[3] On the other hand, what James Baldwin wrote in 1961 about white fantasies of a secure past also remains just as true today:

> The thing that most white people imagine that they can salvage from the storm of life is really, in sum, their innocence ... I am afraid that most of the white people I have ever known impressed me as being in the grip of a weird nostalgia, dreaming of a vanished state of security and order, against which dream, unfailingly and unconsciously, they tested and very often lost their lives.[4]

---

2 Octavia Butler, *Clay's Ark* (1984); in *Seed to Harvest* (New York: Grand Central, 2007), 483.

3 Josephine Rowe, 'Pattern and Forecast (Vol. 5),' *The Believer* (19 March 2019): http://web.archive.org/web/20190320104756/https://believermag.com/logger/pattern-and -forecast-vol-5/.

4 James Baldwin, 'The Black Boy Looks at the White Boy,' *Esquire* (1 May 1961); rpt *Nobody Knows My Name* (1961); in *Collected Essays*, ed. Toni Morrison (New York: Library of America, 1998), 269–85, at 270.

The bunker fantasy exists within, and because of, the tension between dread and nostalgia, and between those with the privilege of living within that fantasy and those excluded from it – those who, as poet and music critic Hanif Abdurraqib memorably wrote of the strangeness of listening to Bruce Springsteen's 1980 double album *The River* in 2016, 'don't fear what the future holds as much as [they] fear not being alive long enough to see it.'[5]

The Reagan years had been dominated by dread of and nostalgia for the Cold War years around 1962; the twenty-first century has been dominated by a similarly conflicted inheritance from those Reagan years, even as what once was known as the nuclear age has been reformulated and incorporated into geology's deep-time vision as the Anthropocene. To be sure, there are no explicit nuclear references to be heard on *The River*; however, the album was released at the height of the antinuclear protest movement, and Springsteen had premiered the title song live at the 1979 No Nukes benefit concert in Madison Square Garden, New York. Like everything in the 1980s, the album is permeated by the nuclear condition through and through without ever needing to come right out and say so. The imagery of 'The River,' although explicitly about dreams of youth blasted by the realities of adult life lived too soon, strongly resonates with the language of the postapocalyptic, of a river that has run dry. The river of a better time that Springsteen's dried-up couple remembers is the fabled promise and fiercely guarded innocence that flowed through postwar America; what Abdurraqib calls the fear of the future captured by the singer's bitter nostalgia reminds us that bunkering – responding to that fear by sheltering in a stylized and idealized space of the past – since the 1980s has been a state of mind as much as a fortified place. And to possess that state, Abdurraqib reminds us, as Baldwin had before him, is itself as privileged and racialized a legacy as possessing a backyard fallout shelter had been back in 1961.

Perhaps the most significant development in postapocalyptic writing since the 1980s has been the appropriation of its popular genres by Black writers, Indigenous writers, writers of color, and writers from the global South. When BIPOC fantasy author Rebecca Roanhorse states flatly that 'We've already survived an apocalypse,' she is neither exaggerating nor saying anything new.[6] Given that an estimated 93 percent of the sixty million Native people who were living in the Americas died as the result of European

---

5 Hanif Abdurraqib, *They Can't Kill Us Until They Kill Us* (Columbus, OH: Two Dollar Radio, 2017), 21.

6 Alexandra Alter, '"We've Already Survived an Apocalypse": Indigenous Writers Are Changing Sci-Fi,' *New York Times* (14 Aug. 2020): http://web.archive.org/web/20230311130649/http://www.nytimes.com/2020/08/14/books/indigenous-native-american-sci-fi-horror.html.

6 *After the end*

colonization, it is no stretch to consider that 'the United States itself is a postapocalyptic nation, with its Native people cloaked in the centuries-long shadow of its aftermath: displacement, forced poverty, and genocide.'[7] It is not surprising that, as women writers had opened up the feminist potentialities of SFF in the 1980s, and 'as Black writers wielded Afrofuturism to imagine worlds beyond the grasp of white violence, so too have Indigenous and Native authors turned to science fiction and dystopian literature to expose and interrogate the violence of settler colonialism.'[8] In their surehanded grasp of historical facts only slowly being acknowledged as such elsewhere, contemporary writers find that, creatively misplaced, the popular forms of postapocalyptic fiction 'allow them to reimagine [their] experience in ways that wouldn't be possible in realistic fiction.'[9] Whether we understand such stories as participating within the forms of traditional genres or whether we take them as themselves ontologies – 'true stories, not forms of fantasy,' as Grace Dillon has argued of Indigenous futurisms[10] – their revisionary stance towards the past centuries remains constant.

Whether as an internalized state of mind or as a 'weird nostalgia' one observes from the outside looking in, the enduring grip of the bunker fantasy extends far beyond the material forms in which it was first concretized. But understanding the affective grip of those physical spaces is a first step to understanding what the many permutations emerging from that space afford to post–Cold War culture. The bunker remains today the only built environment expressly designed to enable survival of nuclear war; in addition to the range of threats in the prepper's 'A-B-C' of apocalypse (atomic-biological-chemical warfare), its form has been updated in the twenty-first century to incorporate shelter from the fear of human predation resulting from climate change, pandemics, and other cataclysmic events. In its design to survive apocalypse, the bunker exists on a nebulous borderline between military reality and social fantasy; survivalism gets a lot of attention, but most contemporary disaster scenarios don't actually model survival at all, and many others directly confront the unlikelihood of oneself, not to mention

---

7 Will Preston, 'Apocalypse Burnout,' *Full Stop* (8 Feb. 2021): http://web.archive.org/web/20221002200933/https://www.full-stop.net/2021/02/09/reviews/will-preston/apocalypse-burnout/.

8 Preston, 'Apocalypse Burnout.' On feminist SFF in the 1980s, see Pike, *Bunkered Decades*, 219–62.

9 Alter, 'We've Already Survived an Apocalypse'; on women writers in the 1980s, see Pike, *Bunkered Decades*, chapter nine.

10 Grace L. Dillon, 'Introduction,' in *Walking the Clouds: An Anthology of Indigenous Science Fiction*, ed. Dillon (Tucson: University of Arizona Press, 2012); qtd in Chelsea Vowel, 'Writing toward a Definition of Indigenous Futurism,' *Literary Hub* (10 June 2022): https://lithub.com/writing-toward-a-definition-of-indigenous-futurism/.

After the imminent apocalypse

one's family or friends, making it to the bunker in time to shelter. The global pandemic of 2020 established the reality of plague – whether spread accidentally or militarily – as an apocalyptic device; however, the threat of nuclear war has hardly disappeared since 1989, either. As of early 2022 (just before the Russian invasion of Ukraine), an estimated 12,700 nuclear devices survived globally, around 90 percent in the possession of the US and Russia, just over two-thirds of them in military stockpiles, 3,730 'deployed with operational forces,' and approximately 2,000 on high alert status.[11]

A global imaginary continues to deploy the bunker fantasy in a myriad of contexts from isolated survivalists, or 'preppers,' to a wide-ranging obsession with securing borders and boundaries the world over, to a burgeoning tourism industry around the physical remains of a Cold War architecture engineered to be literally indestructible. I argue here that the nuclear imaginaries generated around 1962 and around 1983 and analyzed at length in *The Bunkered Decades* have not in fact moved beyond or away from the apocalyptic purview. Rather, the nuclear condition has become a second nature informing pretty much everything about how we imagine and inhabit the world today, including nonnuclear catastrophes and pandemics. Understanding the key issues in these imaginaries opens up new ways of understanding those decades and speaks directly to contemporary issues around borders, migration, and national, regional, and personal security.[12]

To most mainstream writers at the time, the Cold War and the nuclear condition it introduced to the world were as unforeseen and unprecedented as the genocides that had preceded them. As I argue in *The Bunkered Decades*, what has often been called the 'Nuclear Age' can be characterized by a slow process whereby the previously unaccountable and unrepresentable slowly but surely etched its way into the conscious world to the point where it could no longer be ignored or repressed. Viewed in retrospect, there had (sadly) been nothing very new or unexpected about any of these events. Rather than putting a promised end to genocide and oppression, modernity had been driven since its inception by the forced enslavement of Black Africans and the organized eradication of Indigenous Peoples by colonizing forces. Cities have been eliminated wholesale for as long as cities have existed, either by force of arms or by acts of nature. And, of course, war has been atrociously violent and fundamentally dehumanizing for as long as there has been war. The term 'Cold' War itself is a misnomer, argues Andrew

---

11 Hans M. Kristensen and Matt Korda, 'Status of World Nuclear Forces,' *Federation of American Scientists* (Feb. 2022): https://fas.org/issues/nuclear-weapons/status-world-nuclear-forces/; accessed 22 Nov. 2022.

12 The following paragraphs have been excerpted, condensed, and updated from Pike, *Bunkered Decades*, 1–33.

Hammond, for a historical epoch that 'resulted in over a hundred wars throughout the Third World and a body count of over 20 million.'[13] Any counterdiscourse to the Cold War verities was strongly marginalized in the decade around 1962; however, the decade around 1983 had been primed by successful movements for Civil Rights, women's rights, gay rights, and environmental justice to understand the limited application of those verities and to contest their invocation as the foundation stone of Reagan's nostalgic revival of the prior generation's America and its cultural politics. Yet even those protests remained framed from within the nuclear condition.

The bunker fantasy frames of 1983 and 1962 *afford* certain kinds of imaginings and constrain others. I draw the term *affordance* from literary critic Caroline Levine's book *Forms*. Levine defines *affordance* through design theory to describe the 'limited range of potentialities' that 'each shape or pattern, social or literary, lays claim to.'[14] Just as glass, steel, or cotton affords certain qualities and uses but not others, so, Levine argues, do different forms. Forms pattern sociopolitical institutions just as much as they pattern literary fabrications. 'Literary forms and social formations,' Levine continues, 'are equally real in their capacity to organize materials, and equally unreal in being artificial, contingent constraints.'[15] Rather than being reducible to or molded by a single dominant or overarching form, individual experiences, sociopolitical life, and aesthetic creations are composed of an 'extraordinary density' of intersecting and interacting forms.[16] The bunker fantasy, in this sense, is not a single cohesive system; it's an imaginary that assembles 'many forms, all trying to organize us at once'[17] within a single spatial and conceptual unit: the shelter.

These forms can be used conventionally or 'in unexpected ways that expand our general sense of the form's affordances'; nevertheless, there are always things they can do or are suited for and things they cannot do or are unsuited for.[18] 'All forms,' Levine continues, 'do share one affordance … [S]hapes and patterns are iterable – portable.'[19] Like the bunker and many of the other mechanically reproducible products of industrial and military architecture, forms can be precisely duplicated without thereby

---

13 Andrew Hammond, 'From Rhetoric to Rollback: Introductory Thoughts on Cold War Writing,' in *Cold War Literature: Writing the Global Conflict*, ed. Hammond (New York: Routledge, 2005), 1–14, at 1.
14 Caroline Levine, *Forms: Whole, Rhythm, Hierarchy, Network* (Princeton: Princeton University Press, 2015), 6.
15 Levine, *Forms*, 14.
16 Levine, *Forms*, 22.
17 Levine, *Forms*, 22.
18 Levine, *Forms*, 7.
19 Levine, *Forms*, 7.

After the imminent apocalypse   9

losing the affordances specific to them. 'Enclosures,' she writes, 'afford containment and security, inclusion as well as exclusion.'[20] Bunkers in all of their physical variants share the affordances Levine attributes to enclosures. However, as the forms travel, their meaning is subject to change from the unforeseen possibilities of what Brazilian critic Roberto Schwarz termed 'misplaced ideas,' which I understand here to encompass the combination of pitfalls and unforeseen possibilities available when functions and meanings of ideas, tropes, and spaces are adapted to new spatiohistorical imaginaries.[21] Misplaced in space or in time, bunker fantasies open up to different potentialities without thereby fully losing their core affordances, as when Butler misplaced white male nostalgia for the early 1960s and white ghetto imaginaries of the early 1980s into a disorienting and Afrofuturist but no less heavily bunkered-up 2021.

As visible manifestation of the nuclear condition, the bunker form affords a precise and novel relationship to temporality. In their promise to guarantee survival beyond the apocalypse, bunkers function as an enclave of space outside of temporality. This makes them a specific variant of what Fredric Jameson characterizes as utopian space, 'an imaginary enclave within real social space … [T]he very possibility of Utopian space is itself a result of spatial and social differentiation. But it is an aberrant by-product, and its possibility is dependent on the momentary formation of a kind of eddy or self-contained backwater within the general differentiation process and its seemingly irreversible forward momentum.'[22] Bunkers *afford* utopian space within the nuclear condition and thus within the Anthropocene. Moreover, bunkers spatialize the complex dynamic of partial knowledge that enables any utopian imagination. The bunker is the spatial form we summon to assess the balance sheet of nuclearity. This was true in the form's heyday around 1962; it remained true as the culture of the 1980s reimagined its present in relation to a feared and desired past around 1962; and it remains true today as we try to make sense of a contemporary world formed out of the dreams and policies of the 1980s.

As late capitalism has closed off alternatives in the future, in particular the nineteenth-century dream of revolution as a historical phenomenon emerging inevitably or linearly out of present conditions, apocalypse continues to promise a pathway to those alternatives. It is no longer a pathway into

---

20 Levine, *Forms*, 7.
21 Roberto Schwarz, 'Misplaced Ideas,' in *Misplaced Ideas: Essays on Brazilian Culture* (New York: Verso, 2002), 19–32. Originally published in 1973 as 'As idéias fora do lugar.'
22 Fredric Jameson, *Archaeologies of the Future: The Desire Called Utopia and Other Science Fictions* (London: Verso, 2005), 15.

the future, however; instead, nuclear apocalypse and the other versions of cataclysm that have emerged in its wake promise the unmooring of history from temporality altogether. The Anthropocene simply does not afford the imagination of change without apocalypse. Whether the world is going to end and humanity be extinguished, whether nuclear war or global plague or climate crisis will blast humanity back into a neobarbarian stone age or some unforeseen hybrid of technology and feudalism, or whether posthumans will awaken in some distant future and emerge from their shelters into an unrecognizable present, the bunker is the spatial enclave that promises to preserve continuity with what we know and want to retain; the link, however tenuous, between the present world and whatever alternative is being imagined.

Where the possibility of linear thinking appears foreclosed, the bunker promises a different form of ontology. The bunker spatializes the state of being in the world which philosopher Slavoj Žižek, following Ernst Bloch, terms an '"open" ontology': 'In contrast to the idea that every possibility strives to fully actualize itself, one should conceive of "progress" as a move of restoring the dimension of potentiality to mere actuality, of unearthing, in the very heart of actuality, a secret striving toward potentiality.'[23] To live the end of the world is also to open up the possibility of living beyond it, to 'restore the dimension of potentiality' to a 'mere actuality' that otherwise seems an ontological dead end. Even in its present-absence from the nuclear scene, the bunker affords not simply the promise of survival but the insistence that something always remains of the present in whatever strange alternate world one may find oneself stranded. Such an open ontology resists the simple negation or ironic citation of the past. As writer Robert Macfarlane argues, 'To disallow its possibilities for future life, to deny reparation or hope is another kind of oppression.'[24] To describe the 'way of seeing such landscapes' that would attend to their 'dissonance,' Macfarlane adapts the nautical term 'occulting': 'a light that flashes on and off, and in which the periods of illumination are longer than the periods of darkness.'[25] Because the architectural forms of the nuclear age – from the bunker to the missile silo to the arid test site, the hidden laboratories, and the secret control centers – readily adapted themselves to the brutalist dictates of modernity triumphant, their range of meanings and their affective potentialities are all

---

23 Slavoj Žižek, 'Preface: Bloch's Ontology of Not-Yet-Being,' in *The Privatization of Hope: Ernst Bloch and the Future of Utopia*, ed. Peter Thompson and Žižek (Durham: Duke University Press, 2013), SIC 8, Kindle loc. 289–94.
24 Robert Macfarlane, *Underland: A Deep Time Journey* (New York: W. W. Norton, 2019), 229.
25 Macfarlane, *Underland*, 229.

but invisible. One way to restore their range and affect to them is, in fact, to rediscover their textuality, their formal qualities, and, consequently, the ambiguity of meanings afforded by them: their 'occulting' effect of dark and light together.

What I argued in *The Bunkered Decades* is that the end of the Cold War and our growing historical distance from the events of the middle of the last century have begun to enable us finally to deal with the bunker fantasy *as* fantasy, even as what had been fantasy has, in so many ways, been rationalized as history. When philosopher Jacques Derrida pronounced in 1984 that 'Literature has always belonged to the nuclear epoch,'[26] the only available meaning at the time was in the deconstructionist terms that rejected the possibility of any kind of positive meaning, any materiality at all. Four decades on, it is easier to read Derrida against the grain and to argue that, in retrospect, the 'dissident temporality' of the nuclear condition has in fact changed our understanding of the pre-nuclear as also of the post–Cold War. For Derrida as for many of us who lived through the 1980s, this transformed history of the past was a prospect of infinite darkness. But from the vantage point of the twenty-first century, we might also choose to understand that darkness in relation to its occulting effects. With queer theorist Paul Saint-Amour, we might equally inquire of the nuclear condition:

> what new forms of resistance, community, affiliation, or expression might be produced, like mineral allotropes, in the high pressures of the pre-traumatic. Are there situations ... in which an evidently closed, apocalyptic futurity, far from draining our acts of responsibility or critical purchase, might be the only condition under which a certain kind of critique may be tendered, or a certain kind of kinship imagined; might be the catalyst for attending to negative affects instead of dismissing them as fatalism or quietism?[27]

Let me stress that by proposing this 'occulting' description of the dissident temporality of the Cold War and its legacies, I do not fundamentally disagree with the still prevalent critical viewpoint that the exposed bunker's primary value is the ways its out-of-placeness and incommensurability with the landscape around it remind us of the structures of power that drove the tragic absurdities of the Cold War and that persist, pernicious and hidden, today. Nor do I deny that any redemption, reuse, or otherwise vitiation of this profound ambivalence risks compromising that primary value.[28] To reckon

---

26 Jacques Derrida, 'No Apocalypse, Not Now,' *Diacritics* 14.2 (1984): 20–31, at 27.
27 Paul Saint-Amour, *Tense Future: Modernism, Total War, Encyclopedic Form* (New York: Oxford University Press, 2015), 30.
28 John Beck, 'Concrete Ambivalence: Inside the Bunker Complex,' *Cultural Politics* 7.1 (2011): 79–102. Beck's thoughtful and well-argued essay neatly summarizes the stakes of this position.

12 *After the end*

fully with the bunker fantasy requires a critical perspective that, like the bunker, grasps wholesale negativity in the same gesture as wholesale utopia, and grasps both in their occulting relationship. It is as profoundly human and as profoundly uncomfortable to be joyful at the fact or contemplation of survival as it is to continue to acknowledge and to bear the weight of its unbearable costs; and it is perhaps most human of all to do both at once.

The bunker fantasy, here and there

Delhi-born and Mumbai-raised author Vikram Chandra's epic 2006 novel *Sacred Games* opens on a mystery: a gangster run to ground in an antinuclear bunker in the middle of Bombay. The gangster is killed before he can talk, and the police detective attempts to unravel a puzzle that seems out of a Western crime novel:

> In the stack of books at his bedside, ... there are these fictions that he reads for pleasure, often to laugh at the wild extremities of the scenarios that they create, the millions of dead and the dastardly plots and the brave, selfless heroes. In these books, and only in these books, bombs sometimes explode, taking whole cities. Only in these books is there the smoking aftermath, that silence without birds.[29]

Then the scenario comes closer to home:

> But you always shut the book, you put it back on the night-stand, you drink your little sip of water, you turn over and go to sleep. No need to build grim little bunkers in the middle of Bombay, no need for gangsters to run from their safe foreign refuges and into danger, no need to look for three sadhus. No need at all. But Gaitonde is dead. Why?[30]

Later on, the well-read detective finds himself compelled to explain what is going on to his less cosmopolitan partner:

> 'I am telling you now. Listen. That house you found Gaitonde in, that was a nuclear shelter.'
>
> 'A what?'
>
> 'A shelter to protect from a bomb. An atomic weapon. The building was constructed according to a well-known architectural model. It is in books, and you can find it on the internet.'

---

29 Vikram Chandra, *Sacred Games* (London: Faber & Faber, 2006), 322.
30 Chandra, *Sacred Games*, 322. A *sadhu* (the Sanskrit word for a religious ascetic, mendicant, or any holy person in Hinduism, Buddhism, and Jainism who has renounced the worldly life) is central to the novel's apocalyptic plot.

After the imminent apocalypse

Figure I.1 Sartaj Singh (Saif Ali Khan) negotiating with the bunker in Mumbai in *Sacred Games*.

Figure I.2 'Every golden age must be preceded by an apocalypse': the multilingual fantasy of '*pralay, qayamat*, apocalypse' in *Sacred Games*.

'Why would he need that? Here?'

'That is what I want to know.'[31] (Figures I.1 & I.2)

A misplaced antinuclear bunker built by a local gangster beneath a lot in Bombay initiates a police procedural and retrospective that interrogates India's place in the world and the consequences of its nuclear policy and

---

31 Chandra, *Sacred Games*, 481.

14 *After the end*

imbrication in global trade networks. Just as the American bunker fantasy in Butler's imagined 2021 ripples through time from the decade around 1962 through the decade around 1983 and into the present day, so its form travels the world, doing its cultural work according to local needs.

While its center of gravity was always and continues to be the United States, the American bunker fantasy not only traveled the globe; it was in turn seeded and altered by the spatial permutations circulated back to it. The postwar hegemony of American and Soviet imperialism and the Cold (and hot) wars generated by their conflict subjugated the entire world to its bunkered imaginary. 'We're by-products of the mid-twentieth century,' concludes one character in American Canadian writer Ruth Ozeki's 2013 novel, *A Tale for the Time Being*. 'Who isn't?' responds another.[32] From mid-century until near its end, this subjugation was as totalizing and traumatic as the threat of nuclear apocalypse at its dense core; however, it was neither uniform nor comprehensive in its dissemination or effects. This cluster of misplaced ideas continually takes on new and travestied functions and meanings in new spatiohistorical sites and imaginaries. In my reading of Schwarz's concept, such misplaced ideas, tropes, and spaces are subject to both temporal *and* spatial dislocations; moreover, the more time passes, the more alternate bunker fantasies in the present reveal similarly alternate traces in the past. Not only did the Cold War irrevocably transform the world that came after it, but that after-world similarly transformed the meanings of the Cold War. This reciprocal process was captured by German philosopher Walter Benjamin in the oft-cited sixth of his theses 'On the Concept of History' regarding the historian's duty to the ontological instability of the past: 'The only historian capable of fanning the spark of hope in the past is the one who is firmly convinced that *even the dead* will not be safe from the enemy if he is victorious. And this enemy has never ceased to be victorious.'[33] In its strictly ideological meaning, the bunker fantasy created a post–Cold War world permanently confined to an ontological bunker by a ceaselessly victorious enemy above.

At the same time, dwelling in a permanently bunkered and postapocalyptic condition affords several insights that clinging to the fantasy of a preapocalyptic way of life surviving under the nuclear condition does not. Recognized as ontological, the bunker fantasy ceases to operate exclusively as a powerful tool for legitimating surveillance, separation barriers, and enclosure in the name of enhanced security; it can be wielded critically. I adapt the term

32 Ruth Ozeki, *A Tale for the Time Being* (New York: Penguin, 2013), 32.
33 Walter Benjamin, 'On the Concept of History,' in *Selected Writings, Vol. 4, 1938–1940*, ed. Howard Eiland and Michael W. Jennings (Cambridge, MA: Harvard University Press, 2003), 389–97, at 391.

'ontological bunker' from English SFF writer J. G. Ballard's description of the ruins on a South Pacific island of the extensive bunker architecture designed solely to receive and observe nuclear blasts, as an 'ontological Eden': as if the prehistoric traces of some vanished culture and an animistically rendered spatiotemporal truth outside of which the protagonist Traven is simply unable any longer to live.[34] Like the figure of *Homo hydrogenensis* Ballard describes as adequate to this nuclear spacetime, the ontological bunker is simultaneously a thorough critique of the fatal conclusion to which the nuclear condition inevitably leads and also an opening, an exploration of the dissident temporality and wholly unforeseen possibilities that might emerge on the way to the logical conclusion of the nuclear condition. Dwelling on an irradiated Enewetak in a physical sense is untenable; fully dwelling in an imaginative sense on Enewetak opens up the ontological bunker to alternate meanings not afforded anywhere else.

The ontological bunker naturalizes the condition in order fully to study its phenomenological range within a Cold War spacetime in which no other option appeared available. Post-1989, a new way of understanding bunkering has also become available. What we can term the *epistemological* bunker makes visible the bunker fantasy as a system of knowledge production in ways that the ontological bunker affords affectively and experientially. Viewed as epistemology, the bunker promises shelter from the traumas and categories of the past even as it reminds us that we continue to inhabit the world created by it. Rather than emerging from that world, we remain within its parameters and must find ways of reworking rather than simply presuming we can step outside them whenever we wish. The epistemological bunker can also help to understand the spatiocultural history of the security imaginary that makes these measures welcome to some, tolerable to some, and abhorrent to others.

We can glimpse this distinction, for instance, in a moment early on in Japanese writer Haruki Murakami's 2010 novel of parallel 1984 worlds, when one of the two protagonists finds herself watching *On the Beach*, which chronicles the behavior of a mixed group of characters waiting in Melbourne for the inevitable fallout of a nuclear war in the global North to float far enough south that it will kill them (Figure I.3). We thus begin in the ontological bunker of 1959, in which 'The extinction of the human race was simply unavoidable. The surviving human beings there could do nothing but wait for the end to come. They chose different ways to live out their final days. That was the plot. It was a dark movie offering no hope

---

34 J. G. Ballard, 'The Terminal Beach' (1964), in *The Complete Stories of J. G. Ballard* (New York: Norton, 2009), 589–604. For a detailed reading of this story, see Pike, *Bunkered Decades*, 136–8.

Figure I.3 Waiting for the end of the world: the deserted streets of Melbourne, Australia, at the end of the slow death of the world from nuclear war in the north in *On the Beach*.

of salvation.'[35] But then the narrator opens out a parenthesis that briefly suggests an epistemological insight into the bunker fantasy that the alternate version of the Cold War bunker fantasy might have afforded: '(Though, watching it, Aomame reconfirmed her belief that everyone, deep in their hearts, is waiting for the end of the world to come.)'[36] Through Aomame's 1984 experience, the twenty-first-century narrator is simultaneously able to dwell ontologically in the bunker fantasy of *On the Beach*, to experience its affective power epistemologically as secondhand inheritance, and jointly to articulate the contradictions condensed within that power.

Dwelling in the bunker epistemologically enables us to recognize our relationship to apocalypse not solely as the cataclysmic, unique, and always deferred rupture in time that a nuclear war surely would be, but as an ongoing historical condition always affecting a certain – and substantial – number of individuals and groups within unequal societies, affecting them unequally, and affecting them in intersecting but not always commensurate ways. Epistemological dwelling does not remove us from an ontological relationship to a bunkered world; however, it does open up that ontology

---

35 Haruki Murakami, *IQ84*, trans. Jay Rubin and Philip Gabriel (New York: Vintage, 2011 [2010]), 19.
36 Murakami, *IQ84*, 19.

After the imminent apocalypse　　　　　17

both in terms of the ways it is produced and in terms of the alternate ways of dwelling it might afford. This is the insight gained from historicizing the *imagination* of nuclear apocalypse as distinct from its potential *reality*. The bunker fantasy is a powerful means whereby those less directly affected by catastrophic circumstances are able to visualize and also to distance their relationship to those circumstances. By the same token, the bunker fantasy also affords survivors and oppressed individuals and communities a spatiotemporal imaginary that gives form and articulation to their situation. It can reveal to us, as critical geographer Katherine McKittrick writes, that 'Physical geographies ... are not static. Instead, they are permeable and material indications of the uncertainty of place.'[37] The 'spark of hope' that Benjamin termed a life-and-death struggle by the historian over the meaning of the past in a classically polarized mid-century formulation remains accessible even within an apocalyptic moment. And it remains accessible – in McKittrick's example – even within 'the perimeters and buildings of an antebellum plantation'[38] misplaced into a variegated and open ontology of alternate pasts and futures irreducible to a singular or cohesive meaning.

As both Benjamin and Bloch had presciently argued during the 1930s, the most fertile contemporary sources for identifying and opening up alternate potentialities within an ostensibly fixed and determinate contemporary or historical record are usually found in ephemeral cultural productions and material practices that were less concerned or careful about maintaining ideological consistency. In this book, as in *The Bunkered Decades*, I rely heavily on examples from genre fiction, comics, music, and vernacular architecture not because I consider these sources necessarily truer to their age or privileged in their meanings but because their popular forms afford misplacement in their very inception. My specific positionality as a white American man born in the early 1960s, trained as a scholar in the 1980s, and writing in the post–Cold War decades deeply informs this methodology in ways both within and beyond my control. To paraphrase another of Benjamin's theses, my personal historical relationship to the three moments at stake in this book helps me to recognize every image of these pasts as one of my own concerns in the present.[39] Where my own position differs from Benjamin's tragic moment in the 1930s is that rather than 'an irretrievable image which threatens to disappear,' the Cold War past with which this book is concerned threatens instead to remain irretrievably *present*.

37 Katherine McKittrick, *Demonic Grounds: Black Women and the Cartographies of Struggle* (Minneapolis: University of Minnesota Press, 2006), 2.
38 McKittrick, *Demonic Grounds*, 2.
39 Benjamin, 'On the Concept of History,' 391.

Writing from the epistemological bunker affords little if any of the view from without as which Benjamin defined the redemptive stance; instead, it affords innumerable spatiotemporal misplacements of a singularly powerful twenty-first-century imaginary. I understand my own stance in terms of Lily Wong's concept of *dwelling*, which she argues is similar to Benjamin's leftist melancholy but 'without fetishizing ... past political models ... to a point of debilitation.'[40] Writing of the term in its simultaneously 'affective and structural dimensions,' Wong calls for 'a strategic recollection of the past that repoliticizes our relationship to cultural and historical formations in the contemporary. ... [T]o dwell is to reside continuously in the past. It is actively inactive: ongoing, consistently in a state of suspension, relentlessly becoming with no clear origin or end point.'[41] Wong distinguishes without quite drawing a line between critical and noncritical dwelling; for me, the bunker fantasy, as other forms of dwelling in spacetimes of the past, is always both, simultaneously. The bunker fantasy is certainly driven by noncritical, ontological dwelling in an imaginary past given affective form and material substance by the physical and metaphorical shelters of the Cold War. At the same time, the more we recognize it, and ourselves, as dwelling in the Cold War past, the more that past becomes epistemologically available for something other than simply melancholic or simply wish-fulfilling repetition. Such critical dwelling helps to understand the temporal rings that formed today's bunker fantasy, while also making visible the many misreadings, displacements, and appropriations that have occurred as it has circulated in space and time.

The peculiar dynamics of the bunker fantasy inform today's security state and responses to the current threats posed by the climate crisis, just as they inform literary and cultural imaginations around those threats and policies. For both circumstances, the bunker fantasy offers the most adequate epistemological framework available but also remains fundamentally unsuited to the task at hand. Its contradictions capture well the contradictory individual responses to apocalypse-level threats; however, such contradictions impact far differently as policy than as personal affect. As philosopher Lauren Berlant noted,

> One really big difference between political institutions and people is that people are able to manage ordinary affective incoherence and disorganisation with much grace as long as their anchors in the ongoing world or the ordinary feel sufficiently stable ... We can bear a lot of wobble, but when the media and state-interested institutions orchestrate all kinds of situations as crises and

---

40 Lily Wong, 'Dwelling over China: Minor Transnationalisms in Karen Tei Yamashita's *I Hotel*,' *American Quarterly* 69.3 (2017): 719–39, at 721.
41 Wong, 'Dwelling over China,' 721.

as threats to the infrastructures that organise nextness and vague senses of
the projected out future, anxiety levels rise that are not just about the singular
situation but about ongoingness itself.[42]

The ontological bunker, in other words, may be a tenable or a psychologically
necessary position or even a critically astute option for individuals dwelling
in a nuclear world. But when bunker fantasies drive political measures to
build walls or police borders or seal off societies, the effect can quite literally
be catastrophic.

After the End thus proposes reading the bunker fantasy not only in the
occulting effects of its dissident temporality but equally in what we can call
its dissident spatialities. Precisely because it imagines an enclave displaced
in space and time that would open into a new, survivable world, the ontological bunker offers the possibility of imagining alternate spacetimes both
linked to the material present and also profoundly other to them. Quite the
opposite of confinement to a sealed underground shelter, dwelling in the
epistemological bunker can open up as many possibilities for imaginative
traveling as it forecloses difference in a bunkered mind. All bunker fantasies
blink between light and dark in this way; this book explores the affective
dissidence even in the most bunkered of survivalist fantasies as well as the
inevitable foreclosure that frames even the wildest speculations.

Overview of the book

The Bunkered Decades proposed a taxonomy of five primary and overlapping
bunker forms mobilized in the years around 1962 and affording different
associations to social and cultural fault lines of Cold War America: the
basement or backyard shelter, suburbia, and the nuclear family; the cave,
tribalism, and feral humanity; the private supershelter, survivalism, and
self-reliance; the community shelter, infrastructure, and urban bunkerism;
and the government supershelter, paranoia, and paternalism. When the
imaginary around 1983 revisited the Kennedy-era bunker forms, those
associations had not exactly disappeared. Instead, they were subsumed within
a broader repulsion from or nostalgia for the shelter society more generally.
At the same time, new spatial forms emerged that were related to but distinct
from bunkered spaces per se in both their morphology and their affordances.
These literal and figurative forms – in particular, the dome, the separation
wall, the tunnel, and the silo – have similarly been subsumed since 1983

---

42 Lauren Berlant and Jordan Greenwald, 'Affect in the End Times: A Conversation
with Lauren Berlant,' *Qui Parle* 20.2 (2012): 71–89, at 76.

within the broader imaginary of the bunker fantasy around the core contemporary issues of security and mobility. In a world where mobility of goods, ideas, people, and viruses is simultaneously a core principle of late capitalism and a physical or ideological threat to society or sovereignty, this spatial imaginary is where security and mobility are argued and balanced. To be able to tell persuasive stories around the bunker fantasy is essential no matter one's politics or allegiances. No wonder such stories of apocalypse and postapocalypse have proliferated beyond counting in the current century.

Chapters 1 and 2 of *After the End* begin this study with a look at the one area in which the bunker form most strongly has retained its identity qua bunker: the shelter as talismanic space for real-life survivalists through to the present (Chapter 1) and the shelter as time-travel device and fictional emblem (Chapter 2), explicitly making comparisons between the years around 1962, the years around 1983, and whenever the present happens to be. These chapters study the bunker and survivalism primarily within America but also in relation to the changing meanings attributed to Hiroshima, Japan, as a space and a nuclear imaginary. Across the varieties of sheltering, the dome manifests as the open-air alternative to the sealed-off bunker. Radical openness and reactionary foreclosure, lightness and darkness, utopia and dystopia play out against each other in the spaces of survival. Chapter 3 explores the global bunker fantasy from postwar through the present via case studies of the extremes it reached in the almost unimaginably vast civil defense infrastructures constructed by Taiwan, Switzerland, and Albania during the Cold War, and the less extreme but no less formative measures taken by other nations. Misplaced from its origins in American nuclearity, the bunker fantasy proved able both to model fundamental principles of democracy and the right to shelter and to spatialize the insanity of totalitarianism. Chapters 4 and 5 study the global legacy of the bunker fantasy through ways the spatial forms of the Cold War have been appropriated and repurposed for tourism, for capitalism, for infrastructure, and for imagining alternate pasts, presents, and futures. Chapter 4 studies cultural practices and the built environment, in particular nuclear tourism and the various functions in the years after 1989 of the Cold War spaces discussed in Chapter 3. Chapter 5 analyzes new forms of postapocalyptic fictions and practices emerging out of the Cold War: zombie apocalypse, future noir, the Afrofuturism of Octavia Butler, Nalo Hopkinson, and Nnedi Okorafor, and distant-future speculations. I argue, first, that these practices began and existed throughout the Cold War and, second, that they have been transformed since 1990, especially in terms of a new global imaginary of neoliberalism that is itself a misplaced Cold War idea. Chapter 6 addresses the practical ramifications of spatial divisions in imagining the twenty-first-century nation-state and its boundaries, including the growing frequency of separation

After the imminent apocalypse 21

barriers such as on the Mexico–US border and between Israel and Palestinian territories. These borderlands and barriers manifest many of the same spatial fears and dreams of security as the Cold War bunker fantasy, misplaced into the very different geopolitics of the twenty-first century. Far from having been left behind with the end of the Cold War, the bunker fantasy has molded and continues to mold the world today, but as second nature, the internalized truths of the 1980s no longer even recognized as such. The book's conclusion considers the twenty-first-century move toward biosecurity, sheltering, and siloing as a continuation of the Cold War bunker fantasy become ontology: what are the consequences of the ontological bunker and what new liberatory potentials might be opened up by this very fact of being shut in? Rock around a bunker, after all, is both a liberating beat and an inorganic shell, both Hitler's downfall and the Comets' rise. What can we learn from the sacrilege of this pairing beyond its still-powerful charge of transgression?

1

The fantasy of 1980s survivalism since the Reagan years

[For this epigraph, please read the lyrics of or listen to the second verse of the referenced song]

Destiny's Child, 'Survivor' (2001)

While there have always been survivors, while survivors have been known as 'survivalists' at least since the 1920s, and while survivalists began to be identified with rightwing extremism during the early 1960s, it was only during the resurgence of Cold War intensity in the early years of the 1980s that the practices and ideologies of *survivalism* as such came into being. And it is in the bunker as talisman of and popular emblem for the newly imagined form of the nuclear condition known as survivalism that the doubled legacies of the 1960s and 1980s persist most overtly into the present day. A strong tension persists within both self-identified survivalism and the culture of survival writ large: a tension between the libertarian ideologies of isolationism and every-man-for-himself-ism, on the one hand, and the adaptation of survival tactics for the perpetuation of civilized society, on the other. As the veteran captain of the trimaran *Vagabond* concludes of what is functionally a floating fallout shelter in the 1983 nuclear war novel *The Long Voyage Back*, 'We're all trying to survive. Everyone on this boat, everyone, will lie, steal, cheat, and kill in order to survive. That speech served one purpose: to let their survival instinct know that the first thing it has to consider is me and whatever promotes the survival of this ship.'[1] In its struggle with the primal force and the social conundrum of the bunker fantasy, a comprehensive understanding of this 'cold will to survive'[2] is a necessary starting point for understanding Cold War culture since the Cold War.

---

1 Luke Rhinehart, *The Long Voyage Back* (Permuted Press, 2014 [1983]), Kindle edition, loc. 2034.
2 Rhinehart, *Long Voyage Back*, loc. 1669.

The emergence of survivalism out of the bunker

Although its early practitioners drew from counterculture and opposition sources both left and right, the latter-day survivalist has since the Reagan years been strongly identified – and strongly self-identified – as rightwing, libertarian, white nationalist, and militia-focused. Partly because of the sociopolitical threat it represents and partly because it makes such a potent satirical target, that imaginary has tended to overshadow other permutations of survivalism, including the elite supershelter builders currently identified as 'preppers' and the equally select beneficiaries of the potential protection offered by government supershelters. Similarly, while by no means fully erroneous, this identification has obscured the ways in which survivalism has infiltrated apocalyptic thinking across the political spectrum, including progressive opposition to nuclear proliferation and to survivalism itself. Such a comprehensive understanding in no way reduces the political threat or the ideological odiousness of hardcore white supremacist survivalism. Nevertheless, disentangling the meanings and cultural work of survivalism writ large from the specific meanings it bears and the cultural work it does within its rightwing extremist manifestation can help to clarify its allure, while also tracing what it shares with and how it differs from other manifestations of this fundamental response to the nuclear age.

The 'brawny survivor in combat fatigues squatt[ing] near the entrance of a bomb shelter' to whom 'nuclear war was the best thing that had ever happened' has long signified a lunatic fringe response to the nuclear condition.[3] This is true as much for left-liberal satirists such as James Morrow in *This Is the Way the World Ends* (1986, cited above) as for the serialized men's action fictions of the 1980s that form the largest repository of images of this fringe.[4] And it is true even as the protagonist heroes of those fictions always also define themselves as bearing the torch of civilization over against the antisocial, Hobbesian 'survivalist.' Defined by his bomb shelter or hidey-hole, the survivalist provides a limit-case of what distinguishes savage individualists from human society. The typically ironic or dismissive representation of these figures ignores the social critique afforded by survivalism's forms and precludes any analysis of the ways in which the extremes of survivalism since the 1980s, despite and because of their extremism, intersect with and diverge from ideas around 'survival' that have infiltrated global society more broadly.

---

3 James Morrow, *This Is the Way the World Ends* (New York: Harcourt, Brace, 1986), 113–14.
4 On men's action fiction during the 1980s, see chapter seven of Pike, *Bunkered Decades*.

24 *After the end*

Put simply, the survivalist is what remained from the failure of the individual sheltering project in the United States around 1962. It is not that survivalism did not exist as a practice before the 1980s. Rather, what began to be called survivalism had been so mainstream in the early 1960s that it had not yet even been termed 'survivalism'; it had simply occupied the accepted center of the national conversation. In 1961, a Gallup poll had found that 5 percent of those surveyed had made changes aimed at sheltering; private ownership of shelters would soon peak at 2.2 percent.[5] The death of President Kennedy in November 1963 effectively marked the end of even a limited consensus on sheltering and civil defense. But we should not underestimate the 1961 poll or the long afterlife of this endeavor. Measured in terms of the 1962 population of 186.5 million, that limited percentage would still indicate over four million shelter owners and over nine million Americans identifying as what the twenty-first century would come to term 'preppers.' Given that recent scholarship regards an estimate of three million preppers, just under 1 percent of the current population, as substantive evidence of the twenty-first-century 'mainstreaming' of survivalism, we should perhaps take the current claim with a grain of salt and the earlier numbers a bit more seriously than many scholars currently do.[6]

This chapter charts changing attitudes towards nuclear apocalypse and environmental transformation in terms of different and changing approaches towards survivalism as it emerged on its own terms during the 1980s and as it has developed in sometimes predictable and sometimes surprising ways since that time. When treated on these terms, survivalism serves several functions. As any search online will reveal (and as *The Bunkered Decades* explores in depth), the survivalist since the 1980s has become an effective thumbnail figure for rightwing libertarian fanaticism in particular and for critically engaging with masculinity in general. The men's action fictions that emerged in the 1980s and continue to be published today, some in ongoing volumes of long-running series that date back to that earlier decade, tend to employ this same thumbnail to distance their own superhuman protagonists from the charges of fanaticism and bigotry mobilized by this image. This chapter touches on enduring clichés of hardened masculinity

---

5 John Gregory Stocke, '"Suicide on the Installment Plan": Cold-War-Era Civil Defense and Consumerism in the United States,' in *The Writing on the Cloud: American Culture Confronts the Atomic Bomb*, ed. Alison M. Scott and Christopher D. Geist (Lanham: University Press of America, 1997), 46–60, at 46.

6 Gwendolyn Audrey Foster, 'Consuming the Apocalypse, Marketing Bunker Materiality,' *Quarterly Review of Film and Video* 33.4 (2016): 285–302, at 296; Casey Ryan Kelly, 'The Man-pocalypse: Doomsday Preppers and the Rituals of Apocalyptic Manhood,' *Text and Performance Quarterly* 36.2–3 (2016): 95–114, at 95.

The fantasy of survivalism since the 1980s 25

but focuses primarily on two forms of survivalism that take the concept very seriously, either on its own terms or as an effective device for historical comparison in either a tragic or a comic mode.

The following section frames the chapter in terms of the countercultural forms of the 1970s that 1980s survivalism both appropriated and repudiated, in particular, the *Whole Earth Catalog*'s enthusiastic embrace of dome architecture and the pragmatically optimistic DIY survival techniques that emerged from the Oak Ridge National Laboratory in Tennessee, where scientist and inventor Cresson Kearny had worked from 1964 and which published his *Nuclear War Survival Skills* in 1979. The chapter then treats 'real world' survivalism on its own terms, from early theorists and proponents such as Kurt Saxon through 1980s radicalism and religious millenarianism to current 'prepper' sites and reality television series such as the National Geographic Channel's *Doomsday Preppers* (2012–14). Chapter 2 shifts to fictional depictions of survivalists and images of survivalism.

Domes, bunkers, and proto-survivalism in the 1970s

The sources of 1980s survivalism certainly derive from the counterculture, but the counterculture they derive from was far more mainstream than the survivalists who would be inspired by it. Notably, these sources include the bible of the counterculture, *The Whole Earth Catalog*, first published in 1968 and reissued periodically until 1998, and its 'primary competitor,' *Mother Earth News*, founded in 1971 and still published today.[7] *Whole Earth* was polemically eclectic and ecumenical in its approach to survival as to everything else; a single page promoted both *The Survival Book* ('the best we've seen of the military survival manuals') and *Survival Arts of the Primitive Paiutes* ('a rare book: it shows in exhaustive well-illustrated detail how one tribe managed its daily survival').[8] Although editor Stewart Brand proclaimed the 'power of the individual to conduct his own education, find his own inspiration, shape his own environment, and share his adventure with whoever is interested,' the focus was in the present and with an open community of 'whoever is interested.'[9] Survivalists, like the fictions they consumed, stressed private shelters and the critique or outright destruction of any form of organized community; the lede of Kurt Saxon's first *Survivor* newsletter in 1976 was

---

7 Andrew G. Kirk, *Counterculture Green: The Whole Earth Catalog and American Environmentalism* (Lawrence: University Press of Kansas, 2007), 85.
8 Stewart Brand, *Whole Earth Catalog: Access to Tools* (San Rafael, CA: Point Foundation, 1998 [1968]), 46.
9 Brand, *Whole Earth*, 2.

26   *After the end*

'Survival Is Looking after No. 1.'[10] In contrast, *Whole Earth* insisted that new spaces would make visible the '99 percent invisible activity' which guiding spirit Buckminster Fuller had argued was 'coalescing to reshape our future.'[11] Both claims are apocalyptic in form; however, the counterculture approach was to embrace cataclysmic change and bring it out into the open rather than the survivalist's choice to hide from it until forced to fight. 'Reshape environment,' Fuller urged, 'don't try to reshape man.'[12]

In *Shelter*, his seminal building guide to vernacular architecture, first published in 1973 and still in print today, Lloyd Kahn celebrated 'simple homes, natural materials, and human resourcefulness' as well as 'discovery, hard work, the joys of self-sufficiency, and freedom.'[13] Kahn was closely associated with *Whole Earth*, to which he contributed the popular 'Shelter and Land Use' section.[14] Although *Whole Earth* offered practical advice in the basic skills of living off the grid along with what became known as its 'hippie' ideology, the emblematic spatial form of its section on 'Shelter and Land Use' was not the bunker but Fuller's geodesic dome. Nearly a third of the 175 outsized and heavily illustrated pages are devoted to varieties of dome accompanied by designs and techniques for their construction. Kahn described the dome as 'one of man's earliest shelters' newly revived as a form 'associated with a new lifestyle, the subculture, doing "more with less," living in the round, and ecology'; despite a brief feature on the continuing threat of nuclear war, not a mention is made of the bunkered form that would readily have been conjured up by the book's title in the early 1970s.[15] Rather, the entire volume reads as a conscious effort to renovate the concept of shelter as 'more than a roof overhead.'[16]

Due primarily to Kahn's contributions here and in the two *Domebooks* he had published prior to *Shelter*, the dome became, in historian Andrew Kirk's words, 'the standard architectural form for communes, mavericks, and iconoclasts all over the American West ... a statement of a sensibility as much as a place to live and work.'[17] It is a testimony to the enduring

---

10 Kurt Saxon, *The Survivor Volume 1* (n.p.: n.p., 1976), 1: https://archive.org/details/THESURVIVOR1/page/n1/mode/2up; accessed 31 Aug. 2023.
11 Buckminster Fuller, 'WDSD Document 1,' in Brand, *Whole Earth*, 3.
12 Fuller, 'WDSD Document 1,' 4.
13 *Shelter*, ed. Lloyd Kahn, co-ed. and design Bob Easton (Bolenas, CA: Shelter Publications, 2000 [1973]), 3. Kahn reports that the original edition of *Shelter* sold 'over 185,000' copies 'by word of mouth' during the 1970s (174) and as of the 2nd edition had sold 'over 300,000 copies' worldwide.
14 Kirk, *Counterculture Green*, 85.
15 *Shelter*, ed. Kahn, 109, 116.
16 *Shelter*, ed. Kahn, 3.
17 Kirk, *Counterculture Green*, 85.

power of the dome imaginary that, despite *Shelter*'s presentation of an 'intriguing variety of building methods from all over the world,' its argument for 'the advantages of rectilinear construction,' and its insistence on the 'disadvantages of domes' as practical constructions, the form still dominated the reception of the new book.[18] Kahn even bowed to popular demand by releasing a new booklet, *Refried Domes*, in 1989, in part, 'To present our hard-earned opinion of domes as homes. (They don't work.)'[19] As he had written in *Shelter*, distinguishing between the practical and symbolic value of the form, 'there continue to be many unsolved problems with dome homes' but 'Metaphorically, our work on domes now appears to us to have been smart.'[20]

The open-air bunkering of the dome proposed a utopian resolution to the American oxymoron of the public shelter that had never managed to gain a foothold in a dominant American imaginary steeped in anticommunist individualism. Especially in SFF fiction and in comics, the spatial dynamics of the dome expressed a direct response to the sterile, antisocial, and masculinist associations of the bunker space during the 1980s.[21] This resolution applied primarily in the speculative future of feminist SFF or the futuristic spectacle of Spaceship Earth in Walt Disney World's Epcot Center (opened in 1982); in the present day, it simply gave up any pretense of survival in favor of directly transforming the present. As Brand wrote of Drop City, whose *Dome Cookbook* was authored by designer Steve Baer, it was 'a rural vacant lot full of elegant funky domes and ditto people. ... instead of dying of dissertation dry rot, his notions stand around in the world bugging the citizens' (Figure 1.1).[22] Utopian communities such as Drop City (founded in Colorado in 1965) and Arcosanti (established by architect Paolo Soleri in 1970 in the Arizona desert and still holding on into the twenty-first century) embraced the openness and organicism associated with the dome; they were similarly featured in the pages of *Whole Earth* as part of the same counterculture. Writer and photographer James McGirk, for instance, recalls discovering 'Soleri's drawings as a teenager in my parents' bound copy of *The Last Whole Earth Catalog* [1971].'[23] Writing of the original dome in 1989, architect Wendell Burnette rhapsodized in the *Whole Earth*

---

18 Lloyd Kahn, 'Refried Domes' (1989): http://web.archive.org/web/20230202231818/https://www.shelterpub.com/domes; accessed 31 Aug. 2023.

19 Kahn, 'Refried Domes.'

20 *Shelter*, ed. Kahn, 112.

21 Pike, *Bunkered Decades*, 246–62.

22 Brand, *Whole Earth*, 15.

23 James McGirk, 'Remembering Life in Arcosanti, Paolo Soleri's Futuristic Desert Utopia,' *Wired* (11 April 2013): http://web.archive.org/web/20221226074258/http://www.wired.com/2013/04/arcosanti-paolo-soleri/.

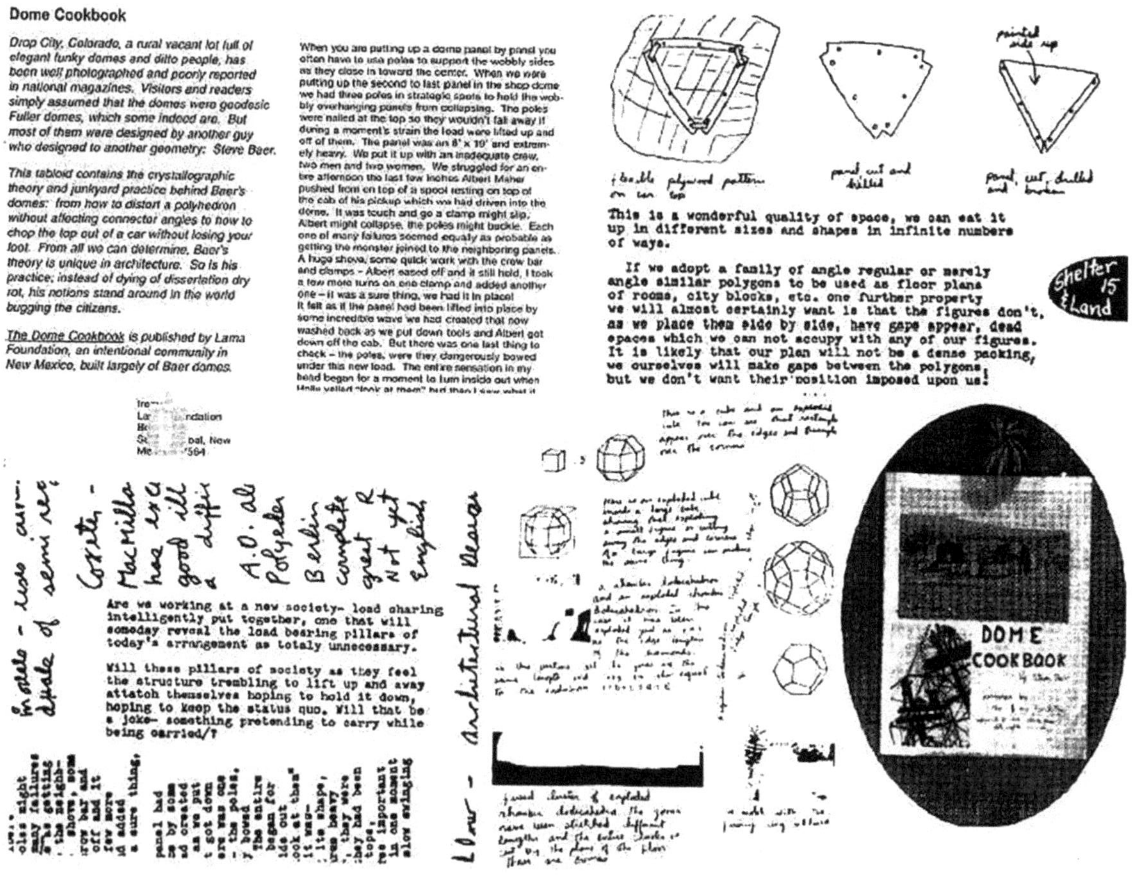

Dome Cookbook

Drop City, Colorado, a rural vacant lot full of elegant funky domes and ditto people, has been well photographed and poorly reported in national magazines. Visitors and readers simply assumed that the domes were geodesic Fuller domes, which some indeed are. But most of them were designed by another guy who designed to another geometry: Steve Baer.

This tabloid contains the crystallographic theory and junkyard practice behind Baer's domes: from how to distort a polyhedron without affecting connector angles to how to chop the top out of a car without losing your foot. From all we can determine, Baer's theory is unique in architecture. So is his practice; instead of dying of dissertation dry rot, his notions stand around in the world bugging the citizens.

The Dome Cookbook is published by Lama Foundation, an intentional community in New Mexico, built largely of Baer domes.

When you are putting up a dome panel by panel you often have to use poles to support the wobbly sides as they close in toward the center. When we were putting up the second to last panel in the shop dome we had three poles in strategic spots to hold the wobbly overhanging panels from collapsing. The poles were nailed at the top so they wouldn't fall away if during a moment's strain the load were lifted up and off of them. The panel was an 8' x 10' and extremely heavy. We put it up with an inadequate crew, two men and two women. We struggled for an entire afternoon the last few inches Albert Maher pushed from on top of a spool resting on top of the cab of his pickup which we had driven into the dome. It was touch and go a clamp might slip, Albert might collapse, the poles might buckle. Each one of many failures seemed equaly as probable as getting the monster joined to the neighboring panels. A huge shove, some quick work with the crow bar and clamps – Albert eased off and it still held, I took a few more turns on one clamp and added another one – it was a sure thing, we had it in place! It felt as if the panel had been lifted into place by some incredible wave we had created that now washed back as we put down tools and Albert got down off the cab. But there was one last thing to check – the poles, were they dangerously bowed under this new load. The entire sensation in my head began for a moment to turn inside out when

This is a wonderful quality of space, we can eat it up in different sizes and shapes in infinite numbers of ways.

If we adopt a family of angle regular or merely angle similar polygons to be used as floor plans of rooms, city blocks, etc. one further property we will almost certainly want is that the figures don't, as we place them side by side, have gaps appear, dead spaces which we can not occupy with any of our figures. It is likely that our plan will not be a dense packing, we ourselves will make gaps between the polygons, but we don't want their position imposed upon us!

Are we working at a new society- load sharing intelligently put together, one that will someday reveal the load bearing pillars of today's arrangement as totaly unnecessary.

Will these pillars of society as they feel the structure trembling to lift up and away attatch themselves hoping to hold it down, hoping to keep the status quo. Will that be a joke- something pretending to carry while being carried/?

Figure 1.1 From Stewart Brand's pages in the first *Whole Earth Catalog* on Drop City: 'a rural vacant lot full of elegant funky domes and ditto people.'

style that, 'Soleri and Mills created not just a glass house in the desert, but a compatible marriage of past and future.'[24] Not all counterculturists were so enamored of 'dome mania' – environmentalist Edward Abbey found them 'ugly ... like pimples across the face of the splendid American Southwest ... both symbol and symptom of the Plastic Plague, the Age of Junk'[25] – but their primacy in Abbey's circles went unchallenged until the 1980s.

As Kirk argues, *Whole Earth* set many of the terms of the environmentalist movement that gave rise to the mainstreaming of antinuclear protest in the 1980s.[26] Its repudiation of cities and the institutions of 'government, big business, formal education, church,'[27] along with its recipes for living off the land, also provided key resources for the survivalists to take down into their doomsday bunkers. When the preppers of the 2010s eschewed the negative associations of those bunkers, however, they brought no new communal vision or geodesic dome inspiration to take its place. Instead, they argued, either implicitly or explicitly, that the neoliberal individual was inherently a prepper and that there was no need for bunkers because every space in the global North was now or soon would be effectively bunkered. The new domes of twenty-first-century pop culture, as we will see below, remained transparent, but they no longer typically embraced and sheltered utopian enclaves imagining postapocalyptic survival. Instead, they simply became giant traps.

1980s survivalists would filter what they saw as the best practices of *Whole Earth* through the militarized expertise of Oak Ridge National Laboratory scientist and inventor Cresson Kearny's *Nuclear War Survival Skills*, first published in 1979, updated in 1987, and still available for download online today. According to a well-informed character in Dean Ing's survivalist novel, *Pulling Through* (1983), 'Fellow named Kearny ramrodded several projects at Oak Ridge oriented toward nuke survival ... and his team deserves top marks.' What's more, the narrator emphatically added, 'The damned manual was in the public domain!'[28] Published just

---

24 Karissa Rosenfield, 'The Dome in the Desert by Wendell Burnette,' *ArchDaily* (14 April 2013): http://web.archive.org/web/20220808193351/https://www.archdaily.com/359748/the-dome-in-the-desert-by-wendell-burnette.

25 Edward Abbey, 'Home Is Where the Hearth Is,' review of *Shelter* (1973): http://theshelterblog.com/shelter/_shelter/abbey.html; accessed 6 April 2018.

26 Kirk, *Counterculture Green*, 30. Although he makes clear that Brand's advocacy of space exploration and nuclear power as part of his 'environmental pragmatism' put him at odds with 'nature purists' (180), Kirk's account also makes evident that both visions of 'appropriate technology' were under siege during the Reagan years (211).

27 Brand, *Whole Earth*, 2.

28 Dean Ing, *Pulling Through* (New York: Ace, 1983), 37.

30 *After the end*

before Kearny's book, Saxon's newsletter (1976–78) approvingly cited *Whole Earth* and *Mother Earth* and included information on building a fallout meter based on Kearny's main source.[29] Rather than 'reshaping' anything, Kearny's book-length pamphlet was based on an ideology of 'self-help civil defense,' or making do on one's own.[30] *Nuclear War Survival Skills* was built around a single concept, a core device, and an essential space. The concept was 'hormesis,' or the difference between small beneficial doses of a 'substance or agent' and large deadly ones; the device was the KFM, or homemade fallout radiation meter (Kearny was fond of naming his survival devices after himself); and the space was the 'expedient shelter ... the greatest need.'[31] More than half a million copies were in print by the mid-1990s and *Nuclear War Survival Skills* has continued to be updated after the author's death.[32] In a brief introduction to the 2016 edition of Kearny's handbook, Don Mann, 'Nuclear Biological and Chemical (NBC) Program Manager for SEAL Team SIX, during the 1990s,' speaks enviously of the 'many nuclear fallout shelters throughout Europe' and the high level of civic and individual preparedness of their populations.[33] This edition, like the author-approved 2004 version available online through the Oregon Institute of Science and Medicine, reprints Kearny's 1999 'Letter to the American People' as an 'Appendix on Hormesis.' Only long after the Cold War, it seems, was Kearny comfortable mentioning this principle directly, which previously would have caused 'panic' and prevented people from taking his

29 Kurt Saxon, *The Survivor Volume 4* (n.p.: n.p., 1978), 1421–3. First published as a quarterly newsletter between 1976 and 1978, *The Survivor* was reissued by Saxon in 1987 and 1988 in four volumes augmented by large amounts of public domain material, mostly from old issues of *Popular Mechanics*, and totaling over 1600 pages. It remains freely available online.

30 Cresson Kearny, *Nuclear War Survival Skills* (1979), updated and expanded 1987 edition (Cave Junction, OR: Oregon Institute of Science and Medicine, 2004): http://web.archive.org/web/20221101062222/http://oism.org/nwss/nwss.pdf; accessed 31 Aug. 2023.

31 Kearny, *Nuclear War*, 37. Kearny had already published three years earlier the two-hundred-page *Expedient Shelter Construction and Occupancy Experiments* (Oak Ridge, TN: Oak Ridge National Laboratory, 1976); he would incorporate its key lessons into the later pamphlet.

32 Christopher Lehmann-Haupt, 'Cresson Kearny, Expert on Nuclear Survival, Dies at 89,' *New York Times* (12 Jan. 2004): www.nytimes.com/2004/01/12/us/cresson-kearny-expert-on-nuclear-survival-dies-at-89.html.

33 Don Mann, 'Introduction,' in *Nuclear War Survival Skills: Lifesaving Nuclear Facts and Self-Help Instructions*, by Cresson H. Kearny, expanded, updated edition (Skyhorse Publishing, 2016), Kindle edition.

book's advice.[34] In different editions of the book, Kearny neatly segmented the stages of its creation and reception: from his arrival at Oak Ridge in 1964, to the various late 1960s and early 1970s pamphlets on sheltering, to the first publication of *Nuclear Survival Skills* in 1979 under the growing shadow of 'all-out nuclear war,' to his belief in the even greater applicability of its principles to the post–Cold War threat of nuclear terrorism.[35]

Despite its focus on practicalities, *Nuclear War Survival Skills* is also utopian and communitarian in its own way. Kearny confesses that his greatest rewards 'have been the thanks of readers – particularly mothers with small children – for having given them hope of surviving a nuclear war.'[36] He simultaneously rejects the government as useless and affirms his faith in keeping the US alive even in the event of a nuclear war. Like survivalism more broadly, Kearny's brand is simultaneously cynical and hopeful. The concept of hormesis seems elastic enough to encompass not only government – salutary in small doses, fatal in larger ones – but also nuclear war itself, which seemed promising to him in the more limited form he expected it to take in the post–Cold War era. This relatively sanguine attitude to the prospect of tactical nuclear warfare and a fatality rate in the tens rather than hundreds of millions links passive survivalists to the proactive revolutionaries in William Luther Pierce's near-future novel of race war, *The Turner Diaries* (1978), where the terrorist 'Organization' is able to overturn the US government after triggering a Soviet attack on urban centers and military installations.[37] Even when not always actively or explicitly genocidal or white nationalist in its ideology, twenty-first-century survivalism typically embraces, and often revels in, the partial apocalypse promised by tactical nuclear warfare.

Kearny, unlike most of the survivalists he continues to instruct and inspire to this day, does not mention arms, guns, or self-defense anywhere in the book. He began his vision within the constraints of an early 1960s ideology of family survival as a civic and civil duty, and within those constraints the specter of disorder and societal breakdown scarcely raises its head (Figures 1.2 & 1.3). Evidently, the preppers he imagined as his audience would be too busy building their expedient shelters and crafting Kearny Fallout Meters to have time for looting, pillaging, or marauding, much less race war, domestic

---

34 Cresson Kearny, 'A Letter to the American People from Cresson Kearny, Inventor of the KFM,' in Kearny, *Nuclear War*, 1.
35 Kearny, 'A Letter,' 1.
36 Kearny, *Nuclear War*, 9.
37 Andrew Macdonald [William Luther Pierce], *The Turner Diaries* ([Washington, DC: National Alliance, 1978]; the novel is available online at archive.org).

Figure 1.2 Cresson Kearny's cheery DIY update of family survivalism in the backyard shelter: 'This family completed their Protection Factor 200 (PF 200) fallout shelter, a Door-Covered Trench Shelter with 2 feet of earth on its roof, 34 hours after receiving the building instructions at their home.'

Figure 1.3 Early 1960s paternalism alive and well in the 1980s: 'Two non-athletic college girls who completed a 4-person Pole-Covered Trench Shelter in 35 ½ hours, despite tree roots.'

terrorism, or violent revolution. Like his absolute faith in the laboratory tests and predictable scenarios for the survivability of nuclear war, Kearny was disarmingly confident that survival entailed merely following his detailed instructions to the letter. Along with the *Whole Earth Catalog*, this confidence predicted and helped to usher in twenty-first-century Maker culture and its utopian ideology that actively shaping the environment would positively reshape the world. *Whole Earth* and Kearny provided DIY instructions with materials at hand for counterculture and everyday families, respectively. Indeed, Kahn continued to maintain the *Shelter Blog* through at least 2022, with nary a survivalist or a bunker in sight, and to look back fondly from the twenty-first century at the 'classic ... joyful, inspiring' *Shelter*.[38]

This utopian streak has not vanished in the present-day imagination of survivalists, preppers, and the media surrounding them any more than it has from the counterculture; however, the prepper imagination these days is far darker in its pleasures and far more consumerist in its provisioning. The heroes of 1980s survivalist fiction had already demonstrated an acquisitive brand consciousness; this trend has only increased with the growth of Internet commerce.[39] Websites like Chance Hughes's *UndergroundBombShelter.com* rate gear and offer shelters ranging from 'as little as $20,000 all the way up to hundreds of thousands of dollars,' complete with links to sites offering budget financing deals; survivalist sites review preassembled survival kits and bugout bags with links directly to Amazon.com or other online shops; additional webpages are devoted simply to ranking the myriad options available elsewhere.[40] Even here, the competition is fierce; *TopPrepperSites* claims the distinction of its ranking of the top 200 sites because, 'Unlike other sites that rank according to numbers controlled by an obscure internet entity, Top Prepper Sites are ranked by the Preparedness Community.'[41] Back in the late 1950s and early 1960s, the consumerist allure of the bomb shelter was identified as such primarily within the scathingly critical fictions of Philip K. Dick or John Cheever; today, consumerism is worn as a badge of honor.

---

38 The language comes from Kahn's webpage, where *Shelter* is still in print (www. shelterpub.com/building/shelter; accessed Nov. 2022); for more on Kahn and 'the counterculture shelter movement,' see Kirk, *Counterculture Green*, 84–7.

39 Pike, *Bunkered Decades*, 169–81.

40 Chance Hughes, 'Bomb Shelter Guide,' *UndergroundBombShelter.com*: http://web. archive.org/web/20220406035405/http://undergroundbombshelter.com/index.htm; last accessed 3 April 2018.

41 *TopPrepperSites*: http://web.archive.org/web/20230314235020/https://www.topprepperwebsites.com/; last accessed 3 April 2018.

34   *After the end*

Present-day survivalism from the 1980s to the present day

According to the *Oxford English Dictionary*, the term 'survivalist' had been
used since the 1920s to refer broadly to 'One who succeeds in surviving;
one who makes a policy of aiming to survive'; the *OED* dates to a *New
York Times* article of 1982 the earliest usage of the word to refer specifically
to 'One who practises outdoor survival skills, or who trains in the use of
combat equipment for survival.' In fact, self-identified 'Survivalist' Kurt
Saxon claimed in 1980 to have coined the term back in 1976, adding that
'The term "Survivalist" is fast becoming a household word' and that 'It is
mentioned constantly on television, in newspapers, magazines and radio.'[42]
Certainly, there is no question that this was true by the time industrial rock
band Nine Inch Nails released their number one single in 2007: 'I got my
fist, I got my plan, I got survivalism.'[43] A Google Books Ngram corroborates
Saxon's statement: usage of 'survivalist' remained fairly steady (between a
range of 0.0000002854 and 0.0000009213 percent) from 1925 through
1968. From 1969, the frequency of usage climbed sharply until a peak in
2000 at 0.0000119162 percent. As of 2008, it was at 0.0000085746 percent;
Google Trends shows steady low-level interest since that time.[44] There were
certainly already in the 1960s what would now be termed 'survivalists' – we
meet them in such popular novels as Pat Frank's *Alas, Babylon* (1959) and
Robert Heinlein's *Farnham's Freehold* (1964) – but they were not labeled
as such until the resurgence of Cold War politics and the hardening of the
cultural divide around how to live with the nuclear condition brought them
to relative prominence during the early 1980s.

The new term 'prepper' does indeed suggest a relative 'mainstreaming'
of the idea of survivalism since the 1980s, although not so far as during
the Kennedy 1960s. 'Prepper' is nearly always used in contrast to the more
extreme term 'survivalist' and the distinction is frequently drawn spatially
in terms of the eccentric fondness of the latter for the bunker. Keith O'Brien
employed the distinction in the 2012 *New York Times Magazine* feature
that gave new mainstream visibility to both movements, writing that 'The
first thing you notice about Douglas's neighborhood in Frederick, Colo.,

---

42 Kurt Saxon, 'What Is a Survivalist?' (n.p.: n.p., 1980): http://web.archive.org/
   web/20230305220852/http://www.textfiles.com/survival/whatsurv.
43 Trent Reznor, 'Survivalism,' perf. Nine Inch Nails, *Year Zero* (Interscope, 2007).
44 There are two sharp spikes (in March 2007 for 'survivalism' and in February 2016
   for 'survivalist'), both of which correlate with specific popular culture phenomena
   rather than an overall cultural trend: Nine Inch Nails released their single 'Survivalism'
   in March 2007; the British postapocalyptic action movie *The Survivalist* was released
   in February 2016.

about 30 miles north of Denver, is that it's not particularly noticeable. He doesn't have a mountain stronghold or a 20-acre spread. He doesn't have a bunker or anything resembling a barn.'[45] 'Prepper' in this context is a twenty-first-century usage: the *OED* first records it in a quote about Y2K (the short-lived theory that the turn of the millennium would bring software-driven disaster). The desire of the mainstream to distance itself from the lunatic fringe is nothing new, however; the 1980s heroes of survivalist fiction nearly always defined themselves in terms contrasting the two *OED* definitions: as the one who 'makes a policy of aiming to survive' rather than the 'one who practises outdoor survival skills, or who trains in the use of combat equipment for survival.'[46] There is no hard-and-fast distinction between the norm and the eccentric, but since the 1980s the bunker has tended to be a strong distinguishing marker in the cultural imaginary. Indeed, it is a sign of the global aspirations of the neo-Nazi Organization in *The Turner Diaries* that the 'enclaves' its members establish are simply fenced or barricaded rather than buried; the only bunkered space in the novel belongs to the hated Pentagon, 'with blast shutters over all windows and surrounded by reinforced-concrete blast deflectors' that do nothing to protect it from Turner's climactic suicide attack with a nuclear-bomb-equipped airplane.[47]

Types of survivalism remain divided by class associations, as Evan Osnos's 2017 *New Yorker* feature makes clear in the starkly delineated polarities of crackpot DIY poverty versus well-informed conspicuous consumption, red versus blue, and inland versus coastal. 'Survivalism,' Osnos writes, 'the practice of preparing for a crackup of civilization, tends to evoke a certain picture: the woodsman in the tinfoil hat, the hysteric with the hoard of beans, the religious doomsayer. But in recent years survivalism has expanded to more affluent quarters, taking root in Silicon Valley and New York City, among technology executives, hedge-fund managers, and others in their economic cohort.'[48] To summarize Osnos's vision: the one percent are prepping, the middle class is barely surviving, and the rural poor are all already survivalists out of necessity. Don DeLillo's 2016 novel *Zero K* speculates on the bunker fantasies of the ultrarich to imagine the Convergence, a subterranean supershelter in a remote location somewhere in the Central

---

45 Keith O'Brien, 'How to Survive Societal Collapse in Suburbia,' *New York Times Magazine* (16 Nov. 2012): www.nytimes.com/2012/11/18/magazine/how-to-survive-societal-collapse-in-suburbia.html. The subject of the profile, Ron Douglas, was an entrepreneur of 'self-reliance.'

46 Oxford English Dictionary, s.v. 'survivalist, n.,' April 2023: https://doi.org/10.1093/OED/7466077643.

47 Macdonald, *Turner Diaries*, chapter twenty-six.

48 Evan Osnos, 'Doomsday Prep for the Super-Rich,' *New Yorker* (30 Jan. 2017): www.newyorker.com/magazine/2017/01/30/doomsday-prep-for-the-super-rich.

Asian vicinity of Kazakhstan that specializes in cryogenesis. As one convert expresses the utopian terms of the Convergence, 'If our planet remains a self-sustaining environment, how nice for everyone and how bloody unlikely. … Either way, the subterrane is where the advanced model realizes itself. This is not submission to a set of difficult circumstances. This is simply where the human endeavor has found what it needs. We're living and breathing in a future context, doing it here and now.'[49]

As site of the ultimate bunkering of the body and a ne plus ultra of survivalism, the Convergence is primarily satirical in function. Nevertheless, DeLillo works hard to credit the utopianism that also seems to survive here more than anywhere else in the contemporary world. As the narrator concedes to his father's perverse attraction to this place, 'If this is what my father wanted me to see, then it was my corresponding duty to feel a twinge of awe and gratitude. And I did. Here was science awash in irrepressible fantasy. I could not stifle my admiration.'[50] Tellingly, the cryogenic fantasy had already been available to the workingman survivalist back in the 1980s as a symbol of the perpetuation of the nation – Jerry Ahern's eponymous hero cryogenically freezes himself, his family, and some 'badass' compatriots for 481 years between the action of volumes 9 and 10 of *The Survivalist*, a long-running action series begun in the 1980s.[51] In the twenty-first century, the same fantasy had become the personal, if no less utopian, domain of elite individuals.

Acquisition does nevertheless retain some utopian qualities across the class spectrum. Photographer Richard Ross writes about one of the family shelters he visited for his project *Waiting for the End of the World*: 'Here, everything is impeccably in order, whereas the house itself is littered with toys, clothes, and books owned by the family's three children.'[52] We see a similarly tidy order in Charlie Hull's Montana shelter, refuge for some of Osnos's 'religious doomsayers' (Figure 1.4). Such shelters offer the possibility of imagining one's life to be in order even if one is unable fully to abandon the everyday ties that bind one to the world above. As journalist Mark O'Connell suggests, 'Preppers are not preparing for their fears: they are preparing for their fantasies.'[53]

---

49 Don DeLillo, *Zero K* (New York: Scribner, 2016), 238–9.
50 DeLillo, *Zero K*, 257.
51 Jerry Ahern, *The Survivalist #9, Earth Fire* (New York: Zebra, 1984); *The Survivalist #10, The Awakening* (New York: Zebra, 1984).
52 Richard Ross, *Waiting for the End of the World* (New York: Princeton Architectural Press, 2004), 20.
53 Mark O'Connell, *Notes from an Apocalypse: A Personal Journey to the End of the World and Back* (New York: Doubleday, 2020), 33.

The fantasy of survivalism since the 1980s

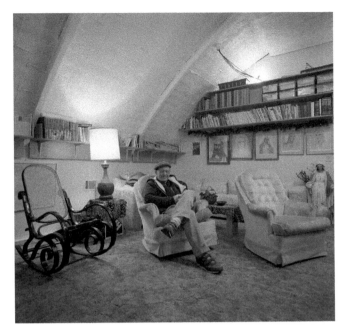

Figure 1.4 An easy chair softens the long wait for the end: the managing partner of the group shelter built in the late 1980s by followers of Elizabeth Clare Prophet's Church Universal and Triumphant.

Most of the imaginary surrounding off-the-grid living is masculinist and rightwing; however, there are alternate versions more closely resembling descendants of the hippie branch of the *Whole Earth* tree. Viggo Mortensen's leftwing anarchist patriarch Ben in *Captain Fantastic* (2016) raises his large family off the grid deep in the woods of the Pacific northwest, instilling in them a practical self-sufficient survivalist ethic that shares little indeed with the consumerist bent of contemporary prepping. Rather than preparing them for an apocalypse per se, he and his partner Leslie are preparing them for a better society and life, period. And the drama in the film results not from external events but from the conflict between his values and those of the society around them, catalyzed by Leslie's suicide but driven by his children's ambivalence towards their life (Figure 1.5). Without the guiding principle of apocalypse to inspire fear and drive by necessity, ideology alone proves insufficient to transform individuals or society.

The narrative lines of *Captain Fantastic* also suggest that countercultural survivalism in harmony with rather than opposition to nature is fundamentally incompatible with masculinist structures of authority and domination. Without

Figure 1.5 Survivalists out of their natural element: *Captain Fantastic*'s countercultural family in a culture clash with the twenty-first century. The younger children's costumes heighten both the alien and the retro context – especially the gas mask.

the mediating figure of the mother, the children begin to reject their father's teaching as brute assertion of paternal authority. Something analogous happens in the more fully postapocalyptic setting of Joan Hegland's 1996 novel *Into the Forest*. But here, the similarly isolated family living at the end of a long dirt road deep in the northern California woods ends up rejecting rather than seeking integration into the structures of the outside world. Hegland figures those structures throughout the novel as masculinist in nature. While the mother had chosen to leave the culture and dance community of San Francisco to raise a family, the father retains a much stronger tie to the outside world, as principal of the school in Redwood, the nearest town, thirty miles away. When the mother dies of cancer and the ills of the late capitalist world speed the slow disintegration of social structures and norms, the only remaining links to society are male, and mediated by the father, who capably has prepped his family to survive and continues the work.

Like Ben, Robert's practical prepping is ideologically driven by a belief in self-sufficiency and adaptive reuse rather than the coming end of the world. But when he dies in a gruesome chainsaw accident while cutting wood, the teenaged sisters must learn to survive psychologically and materially on their own. The only male figures are Eli – a love interest that follows Nell to the woods, seduces her, and tries to lure her away on a classically postapocalyptic journey across America to a fabled sanctuary in Boston – and a nameless marauding survivalist searching for gasoline who rapes Eva and then disappears, lingering only as a lurking fear of predatory masculinity. Nell and Eva survive not by accumulation, but by rejection: the novel

The fantasy of survivalism since the 1980s

concludes with them using their remaining gasoline to burn their home (partly in fear of attracting other human predators) and retreating to the enormous hollow redwood stump deep in the woods that they have converted to a cabin, where Eva was previously able to survive a difficult labor to bear a son, and where they will live off the land using folk knowledge and indigenous ways, at one with a nature that is not nurturing but is accepting. 'Everything else I left ... a whole house of things we once thought we needed to survive, and walked outside.'[54] This, Hegland suggests, is what feminist survivalism might look like. It is a survivalism centrally concerned with and targeted at what it means to enter adult society and reproductive futurism; both *Captain Fantastic* and *Into the Forest* deploy the formal conventions of YA fiction to underpin their critique of systems of authority.

While the full-fledged countercultural or survivalist figure truly drops out of society and off the grid, prepping offers a chance to indulge in the bunker fantasy while continuing to participate fully in the present-day world. Caroline Ross, an English artist who works 'solely with materials she had made herself, and making those materials only out of things she found in nature, or that had been discarded by other people,' dismisses 'doomsday survivalists ... always men ... [who] were interested ultimately not in making things but in equipment.'[55] Survivalism can either forswear equipment and accumulation or revel in them. 'Hull was wistful,' Ross recounts, 'in describing the number of vacations in Hawaii, new boats, or cars that have gone into the shelter.'[56] Given that Hull was managing partner of this group shelter built back in the late 1980s by followers of Elizabeth Clare Prophet's Church Universal and Triumphant, it is safe to assume that he did not in the end regret the choice to dedicate his funds to surviving a nuclear war prophesied to be imminent.[57] But we should equally note the familiar way in which modern evangelical churches balance the demands of the present day with the dream of apocalypse. Hull's group shelter, designed for ninety families, was apparently one among several built to house the nearly three thousand followers of Clare's religion in Paradise Valley near Bozeman in southwestern Montana.[58] 'She said she would like her prophecy of nuclear war to be

---

54 Joan Hegland, *Into the Forest* (New York: Bantam, 1997 [1996]), 239.
55 O'Connell, *Notes from an Apocalypse*, 157, 159.
56 Ross, *Waiting*, 12, 23.
57 Timothy Egan, 'Guru's Bomb Shelter Hits Legal Snag,' *New York Times* (24 April 1990): A16.
58 Egan, 'Guru's Bomb Shelter,' A16. The occasion of Egan's story was a leak from the 31,000 gallons of fuel stored in underground tanks on the site of the Church's larger main shelter; Hull's shelter was apparently one of a number of privately funded shelters near the main compound. According to Egan's piece and to Ross, when Elizabeth Clare's prophecy of nuclear war failed to come true, many followers moved on.

40 *After the end*

untrue,' reported journalist Timothy Egan in 1990. '"I pray regularly that this prophecy will fail," she said. "I would be happy to be a fool for Christ." But if she is right, she said, she and her followers are nearly finished building "a state-of-the-art, masterpiece shelter."'[59]

Although not always in the physical form taken in Paradise Valley, fantasies of safe enclaves and of purged, purified, and uniform societies figure throughout the more militant forms of millennialism that arose in the 1980s, many influenced by *The Turner Diaries*. Christian in heritage but secular in its politics, Pierce's revolutionary fantasy of a new world order enabled by nuclear war had originally been serialized over a span of three and a half years in his neo-Nazi newspaper *Attack!* with the goal of attracting recruits for the National Alliance, which he led until his death in 2002.[60] The doctrines of Identity Christianity to which many bands of paramilitary survivalists adhered similarly included violent resistance to the federal government and a broad and loosely affiliated collection of secessionist movements based on antisemitic and white supremacist views.[61] As political scientist Michael Barkun argues, Identity Christianity radicals intersected with Posse Comitatus organizations, militias who claimed a locally based legal authority not beholden to any federal laws.[62] A touchstone of the movement was the death of tax-resister Gordon Kahl, who killed two federal marshals in a North Dakota standoff before himself being killed after being trapped in 'a bunker-style "safe house" owned by people of similar beliefs.'[63] In the various accounts, Kahl's recourse to such a shelter figures both the dogged resourcefulness of a survivalist and the extreme desperation of a hunted animal run to ground.

Like other violent conflicts between legal authorities and rightwing militias, the incident has had a long afterlife in the visual media and on the Internet. It was made into a TV movie in 1991 starring Rod Steiger, best known for his Academy Award–winning portrayal of a racist Mississippi police chief in *In the Heat of the Night* (1967). *In the Line of Duty: Manhunt in the*

---

59 Egan, 'Guru's Bomb Shelter,' A16.
60 J. M. Berger, 'The Turner Legacy: The Storied Origins and Enduring Impact of White Nationalism's Deadly Bible,' International Centre for Counter-Terrorism Research Paper (2016): 6; http://web.archive.org/web/20230106164845/https://icct.nl/publication/the-turner-legacy-the-storied-origins-and-enduring-impact-of-white-nationalisms-deadly-bible/.
61 Michael Barkun, *Religion and the Racist Right: The Origins of the Christian Identity Movement* (Chapel Hill: University of North Carolina Press, 1997), 200.
62 Barkun, *Religion*, 219–20.
63 Wayne King, 'Link Seen among Heavily Armed Rightist Groups,' *New York Times* (11 June 1983): section 1, p. 1: www.nytimes.com/1983/06/11/us/link-seen-among-heavily-armed-rightist-groups.html.

Dakotas, aka *Midnight Murders*, is available in full only on VHS, but the four-and-a-half-minute sequence in which Kahl kills the marshals can readily be viewed online. Two years after *In the Line of Duty*, self-identified 'anarchist' filmmaker Jeffrey Jackson released the two-hour documentary *Death & Taxes*. Funded originally by England's Channel 4 based on a piece of investigative journalism Jackson had published in *Hustler* in 1989, *Death & Taxes* took Kahl's side; as the *Variety* reviewer wryly noted, 'Non-U.S. viewers will also get a charge out of its conspiracy theme.'[64] The film remains available on Jackson's website in the original VHS, on DVD, and as a six-DVD 'miniseries' containing the full 783 minutes of footage from Jackson's project.[65] The trailer has over twenty thousand views on YouTube, where it shares space with a plethora of material related to Kahl, including a full rip of Jackson's documentary.[66] While Jackson's film works hard to redeem Kahl as hero and as victim of government overreach, survivalist guru Kurt Saxon, himself a former member of some of the most radical far-right organizations of the 1960s, including the John Birch Society, the Minutemen, and the American Nazi Party, and who lived sixty miles from the afore-mentioned 'concrete farmhouse bunker,' claimed by 1983 to have abandoned rightwing ideologies for what he regarded as pure self-reliance.[67] While offering that '[Identity] is like one great big club ... and if you are on the run, a believer will shelter you regardless if he wears the overt label or not,' and remaining in close contact with Identity ideologue William Potter Gale, Saxon maintained that a meeting with Gale was coincidental and that Gale 'didn't know Kahl. I don't think he had any knowledge of the bunker at all.'[68] Bunkers were the safe spaces of the most militant branches of Identity; as a label, they were also the simplest way for figureheads of the movement such as Saxon and Gale to differentiate and distance themselves from the most extreme proponents of that movement. In this context, as in much of the fiction of the 1980s, the bunker came to represent the final step in the hardcore survivalist's rejection of organized civil society.

64 Derek Elley, 'Review: *Death & Taxes*,' *Variety* (30 Nov. 1993): http://web.archive. org/web/20170916140717/http://variety.com/1993/film/reviews/death-taxes -1200435039/.
65 Taos Land & Film Company, http://web.archive.org/web/20230131181325/https:// www.taoslandandfilm.com/independent-films/Death-and-Taxes-Gordon-Kahl/#. Y9laSB_P2Mo; accessed 9 April 2018.
66 Taos Land & Film Company, *Death & Taxes Movie Trailer (The Gordon Kahl Story)*, published 31 Oct. 2011: www.youtube.com/watch?v=EHStX0iyyMk; accessed 19 Nov. 2022.
67 According to journalist Wayne King in a 1983 page-one story in the *New York Times*, 'Mr. Saxon said he was no longer active in right-wing affairs and devoted himself exclusively to survivalism' (King, 'Link,' 1).
68 King. 'Link,' 1.

Prepping, survivalism, and apocalyptic consumerism

The bunker similarly denotes the crackpot line of doomsday preppers in twenty-first-century reality television (RTV) series such as the National Geographic Channel's hit *Doomsday Preppers* (2012–14).[69] Like much of RTV, *Doomsday Preppers* treads a fine line between audience positions of superior mockery and of shared identification; the bunker tends to do the symbolic work of maintaining a line of separation. When 'experts' recommend that he recruit a 'partner' to share the decommissioned SM-65 Atlas missile silo he has bought in central Kansas, hapless prepper Jeff Flaningham lines up a sequence of dates; he breaks the ice first thing by inviting each woman to live with him in his silo.[70] When one of the women, incredibly, agrees to visit the silo, we next see her hesitating to be blindfolded so that the location of his hideout will remain hidden. Presumably because she knows a camera crew will remain present offscreen, she finally agrees. Once inside, she visibly blanches at the twenty thousand square feet of silo, with the required restoration to repair fifty years of vandalism and neglect scarcely begun.

Better funded and more organized, Larry Hall has converted another decommissioned Kansas silo at great expense into a fourteen-story 'luxury survival condominium' for seventy wealthy preppers willing, he hopes, to pay one to two million dollars each.[71] Hall mentions his wife and children and his 'backers,' and otherwise sounds like your typical real estate broker, but we never see anyone sign on the dotted line, although the woman he shows around does express serious interest. Indeed, Hall admits that he has 'given up being socially acceptable.' Despite the trappings of luxury in contrast to Flaningham's dump of a mancave, the episode never disagrees with Hall's own assessment. The tons of concrete in Flaningham's and Hall's 1960s silos may be a far cry from the three-by-seven-foot 'spider holes' survivalist Doug Huffman has dug out and reinforced in camouflaged locations just beneath the ground in a 200-mile network around his rural California compound (Figure 1.6).[72] But as an audience, we are asked simultaneously to admire and to cringe over the regressive fantasies of all three men. No doubt Huffman is playing up for the cameras; his spider hole moment was

---

69 *Doomsday Preppers*, National Geographic Channel, 54 episodes (7 Feb. 2012–28 Aug. 2014).

70 'Solutions Not Problems,' *Doomsday Preppers*, season 2, ep. 13, originally aired 12 Feb. 2013.

71 'You Shall Not Fear,' *Doomsday Preppers*, season 1, ep. 5, originally aired 28 Feb. 2012.

72 'Into the Spider Hole,' *Doomsday Preppers*, season 1, ep. 7, originally aired 13 March 2012.

The fantasy of survivalism since the 1980s 43

Figure 1.6 Self-proclaimed survivalist Doug Huffman demonstrates one of the many camouflaged 'spider holes' scattered across his rural California compound in an episode of *Doomsday Preppers*.

emblematic enough to make the show's credit sequence. But the shots of him in his lair, just like those of Flaningham and Hall, assure us that however much he may be exaggerating, he is definitely not kidding: these bunkers exist, and these men are hardcore survivalists, not just weekend preppers.

Doomsday Preppers ran for fifty-four episodes over four seasons and was the most-watched show in the history of the National Geographic Channel. Top viewership ranged from 700,000 to 1.2 million per episode.[73] The show was successful enough to inspire the spinoffs *Doomsday Castle* (2013, 8 episodes) and *Preppers UK: Surviving Armageddon* (2012, TV movie), copycat competitors from other channels such as *Prepper Hillbillies* (2014, 8 episodes), and the one-shot shows or episodes *Armageddon Arsenal* (2012), *Meet the Preppers: My Pink Pistol* (2012), and *Apocalypse Preppers*

---

73 Wikipedia contributors, 'Doomsday Preppers,' *Wikipedia*, https://en.wikipedia.org/w/index.php?title=Doomsday_Preppers&oldid=817956837; accessed 9 April 2018. To put these numbers in perspective, fewer than watched RTV competitors *Real Wives of OC*, *Shipping Wars*, *Storage Wars*, or *Storage Hunters* or reruns of network shows like *Big Bang Theory* or *Law & Order: SVU*. See Robert Seidman, 'Tuesday Cable Ratings: "Teen Mom 2" Wins Easily + "Tosh.0," "The Game," "Key & Peele," "White Collar," "Justified," "Southland" & More' (8 Feb. 2012): https://web.archive.org/web/20120210095750/http://tvbythenumbers.zap2it.com/2012/02/08/tuesday-cable-ratings-teen-mom-2-wins-easily-tosh-0-the-game-key-peele-white-collar-justified-southland-more/119200/.

(2013, TV movie). As an RTV phenomenon, these shows are descended from the seminal success of *Survivor*, which first broadcast in 1997 in Sweden, in 2000 in the US, and as of 2021 was produced in seventeen different versions worldwide, primarily across Europe.[74] The basic *Survivor* format strands a group of young 'castaways' in an exotic and remote location and pits them against each other until a 'Sole Survivor' is determined. Unlike postapocalyptic or dystopian forms of the 'contest' narrative such as *Battle Royale* (novel 1999, movies 2000, 2003), *The Hunger Games* (novels 2008–10, movies 2012–15), or South Korea's *Squid Game* (2021, 9 episodes), and unlike typical survivalist and prepper fantasies of fighting off 'marauders,' the *Survivor* model is a limited duration contest rather than a fight to the death. The first eleven seasons of *Survivor* rated among the top ten most-watched shows on television, and it is widely credited (or blamed) with popularizing RTV as we now know it.[75] *Doomsday Preppers* shows this influence not only in the dominant theme of survival (indeed, copyright concerns may well be one reason the less familiar term 'prepper' was used in the title) but also in the 'judging' by experts of the three prepper plans at the end of each episode. The key difference is also what makes *Survivor* in the end a mainstream and *Doomsday Preppers* more of a niche success: the former features 'normal' people surviving a staged disaster; the latter features fringe individuals preparing for imagined disaster. The premise for *Survivor* is removal from one's home; the premise for *Doomsday Preppers* is fortification of that home. The same skills learned from *Whole Earth* or Kurt Saxon might come in handy in either scenario, but only the latter show directly engages with the bunker fantasy.

It is easy enough to argue, as Foster does, that '*Doomsday Preppers* cultivates and affirms the values of doomsday preppers' and is 'a decided return to Cold War values' or, as Kelly does, that 'doomsday RTV recuperates hegemonic masculinity by restaging the plausible real world conditions under which the performance of manly labor appears instrumental to collective survival'; there is no question that these values are available as viewing positions of these shows.[76] But these are by no means the only available viewing positions. Nor, as I argue above, are these the stances most readily afforded the viewer by the show's own form. While unarguably concerned, as are all bunker fantasies, with masculinity, gender relations, and 'Cold War values,' these shows comprise a repository of a twenty-first-century

---

74 Wikipedia contributors, 'Survivor (Franchise),' *Wikipedia*, https://en.wikipedia.org/w/index.php?title=Survivor_(franchise)&oldid=835322835; accessed 9 April 2018.
75 Wikipedia contributors, 'Survivor (Franchise).'
76 Gwendolyn Audrey Foster, *Hoarders, Doomsday Preppers, and the Culture of Apocalypse* (New York: Palgrave Macmillan, 2014), 26; Kelly, 'Man-pocalypse,' 96.

Figure 1.7 Collective survivalism, Canadian style. Retired scientist Bruce Beach and two grandchildren set to work on improvements to 'Ark 2' in an episode of *Doomsday Preppers*.

imaginary rather than a fixed, reductive, or coherent argument about that imaginary. Nor is the range of the imaginary exhausted by the determination to avoid at all costs the suffering that rugged survivalists and weekend preppers alike are certain awaits the unprepared around them, a determination O'Connell accurately diagnoses as a 'void of empathy.'[77]

Something else, for instance, is at stake in the prepping of retired Canadian scientist Bruce Beach, who, since he emigrated to Canada from Chicago 'to ride out the coming nuclear war' at the end of the 1960s with Kennedy's backyard-shelter initiative still planted in his mind, has been building a ten-thousand-square-foot shelter that would serve as an underground orphanage (Figure 1.7).[78] Rather than decommissioned missile silos, however, Beach has buried and linked up forty-two cheaply acquired school buses beneath concrete and dirt to form 'Ark 2' in southern Ontario, which he has been working on since 1980. Asked by a high school student on one of the tours he regularly gives to his target audience, 'Do you ever get tired of waiting for the world to end?' Beach responds, 'We are not about survival, we are

---

77 O'Connell, *Notes from an Apocalypse*, 36.
78 Joe O'Connor, 'How a Canadian Built a DIY Nuclear Bunker from 42 Buried Buses and Plenty of Concrete,' *National Post* (Toronto) (13 Oct. 2017; updated 17 Dec. 2018): https://nationalpost.com/news/canada/inside-ark-two-canadas-largest-diy-nuclear-shelter.

46

After the end

about reconstruction.'[79] Rather than being filmed in isolation or during awkward social interactions like Flaningham, Hall, or Huffman, Beach is surrounded by his family, including two grandchildren who spend their free time working with him on cheap DIY additions and replenishing the supplies in the now forty-year-old Ark. The grandchildren seem simply to accept that this is who their grandparents are, although a feature in Toronto's *National Post* suggests the older members of the family may not fully agree: 'His two adult children are no longer interested in hearing their Dad prattle on about nuclear war. Even Jean, sweet as she is, gets tired of her husband's apocalyptic monologues.'[80] Beach's altruistic survivalism is no more nor less marginal than any other – he tells one adult visitor, 'We have room for your children, but we don't have room for you' – but there is nothing of mainstream Cold War culture in his community shelter plan and nothing of 'hegemonic masculinity' or 'the performance of manly labor' in the garbage bags we see this gentle old man patiently taping together or the menial chores we see his grandchildren or wife cheerfully performing at his side. We might well regard his archaic collectivism born of 1980s activism as an implicit antidote to the self-absorbed solipsism of the mostly younger prepping men on the show; however, that very dissent suggests a less coherent and more polyvocal imaginary than one might initially expect from the show's overt sensationalism.

In addition to the range of 'prepper' behavior shown, of viewer positioning towards that behavior, and of the show's overall goals, it is also important to note the formal choices made in framing and presenting 'preppers' for us. It is instructive to compare the RTV portrayal of Larry Hall and his Survival Condo with Osnos's profile of Hall in the *New Yorker*, which presents Hall's $20 million investment in twelve luxury units deadpan as a sound business calculation. 'Most preppers don't actually have bunkers,' Osnos accurately states, because 'hardened shelters are expensive and complicated to build.'[81] Information about his education and background in the defense industry further bolsters Hall's credibility. The only moment Hall starts to sound like an extremist is when he responds to Osnos's questions about 'survivalists' threatening to 'seize' his 'exclusive refuge for the rich' in the event of a crisis with the simple reminder that 'we have a sniper post.'[82] We find a similar moment in journalist O'Connell's profile of Robert Vicino, whose company Vivos develops decommissioned missile

---

79 'It's Gonna Get Worse,' *Doomsday Preppers*, season 1, ep. 8, originally aired 27 March 2012.
80 O'Connor, 'How a Canadian Built a DIY Nuclear Bunker.'
81 Osnos, 'Doomsday Prep.'
82 Osnos, 'Doomsday Prep.'

The fantasy of survivalism since the 1980s   47

silos into high-end bunkers in South Dakota, elsewhere in the US, and also in a Soviet-era mountainside munitions depot in Thuringia in what used to be East Germany. Vicino presents like a typical real estate broker intent on flipping a slightly unusual home – except when he veers into apocalyptic conspiracy theories about rogue planets, deep states, and 'a hoard of marauding cannibals baying for the flesh of his daughters.'[83] In contrast, when Hall outlines on *Doomsday Preppers* the four levels of security he has installed at the bunker, the lack of context and comments by a security expert make it sound like he's throwing money down the drain; when Osnos brings it up we simply witness one more brick in the wall sealing off the one percent from the rest of the world, all of them either preppers or survivalists.

Back in 1982, Edward Myers had argued of the new survivalists that, in contrast to the early 1960s original, '[M]ost live rather ordinary – even banal – lives in the here and now. The stereotype of the survivalist as a paramilitary nut,' he maintained, 'is a risky oversimplification.'[84] Rather than a separate shelter as their predecessors had built, Myers added, 'It isn't simply a question of a *structure* – although blast and fallout shelters enter into the overall scheme. Rather, it's a matter of a whole context of beliefs, decisions, activities, and consequences which change the survivalists' lives deeply and intricately. Shelter – to put it bluntly – can be a matter of withdrawal from mainstream society.'[85] The bunker remained the material emblem of sheltering, but Myers's formulation argued that this emblem now marked a social schism rather than the earlier era's division over the degree to which one followed through on or resisted a broad consensus on how and why to shelter. Writing about a member of the prepper community known as 'Survival Mom' during the first year of the COVID-19 pandemic, journalist Mira Ptacin sets the scene with a similar emblem of isolation: the mostly accurate 'stereotype' she finds of 'the prepper as a rural, military-minded dude who gathers canned food, guns and ammo, and heads to the hills to wait out the zombie apocalypse,' armed to the teeth in his bunker.[86] She then counters this image of whacked-out male preppers with her embrace, through Survival Mom's practical DIY advice, of the home as shelter, the homemaker as self-sufficient prepper, and prepping as 'a form of activism

---

83 O'Connell, *Notes from an Apocalypse*, 61.
84 Edward Myers, *The Chosen Few* (South Bend, IN: and books, 1982), 18.
85 Myers, *Chosen Few*, 84.
86 Mira Ptacin, 'I Am Not a Housewife. I'm a Prepper,' *New York Times* (24 Sept. 2020): www.nytimes.com/2020/09/24/opinion/sunday/i-am-not-a-housewife-im-a-prepper.html.

and preparedness. ... [that] meant feeling more connected to my neighbors, not less connected.'[87] Or, in the words of fictional 'survival mom' Grace, trying to keep it together after the sudden death of her husband in Melissa Scholes Young's 2020 novel *The Hive*, 'Some of them thought it was a game. It wasn't. She preferred the term survivalist to prepper because surviving this marriage, this family business, and this life was a war she knew how to win.'[88]

In the 1980s, the bunker began to demarcate an ideological divide between whether one was willing or not to accept the cost of survival – that is, how one chose to approach the impending end of the world. Even Myers felt obligated to conclude his summary of survivalism on a note of moral warning about 'the struggle to survive at any cost – even at the cost of ... membership in the wider community of men and women.'[89] What we find in twenty-first-century prepping is a renewed consensus on the possibility and necessity of survival but a dwindling of the moral stakes. The new divide within a global neoliberal community is economic rather than ideological, but its imaginary continues to circle the bunker. 'Could Doomsday Bunkers Become the New Normal?' asked a *New York Times* feature in the summer of 2020 on the rising popularity of ready-made backyard bunkers during the pandemic, proposing the widespread acceptance of prepping while at the same time rhetorically holding it at arm's length. One Washington DC purchaser explained that he had installed the bunker at the same time as a new pool. 'So no one knew what we were building,' he continued, asserting bluntly: 'I'm not a prepper.'[90] 'I'm not one of the paranoid kinds of people,' claims a construction-company owner who is moving his wife and daughters from small-town Indiana into one of Vicino's converted bunkers in the Black Hills of South Dakota.[91] A similar distancing gesture distinguished the taunting hashtag #BunkerBoy that greeted reports that then-President Donald Trump 'had been taken to the White House's underground bunker' when a Black Lives Matter protest march for racial justice had apparently come too close for comfort during the summer of 2020.[92] As prepping mainstreams, we

---

87 Ptacin, 'I'm a Prepper.'
88 Melissa Scholes Young, *The Hive* (Nashville: Turner Publishing, 2020), 21.
89 Myers, *Chosen Few*, 172.
90 Mira Ptacin, 'Could Doomsday Bunkers Become the New Normal?' *New York Times* (26 June 2020): www.nytimes.com/2020/06/26/realestate/could-doomsday-bunkers-become-the-new-normal.html.
91 Annie Lowrey, 'The Bunker Magnates Hate to Say They Told You So,' *Atlantic* (15 Sept. 2020): www.theatlantic.com/technology/archive/2020/09/rising-s-vivos-and-the-booming-bunker-economy/616240/.
92 Susan Glasser, '#BunkerBoy's Photo-Op War,' *New Yorker* (3 June 2020): www.newyorker.com/news/letter-from-trumps-washington/bunkerboys-photo-op-war.

The fantasy of survivalism since the 1980s

can trace the development of its imaginary especially well through fictions of survivalism and narratives of bunker emergence in literature and film, which not only display the double consciousness of the fantasy at the foundation of survivalism's bunkered masculinist ontology, but constantly question the epistemological premises of that fantasy from within the bunker's confines. We turn to these fictions in Chapter 2.

2

Survivance in fictions of survivalism since the Reagan years

[For this epigraph, please read the lyrics of or listen to the referenced song]
Radiohead, 'Idioteque' (2000)

A key episode in Chuck Wendig's 2019 novel *Wanderers* brings together survivalists, preppers, and white supremacists within the contemporary context of rightwing politics. The villain of what one reviewer termed a 'deconstructed apocalypse,'[1] Ozark Stover is a figure pulled from the extremes of survivalist fiction and RTV caricatures such as *Duck Dynasty*. Ozark name-checks the long-running series of postapocalyptic libertarian separatism, *Out of the Ashes*; mocks *Wanderer*'s populist (and usurper) president Creel as a millionaire prepper ('He has a compound out in Kansas, one of those ex-missile-silo "survival compounds," condos for the richest preppers. ... Cost him around ten million, place is full of apartments for the rich and elite asshole buddies'); and imprisons the Reverend Matthew Stark 'in a basement underneath the shed that sat adjacent to Ozark Stover's Morton building. The shed was built like a bomb shelter bunker, which reportedly was one of its potential functions – Stover said he had many such bunkers across his property.'[2] Ranged against Stover's sadistic militia is a diverse assemblage of 'shepherds' and their 'flock,' whom AI Black Swan will lead to Ouray, Colorado, to ride out the apocalypse in open-air-style sheltering, not a bunker in sight. Wendig pulls freely from the twenty-first-century bunker imaginary to articulate the stark political stakes his novel formulates: a bunkered toxic masculinity versus an emergent alliance of freedom.

In Chapter 1, we examined the practices of survivalism from the inside; this chapter studies the treatment of survivalism outside of survivalism's principal subcultures. This includes mainstream novels and movies such as

---

1 Gabino Iglesias, 'These "Wanderers" Are Heading for the End of the World,' *NPR. org* (6 July 2019): http://web.archive.org/web/20220714180421/https://www.npr.org/2019/07/06/738974776/these-wanderers-are-heading-for-the-end-of-the-world.
2 Chuck Wendig, *Wanderers* (New York: Del Rey, 2019), 463, 557, 738, 455.

Tim O'Brien's *The Nuclear Age* (1985) and Jeff Nichols's *Take Shelter* (2011) that burrow inside the survivalist ontology as a means for identifying and diagnosing broad crises in masculinity. The chapter also treats 'realistic' bunker emergence narratives from *Radioactive Dreams* (1985) through *Blast from the Past* (1999) to *Unbreakable Kimmy Schmidt* (2015–20) that deploy the bunker fantasy in a primarily comic mode to make temporal comparisons between periods and cultures. In the twenty-first century, the comedy of bunker emergence became a critical tool for calling out the dominance and abuses of a white male hegemony rooted in Cold War geopolitics and readily imagined ensconced underground. Whether in comic mode, in tragic mode, or balancing both, critical survivalist fictions and bunker emergence comedies use the bunker as space and as imaginary to evaluate the balance and tension between the bunker fantasy – the impetus that drives the survivalist and has created the protagonists of emergence comedies – and the factors dismissive of that same fantasy. The chapter concludes with a return to the dome in Anishinaabe writer Gerald Vizenor's postmodernist novel *Hiroshima Bugi: Atomu 57* (2003) and the concept of *survivance*. In contrast to 'the commerce of reactive survivalists,' survivance for Vizenor is 'a creative, concerted consciousness that does not arise from separation, dominance, or concession nightmares.'[3] Survivance is not so much escape from the ontological bunker as misplacing and repurposing its affordances. In its understanding of survivance and its narration of an intersectional play between Japan and America, *Hiroshima Bugi* transitions this book's argument from the direct reckoning with the spatiotemporal legacies of America around the Cuban Missile Crisis and during Reaganism in the first two chapters to examine appropriation, revisions, and adaptive reuse imagined from that focus, across the globe, in the next four chapters.

Fictional survivalists from the late 1950s to 2023

Survivalism since the 1980s has afforded a privileged position from which to imagine white masculinity even as its practices may have been adopted at times by a wider population. During the late 1950s and early 1960s, white, straight, cisgender masculinity was simply the presumed national identity and the nation was oriented around the shelters it built and everything else they contained or shut out; it has remained the default position in later imaginings through this period and ever since. 1980s survivalism invoked the 1960s bunker to imagine masculinity under siege from outside forces,

---

3 Gerald Vizenor, *Hiroshima Bugi: Atomu 57* (Lincoln: University of Nebraska Press, 2003), 9.

52   *After the end*

and mainstream writers did the same. Whereas Kurt Saxon would polemically voice the survivalist fantasy evident in men's action fiction of the 1980s – that 'a nuclear holocaust will be a blessing for the survivors'[4] – realist fictions about survivalism unleashed the same figure in the 'normal' world to document the ensuing havoc and to diagnose its causes. Notably, O'Brien's *The Nuclear Age* (1985) uses its protagonist's obsession with self-protection to retell its titular history beginning in the early 1960s from the vantage point of the narrator's 'present' in a future 1995. Twenty-first-century heirs to O'Brien's realism use the bunker to imagine a similar crisis in the present day. As the default position of turn-of-the-millennium neoliberalism, white Western masculinity continued to afford a space for locating and visualizing crisis; however, while the survivalist's approach remains suspect, he nearly always turns out also to have been right nevertheless. Recent novels, films, and television series such as *Sacred Games* (2006, see Chapter 4), *Take Shelter* (2011), *The Purge* (2013), *Fallout* (2013), *10 Cloverfield Lane* (2016), and *A Quiet Place* (2018) create reasonably sympathetic but deeply flawed prepper and survivalist characters whose shelters help to imagine the crisis to come. There is no longer any doubt in these texts; the only question is what to do when the end comes.

Todd Strasser's 2013 YA novel *Fallout* makes the historical periodization explicit, combining a coming-of-age story in a 1962-era bunker with a present-day coda around the narrator's father. The body of the novel is an unremarkable amplification of the influential 1961 *Twilight Zone* episode 'The Shelter,'[5] tightly constrained by the perspective of early teen Scott and the unflattering but sympathetic portrait of his flawed father. The 'Author's Note' returns to Strasser's actual childhood home on Long Island, looking for the shelter his father had built and dispelling the myths neighbors have told the new owner about the past, including a 'twelve-foot fence' to hide the construction and his father's pouring 'every square cent my family had' into the project.[6] Unsurprisingly, it was the myths and not the more prosaic reality Strasser remembers that he chose to incorporate into the fictional plot. For the author as a child in the later 1960s, apparently, the shelter was one more token of a middle-class suburban childhood to show off to visiting friends, just as the new owner proudly shows it to him:

> We go into the first bedroom – decorated in pink, a color virtually nonexistent in the male-dominated home of my childhood – and the owner opens a closet door. He clears away some shoes and dolls from the carpeted floor. 'Listen.'

4 Qtd Myers, *Chosen Few*, 127.
5 'The Shelter,' season 3, ep. 3 of *The Twilight Zone*, originally aired on CBS television 19 Sept. 1961; see also Pike, *Bunkered Decades*, 55–60.
6 Todd Strasser, 'Author's Note,' *Fallout* (Somerville, MA: Candlewick, 2013), 259.

Survivance in fictions of survivalism

He raps the carpet with his knuckles, producing a dull, echoing clang. 'We never had it removed.' He means the metal trapdoor. He can't show it to me without pulling up the carpet, but it evokes a memory just the same – of the Cuban Missile Crisis and the years after, when the threat of nuclear war had diminished, and the trapdoor practically vanished under toys and balls and other sports equipment. The trapdoor has been permanently sealed. No one will ever open it and climb down, as I did as a teenager to show my friends the shelter.[7]

From a childhood of masculine spaces, Strasser meditates on the warmongering of 'mere handfuls of influential men,' arguing that it was not so much Kennedy's assassination as the 'nuclear arms race' that had put paid to the 'era of post–World War II American innocence.'[8]

Curiously, despite a more feminized household and a post–Cold War perspective, the current owner has not eliminated the shelter. Instead, at some cost and trouble, he has not only preserved it but made a new, external entrance that proved quite expensive because Strasser's father had lined his shelter with 'quarter-inch thick iron plating' sandwiched between two walls of cinder-block concrete: '"Your father really wanted to protect you," the owner says as he leads me down the entrance steps.'[9] Strasser does not provide dates for the renovation, but the likeliest scenario given evidence of recent neglect (the walls are 'shrouded in spiderwebs' and his guide confesses that he, 'rarely comes down to the shelter anymore'[10]) is that the 'new' owner did his own renovations during the 1980s. Neither Strasser nor he is a contemporary survivalist; they belong to their respective epochs: the 1960s and the 1980s.

Within the survivalist diegesis of Strasser's fiction, however, contemporary masculinity is doubtless still in play. The only patriarch on the block who has built a shelter, Scott's father finds his family besieged by violent neighbors, one of them causing his wife to fall down the entrance tube of the tunnel; she lies comatose for the rest of the novel. Like Kearny, Strasser assumes a limited war and a two-week limit to the fallout, building the discomforts of the cramped quarters out of an adolescent boy's bodily and social anxieties. As often with recent nuclear fiction, the feeling at times is that the bomb is an excuse for the story rather than vice versa; one reason Strasser assumes a rosy scenario is that survivalism is the hook but not the primary interest. The novel's most ambivalent character, Mr McGovern, who has fought his way into the shelter with his daughter but not his wife and who constantly

7 Strasser, 'Author's Note,' 259.
8 Strasser, 'Author's Note,' 259.
9 Strasser, 'Author's Note,' 259.
10 Strasser, 'Author's Note,' 259.

54   *After the end*

challenges the authority of Scott's father, makes a number of cruelly pragmatic arguments for pushing Scott's injured mother out of the shelter so that the others may survive. 'This isn't arbitrary – it's a matter of survival,' he argues. 'It's what has to be done if we're going to stay down here long enough to let the danger subside up there. ... It looks to me like we can either adapt to the reality of this situation or starve to death.'[11] As the novel concludes, McGovern is proven wrong: they have all survived and the mother has at least somewhat revived. The last word goes to the neighbor Mrs Shaw, who dismisses the survivalist dilemma of the bunker. 'It's horrible,' she says of the bodies scattered around the entrance, 'but we all couldn't have survived.'[12] McGovern, finally, is equally conciliatory: 'I'm sorry. We all made mistakes.'[13] With its coda and the historicism of its characterizations, *Fallout* subtly incorporates three epochs of attitudes towards sheltering, correcting the polarized debates of 1962 via the 1980s with an eye towards the ethics of the present.

We find a similar dynamic in the more tragic outcomes of O'Brien's 1980s novel and more recent films like *Take Shelter* and *The Purge*, which consciously evoke the earlier decades of survivalism in the context of the present day. For example, in her 1984 novel *Machine Dreams*, Jayne Anne Phillips uses a war veteran father's proposal to build a shelter at the time of the Cuban Missile Crisis to set off a 'domestic crisis.'[14] Staging the argument across an ironing board from the perspective of the younger wife, Phillips frames the proposed shelter as a masculine space eating up resources the mother would prefer to use for the children's coats, a 1960s dynamic bleeding into the 1980s.[15] *The Nuclear Age* similarly moves between epochs: the late 1950s to 1960s of William Cowling's childhood through college years, the 1979–85 of the novel's publishing history, and the 1995 future of the diegetic present where a crazed father takes his drugged wife and daughter into a giant hole he plans to turn into a fallout shelter, to blow the three of them up.[16] Curiously, as Daniel Grausam notes, Cowling's 'symptoms' of anxiety, quietened after their first manifestation in a ping-pong-table shelter in 1958 by a game with his father atop the 'shelter,' 'come back strangely unmoored

---

11 Strasser, *Fallout*, 125–6, 180.
12 Strasser, *Fallout*, 256.
13 Strasser, *Fallout*, 257.
14 Daniel Cordle, *States of Suspense: The Nuclear Age, Postmodernism and United States Fiction and Prose* (Manchester: Manchester University Press, 2008), 28.
15 Jayne Anne Phillips, *Machine Dreams* (New York: Vintage, 1999 [1984]), 162–3.
16 Tim O'Brien, *The Nuclear Age* (New York: Knopf, 1985). Various parts of the novel were published individually from 1979; the final novel was published in 1985.

from any of the key crisis events of the Cold War.'[17] Like O'Brien's decision to make Cowling an outlier rather than an everyman, the temporal disjunction shifts the novel out of the realm of historical fiction and into some other indeterminate genre, be it satire (Heberle), metafictional games (Grausam), or ecofeminism (Schweninger).[18] Cordle's reading of the novel as 'nuclear anxiety fiction' is more equivocal since the argument is primarily thematic, finding that, '[T]he novel is about the idea of security and ... demonstrates that security in the home is intimately bound to security in the homeland.'[19] Given O'Brien's choice to render the narrative through the unreliable first person of Cowling's voice, it is difficult straightforwardly to extrapolate from Cowling's obsession with security and Cowling's analogy between a secure home and a secure homeland to Cordle's 'demonstration.' At the same time, O'Brien's evident concern with the near-tragic impact of Cowling's obsession on his life and his family does support a broader reading of the crisis of masculinity embodied in that obsession, fixated in the 1995 bunker project, and grounded in Cowling's review of a life defined by survivalism since the late 1950s.

As Grausam notes, Cowling's life-review remains unable to make sense of how he has ended up in a hole with his family hostage to his mania.[20] For David Seed, herein lies the fundamental ambiguity over 'whether Cowling's hole is expressing anything beyond his futile and obsessive search for a shelter, and thereby demonstrating the pathology of the nuclear age.'[21] O'Brien's own statement at the time of writing suggests the resolution that he saw as available: '[T]here is another real bomb shelter. No metaphor, no image. Real! Real! ... [W]e *won't* survive if we can't stop thinking of nuclear weapons as mere metaphors.'[22] *The Nuclear Age* was not so much questioning the efficacy or pathology of survivalism as getting inside them

---

17 Daniel Grausam, *On Endings: American Postmodern Fiction and the Cold War* (Charlottesville: University of Virginia Press, 2011), 78.

18 Mark A. Heberle, *A Trauma Artist: Tim O'Brien and the Fiction of Vietnam* (Iowa City: University of Iowa Press, 2001), 144; Grausam, *On Endings*, 85; Lee Schweninger, 'Ecofeminism, Nuclearism, and O'Brien's *The Nuclear Age*,' in *The Nightmare Considered: Critical Essays on Nuclear Criticism*, ed. Nancy Anisfield (Bowling Green, OH: Bowling Green State University Popular Press, 1991), 177–85.

19 Cordle, *States of Suspense*, 130.

20 Grausam, *On Endings*, 78.

21 David Seed, *Under the Shadow: The Atomic Bomb and Cold War Narratives* (Kent, OH: Kent State University Press, 2013), 74.

22 O'Brien, interview in *Anything Can Happen: Interviews with Contemporary American Novelists*, ed. Tom LeClair and Larry McCaffery (Champaign: University of Illinois Press, 1983), 271; qtd Seed, *Under the Shadow*, 74.

56 *After the end*

to figure out what could be salvaged. So, when the hole is speaking to Cowling at the novel's end, the reader recognizes the speech as a hallucination; however, this recognition does not discount the validity of the overwrought words it speaks:

> *I am all there is*, it says. *Keyhole, rathole, asshole, eyehole, hellhole, loophole, knothole, manhole, peephole, foxhole, armhole, sinkhole, cubbyhole, pothole, wormhole, buttonhole, water hole, bullet hole, air hole, black hole, hidey-hole ... I am that I am. I am that which nearly was but never will be, and that which never was but always will be. I am the unwritten masterpiece. I am the square root of infinity. I am one hand clapping. I am what happened to the dinosaurs. I am the ovens at Auschwitz, the Bermuda Triangle, the Lost Tribes, the Flying Dutchman, the Missing Link. I am Lee Harvey Oswald's secret contact in Moscow. I am the anonymous tipster. I am Captain Kidd's treasure. I am the uncaused cause, the unnamed source, the unindicted co-conspirator, the unknown soldier, the untold misery, the unmarked grave. I am, in modesty, Neverness. I am the be-all and end-all. I am you, of course. I am your inside-out – your Ace in the Hole.*[23]

In O'Brien's late–Cold War 1985, the 'hole' had swallowed everything; it was all there was. Everyone was a survivalist in a hole; the only question was how to make survivalism something other than the toxically male paranoia Cowling's trajectory demonstrates it to be.

The novel's resolution – Cowling abandons his plan in the face of his daughter Melinda – requires him not so much to identify his bunker fantasy as fantasy, as to persuade himself to believe that he has done so: 'I know this, but I believe otherwise.'[24] Within the Cold War polarizations of the 1980s, this choice meant knowing that 'The world will surely end' while also believing in the normal life of his family, 'what cannot be believed.'[25] 1980s survivalism framed this paradox in terms of a life-and-death conflict between a masculinized war footing and a feminized domesticity, between Cowling's bunker-under-construction and his family. Within the survivalist calculus, one side took measures, the other lived convinced that measures were irrelevant – Myers, like many survivalists, terms this calculus the 'Ant-and-Grasshopper routine'[26] – and no alternative existed: 'Real! Real!' After the Cold War ended, the ground would shift around the bunker fantasy. Whatever the relative risk of nuclear war, the fault line was no longer drawn by the bombs; instead, the survivalist recognized that all of society had itself become apocalyptic and toxic. In O'Brien's 1985, there

---

23 O'Brien, *Nuclear Age*, 298.
24 O'Brien, *Nuclear Age*, 312.
25 O'Brien, *Nuclear Age*, 312.
26 Myers, *Chosen Few*, 11.

could still be ambiguity about Cowling's delusions. In twenty-first-century critical fictions of survivalism, the doubt lasts only as long as the drama and not beyond, for the denouement no longer redeems the survivalist. Instead, his worst fears are confirmed, and usually at the cost of his life.

Approximately twenty-five years after O'Brien, writer-director Jeff Nichols revisited the scenario of *The Nuclear Age* on screen in *Take Shelter* (2011). Like William Cowling, Curtis LaForche's (Michael Shannon) visions of apocalypse compel him to protect his young family. Like Cowling, LaForche responds to this compulsion by digging a very large hole in his backyard into which he pours all the money his family has and more, alienating himself from the community and from his loved ones. Like Cowling's hole, LaForche's dig, although sealed up, is ugly and uncomfortable, with canvas cots, bare walls, and a roughly hewn opening from the (much better made) Midwestern storm shelter into the container. There's no fantasy of order and renewal here, only the barest bones of a shelter. Finally, like Cowling, LaForche ends up bringing his reluctant wife and child into the shelter by force before finally giving way to their love and trust (Figure 2.1). Even more than Cowling, LaForche is simultaneously persuaded that he is delusional and unable to ignore the visions of apocalypse that spur him to action. Nichols cleverly films the visions in such a way that the audience is unable immediately to determine whether they are meant to be diegetically 'real' or not; the effect is that the viewer partly participates in LaForche's own psychosis. Unlike *Nuclear Age*, *Take Shelter* does not shift in time or space from in and around its small-town setting in Lagrange, Ohio, until the final scene on Myrtle Beach, South Carolina. Similarly, Nichols grounds his protagonist's hallucinations in medical science: LaForche's mother has a history of paranoid schizophrenia, he consults with a psychiatrist, and he

Figure 2.1 The modern family, masked, prepped, and trapped in Curtis LaForche's rudimentary backyard shelter in *Take Shelter*.

58   *After the end*

spends much of his time in the bunker researching his condition in medical textbooks. Unlike O'Brien's distancing narration and the allegorical sweep of the decades narrated, Nichols keeps LaForche's bunker ontological. It becomes less important whether or not he is living with a mental illness and more important whether or not he is right.

Because of this shift in emphasis and because of the visceral power of images, *Take Shelter* pulls the audience deeply into the family's emotional turmoil. We feel with LaForche the compulsion to act on what he sees and we feel for his wife (Jessica Chastain) as she watches him lose control of his life and threaten to destroy hers and their daughter's. The affective charge of the film is all the more effective in that it sidesteps a straightforward narration of mental illness and disintegration. Instead, Samantha somehow manages to keep the family together, allowing the film to focus on the emotional impact of survivalism on an otherwise unexceptional lower-middle-class Midwestern family. The lack of any breakup makes the final image even more of a piece with what has come before, as Samantha and Curtis together watch a tidal wave descending on the beach house where they are staying. Nichols in an interview explains that the ending was 'specifically designed to be ambiguous ... What's important to me is that these two people are on the same page and are seeing the same thing.'[27] Like the world around them, LaForche's survivalism is what it is, and Samantha approaches it as pragmatically as she does everything else in her life. We can recognize class- and geography-specific elements to their crisis – the evangelical emphasis on apocalypse, the Midwestern necessity of storm shelters for tornadoes – just as we recognize ways the traditional gender roles of their relationship exacerbate the crisis and his delusions. But these same elements also afford the conflict's resolution, where both parties force themselves to give ground. The question is not in the end *whether* they should shelter, but whether LaForche's ugly, expensive, and impractical shelter will protect them from the modern world better than their home and their community will – whether, from the meager options available to them, they should choose the male bunker or the domestic household.

The ambiguously conciliatory resolution of *Take Shelter* formally differentiates it from the typical survivalist drama. The crudeness of LaForche's bunker visually informs us that there is nothing desirable to be found there, no matter how *true* his visions may be. Other films of contemporary survivalists use the conventions of horror fantasy to make the bunkers more alluring and the bunker-master threatening and irredeemable. The full ninety minutes

---

27 Matt Singer, '"Take Shelter" Director Jeff Nichols Clears the Air,' *IFC.com* (29 Sept. 2011): http://web.archive.org/web/20151126131050/https://www.ifc.com/2011/09/jeff-nichols-take-shelter-interview.

of James DeMonaco's hit low-budget horror movie *The Purge* (2013) are set in and around a single bunkered mansion in an elite suburban enclave, occupied by home-security salesman James Sandin (Ethan Hawke) and his wife, daughter, and son. Sandin's specialty is securing homes at premium cost against the 'purge,' a twelve-hour period once a year in which all criminal activity is temporarily legal, encouraged, and unpunished, and no public services of any kind are available. Violent crime has been radically cut back during the other 364 days in this dystopian near-future America, although whether this is due to the release provided by the purge or because the twelve hours of mayhem disproportionately winnow the irredeemably criminal along with the poor and vulnerable is left an open question. As the movie begins, the Sandins prepare to shelter in place. Sitting in the interior control room surrounded by security cameras, they press the button that brings steel shutters down over all windows and doors. Slyly, DeMonaco shows the bunker to be compromised not only by human error and irrationality, as expected, but also by a security system that, like the fallout shelter in *Matinee* (1993, see below), is itself mostly cosmetic – a visual deterrent rather than actual protection or fortification. As Sandin eventually rationalizes to his wife, 'It's not built for worst-case scenarios.'[28] Like Shirley Jackson's short story 'The Lottery' (1948), to which many reviewers compared the film, *The Purge* ritualizes as normal and makes explicit an unspoken social pathology. Survivalism has become a self-fulfilling prophecy.

In borrowing its premise from Jackson's story and from the 1967 *Star Trek* episode 'Return of the Archons,' and its imagination of neighbors turned feral from the *Twilight Zone* episode 'The Shelter,' DeMonaco roots the movie's nastily contemporary edge firmly within Cold War cultural forms. In contrast, the economic and racial politics are purely of its twenty-first-century moment. Sandin's neighbors are envious and bitter that he has grown rich on their money, securing their homes. The most dangerous threat turns out not to be nonwhite or immigrant members of the urban poor or gun-toting survivalists from the heartland but the Sandins' own peers: the neighbors and the racist and amoral scions of the white elite who batter down the home when the Sandin family's son shelters a Black man targeted by the archly named Polite Leader. Although it does not flip the script as fully as Jordan Peele's horrific normalizing of survivalism as the cynical behavior of the white elite in the basement clinic of a suburban estate in *Get Out* (2017), *The Purge* does directly target white male privilege and

---

28 *The Purge*, wr. and dir. James DeMonaco, Blumhouse Productions, dist. Universal (2013). Low budget and extremely popular, the film spawned four sequels between 2013 and 2021, with another in development as of 2023, as well as a twenty-episode Netflix series (2018–19).

the female complicity underpinning it, taking aim early at Sandin's complacent self-importance and later at the moral vacuity of privileged white youth.

Unlike in *Get Out*, moralizing social critique in *The Purge* mostly takes a back seat to thrills and violence, however, and Sandin is allowed to redeem himself for his ethical failure, although not enough to survive. Where *Get Out* productively misplaces the tropes of survivalist extremism into the genteel heart of white power engaged in business as usual, DeMonaco's film suggests that playing at survivalism is a lot more gratifying than actually living it, and that the only ones who gain from prepping are the ultrarich and the pathologically criminal; the rest of us simply risk giving in to our worst impulses. What pleasures remain in this bunker fantasy are nasty, brutish, short, and not so different from those offered by the zombie genre: not the ability to shelter in quiet and safety but the freedom to defend your home from marauders with impunity. The viewer will likely be too busy rooting for the family to kill the evil preppies to notice that, because of the purge, the surviving Sandins won't even have to account afterwards to the police for the final mayhem. Survival may not be enough, *The Purge* tells us, but it can still be entertainingly cathartic to watch on screen. For every prepper who actually built enough to make it onto the National Geographic show and for every hippie who erected a dome in Drop City, there were hundreds if not thousands of others for whom the fantasy or the secondhand view was sufficient. For all their talk of marauders and ends of days, most survivalists and preppers preferred the fantasy straight on and in the comic mode of RTV, while *The Purge* cloaks it in horror. Like fictional survivalists in realist fiction and film, these films imagine survival in the tragic mode with no apparent exit.

Where *The Purge* posits a would-be-decent father who knows exactly what is coming but turns out to be a failure at prepping, *10 Cloverfield Lane* (2016) introduces its viewers to a criminal but dedicated prepper who turns out also to have been right all along.[29] Although the film plays with audience sympathies by presenting different versions along the way, the basic scenario is that Howard Stambler (John Goodman) has kidnapped Michelle (Mary Elizabeth Winstead) to his survivalist bunker, a textbook shelter he has painstakingly built and equipped in his backyard. When she

---

29 *10 Cloverfield Lane* came with a strong twentieth-first-century pedigree of white guys from the bunkered decades. Co-produced by the prolific and successful SFF filmmaker and 1960s child J. J. Abrams (b. 1966) from a screenplay co-written by Academy Award–winner and 1980s child (b. 1985) Damien Chazelle, the film marked the directorial debut of 1980s child (b. 1981) Dan Trachtenberg. It also inspired a 'mod' to the postapocalyptic videogame *Fallout 4* (2015): a player home modeled on Stambler's bunker.

Survivance in fictions of survivalism 61

Figure 2.2 The ambiguous status of Howard Stambler's (John Goodman) bunker: the room Michelle (Mary Elizabeth Winstead) is handcuffed to at night, and her imagination of the fallout shelter in *10 Cloverfield Lane*.

Figure 2.3 The ambiguous status of Howard Stambler's bunker: the common space and his imagination of the fallout shelter in *10 Cloverfield Lane*.

awakes, chained to a pipe, and asks what he is going to do to her, he answers, paternally, 'I'm going to keep you alive' (Figure 2.2).[30] Like the shelter-child Adam in *Blast from the Past* (1999, discussed below), Stambler is happier in his bunker than he was aboveground; he enthusiastically shows and tells its many innovations and amenities, from double blast doors and state-of-the-art ventilation to a jukebox stocked with oldies and a pantry filled with decades worth of supplies of his favorite foods (Figure 2.3).

30 *10 Cloverfield Lane*, dir. Dan Trachtenberg, prod. Bad Robot, dist. Paramount Pictures (2016).

Goodman has a knack for playing sympathetic reprobates, and his iconic presence amongst unknown faces heightens the ambiguity of his character through the middle section of the film. When the Grand Guignol effects roll out and Michelle resourcefully eliminates Howard to escape, *Cloverfield Lane* looks ready to settle down into a typical bunker escape drama. But the final twist is that there is not much of anyone or anywhere left above to escape to, although the apocalypse is due to alien invasion rather than the A-B-C attack Howard had imagined he was prepping for. *Cloverfield* asks us to take Stambler's prepping and his damaged masculinity seriously as a proposition; he has, indeed, kept Michelle alive, and when she emerges from the bunker she's wearing a homemade hazmat suit, the design copied from Stambler's *Surviving Doomsday* book (Figure 2.4). At the same time, *Cloverfield* apparently condemns his methods. Or, perhaps, it is suggesting that without the unprovoked attack Stambler might have been talked down from his psychosis. Perhaps all that separates a deranged and dangerous survivalist like LaForche from a deranged and dangerous survivalist like Stambler is the lack of a loving wife who knows the right way to keep him on the straight and narrow. Popular genres afford problems and permutations, not coherence or resolution.

Where protests in the 1980s held the white male establishment responsible for the nuclear condition that had made everyone a survivalist, the 2010s apparently held no one responsible, least of all the establishment, but continued to recognize that white men have a privileged relationship to the spaces we need to imagine in order understand what has happened. Unfortunately, their own psychoses tend to make those bunkers the most dangerous

Figure 2.4 Empowered by the ambiguous bunker in *10 Cloverfield Lane*: the hazmat suit that Michelle believes is necessary for her to survive aboveground, made from a book in Stambler's shelter library.

Survivance in fictions of survivalism 63

if also still the necessary spaces for everyone threatened by that same white masculinity. After all, as 'Bloody Stranger' (Edwin Hodge) in *The Purge* can well attest, Sandin's security certainly helped to save *his* life. The current dispute between the survivalist and the non-survivalist can be framed in the following way. For people of privilege or people feeling disempowered and deserving of privilege, prepping and survivalism promise a changed world in which they maintain some kind of agency and control. For the rest of the world, conditions have pretty much always felt – and often have in fact been – apocalyptic, so there's no need and little reason for any radical adjustment to the current situation, although recognizing this fact might help make things better. Reviewing the dicta of 'Survival Mom,' Mira Ptacin 'heard echoes of my Polish grandmother's and my own mother's upbringing in the little town of Zakopane. They were resourceful because they had to be.'[31] Faced with the prospect of apocalypse, the daughter adopted into white privilege in Turtle Mountain Chippewa author Louise Erdrich's novel *Future Home of the Living God* (2017) asks her birth father what's going to happen:

> 'Indians have been adapting since before 1492 so I guess we'll keep adapting.'
>
> 'But the world is going to pieces.'
>
> 'It is always going to pieces.'
>
> 'This is different.'
>
> 'It's always different. We'll adapt.'[32]

Throughout the Cold War, survivalism was the default position; in the 2010s, that default was under siege from many different directions. What was at issue was not the crisis or even where best to think about the crisis; what was at issue was how best to face it.

One more survivalist tragedy can transition us to the somewhat cheerier genre of bunker escape comedies in the next section, for John Krasinski's postapocalyptic horror film *A Quiet Place* (2018) straddles both forms. On the one hand, paterfamilias Lee Abbott (Krasinski) is the acknowledged master at surviving the coming plague of blind, anosmic aliens whose pindrop hearing makes them deadly hunters nonetheless. Abbott's creation of a soundproofed farmstead from his high-tech basement control room is nothing

---

31 Ptacin, 'I'm a Prepper.'
32 Louise Erdrich, *Future Home of the Living God* (New York: HarperCollins, 2017), 28.

64 *After the end*

short of astonishing and just manages to save his family in the extended crisis that constitutes most of the film's narrative arc. On the other hand, Lee himself is still unable to protect his family: the youngest son is snatched in the opening teaser scene; his wife (Emily Blunt) is left to give birth on her own; the safe space he has painstakingly created to muffle the newborn baby's crying is flooded with water and doesn't keep out the monsters; his children are stranded in a derelict pickup truck at the mercy of one of the aliens and his only, very temporary, solution is to sacrifice himself to save them. Most damning of all, he forbids his teenaged daughter from entering the basement, for no reason the film ever provides. If he had not, she would likely have stumbled sooner on the rudimentary Achilles heel of the otherwise invincible aliens. To give Lee credit, he loves his family, he suffers over every one of his shortcomings, and, even more readily than Sandin in *The Purge*, he is willing to sacrifice his life for them. In other words, he is a good father but a flawed man, and according to the film's logic none of it is really his fault. That's the form typically taken by critical survivalist fiction, and it ends tragically.

There is an alternate reading available. Since the remaining four family members survive the siege of the bunker to emerge, alive and ready for a sequel, we can plausibly read the movie not as a survivalist drama but as a bunker emergence comedy whose protagonist would be not the flawed father but the capable teenager Regan (played by deaf actor Millicent Simmons). At the moment of crisis, Regan has, in fact, already left, having run off after an argument with her father over the bunker, to visit the grave of her baby brother for whose death, she, like Lee, feels responsible. Regan is likely also responsible for the family's initial survival since the necessity of learning sign language would have left them unusually well-equipped to deal with this particular apocalypse. She is well capable of performing survivalist tasks like hunting and fishing, although Lee refuses to take her, preferring to train the clearly less capable younger brother Marcus (Noah Jupe). Regan's quick analytical thinking and decisive action succeed in dealing the death blow to the aliens. If this newly nonnuclear family is going to survive post-patriarchy, she will need to lead the way; her mother, for all her toughness, appears to have been trained, like the Cold War galactic housewives before her, for nothing but farm labor, housework, child-bearing, and silent stoic suffering.[33] *A Quiet Place* takes a classic Cold War survivalist drama akin to 1962's *Panic in Year Zero!* or 1964's *Farnham's Freehold* and unfolds it in almost shockingly conventional fashion for its own time,

---

33 And, indeed, Regan has a greatly expanded role in the movie's sequel, *A Quiet Place Part II* (2020).

Survivance in fictions of survivalism 65

only to tack on a highly unconventional ending, as perfectly suited to 2018 as the first eighty minutes were suited to the early 1960s.[34] The bunker emergence stories discussed in the next section similarly flip the tragic tale of masculinity into a comic tale of intersectionality; the space remains determinative even as the perspective changes radically.

Survivors of bunkering from the 1980s to the future

Not all of twenty-first-century culture accepts the survivalist creed that the world is going to end. Alongside the survivalist dramas discussed above there is a counter-thread in the comic mode that imagines what happens to survivalists when the world does not in fact end as predicted. There was no room for such a stance in the mainstream imaginary of the Kennedy-era Cold War period; the world was seldom ended by a war, but neither were any happy near-future endings ever imagined. The closest to a bunker emergence comedy in those years was the 1961 *Twilight Zone* episode 'The Shelter'; however, there is nothing comic or resolved about the fractured civic society left for the emerging shelterers after what turns out to have been a false alarm. In contrast, the werewolf's father's basement shelter in *Full Moon High* (1981), the bunker seduction scene in *Grease 2* (1982), the frame tale of *Radioactive Dreams* (1985), the drug-addled 'psychic fallout shelter' of Marty Asher's *Shelter* (1986), the bunker-raised wild children of *Shelf Life* (1992), and the huckster spectacle of *Matinee* (1993) all suggest, for starters, as critic Kim Newman memorably put it, that for many in the 1980s, '[O]wning a bomb shelter is almost as embarrassing as driving an Edsel.'[35] That premise suggests that the bunker affords these films a comic space of social critique that tacks between the early 1960s and the 1980s. Within this space, the bunker fantasy became the measure, once again, of what it means to survive and what survives with you when you do.

---

34 When film critic Richard Brody took *A Quiet Place* to task for the whiteness of its frontier vision, he was perfectly well on target; however, not taking account of the odd conclusion means that what he accurately termed the film's 'unconscious and conspicuously regressive ... symbolic,' which I argue dates back to 1962, in fact neatly sets in relief the absolutely current politics of intersectionality mobilized in the conclusion, if also perhaps in an equally 'unconscious' way ('The Silently Regressive Politics of *A Quiet Place*,' *New Yorker* (10 April 2018): www.newyorker.com/culture/richard-brody/the-silently-regressive-politics-of-a-quiet-place; accessed 11 April 2018).
35 Kim Newman, *Apocalypse Movies: End of the World Cinema* (New York: St. Martin's Griffin, 2000 [1999]), 67.

66 *After the end*

During the 1980s, the survivors of the early Cold War continued to be themselves embodied in white men even as the primary target of the 1980s was the ideology of Reaganite conservatism and the retro early Cold War fantasy within which it was imagined. In contrast, 2010s bunker survival fictions, as suggested in the discussion of *Quiet Place* above, imagined emergence from the bunker as escape from white masculinity itself. Dark enough at times to be considered 'comic' only in the Aristotelian sense of ending better than they began, the TV series *Unbreakable Kimmy Schmidt* (2015–20) and the movies *Room* (2015), *Get Out* (2017), and *The Shape of Water* (2017) imagined the bunker as hellish imprisonment by the very social categories taken for granted in the 1960s and mostly elided in the 1980s focus on the reality of war. The bunker metaphorized not so much an escape from the nuclear condition as a place from which to recognize and call out the world that condition had led us down into and to imagine how one might emerge again from its constraints.

In an episode late in season three, *Unbreakable Kimmy Schmidt* took direct aim at the survivalist industry and the toxic white masculinity it found bunkered within it. The show's premise has Kimmy (Elle Kemper) move to New York City after being rescued from a doomsday bunker where she was imprisoned for fifteen years with several other women by 'The Reverend,' who successfully persuaded his prisoners, among other things, that the world above had ended. When Kimmy visits a fellow survivor at Manhattan's Javits Center, Cyndee is working at the '2017 EschaCon Doomsday Preparation Convention,' dressed as a 'mole woman' in front of a replica of The Reverend's bunker, pitching rape culture as a corollary of survivalism: 'Let me tell you, sir, if I'd been kept in a BunCo bunker, I never would have gotten out,' she asserts. 'This is great,' a conventioneer responds. 'Can you struggle with the door a little bit?' Her final pitch: 'So, you've got her in your van. Now what? BunCo – ' (Figure 2.5).[36] A position within the bunker affords the most effective perspective from which to understand the workings of its fantasy, since leaving the bunker simply makes that same fantasy harder to see. The bunker's promise of certainty, meaning, and shelter is nearly impossible to resist, especially when its promise is backed up economically: this is the job Cyndee's life has trained her for and likely the best offer she has had since emerging. That 'bunco' is a synonym for fraud or swindle only sharpens the dark gag. The wonder of the show, and where it captures the full power and range of the bunker fantasy in all its ambiguity, is not its skewering of the Reverend, however; the show's writers equally argue that Kimmy's very experience is what has made her 'unbreakable.' Her ability stubbornly to

---

36 'Kimmy and the Trolley Problem!' *Unbreakable Kimmy Schmidt*, season 3, ep. 12 (19 May 2017), Netflix.

Figure 2.5 Cyndee Pokorny (Sara Chase) in the ontological BunCo: the challenges of emerging from the bunker in *Unbreakable Kimmy Schmidt*.

refuse the bunker fantasy in all its manifestations comes from the same source as the insidious world she smilingly resists. This tension is reiterated by the opening credits, a visually miraculous sequence that shows the bunker door pulled back, light streaming in from above, and then cuts to an extreme long shot of Kimmy emerging through a hidden door into a green field, before the camera whip-zooms into her blissfully smiling face, exclaiming, amazed, 'It's all still here' (Figure 2.6).

This open-eyed gaze into and out of the abyss is what the comedy of bunker emergence affords; that its gaze is also bunco – exaggerated, irreverent, and impossible to take completely seriously – is the other side of the comic bargain offered by this form. An instructive example is 'Let's Do It for Our Country,' a musical number from *Grease 2* (1982, dir. Patricia Birch) that sets a fraudulent seduction scheme within a backyard fallout shelter. Embedded within a film produced to capitalize on nostalgia for the Kennedy-era Cold War, the sequence plays on the repressed sexuality contained within the original bunker fantasy while equally exposing the sexual politics now made visible for at least some members of the 1980s audience by 1970s feminism. Given the film's release in the middle of Reagan's first term, it easily lends itself to a reading in terms of the president's callow seduction of a credulous populace with cynical warmongering and fake patriotism whose only goal is to take it for a ride. Nor is it difficult to argue that the awareness that permits the scene to thwart and mock the culture of containment emerges from a similarly feminist place to the one that led six years later to the

Figure 2.6 'It's all still here.' Cyndee (left) and Kimmy Schmidt (Elle Kemper, right) experience the wonder and the horror of emerging from bunker captivity in the opening credit sequence to *Unbreakable Kimmy Schmidt*.

influential argument in sociologist Elaine Tyler May's *Homeward Bound* that the postwar suburban home as such was imbued with and designed to contain the effects of nuclearity.[37] This is certainly not an argument that was made at the time, and the characters themselves betray no awareness of the stakes that are now readily apparent in retrospect.[38] But this is how the comedy of bunker emergence functions. In 'Let's Do It for Our Country,'

---

37 Elaine Tyler May, *Homeward Bound: American Families in the Cold War Era*. Rev. ed. (New York: Basic Books, 1999 [1988]).
38 As Rachel Syme informed the film's star in a 2021 interview, 'Gen Z loves that movie. … People post the songs on TikTok. They have rediscovered it.' ('Michelle Pfeiffer Chooses Carefully,' *New Yorker* (31 Jan. 2021): http://web.archive.org/web/20230129042317/https://www.newyorker.com/culture/the-new-yorker-interview/michelle-pfeiffer-chooses-carefully) For some recent reappraisals of the film in this context, see Jamie Graham, 'In Defence of … *Grease 2*, Michelle Pfeiffer's Much-Maligned Sequel,' *Digital Spy* (22 March 2014): http://web.archive.org/web/20181129111310/http://www.digitalspy.com/movies/feature/a557626/in-defence-of-grease-2-michelle-pfeiffers-much-maligned-sequel/; Nic Holas, '"Grease 2" Was a Way Better Film than "Grease" and I Won't Be Told Otherwise,' *Junkee* (23 Jan. 2015): http://web.archive.org/web/20221206095457/https://junkee.com/revisited-grease-2-was-a-way-better-film-than-grease-heres-why/49561; Louisa Leontiades, 'Why My Mother Hated Grease 2… Along with the Rest of the World,' *Huffington Post* (30 March 2015): http://web.archive.org/web/20220630021535/https://www.huffingtonpost.co.uk/louisa-leontiades/grease-2-feminism_b_6561752.html; all accessed 31 Aug. 2023.

Figure 2.7 Revisionary patriotism and shelter as trap in *Grease 2*: playacting war as seduction or as rape, depending on the decade and the perspective. Louis (Peter Frechette) and Sharon (Maureen Teefy) sing 'Let's Do It for Our Country' in a backyard fallout shelter.

Sharon (Maureen Teefy) narrowly escapes being raped in the bunker by her boyfriend (Peter Frechette). This scene establishes more than any other in *Grease 2* the fraught relationship between the film's ostensible nostalgia for 1961 and the present day of its production (Figure 2.7).

Although a critical stance typically afforded only in the camp performance and the winking self-awareness of genre nostalgia, these traits underlie the bunker emergence comedies of the 1980s more generally, as they had already manifested in Serge Gainsbourg's 1975 LP *Rock around the Bunker* (discussed in the Introduction). They are one way, in fact, that the popular cinema of the time pushed back against the survivalist masculinity that dominated mainstream public discourse. So, the teen-werewolf comedy *Full Moon High* sets its origin story in the Kennedy-era Cold War, where the military officer father of titular protagonist Tony (Adam Arkin), played by 1960s and 1970s TV icon Ed McMahon, keeps a framed photo of his late, lamented hero Joseph McCarthy in the basement shelter (Figure 2.8). In a travesty of cross-generational conflict, Tony's father locks himself in the bunker to escape his feral son, vents about his misfortunes to the McCarthy photo, tries to shoot the snarling wolf through a porthole, and ends up shot dead himself when the bullet ricochets around the walls of his fortified Quonset hut. Cursed to remain a teenaged werewolf for the next twenty years, Tony fulfills his destiny, naturally, in 1981. As blogger Matt Wedge sums it up,

---

39 Matt Wedge, 'The Cohen Case Files: Full Moon High (1981),' *Obsessive Movie Nerd* (8 March 2011): http://web.archive.org/web/20221128042642/https://obsessivemovienerd.com/2011/03/08/the-cohen-case-files-full-moon-high-1981/; accessed 10 April 2018.

Figure 2.8 Revisionary patriotism and shelter as trap in *Full Moon High*: the father (Ed McMahon) of teen werewolf Tony (Adam Arkin) seeks refuge in the icons of his vanishing world: Joseph McCarthy, a hunting rifle, and a well-stocked fallout shelter. He will soon die from the architecture of his time when the rifle shot aimed at his son ricochets around the Quonset hut.

Full Moon High is 'a stupid movie [that] knows it's a stupid movie and revels in the fact.'[39] The shelter scene and the setup between 1960 and 1980 are part of the broader mockery and genre mashup in writer-director Larry Cohen's early feature. But there will be no emergence for Tony; this context and the monster movie genre's convention that he must die tell us that the present remains indelibly trapped by the Eisenhower–Kennedy world as reimagined by Reagan, cursed by the father's politics.

Radioactive Dreams is more self-consciously historicizing than *Full Moon*; its retro is more retro and its present-future more current. Sealed in a mountainside bunker when nuclear war breaks out in 1996 by a pair of men whose distinguishing feature seems to have been their love for hard-boiled pulp fiction, the orphaned 'Philip Chandler' and 'Marlowe Hammer' are left with little affection for their survivalist saviors. 'The creeps that locked us in here,' they conclude as they break out, 'were not our fathers.'[40] Philip and Marlowe emerge from their shelter and from scenes filmed on black-and-white stock into a 2010 in living color as clueless young adults who have gleaned their view of the world from old gangster movie clichés. Rather than futuristic, however, 'Edge City' in 2010 looks like nothing more than

---

40 *Radioactive Dreams*, wr. and dir. Albert Pyun, dist. DeLaurentiis Entertainment Group, 1985.

a postpunk underground circa 1985, complete with four songs and an onscreen performance of the title song by LA new-wave band Sue Saad and the Next. For all its DIY costumes and effects, the postapocalyptic CBGB in the 1980 video to Blondie's hit single 'Atomic' looked more futuristic than the one in Edge City.[41] While Philip and Marlowe are mildly nostalgic for their shelter ('I mean, it was the only world we'd ever known'), there is nothing that tempts them either in that sterile mancave or in the boiler-plate future noir they emerge into. 'Get me out of this nightmare of radioactive dreams,' sings Sue Saad, suggesting that the film's future is as trapped in the retro-culture of the 1980s as the two young men were in their bunker. Given the song's history, this is not surprising. According to the artist, growing up in Las Vegas in 'a culture of war, fear, and the end of the world ... As a kid I couldn't imagine how much more of a wasteland it could become. I had moved from Santa Monica, California. It felt like I was living in the aftermath of a nuclear attack already.'[42] The 'wasteland,' in other words, was not only the feared apocalypse to come but quite literally the apocalypse being lived in the present day.

Radioactive Dreams could just as well have been the title of *Matinee*, Joe Dante's 1993 homage to 1950s monster movies; however, perhaps with the Cold War now behind him, Dante was able to look back on 1962 with more fondness and insight than horror and disgust. Starring John Goodman as Lawrence Woolsey, a huckster filmmaker promoting a belated entry to the 1950s mutant monster movie genre, *Matinee* plays self-referentially with atomic war as a hook and a spectacle rather than a real danger. Despite the setting on and around a Key West Air Force base, *Matinee* argues for the cinema as a safe space to overcome real fear by taking it in as overblown spectacle. Woolsey's hokey 'Atomo-Vision' literally brings the action to the audience, complete with a movie screen 'ripped' open by the half-man, half-ant 'Mant' as he pursues the movie's starlet into the aisles. While the crowd panics and flees, destroying the cinema, a second drama is being enacted in the paranoid theater owner's state-of-the-art basement bunker. Here, in a consensual variation on *Grease 2*, teen protagonist Gene Loomis (Simon Fenton) and peacenik heartthrob Sandra (Lisa Jakub) are accidentally sealed into the impregnable bunker with a timed lock of several months' duration; kissing and heavy petting ensue. On the other side of the airlock, parental authorities gather and despair until the knowing Woolsey helpfully informs them that the shelters are as bunco as the actor in a Mant suit; he easily breaks it open for the embarrassed young couple to emerge (Figure

41 Blondie, 'Atomic,' dir. David Mallet, Capital Records, 1980.
42 Susan Boecker (née Saad), email communication, 18 Feb. 2021.

Figure 2.9 It takes one to know one: Cold War huckster Lawrence Woolsey (John Goodman) shows what the sheltering craze was really made of in *Matinee*, Joe Dante's homage to atomic spectacle and blinkered politics.

2.9). In the giddy years following the Cold War and following the Reaganite 1980s, Dante assures his audience that the security had been as illusory as the threat; the only legacy worth keeping was the era's endearingly bad movies.

It would be too easy to ascribe *Matinee*'s high spirits solely to the end of the Cold War, however; we can find a similar giddiness seven years earlier in *Shelter*, book editor Marty Asher's short and hallucinatory romp through the previous twenty-five years. Where *Matinee* looked back to monster movies, *Shelter*'s protagonist Billy medicates his debilitating nuclear fears with heavy doses of the Beatles. 'Billy's musical life ended,' we read, 'in 1970 with the release of *Abbey Road*.'[43] Billy, too, is locked into a bunker from which he appears never to emerge, 'his pharmaceutical box – his psychic fallout shelter in case the end came.'[44] He is a pure child of the 1960s, full of marijuana and self-indulgence, and blessed with an absurdly indulgent flower-child wife who runs the Gourd, a natural foods restaurant in the Hudson River valley. Their older son is starting a punk band, while the younger one is obsessed with fire engines as a result of the allegorical stories of nuclear war his father tells him. They won't follow him into his psychic fallout shelter, which, like the novel's title, references both the solipsism of rock music (the Rolling Stones' song 'Gimme Shelter') and the civil

---

43 Marty Asher, *Shelter* (New York: Arbor House, 1986), 12.
44 Asher, *Shelter*, 70.

Survivance in fictions of survivalism 73

defense schemes of Ronald Reagan. Instead, he will be visited by a resurrected John Lennon, who will teach him how to change the world. The process begins with a deep reading of the messages hidden within each song of *Sgt. Pepper's Lonely Hearts Club Band* (1967); it then leads to a riotous parody of both sheltermania and hippiedom, including no doubt the previous year's *Nuclear Age*:

'You've got to dig. Dig?'

Billy laughed. 'Yeah, I dig.'

'No,' John said. 'Dig. Dig?'

John handed him a shovel. Billy dug ... 'Now fix the hole! Fill it in!'

'But you're inside it.'

'But I'm dead. It doesn't matter.'

'But the music.'

'That's dead, too.' Billy bolted.[45]

The wordplay intimates the affiliation of pop music with nuclearity even as it dismisses careful reading as ridiculous – what Billy is told by Lennon to bury is his manuscript of notes on the secret meanings of 'Fixing a Hole' and the rest of *Sgt. Pepper's* pop songs. It's a refusal of bunkering as absurdity. But there is not really anything else on offer. After Billy brings back the Beatles to play a concert for peace in front of four million people in Central Park, he is brought home by his white wife Sara and his Black college roommate Roland, who is a postal worker, genius slacker, and jazz enthusiast. Billy coins a new bumper sticker slogan, 'Sometimes the only solution is to find a new problem.'[46]

Like the other 1980s comic bunker emergences discussed in this chapter, *Shelter* believes neither in bunkers nor in emergence. What it does posit is a different relation to the past than the one being promulgated through Reaganism. The bunker afforded a space for imagining and representing that different relationship. The emergence narrative suggested the necessity of leaving the bunker behind or putting it into context, whether or not the solution was actually possible to achieve. And although all concerned in various ways with conflicting and updated forms of paternity and masculinity, none of these texts is directly critical in the manner of the realist fictions discussed above or later bunker emergence comedies such as *Kimmy Schmidt* or *The Shape of Water*. The Brendan Fraser–Alicia Silverstone vehicle *Blast*

45 Asher, *Shelter*, 119.
46 Asher, *Shelter*, 131.

Figure 2.10 The galactic housewife (Sissy Spacek) shopping in her husband's bunkered vision of a 1962 stuck in time in *Blast from the Past*.

from the Past (1999) provides something of a bridge between the earlier films still steeped in the Cold War relationship of the 1980s to the 1960s and the later films and novels from the 2010s that open up the Cold War imaginary to address directly what was occluded by the containment narratives, what can be rescued from them, and what genuine and complete emergence might look like.

Blast from the Past was directed by Hugh Wilson from a thoughtful and detailed screenplay by Bill Kelly. One sign that the 1980s had long been over is that the camera is allowed to linger lovingly on the bunker to which Adam's soon-to-be parents retreat on the night of Kennedy's Cuban Missile Crisis speech in the false belief that war has begun. Adam is born the next day, and the film develops the lives of the characters through the shelter, likely based on an actual home built in Las Vegas in 1978 by the owner of the 1960s company Underground World Homes.[47] Adam's parents are played by Christopher Walken and Sissy Spacek, two actors who were born in the 1940s, raised into the Cold War, and became iconic figures of 1970s and 1980s Hollywood. Calvin Webber is an eccentric anticommunist scientist-inventor who has struck it rich and invested everything in a supershelter beneath his house with blast doors designed to hermetically seal themselves for thirty-five years to preclude any temptation to court the danger of residual radiation. Calvin has obsessively designed the shelter to mimic a controlled version of the house and outside world above, complete with a massive storeroom through which Helen can 'shop' with a pushcart (Figure 2.10).

[47] Mark Voelker, 'I Live in a 15,000 Sq Ft Underground Nuclear Fallout Bunker with a Swimming Pool,' *Newsweek* (3 Feb. 2022): http://web.archive.org/web/20220203100457/https://www.newsweek.com/underground-home-nuclear-fallout-shelter-1675286.

Survivance in fictions of survivalism

And he has never been happier, home-schooling Adam into a boy genius and endlessly tinkering with his greatest invention. Calvin's bunker perfectly simulates the containment culture of the early Cold War; no wonder Helen is as miserable as he is happy in her confinement. 'Your favorite, Calvin, not mine,' she ruefully corrects him at one point. Helen puts on a brave face for her son and husband while nipping from every bottle of cooking sherry she can lay her hands on in the well-stocked larder. When Calvin finally ventures out for the first time in thirty-five years, dressed in his hazmat suit, and finds a clichéd ghetto – dark, rainy, and graffiti-filled, replete with transgender sex workers, adult bookstores, and hoods in low riders waving guns – he decides he is happier down below in an eternal 1962 than living with what he regards as the 'sub-species mutants' above.[48]

When Adam (Brendan Fraser) must make the same journey for supplies, he encounters instead Alicia Silverstone's Eve. The 'surprise' is that, despite his father bearing all the trappings of toxic white masculinity and maniacal survivalism, Adam's naive gentleman-polymath turns out to be just the antidote for Eve's poisonous 1990s cynicism and hopeless taste for abusive men. Punctuated by predictable rom-com mishaps and misunderstandings, Adam negotiates the turn-of-the-millennium city with aplomb, from the fashion tips bestowed by Eve's requisite gay best friend to the physical threat of her most recent ex. The bunker fantasy may have ruined one woman's life and made one father a monster, but it has somehow managed to produce the perfect man out of time for the new millennium.

Blast from the Past plays Helen's plight for laughs, but not so much as to preclude awareness of the trap she is in. We catch a glimpse of the more frightening correlative of her captivity narrative in Eve's initial reaction to Adam's big reveal. When he finally confides to her about the shelter, she thinks he is trying to lure her underground à la *Silence of the Lambs* (1991), and she calls the authorities on him. The threat to women of bunker captivity, as we have seen, is never far removed from the white man's bunker fantasy. The film's denouement briefly returns to the supershelter suburban home, which Adam will go on to reproduce in two different contemporary forms aboveground using the millions his father's baseball card collection and stock options had accumulated over thirty-five years. First, he transforms the dive bar that had been built above the shelter as urban sprawl overtook the 1962 suburban home. Wilson has used the bar's various incarnations to mark the passage of years, accompanied by appropriate music: from surf pop in Mom's 1960s soda shop to Barry White in the 1970s to grunge in the 1990s to an evangelical cult devoted to the scripture of the gods who

---

48 *Blast from the Past*, dir. Hugh Wilson, wr. Bill Kelly, dist. New Line Cinema (1999).

Figure 2.11 1962 appropriated for the coming twenty-first century in *Blast from the Past*: the final incarnation of the lot above the bunker renovates its concept as a retro-futurist diner.

rise in the elevator through the floor, in a nice, end-of-millennium twist on the familiar ghetto-church storefront. The new conversion, naturally, transforms the space into a gentrifying retro diner called Shelter (Figure 2.11). For the second bunker renewal, Adam builds a precise aboveground replica of the shelter space on land he has purchased beyond the reach of the city. Like Kimmy Schmidt after him, the bunker fantasy tells us that the resolute naivete, niceness, and ability to accomplish everything in spite of it are all qualities inculcated only in the misery of the shelter. And although Adam's misery is a different order than Kimmy's, Helen's slow burn reminds us of how truly awful it must have been to be stuck with her husband for thirty-five endless repetitions of his version of the year 1962. *Blast from the Past* gently but firmly rejects everything that year stood for, all the while telling us that what containment produced nevertheless still cannot be beat. That the bunker fantasy only really suits straight white men is something the late 1990s comic form of *Blast from the Past* can only hint at.

Paul Bartel's 1993 three-hander *Shelf Life* shares with *Blast from the Past* not only the southern California location but also the origin story of a bigoted but loving father, a confined and mildly alcoholic mother, a mistaken decision to shelter long term, and a younger generation fully formed by life spent in a bunker. From that shared premise, *Shelf Life* takes a decidedly different path: following a brief opening on the day of Kennedy's assassination in 1963 that prompts the father to lock them in, the film jumps thirty years to a post–Cold War present shared by a trio of middle-aged adults who have raised themselves ferally after their parents died, apparently quite early on, from a tainted tin of food. The film documents a day in the life of

Survivance in fictions of survivalism 77

Figure 2.12 *Shelf Life* shows the impending end to the Cold War promise of endless plenty in Grandma's pantry.

siblings Pam, Tina, and Scotty, observing their rapidly shifting play between ritual and improvisation in an absurdist mashup of TV serials, comics, ads, Christianity, parental nostrums, and public service announcements. While intimating a tragic breakdown of society on the model of *Lord of the Flies* or 1980s cultural critique, the force and imagination of the three performers suggest more of a functional technique of survival within the debased, contained, and bunkered culture that was the Cold War around 1963 and in Bartel's 1980s. Rather than producing Adam's ideal Gen X male, this Cold War couple has birthed a hermetic, private language that hopelessly garbles mainstream values while somehow providing affective meaning and social cohesion to the three siblings: they survive until, just after the camera has revealed the exhaustion of their seemingly endless food supply, they bid each other goodnight, sunlight breaks in through the roof, and a construction worker (played by the director) peers into the bunker and, in a tight close-up, breaks into open-mouthed astonishment (Figures 2.12 & 2.13). The frame freezes and the film concludes, granting the audience the comic ending of emergence and survival but declining to speculate on what will happen to the siblings in the 'normal' world above.

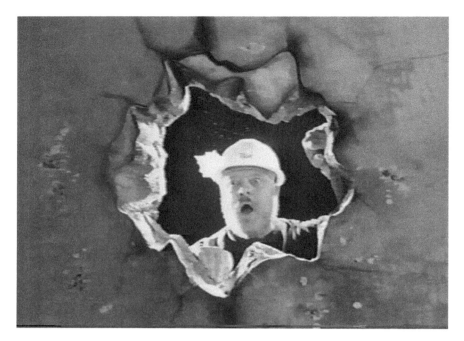

Figure 2.13 The concluding surprise of emergence into an unknown but essentially comic and open future in *Shelf Life*.

Both *Blast from the Past* and *Shelf Life* hint at the essentially sociopathic core of the father's need to confine and control his family in a bunker of his own design even as they temper that core with the assertion of his good intentions. But in its gender split between a happily confined man and a miserably confined woman or children, the captivity narrative has always existed uneasily alongside the bunker fantasy. *Silence of the Lambs* used a female protagonist, but still told its tale primarily from the perspective of the liberator rather than the captive. More recent iterations such as Denis Villeneuve's *Prisoners* (2013) and Atom Egoyan's *The Captive* (2014) focus primarily on the father's insistent search for his daughter and the social cost of that search; the rescue ends any relationship with the captive space. South African novelist Lauren Beukes tweaks this dynamic in her 2020 postapocalyptic thriller *Afterland*, where an XY-specific pandemic has killed all but an anomalous number of men, and most of the few survivors are imprisoned in a top-secret five-story 'luxury bunker facility' called Ataraxia. Rumored to be located in California, it was built by an ultrarich prepper who succumbed to the virus; it was then requisitioned by the all-female government and dedicated to perpetuating the species. Rather than the home shelters

Survivance in fictions of survivalism   79

and subterranes that typically imprison female victims, Ataraxia boasts 'a state-of-the-art hospital, luxury accommodation for twenty families and slightly less sumptuous accommodation for fifty staff, a subterranean hydroponic greenhouse, a running track, classrooms, a recreation center with a gym, a wine cellar, a goddamn swimming pool fed by a borehole, and ... most absurd: a jungle-theme tiki bar.'[49]

The plot of *Afterland* turns around the boy whose mother breaks him out of Ataraxia in a bid to escape back to a saner, safer South Africa and the sociopathic sister's attempts to kidnap her nephew to sell on the black market. Beukes writes the gender inversion as a darkly comic road trip, seeking alienation effects from the absence of 'cannibal biker gangs ... shambling undead, small-town utopian havens with dark underbellies, highwaymen ... crazed militias' and other 'apocalypses of pop culture.'[50] There are a surprising number of towns still functioning and other cars on the road. But while the familiar emblems of toxic masculine apocalypse are missing from the imagined future, women have easily stepped into every position in an oppressive and corrupt system of crime networks and militarized government that has changed very little beyond its gender. Beukes thus skewers the masculinist fantasies of apocalypse while casting an equally jaundiced eye on a capitalist system that corrupts irrespective of gender. Even so, Cole and Miles escape from Ataraxia, escape from a locked-down America, and grow in the process, a process the bunker emergence comedy affords as a form.

Despite a subject matter painfully steeped in the trauma of conventionally gendered captivity tales, *Room* (2015), directed by Lenny Abrahamson from a script adapted by Emma Donoghue from her 2010 novel, fits neatly within the form of the bunker emergence comedy it shares with *Afterland* as much as it shares its mother–son dyad. As the tagline on the poster asserted, 'Love knows no boundaries'; the characters, of course, do know them. The first half of the film takes place entirely within the eleven-foot-by-eleven-foot room in a backyard shed in which twenty-four-year-old Joy Newsome (Brie Larson) has been imprisoned since she was abducted at seventeen. She shares the room with her five-year-old son Jack (Jacob Tremblay) and with her captor, who visits her weekly to rape her. During these visits, Jack is shut into the even smaller space he calls Wardrobe.

Joy's captor (Sean Bridgers), whom she calls Old Nick (after an archaic alias of the Devil), closely resembles an abusive husband. He keeps her confined, brings her the stuff she needs to survive, grants her special requests for outside goods after each conjugal visit, and beats her when he is dissatisfied

---

49 Lauren Beukes, *Afterland* (New York: Little, Brown, 2020), 133.
50 Beukes, *Afterland*, 10, 33.

with her behavior. Because the room is fully equipped with TV, kitchenette, tub, and toilet, like a tenement apartment, it more closely resembles a bunker than a prison. That is, it presents as a regular dwelling, except that they are unable to leave. This fact makes Joy's five-year endeavor to persuade Jack of the normality and even wonder of his world both credible and poignant – how many parents, especially mothers, living in poverty, conditions of war, or other kinds of confinement or abuse, don't do the same for their children every day? Abrahamson and Donoghue strengthen this existential quality through the phenomenological way in which Jack interacts with his space as if it were sentient and benevolent: Room, Door, Skylight, and Wardrobe are the marvels of his existence. What are terrors to his mother, he accepts matter-of-factly just like any child who knows nothing else.

When they escape the room at midpoint in the film, the long time spent in the bunker pays off in the viewer's shared understanding of the pressures of the 'normal' outside world and the ways in which her parents' house, which Joy has been yearning to return to for seven years, is nearly as confining and stifling a bunker as the room was. What is worse, so now is Jack. The bunker fantasy has marked them, and perhaps spoiled them, for the 'real world.' Here, too, one can imagine that Jack would survive and eventually thrive after leaving the space he loved and sometimes misses, partly because of the undivided love and attention he had received there from his mother. His confinement naturally mirrors the trajectory of childhood; the separation would always have happened, if not always so starkly. And one can imagine that Joy would be permanently scarred, for her confinement is perverse and works only to show every way in which her life might trap and betray her.

The film concludes with a final return to the room, at Jack's request. It looks different, shrunk, Jack comments. Then he chillingly corrects this facile allegory of childhood, reasoning that, 'It's because Door's open. It can't really be Room if Door's open.' The bunker is only a bunker when sealed. *Room*'s bunker fantasy is deeply troubling; as movie critic Anthony Lane challenged, 'Does that lesson not come at too great a cost?'[51] The cost of the lesson is what makes the bunker fantasy such a powerfully resonant space; it locates and expresses ethical stakes in the starkest, most visceral terms. After all, Jack, whom the film painstakingly brings the viewer to love and to treasure, is the child of Joy and her captor; his very existence is predicated on one of the most pernicious and extreme forms the bunker fantasy can take. The ontological bunker stresses the power of the imagination

---

51 Anthony Lane, 'Room,' *New Yorker* (24 Feb. 2016): http://web.archive.org/web/20190701093401/https://www.newyorker.com/goings-on-about-town/movies/room.

over the reality of abduction, abuse, and confinement, and this is how *Room* was marketed. Only in this perspective of 'an extraordinary story of hope and survival' can one grasp the evident paradox of Donoghue's later adaptation of her novel as a Broadway show. "Brought to life with music and imagination," *Room* opened in 2023; it starred Adrienne Warren, best known for her Tony Award–winning performance as domestic abuse survivor Tina Turner.[52]

While *Room* grounds its setting very loosely in an anonymous Toronto suburb masquerading as present-day Akron, Ohio, the fantasy-horror films *Get Out* and *The Shape of Water* (both 2017) draw strong and explicit connections to the Cold War past. Jordan Peele makes iconic use of George Romero's then-unprecedented casting of a Black actor in the middle of a white countryside in *Night of the Living Dead* (1968) and of the dystopian vision of zombified suburban housewives eagerly embraced by their complicit husbands in *The Stepford Wives* (1975). The Cold War bunker, Peele implies, lurks beneath every respectable white household like a sadistic repository of all that was and remains wrong with American society. Guillermo del Toro similarly employs the tropes and iconography of Cold War monster movies and myriad images of secret underground research facilities to craft a contemporary fable that, rather than coming to terms with atomic mutation, embraces alienness for its own sake in an ostensibly 1962 Baltimore. In each film, the imprisoned character – Black protagonist Chris (Daniel Kaluuya) and 'Amphibian Man' (Doug Jones), respectively – escapes what initially feels like a bunker out of time but which the viewer must come to accept as part and parcel of the contemporary world.

Neither film is explicitly concerned with the bunker qua bunker the way *Blast from the Past* or *Kimmy Schmidt* is; nevertheless, their subterranean spaces afford similar qualities within their forms. In both films, scientific cruelty and criminal torture performed by supposedly reputable white male community members are hidden underground. *Water*'s bunkered laboratory is military while *Get Out*'s is a private enterprise; however, both spaces are defined by those who control them as designed for the benefit of the future. In the 1962 of *Water*, that benefit is defined socially and eventually trumped by the ethics and individual desires of marginalized citizens Elisa Esposito (Sally Hawkins), Giles (Richard Jenkins), and Zelda Delilah Fuller (Octavia Spencer). The trio's intersectionality – Latinx, mute, gay, female, Black – is at once programmatic and mobilized to underpin the far more transgressive inclusion of Amphibian Man, a humanoid but strongly alien creature, within

---

52 *Roombroadway.com*: http://web.archive.org/web/20230311041330/https://roombroadway.com/; accessed 31 Aug. 2023.

82 *After the end*

the ranks of those shut out of the bunker of Michael Shannon's exaggeratedly evil antagonist Colonel Richard Strickland. In the 2017 film *Get Out*, civic good is cynically defined as whatever meets the wishes of the white elite who pay for the Armitage family's services in transplanting their brains from aging white to talented, fit, and young Black bodies. The bunker spaces are the linchpin of the two films not only because of the secrets they reveal and the truths they contain, but because they are so familiar to the audience in their resonance as shelters from nuclear fear and underground sources of knowledge from which one returns – *if* one returns – wiser and enlightened. Precisely because the bunker fantasy has not lost its resonances within the Cold War culture it emerged from, the betrayal both films reveal, despite its absence from the overt imagination of that culture, nevertheless rings true.

One of the fault lines within *Kimmy Schmidt* is the uneasy way the show vacillates between affirming the horrible particularity of her bunker experience and extending the bunker as a metaphor to cover pretty much any formative hardship. As her Black, gay roommate Titus Andromedon (Ronald Wilkerson) puts it when he tells her his own backstory for the first time, 'Mississippi was my bunker. ... It took all the courage I had to escape.'[53] Then, in the third season, meteorologist Drench Thunderman (Michael Torpey) hypes Hurricane Tammi with the same image: 'If you've got a bunker, get in it and close the hatch.'[54] Kimmy eventually decides herself that 'a bunker can be a good thing' and that she is going to turn their apartment into a bunker, but her way: 'fair' and 'fun.' There's a not-so-implicit argument that the world is bunkered between the one percent and the rest. As Kimmy explains to Thunderman about his hyperbole, 'You make the movie *Overboard* look like a lighthearted comedy instead of a messed-up story about a handyman enslaving a woman with a brain injury.'[55] In comedy, it is always both at once. *Kimmy Schmidt* certainly makes radically reductive claims distinguishing the bunker survivors in New York City and the bunkerers pretty much all over everywhere else. It is both savage and forgiving in its attacks; however, in comparison to *Room*, *Get Out*, or *Shape of Water*, one could argue that it approaches the Reverend and the bunker experience with angry equanimity. The show needs the depth of Kimmy's suffering in order to motivate and

---

53 'Kimmy Goes Roller Skating!' *Unbreakable Kimmy Schmidt*, season 2, ep. 1 (15 April 2016), Netflix.

54 'Kimmy Learns about the Weather!' *Unbreakable Kimmy Schmidt*, season 3, ep. 7 (19 May 2017), Netflix.

55 For anyone that missed it, the 1987 film *Overboard* is a lighthearted comedy about a handyman enslaving a woman with a brain injury. It would be remade in 2018 with the genders of the two characters reversed.

Survivance and the Atomic Bomb Dome

make her Pollyanna character believable and tolerable to the audience. It continues to argue that the comedy in *Overboard* or the origins of Kimmy's strength and moral compass emanate from the same source as their 'messed-up stories' of abuse. You can't have one without the other, *Kimmy Schmidt* tells us, and a survivor who has not lost sight of what matters remains a survivor, even while she is always also more than that.

Survivance and the Atomic Bomb Dome

In *Hiroshima Bugi: Atomu 57* (2003), his hybrid experimental fiction of Japan, nuclear war, and Native American identity, Gerald Vizenor's narrator coins the term *survivance*, which he contrasts with '[T]he commerce of reactive survivalists, mere liturgy, ideology, or the causative leverage of a sworn witness.' Survivance, the narrator tells us, 'is a creative, concerted consciousness that does not arise from separation, dominance, or concession nightmares. Our stories create perfect memories of survivance.'[56] Survivance accurately characterizes the bunker emergence comedy, finding a different and redemptive means of negotiating past trauma that neither accepts personal survival as a sine qua non nor lives life according to the 'reactive' fantasies of survivalism. As Annalee Newitz clarifies, 'The difference between survival and survivance is the difference between maintaining existence at a subsistence level and leading a life that is freely chosen.'[57] Vizenor grounds the concept of survivance in the paradigmatically hybrid character Ronin Ainoko Brown, orphan son of Okichi, a Japanese dancer, and Nightbreaker, an Anishinaabe soldier from White Earth Reservation who was in Japan postwar as General MacArthur's interpreter. Before his death, Ronin had been living with a homeless community of 'roamers' and 'storiers' in the Hiroshima Peace Park, devoting himself among other things to subversive appropriations and misplacements of the innocuous 'peace' narrative. The novel is composed of his notes and stories interspersed with the narrator's discussion and annotations, per Ronin's request. The site of the novel and the focus of Ronin's survivance is the Atomic Bomb Dome, the building nearest to the bomb's ground zero left standing in any recognizable form, 'the steel frame of the dome and the outer walls of the building,' protected, 'with no intended irony ... on the World Heritage List' (Figure 2.14).[58] The Dome, the narrator informs us, 'is the actual ruins of the Hiroshima Industrial Promotion Hall.

---

56 Vizenor, *Hiroshima Bugi*, 9.
57 Annalee Newitz, *Scatter, Adapt, and Remember: How Humans Will Survive a Mass Extinction* (New York: Doubleday, 2013), 102.
58 Vizenor, *Hiroshima Bugi*, 10.
59 Vizenor, *Hiroshima Bugi*, 10.

Figure 2.14 Survivance and nuclear tourism: the unintended irony of an atomic ruin as World Heritage Site.

The Dome, however, is not as real to many tourists as the simulated miniature dome constructed inside the Peace Memorial Museum.'[59]

To Ronin, for whom 'The perception of the real must be sincere, yet the sense is ironic, never actual,' the 'plastic' Dome is an affront.[60] In his description:

> There are hundreds of miniature letters etched on metal and mounted as a permanent exhibit on a huge column in the museum, a prominent pillar under the new simulated dome. The scale model plaster dome is a stagy, contemptible memorial of atomic destruction. ... Many people were critical of the real dome because of the land values, a constant reminder of the war and hibakusha, the survivors of the atomic bomb. The detractors conspired to raze the real to save the faux as a museum catchword, but proxy politics did not prevail. The Atomic Bomb Dome was recognized as an international historic site and registered, along with the Great Wall of China, on the World Heritage List. I live with roamers in the real dome in the ruins of the atomu bomb and despise the models. The museum is a cynical theme park of human misery, and the miniature letters are a testament to the arrogance and deceptions of political peacemongers.[61]

60 Vizenor, *Hiroshima Bugi*, 69.
61 Vizenor, *Hiroshima Bugi*, 80–1.

Survivance in fictions of survivalism 85

A similar flattening of the experience of Hiroshima within the global economy of heritage sites and war memorials is evident in the use of a photograph of the Atomic Bomb Dome since the 1980s as the cover design of the English-language edition of Masuji Ibuse's 1969 novel *Black Rain* despite the fact that the landmark and symbol is not mentioned within its pages. Instead, in a form certainly encompassed by the concept of survivance, and characterized by its translator as 'a documentary novel,'[62] *Black Rain* incorporates actual records and journal entries into the experience of its fictional characters to register the diverse effects of the bombing and subsequent surrender on the everyday life of the Japanese who lived through it.

Ronin's related obsession with 'authenticity,' his perverse yet principled rejection of the hypocrisy of 'peacemongers,' his paradoxical insistence on an 'ironic' rather than an 'actual' stance towards the 'real,' and the formal alternation of his 'authentic' notes with the narrator's analytic voice mark the novel as classic postmodernist fiction. Similarly, Ronin's hybridity blends and disrupts categories of center and margin, of colonizer and colonized, of power and impotence: his father was both a Native American veteran and a member of the occupying forces working for MacArthur, where he sired a child with a 'hostess' servicing the occupying forces, and the Japanese themselves are simultaneously victims and self-denying aggressors. Through Ronin's intersectional identity, Vizenor claims the right to speak both from within and from outside of a survivor's perspective about Hiroshima.

Laguna Pueblo writer Leslie Marmon Silko in her 1977 novel *Ceremony* and Cherokee writer William Sanders in his 1999 speculative fiction *The Ballad of Billy Badass and the Rose of Turkestan* had done something similar. Billy Badass is a veteran of the first Iraq war and *Ceremony*'s Tayo is a World War II veteran suffering from post-traumatic stress disorder; each protagonist's slow healing is woven into a story able to encompass and counter what *Ceremony*'s narrator calls 'a circle of death that devoured people in cities twelve thousand miles away, victims who had never known these mesas, who had never seen the delicate colors of the rocks which boiled up their slaughter.'[63] Those 'delicate colors' are uranium in its natural state as ore rock, 'gray stone ... streaked with powdery yellow uranium, bright and alive as pollen; veins of sooty black formed lines with the yellow, making mountain ranges and rivers across the stone.'[64] Tayo is standing at the entrance to the mine-shaft from which uranium was extracted between

62 John Best, 'Translator's Preface,' in *Black Rain* by Masuji Ibuse (Bunkyo-ku, Tokyo: Kodansha International, 1979 [1969]), 5–8, at 6.
63 Leslie Marmon Silko, *Ceremony* (New York: Penguin, 2006 [1977]), 229.
64 Silko, *Ceremony*, 228–9.

1943 and 1945, part of the Grants mineral belt at the intersection of Arizona, Colorado, New Mexico, and Utah that contained two-thirds of US uranium deposits.[65] It is here that he understands why he is haunted by seeing his uncle Josiah's face in a Japanese soldier killed in the war, and later mistakes a Japanese American boy's face for his cousin Rocky, killed by Japanese soldiers in the Philippines.[66]

Ballad of Billy Badass pairs a romance between Billy and Janna, a visiting Kazakh medical technologist investigating the effects of radiation exposure on children in a (fictional) Paiute reservation near Las Vegas in the proximity of underground testing and near a secret nuclear waste dump, with an SFF-horror plot involving a deadly world-destroying alien that feeds on the energies released by nuclear decay and by humans engaged in heightened spiritual or sexual activity.[67] What scholar Miriam Brown Spiers terms the novel's 'radiation monster' defies understanding within human terms; it is first turned aside by a tobacco ceremony and finally destroyed in enigmatic fashion by a more hybrid ceremony: 'the power of all the children around the world who have been harmed by radiation exposure [and] seem to have harnessed the power imparted by the radiation that has so affected them.'[68] Rather than undercut the allegorical fury and historical texture of the Indigenous characters' battle against global nuclear-driven settler colonialism, the deadpan humor, ordinary heroism, and other pulp SFF genre tropes ground it terrifyingly within the everyday.

While Sanders finds it in speculative fiction, Silko names 'story' the form Vizenor will later term survivance: the recognition that dealing with the devastations of the nuclear age comes from within and not from without. Tayo's understanding leads him also to complete a hybrid ceremony, a story recognizing that 'human beings were one clan again, united by the fate the destroyers planned for all of them'; that Indigenous Peoples existed before and created the whites that would colonize and attempt to destroy them and everyone else; and that the nuclear devastation that began at 'Trinity Site, where they exploded the first atomic bomb, ... only three hundred miles to the southeast, at White Sands ... [a]nd the top-secret laboratories where the bomb had been created were deep in the Jemez Mountains on land the Government took from Cochiti Pueblo: Los Alamos, only a hundred

---

65 Kyoko Matsunaga, 'Leslie Marmon Silko and Nuclear Dissent in the American Southwest,' *Japanese Journal of American Studies* 25 (2014): 67–87, at 68.
66 Matsunaga, 'Leslie Marmon Silko and Nuclear Dissent,' 72.
67 William Sanders, *The Ballad of Billy Badass and the Rose of Turkestan* (Holicong, PA: Wildside Press, 1999).
68 Miriam Brown Spiers, '"The Yellow Monster": Reanimating Nuclear Fears in Cherokee Science Fiction,' *Native South* 12 (2019): 52–73, at 68.
69 Silko, *Ceremony*, 228.

miles northeast of him now' had spread across the globe, a nuclear colonialism part and parcel of a much longer colonial legacy.[69] Silko's narrative makes it clear that survivance was a struggle even for survivors of nuclear colonialism. Like Vizenor, she identifies what were long designated the forms of post-modernism as tools to contain and reimagine the brief but deadly timeframe of the nuclear age as merely a brief episode in a much longer struggle against 'witchery' but on Native Peoples' terms. Tayo 'had never been crazy,' he realized. 'He had only seen and heard the world as it always was: no boundaries, only transitions through all distances and time.'[70] Emerging from an epistemological bunker rooted in the uranium mine and the 'government laboratories ... deep in the Jemez Mountains' does not free Tayo from the nuclear condition; however, it restores him to an alternate story radiating out from his people's lands, 'a convergence of patterns' of which the bunker fantasy is the center but not the meaning and not all there is.[71]

Silko's later, much longer novel *Almanac of the Dead* (1991) repurposes the bunker fantasy to frame a vast panorama that radiates out in every direction from the same uranium mine. Set in a speculative near future rather than in a reconceived present, *Almanac* seems to welcome apocalypse within its cosmology. Sterling, a hybrid Laguna Pueblo character similar to *Ceremony*'s Tayo, does not even have the option of a ceremony; instead, he simply finds his way back to the stone snake that had manifested at an open-pit uranium mine. Here, he discovers his own insight: 'The snake didn't care if people were believers or not; the work of the spirits and prophecies went on regardless. Spirit beings might appear anywhere, even near open-pit mines. The snake didn't care about the uranium tailings; humans had desecrated only themselves with the mine, not the earth. Burned and radioactive, with all humans dead, the earth would still be sacred. Man was too insignificant to desecrate her.'[72] In this vision, the nuclear age is simply the culminating moment of a long-predicted heat-death of the human race. 'What mattered,' Sterling realizes, 'was that after all the ground water had been sucked out of the Ogalala Aquifer, then the white people and their cities of Tulsa, Denver, Wichita, and Des Moines would gradually disappear and the Great Plains would again host great herds of buffalo and those human beings who knew how to survive on the annual rainfall.'[73] For Silko, survivance radically decenters not just *Ceremony*'s destroyers but the human race full stop.

---

70 Silko, *Ceremony*, 229.
71 Silko, *Ceremony*, 235.
72 Silko, *Almanac of the Dead: A Novel* (New York: Penguin, 1992 [1991]), 762.
73 Silko, *Almanac of the Dead*, 759.

Vizenor similarly deploys his own identity as an Anishinaabe writer to treat Hiroshima in a tragicomic and absurdist mode that would typically be unavailable to a white male US writer. Like the creators of *Room*, *Get Out*, *Shape of Water*, and *Kimmy Schmidt*, Silko's and Vizenor's identities authorize them to create and to play with a comedy of bunker emergence. As Tayo and Sterling cannot escape what has occurred, so the mark of Vizenor's postmodernism is that there is no escape for Ronin from the bunker of his identities or from the dilemma of maintaining distinctions between plastic and authentic or between war and peace. As Tayo finds resolution in 'the pattern' he identifies that allows him to complete the ceremony, the figure of the dome affords Ronin a certain kind of psychic and physical protection. However, like the traumatized Traven in the nuclear testing ruins of Enewetak Atoll in J. G. Ballard's 1964 short story 'Terminal Beach' (see Introduction above), Ronin is unable to live outside of what we might term, by extension, his 'ontological dome.' As opposed to Traven, who submits to the simultaneously transformative and horrific terms of his ontological bunker, Ronin's identity is as porous as the framework that makes of the Dome a ruin rather than the divinely transparent protection we see in superhero or science-fictional domes. That porosity certainly bears a family resemblance to the geodesic dome and other transparently utopian structures promoted by Buckminster Fuller and the *Whole Earth Catalog* (see Chapter 1), but Vizenor makes clear that any utopia is predicated on survivance exclusively rather than on creating something new. Nevertheless, Ronin prefers this ruin to the impassable rigidity of the ersatz dome enclosed in a museum; indeed, we find an echo of that repulsion in the domes that become entrapping enclosures of horror and death in the alien occupations of the Luna Brothers' comic *Girls* (2005–7) or Stephen King's novel *Under the Dome* (2009) and the subsequent TV series (2013–15), as well as in PRC journalist and activist Chai Jing's 2015 documentary that uses the same title as a metaphor for air pollution. The dome acts like the comic punchline to the invariably tragic straight man of the bunker fantasy. But without that comic turn, domes can be even worse traps than bunkers are – invisible prisons without any promise of survival or escape.

What Vizenor's novel of survivance and the comedies of bunker emergence discussed above suggest in the twenty-first century is that the most effective way fundamentally to challenge the ontological bunker that continues to dominate and inform our understanding and processing of the world around us is by dwelling in its experience and fantasies. Their postmodern or comic modes acknowledge the physical impossibility of escaping a space that is no longer in fact physically dominant as it was during the Cold War. They equally acknowledge that there may be less utility in stepping outside the bunker than in imagining how the step outside might change the ways we

Survivance in fictions of survivalism

understand its fantasies. In this sense, they do not supersede the tragic fantasies of white male survivalism, which tell their own partial truths about where the Cold War led us and why. But these hybrid and intersectional approaches to the bunker fantasy provide an effective perspective from which to approach the spatial and temporal appropriations of the bunker fantasy, its ruins, its intact traces, and its legacies. This perspective firmly resituates the fantasy within a world at large that is always intersectional in its relationship to an America that, conversely, is now visibly seamed with alternate positions that challenge an imagined nation that for so long was univocally and unilaterally identified as united in sameness under the banner of survival.

3

The hedgehog, the tortoise, and the world: Switzerland, Albania, and the global bunker fantasy

> Well, this here verse is for the people in Russia
> Though it is a long long ways away
> They couldn't hear this song in Russia
> But couldn't understand the words anyway
> ....
> So just be glad you live in America
> Just relax and be yourself
> Cuz if you didn't live here in America
> You'd probably live somewhere else
>
> Camper Van Beethoven, 'Good Guys and Bad Guys' (1986)

As northern California band Camper Van Beethoven suggested in 1986, even in the black-and-white opposition of 'Good Guys and Bad Guys,' the bunker fantasy was a collaborative project of Cold War rivals that had more in common than otherwise. Indeed, far more joined the United States and Russia than the 'biology' or love of children on which English musician Sting pinned his hopes for peace in the hit 1985 pop single 'Russians.' Due to the technological reproducibility of its basic affordances, that shared fantasy spread far beyond its twin origin. And as Sting argued of parental love and Camper Van Beethoven of where you live, the bunker fantasy could be filled in with democracy, communism, or any other political ideology around; its basic form and function did not change. What remained consistent as it circulated the globe were the spaces it afforded for mobilizing national political imaginaries against outside forces and for either debate or attempts to limit debate over the identity of those imaginaries. Confined to the figurative lineaments of the nation-state, the bunker fantasy as geopolitical imaginary is restrictive in its capacity to account for difference within national identity; only in the cosmic scale of the SFF forms examined in Chapter 5 below can we see its critical potentialities for unpacking the racial dynamics of the Euro-American nation-state. On the conventional scale of the nation, the global bunker fantasy could only be conceived as all-consuming. Such a

The hedgehog, the tortoise, and the world 91

view was expressed in *The Atom Station*, Icelandic writer (and, at the time, staunch communist) Halldór Laxness's 1948 political satire on his government's agreement to allow a US military base in the newly independent nation, in which a poet declares, 'We belong to the atom bomb. ... The whole world is one atom station.'[1]

This chapter studies the global circulation of the bunker since the end of the Second World War and the ways its spaces and imaginaries continue to be adapted as global responses to various legacies of the Cold War today. The first section brings out the broad stakes of the global bunker fantasy through a survey of bunkering and civil defense in Europe, Russia, and Asia. The following sections deepen this survey through case studies of two small nation-states: Albania, where the totalitarian former Communist leader Enver Hoxha had seven hundred thousand concrete bunkers constructed during the 1970s, and democratic, capitalist Switzerland, which to this day regularly votes to continue mandating shelter facilities in every building constructed in the country. The apparent eccentricities of these smaller-scale extremes of civil defense illuminate the bunker fantasy in ways less openly visible within the dominant American Cold War imaginary. Certainly, they do nothing to lessen the perception of folly that imbues the entire project when viewed from outside and to demonstrate how the struggle between two superpowers engulfed the entire world in its totalizing imaginary and the material consequences of that imaginary. But within the shared affordances of the concrete shelter and other elements of bunker architecture and civil defense practices, the examples of Switzerland and Albania remind us of the range of forms and responses that did and could occur within a seemingly uniform practice. They show us, differently than the speculative visions from within the American model in the 1960s and 1980s from which the survivalism studied in Chapters 1 and 2 emerged, what could go wrong and what might plausibly go right in the bunker fantasy, and how the latter always existed inseparably from the former.

Europe, Taiwan, Russia, and the global bunker fantasy

The bunkerization of Europe, Russia, and Asia is a Cold War story that has continued to resonate into the twenty-first century through foreign policy, the built environment, and cultural traces ranging from physical habitus to literature and film, from overt end-of-the-century reckonings

---

1 Halldór Laxness, *The Atom Station* (Sag Harbor, NY: Permanent Press, 1982 [1948]), 166, 183.

92 *After the end*

such as American novelist Don DeLillo's *Underworld* (1997) and Serbian filmmaker Emir Kusturica's *Underground* (1995) to the more recent rise of bunker-related tourism and the beginnings of a scholarly attempt to address the peculiarities of Cold War architecture on its own terms. The core spatial symbols of a bunkerized Europe were the Berlin Wall and the Iron Curtain of which the Wall was the physical manifestation; the European Union continues to struggle with the consequences of the principle of open borders generated in part as a reaction to that divisive barrier. This book takes up the spatial resonances of walls and borders during and after the Cold War in Chapter 6 below. But there is also much to be learned from the more fully realized and less well-known bunker fantasies of European outliers, as well as from civil defense practices and imaginaries the world over, albeit primarily in the wealthier global North.

The histories of Switzerland and of Albania testify to the geographical analogy between the two nations: their mountainous topography and situation at crossroads between north, south, east, and west of Europe, and between Europe and Asia, respectively, have made them simultaneously vulnerable and easy to defend for millennia. However, Switzerland was able to fend off invasion numerous times before the nineteenth century, gained its neutrality in 1815, and has preserved itself inviolate in the two centuries since, with surrender to Napoleon the exception that proved the rule of its independent and self-reliant identity – he was so impressed with the Swiss army that he hired their guards for his own elite force. Conversely, Albania had undergone a fairly constant string of invasions and occupations since antiquity, with its national hero Skanderbeg commemorating the victorious exception that proved the rule of ignominious defeat, until gaining a precarious independence after the Second World War. And even today, democratic Albania is equally besieged by the forces of global capital, eager for entry into one of the last pristine territories of Europe, while democratic Switzerland struggles to maintain the lucrative anonymity of its banking system. Both countries have a long history of fortification, but both undertook radically new bunkering plans during the 1970s, attempting to safeguard their borders and their neutrality under the sign of armored animals: the hedgehog and the tortoise, respectively. While democratic Switzerland embraced as its strategy the threat at any time of rolling its entire nation into a prickly ball able to repulse any attempt to approach it belligerently, Hoxha's Albania pulled into its shell, festooning its watery and mountainous borders with hundreds of thousands of discrete concrete bunkers, materializations of its withdrawal from commerce with the world.

These two countries offer limit-cases of the role played by civil defense and of the fraught relationship between security and democracy in the modern world. On the one hand, Albania's 'concrete mushrooms' were imposed on the country by fiat, enforced by a police state, and remain a potent symbol for the abuses of a now-fallen dictatorship. On the other hand, Switzerland's policy has been openly debated for centuries, continues to be subject to periodic national votes and other democratic processes, and remains central to a national myth of collective resistance and of 'armed neutrality.' One country has come to stand for, and to identify itself with, the hazards of failing to control borders and maintain sovereignty, while the other has banked its national identity from Roman times and into the age of neoliberal capitalism on its ability to maintain neutrality and sovereignty. As the two most comprehensive realizations on the national scale of the bunker fantasy, the Swiss hedgehog and the Albanian tortoise raise compelling questions about the motivations, promises, and limitations of the bunker fantasy during its Cold War heyday and its legacy in the decades since it appeared to have been made redundant. For, while the animal metaphors neatly conjure the living and breathing force of these myths, they are incapable of dealing with the well-nigh indestructible fact of the inorganic constructions whereby those myths were concretized into the mountainous landscape of these European states.

Switzerland and Albania are by no means the only bunkered nations in Europe, much less the world. To be sure, Switzerland's ability to shelter more than eight million people, well over 100 percent of its population, has long been far and away the gold standard both in number and in preparedness.[2] Sweden has always been especially public about its investment, inviting the international press back in 1953 to tour the three-story shelter for twenty thousand civilians beneath Stockholm's Katarina Mountain.[3] By the mid-1960s, there were forty-three thousand facilities able to shelter nearly half the population; Sweden's per capita civil defense budget during the 1980s was second only to Switzerland's.[4] Only Sweden (7.2 million, 81 percent) and Finland (3.4 million, 70 percent, its entire urban population) approach Switzerland in terms of percentage of population and degree of

---

2 Silvia Bergen Ziauddin makes this claim especially strongly, arguing that 'The Swiss network of catacomb-like structures thus marks the very apotheosis of bunker construction,' in '(De)territorializing the Home. The Nuclear Bomb Shelter as a Malleable Site of Passage,' *Environment and Planning D: Society and Space* 35.4 (2017): 674–93, at 675.

3 Samuel Merrill, 'Striving Underground: Stockholm's Atomic Bomb Defences,' in *Global Undergrounds: Exploring Cities Within*, ed. Paul Dobraszczyk, Carlos López Galviz, and Bradley L. Garrett (London: Reaktion, 2016), 121–3.

4 Merrill, 'Striving Underground,' 123.

94   *After the end*

protection from a nuclear blast or fallout.[5] Outside of Europe, Israel can shelter two-thirds of its population in fortified spaces, although lacking in hermetic seals or ventilation; China, South Korea, India, and Singapore all hover around 50 percent capacity.[6] Moreover, China since the 1980s has developed the 'underground Great Wall,' a tunnel network three thousand miles in extent to shelter and to move undetected its nuclear arsenal.[7] While Albania's plan accounted for around 25 percent of the total population, the proportion of individual shelters is unprecedented in a civil defense project of the scale of Hoxha's plan. The Taiwanese territories of the Kinmen and Matsu archipelagoes are among the most heavily fortified lands in the world, both in number (more than a hundred tunnels seam the twenty-nine square kilometers of Matsu's thirty-six islands) and in scale (Taiwu hill in central Kinmen boasts an auditorium seating a thousand and tunnels on both islands are large enough to conceal naval forces and to drive tanks through).

The example of the Taiwan islands intimates the broader relationship of global bunkering and the timeline of the Cold War to its aftermath. In 1949, Chiang Kai-Shek's Kuomintang troops retreated in defeat to Kinmen Island (Figure 3.1). On 25 October, some ten thousand Communist soldiers crossed the two kilometers from mainland China in fishing boats. They were repelled after a bloody battle and Taiwan (officially the Republic of China, or ROC) has held the islands ever since. They were soon transformed into a frontline defense, often termed a 'mini-Maginot Line,' for the island of Taiwan across the Taiwan Strait (Figure 3.2). The ROC also occupied the islands of the Matsu archipelago, 150 kilometers up the coast, off the Min Chiang estuary. Military bases capacious enough for the one hundred thousand-plus troops (a full third of the ROC's total forces at their peak) were built almost

---

5 Catherine Edwards, 'Why Sweden Is Home to 65,000 Fallout Shelters,' *The Local* (1 Nov. 2017): http://web.archive.org/web/20221121132025/https://www.thelocal. se/20171101/why-sweden-is-home-to-65000-fallout-shelters/; Wikipedia contributors, 'Civil Defense in Finland,' *Wikipedia*: https://en.wikipedia.org/w/index.php?title=Civil_ defense_in_Finland&oldid=821282919; accessed 13 April 2018.
6 Daniele Mariani, 'A chacun son bunker,' Swissinfo.ch (23 Oct. 2009): http://web. archive.org/web/20221115065308/https://www.swissinfo.ch/fre/a-chacun-son -bunker/7485678.
7 The term is Chinese, first used in print in the mid-1990s (Phillip Karber, *Strategic Implications of China's Underground Great Wall* (Washington, DC: Georgetown University Asian Arms Control Project, 2011): www.fas.org/nuke/guide/china/ Karber_UndergroundFacilities-Full_2011_reduced.pdf; accessed 2 May 2018). Estimates of the arsenal contained within these tunnel's ranges from Karber's 3,000 missiles to Hui Shang's 170 ('How US Restraint Can Keep China's Nuclear Arsenal Small,' *Bulletin of the Atomic Scientists* 68.4 (2015): 73–82, DOI: 10.1177/0096340212451433, at 74).

Figure 3.1 Map showing artillery placements on Kinmen and Little Kinmen Islands.

entirely underground, along both the flatter Kinmen beaches and the rugged Matsu coast and beneath the mountainous interiors of both archipelagoes. The islands became a Cold War hot spot during the sustained bombing of 1958 (as many as ten thousand people were killed that year in a single day in August; over thirty thousand shells were fired in under two hours, and a total of half a million over six months). US President Eisenhower sent the seventh fleet to patrol the strait in support of the close US ally's resistance against the People's Republic of China (PRC).

Kinmen was a frequent setting for films of the period, all strongly supporting ROC resistance. These include Dai Pengling's award-winning documentary *Kinmen Today* (*Jinri Jinmen*, 1962) and fiction-feature *Love on Kinmen* (*Jinmen zhi lian*, 1964), as well as the 1962 drama *The Ocean Bay Incident* (*Haiwan Fengyun*; aka *Love Story of Kinmen Island*, or *Jinmen Dao Zhi Lian*), a Japanese–Taiwanese co-production co-directed by Akinori Matsuo and Pan Lei.[8] Produced in 1986, Ding Shanxi's *Kinmen Bombs* (*Ba er san pao zhan*) deployed 'a whole parade of stars, elaborate sets and

---

8 Robert Chi, 'The New Taiwanese Documentary,' *Modern Chinese Literature and Culture* 15.1 (2003): 146–96, at 171–2; Wang Ting-chi, email communication to the author (4 June 2018).

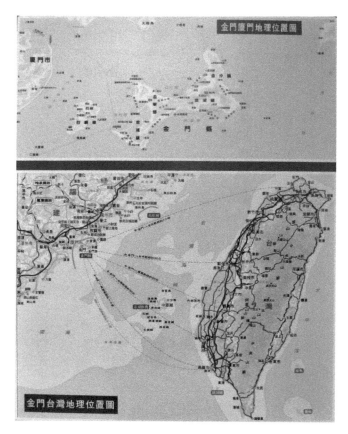

Figure 3.2 Map showing artillery placements on Kinmen and Little Kinmen Islands. Kinmen is at the convergence of the lines from Taiwan, demarcated from the mainland by a gray line.

locations and props, sumptuous pyrotechnics, and an army of extras' to dramatically recreate ROC resistance during the PRC bombing of 1958.[9] Like *Love on Kinmen* and Yang Jiay's 1983 fiction-feature *Women Soldiers on Kinmen* (*Jinmen nü bing*), *Love Story of Kinmen Island* is a woman-centered drama; it tells of the romance between a Japanese agent and a Kinmen woman who are separated by circumstances only to be reunited on Kinmen Island during the spectacularly restaged artillery attack.[10] Primarily shot on location, these films capture the militarized nature and threat of invasion that permeated everyday life on the island and in the region;

9 Chi, 'New Taiwanese Documentary,' 171–2.
10 Wang, email communication.

The hedgehog, the tortoise, and the world 97

individual desires are both inspired by and subordinated to the duties of national and ideological defense.

Another form of individual desire contained within a mobilized populace would become publicly circulated only in retrospect: the 'open secret' that military brothels were operated on Kinmen and Matsu until 1989 (they had been abolished in Taiwan in the late 1960s).[11] At least one (on Matsu) was situated in a tunnel. The revisionist drama *Paradise in Service* (2014) recreates on location a 1969 Kinmen of callow soldiers and the squad of sex workers, identified by number, that service them, some in exchange for shortened prison sentences. (Production was at one point halted when director Doze Niu was charged with smuggling his director of photography into a restricted military zone.)[12] In one plot line, a soldier is 'mercilessly hazed while stationed inside Jhaisan [also Zhaishan] tunnel'; in another, nineteen-year-old Lo Pao-tai (Ethan Juan) takes the women on an excursion to the seashore. Formidable antitank obstacles to repel invasion from the mainland loom behind them as reminders of their bunkered lives; in the foreground sits Pao, handcuffed to two of the women as a pointless security measure. As film critic Maggie Lee summed up the contradiction: '*Paradise in Service* steadily reveals the lies and self-delusions that permeate its characters' lives, depicting the island as both an idyllic beach paradise and a prison.'[13]

Escalation was narrowly avoided, but PRC and ROC troops continued to shell each other until the end of the 1970s. The exchange eventually became ritualized to the degree that the two sides would alternate shelling days, both resting on Sundays, and the contents of the shells were more likely to be propaganda leaflets than explosives (Figure 3.3). The most extensive development of underground construction occurred during the late 1960s and 1970s, when villagers were directed to increase the size and number of their shelters, to excavate extensive tunnel networks beneath and between their homes on the model of the Viet Cong, and in general to live in a state of constant mobilization as 'combat villages' (Figures 3.4 & 3.5).[14] Among other restrictions was the banning of video and motion-picture

11 Yvonne Teh, 'Film Review: *Paradise in Service* Is a Coming-of-Age Story in a Military Brothel,' *South China Morning Post* (8 Oct. 2014): http://web.archive.org/web/20180204072715/http://www.scmp.com/magazines/48hrs/article/1612043/film-review-paradise-service-coming-age-story-military-brothel.

12 Maggie Lee, 'Busan Film Review: *Paradise in Service*,' *Variety* (1 Oct. 2014): http://web.archive.org/web/20221203092054/https://variety.com/2014/film/reviews/busan-film-review-paradise-in-service-1201318199/.

13 Lee, 'Busan Film Review.'

14 Michael Szonyi, *Cold War Island: Quemoy on the Front Line* (Cambridge, MA: Harvard University Press, 2008), 101–19. Szonyi notes that due to the ideological embarrassment of borrowing strategy from 'a Communist enemy,' the strategy was attributed instead to the Republic of Vietnam and the US (109–10).

Figure 3.3 So near, but only birds, bullets, and propaganda can travel between Kinmen and the mainland: video frame grab from *Paradise in Service / Jun Zhong Le Yuan*.

Figure 3.4 Exterior bunker linked to tunnels beneath Qongling Village, Kinmen.

The hedgehog, the tortoise, and the world 99

Figure 3.5 'Combat village' tunnel excavated beneath their homes by the inhabitants of Qongling Village, Kinmen. The villagers now provide tours of the homemade fortifications.

cameras on Kinmen.[15] In 1992, when the PRC's possession of mid-range missiles capable of striking directly at Taiwanese targets had diminished the strategic importance of the islands, martial law was lifted and they were finally returned to civilian government. Kinmen activist and filmmaker Dong Zhenliang, who had been jailed and blacklisted, was finally able to begin filming on the island. Among films he would shoot there is the hybrid 1994 documentary *Every Odd-Numbered Day* (*Dan da shuang bu da*), which intercuts interviews, historical dramatizations, and on-site photography in the present to inform the rest of the ROC about the still little-known

---

15 Chi, 'New Taiwanese Documentary,' 172.

100   *After the end*

experience of life on the bunkered island.[16] Marketed as the first Kinmen film made from a civilian perspective, *Every Odd-Numbered Day* received financial support from the government, was screened in festivals across the Pacific, and toured Taiwan for much of 1995, promoting Kinmen tourism at prize drawings that included round-trip air tickets to Kinmen and island products, such as *kaoliang* (sorghum) liquor aged in the former tunnels and the kitchen knives of Maestro Wu, forged from spent PRC shells (Figures 4.12 and 4.13). Dong had similarly once worked the conversion of war machine into cultural product and performance art by digging up an artillery shell to sell for scrap, 'us[ing] the money to subscribe to the popular Hong Kong movie magazine *Southern Screen*.'[17]

The military mostly pulled out of Matsu in 1996, but it continues to maintain a significant presence on Kinmen. Although tensions rose in 1996 and at varying times thereafter, the primary function of the islands in the relationship between the two governments has transmuted from military to economic symbolism. In 2001, the 'mini three links' (shipping, post, and flight) were established between the islands and nearby PRC ports, permitting, for the first time, travel between Taiwan and the mainland. A robust smuggling trade was mostly shut down, but travel was heavily skewed in favor of the Taiwanese, who benefitted from their government's far more liberal travel policy (only 0.5 percent of travel was undertaken by mainland Chinese in the first years of the policy).[18] Meanwhile, the Taiwanese invested money in land-mine removal and economic support to islands with few indigenous means of achieving self-sufficiency, especially following decades of fortification and military control.

Tensions eased following the election of the pro-unification candidate Ma Ying-jeou, and serious discussions began in 2008 on the construction of a ten-kilometer bridge linking Kinmen with Xiamen, an idea dating back to 2004. Talks were stalled because the project had the strong support of local politicians and businessmen, elicited mixed feelings from the residents, and had made little headway with the Taiwanese government.[19] As one

---

16 Chi, 'New Taiwanese Documentary,' 173–4.
17 Chi, 'New Taiwanese Documentary,' 173–4.
18 The proportion from the mainland has skewed the other way in more recent years, as younger Taiwanese prefer other destinations (Matthew Falco, 'Kinmen on the Front Lines of History,' *Taiwan Business Topics* (7 July 2017): http://web.archive. org/web/20220703170941/https://topics.amcham.com.tw/2017/07/kinmen-front -lines-history/).
19 Rob Schmitz 'On a Rural Taiwanese Island, Modern China Beckons,' *NPR* (11 Sept. 2016): http://web.archive.org/web/20221107142844/https://www.npr.org/sections/ parallels/2016/09/11/493255462/on-a-rural-taiwanese-island-modern-china-beckons; Anna Beth Keim, 'You Ask How Deeply I Love You: Kinmen Island, and the Past

The hedgehog, the tortoise, and the world

resident informed me, 'Most people ridicule these bridges as "floating bridges" because they only surface during election season and sink again once the election is finished.'[20] In August 2018, after three years of construction, water began flowing through an infrastructure project with less direct resonance as a security risk: a ten-mile pipeline from Fujian province to address the island's water shortage.[21] But the bridge continues to be mooted – most recently by Taipei mayor Ko Wen-jo in 2022, who 'said the bridge would not only help promote prosperity on the former Taiwan defence outpost but also ease cross-strait tensions.'[22] The island landscape has been irrevocably transformed by the Cold War, while the bunker infrastructure and the ideology of independence underlining that infrastructure continue to dominate life on Kinmen and Matsu as well as the dominant PRC and ROC attitudes towards them. At the same time, the precise function of the infrastructure continues to change; in particular, as discussed in Chapter 4, new and adaptive uses have now taken their place amidst the ongoing military control. During the Cold War Kinmen and Matsu would not have survived without actual military occupation; today the military and its history continue as the basis of their economic survival.

While Taiwan, like Albania and Switzerland, provides an outlying example that informs through its peculiarities, the Soviet shelter system was at the heart of Cold War discussions of civil defense. Its presence as a focal point of Western debate was almost wholly driven by imagination and surmise, both at home and abroad, because of the Soviet government's penchant for secrecy and reluctance to admit the possibility of nuclear defeat.[23] Although

and Future of Sino-Taiwanese Relations,' *ChinaFile* (12 July 2016): http://web.archive.org/web/20221224145549/https://www.chinafile.com/features/you-ask-how-deeply-i-love-you; Falco, 'Kinmen.'

20 Wang, email communication.

21 'Peace Pipe,' *The Economist* (23 May 2015): http://web.archive.org/web/20170216000239/http://www.economist.com/news/asia/21651874-officials-plan-pump-water-china-its-political-rival-taiwan-peace-pipe; 'Taiwan's Kinmen Island Begins Importing Water from China,' *APnews* (6 Aug. 2018): http://web.archive.org/web/20230307165432/https://apnews.com/article/44646c1d8d734f2e860e3ed237dc3741; Chris Horton, 'Once a Cold War Flashpoint, a Part of Taiwan Embraces China's Pull,' *New York Times* (2 Sept. 2018): http://web.archive.org/web/20220718164114/https://www.nytimes.com/2018/09/02/world/asia/taiwan-kinmen-island-china.html.

22 Lawrence Chung, 'A Bridge Too Far? Taipei Mayor Draws Fire for Proposal to Link Quemoy and Xiamen,' *South China Morning Post* (25 June 2022): http://web.archive.org/web/20220803233247/https://www.scmp.com/news/china/politics/article/3183040/bridge-too-far-taipei-mayor-draws-fire-proposal-link-quemoy-and.

23 Edward Geist discusses this stance and its consequences in some detail in 'Was There a Real "Mineshaft Gap"? Bomb Shelters in the USSR, 1945–1962,' *Journal of Cold War Studies* 14.2 (2012): 3–28.

102   *After the end*

repeatedly deployed rhetorically in political discourse from the 1950s through the 1980s as a target against which US civil defense preparations fell fatally short, the USSR in fact had taken no sheltering measures at all from the end of the war until after the death of Stalin in 1953, and it fully canceled civil defense from the budget in 1959 in the belief that Cold War tensions were on the wane. When tensions rose again in 1961, Khrushchev quickly passed a new set of regulations that aimed 'to rebuild Soviet civil defense along new, modern lines.'[24] Before and during the war, the government had invested heavily in conventional bomb shelters, especially in the deep tunnels of the Moscow Metro, capable of sheltering more than half a million people.[25] Writing in 1962, Leon Gouré, the foremost Western authority on Soviet civil defense of the time, concluded that while there was no doubt that the 'Soviet leaders believe the program to be worth further efforts and continued investment,' shelters were limited both in capacity and effectiveness.[26] Policy researcher Edward Geist corroborates the assessment, estimating that during this period the Soviet Union was devoting over ten times more of its military budget to civil defense than the US was.[27] But Geist also notes that a sizeable portion of that budget went to sheltering the elite rather than the populace as a whole.[28]

Whereas US propaganda stressed self-reliant individual responses to the war and locally organized wardens and community measures, Soviet propaganda hyped the effectiveness of its collective sheltering. Moreover, while the US deemphasized sheltering and civil defense after the mid-1960s, the Soviet Union continued to invest heavily in both.[29] Although the CIA was aware by 1971 of an increase in activity, evidence of specific projects has been available publicly only since 1990, and much of it remains unsubstantiated.[30] A Defense department report from 1991 confirms the construction of an underground supershelter for top officials in Ramenki District near

---

24 Geist, 'Mineshaft Gap,' 22.
25 Geist, 'Mineshaft Gap,' 7.
26 Leon Gouré, *Civil Defense in the Soviet Union* (Berkeley: University of California Press, 1962), 151.
27 Geist, 'Mineshaft Gap,' 20.
28 Geist, 'Mineshaft Gap,' 10, 13.
29 Geist, 'Mineshaft Gap,' 26.
30 Paul Ozorak cites the 1971 CIA report and summarizes 'what has been revealed in the media and on the Internet' in the chapter on Russia in *Underground Structures of the Cold War: The World Below* (Pen & Sword Books, 2012), Kindle loc. 2886–7. The Wikipedia article 'Metro-2,' while less detailed about the extent of Moscow and Russian shelters, details confirmed and unconfirmed elements with documented sources (Wikipedia contributors, 'Metro-2,' *Wikipedia*: https://en.wikipedia.org/w/index.php?title=Metro-2&oldid=832252615; accessed 13 April 2018).

Moscow State University linked to Moscow and perhaps to the government airfield via a dedicated Metro line.[31] Later reports date the construction of this facility, known as 'Underground City' or 'Ramenki-43,' to the mid-1970s and estimate its capacity variously at ten thousand to thirty thousand people.[32] The basic lack of information about the program during the Cold War and the inability to know whether available information was exaggerated, downplayed, basically truthful, or fully mendacious left the Soviet system readily available for projecting onto it whatever Western fantasy or policy required. Gouré's career as a Sovietologist was defined by his insistence that 'Inferiority to the Soviet Union in civil defence could allow Moscow to force America's hand during a nuclear standoff or even embolden Soviet leaders to launch a nuclear attack.'[33] Such projections became especially prevalent during the 1980s, when a vast secret sheltering program was the logical correlative of the assumption of an evil empire. But it also might, in line with Sting's 'Russians,' mean simply that 'they' cared just as much as Westerners about protecting their children. To imagine the Soviets in one's image could lead just as well to apocalypse as to peace, as we see in the plot trajectory of Jerry Ahern's twenty-seven-volume *Survivalist* series (1981–93), where the titular hero in his mountain hideaway is matched move for move by his archenemy in a Ural Mountain supershelter. The bunker fantasy must always allow for both.

Russia by no means terminated its sheltering initiative at the end of the Cold War. As historian Kenneth Rose observed in 2001, 'The one place where there has been a more permanent revival of shelter building is in

---

31 Wikipedia contributors, 'Metro-2.' The construction of military and civilian shelters was often combined with metro construction both for practicality and for deception. Begun deep under Prague during 1960s as a celebration of the 'thaw,' the underground was finished in 1974 as a demonstration of Eastern bloc technology and equipped as a public shelter for 200,000 (Petr Gibas, 'Ideology and Fear: Prague Metro,' in *Global Undergrounds*, ed. Dobraszczyk et al., 161–3). The Pyongyang metro, the deepest in the world, includes capacious and ornate stations à la Moscow, provides an ideological education, and incorporates a secret line for leader Kim Jong-il and, perhaps, 'a vast subterranean command centre' (Darmon Richter, 'Futures Past: Pyongyang Metro,' in *Global Undergrounds*, ed. Dobraszczyk et al., 232–4).

32 Wikipedia contributors, 'Metro-2'; Carey Scott, 'Kremlin Refurbishes Nuclear Bunkers as Fear of Nato Grows,' *Sunday Times* [London] (13 April 1997); Kenneth D. Rose, *One Nation Underground: The Fallout Shelter in American Culture* (New York: New York University Press, 2001), 163.

33 Geist, 'Mineshaft Gap,' 4. Gouré worked for the Rand Corp. from 1954 until 1969, and remained active in the field until his retirement in 2004 (Joe Holley, 'Leon Goure, 84; Cold War Political Scientist Was Expert on Soviet Civil Defense,' *Los Angeles Times* (9 April 2007): http://web.archive.org/web/20151020142442/http://articles. latimes.com/2007/apr/09/local/me-goure9).

104 *After the end*

Russia.'[34] As in the US, Russian shelters were regularly expanded and updated with the goal of ensuring continuity of government and the survival of high-ranking officials. The London *Sunday Times* reported that the Ramenki complex, which included cinemas and a swimming pool, was being overhauled to respond to the new threat posed by NATO expansion eastward.[35] According to Ozorak, construction on Russia's underground military infrastructure continues, including, 'a large complex at Yamantau Mountain near Beloretsk in the Urals 850 miles east of Moscow.'[36] Ozorak concludes his chapter on Russia by citing an evidently less trustworthy authority: 'Peter Pry in his book *War Scare* states that this is just one of many underground facilities being built or improved in Russia.'[37] The secret underground enemy facility continues to spur the imagination nearly as much as the alien-built or deep-state infrastructure suspected in many conspiracy-minded circles to exist below the continental United States.

Like the Russians, the Chinese invested heavily in shelter construction and civil defense following the Sino-Soviet conflict in 1968, including an 'underground city' in Beijing with a reputed capacity of 350,000; unlike in Russia, according to Ozorak, these tunnels and shelters offered little blast protection, the infrastructure has not been maintained since tensions eased in 1978, and much of it has been adaptively reused.[38] Doubtless there continue to exist deep shelters for top officials; if any lesson has been learned from the Cold War, it is that those officials best informed regarding the damage their weapons can do provide lavishly for their own protection. Similar infrastructure is suspected to exist in North Korea – a deep underground railway linking military facilities in and around Pyongyang to the airport, the palace, and 'an underground command post at Mount Chidang in the Sosong district' that can shelter up to one hundred thousand personnel.[39] While most leaders of most countries provide for themselves and for their military, very few countries indeed attempt to provide shelter for their citizens universally, and even fewer strive for any kind of protection from nuclear attack or fallout. Those that do – such as Sweden and Finland – periodically consider cutting back, only to change their minds when a new perceived danger appears. The ways in which two other countries – Switzerland and Albania – provided for universal shelter, and the afterlife of those provisions, raise the question of shelter and citizenship in an especially pointed manner.

34 Rose, *One Nation Underground*, 224.
35 Scott, 'Kremlin Refurbishes Nuclear Bunkers.'
36 Ozorak, *Underground Structures*, loc. 3264–5.
37 Ozorak, *Underground Structures*, loc. 3269–70.
38 Ozorak, *Underground Structures*, loc. 2621–2. On Beijing's 'Underground City,' see Ross, *Waiting*, 92–3.
39 Ozorak, *Underground Structures*, loc. 2621–2.

Switzerland as hedgehog: the principle of reduction

With a visual correlative in the jagged mountains of the nation's southern, alpine borders, the hedgehog has resonated as an image throughout Swiss history. However, the defining moment of its identity as a fortified nation crystallized around a geographic amplification of that image, the conception of the 'Réduit national' or 'Alpenreduit,' the national Redoubt proposed by General Henri Guisan in his Rütli Report of 25 July 1940.[40] In this report, Guisan articulated a new defensive strategy in the light of three factors: French defeat, a geographical position sandwiched between the Axis forces of Germany and Italy, and the likelihood of invasion from either direction. Guisan took the radical decision to 'reduce' the defense of Switzerland to a fortified enclave defined by its topography and to concede the loss of the central plateau in order to create, in effect, 'the largest fortress in Europe.'[41] By blocking passage from the north as well as from the south, the Redoubt would function as a double Maginot line. Excavating deep within the mountains themselves would create a networked shelter-fortress capable of garrisoning the entire Swiss army. How much of the retreating civilian population would also have been brought into this enormous fortress is still debated today. This is a fundamental question, since the strategy of withdrawal necessitated the sacrifice of the *Mittelland*, the central plain where most of the Swiss population lives, works, farms, and produces.

As the eminent leftwing Swiss writer Friedrich Dürrenmatt trenchantly expressed the issue in the postwar years, 'The idea of the Redoubt was a brilliant idea. It consisted in the army saving itself and leaving the people in the lurch.'[42] Or, as American essayist John McPhee put it more charitably and abstractly, 'The only place that will never need defending represents what the Swiss defend.'[43] Although undertaken on a vast physical scale in the Swiss landscape during and after the war years, the Redoubt was also a profoundly symbolic gesture aimed at persuading the Nazis that the Swiss had the resolve to sacrifice their vulnerable heartland and general populace in order to enable effective long-term resistance. In short, the Redoubt depended upon the equation of Switzerland as a nation with the entity of

---

40 German-language sources also use the French term *réduit* to describe the strategy.

41 Jean-Jacques Rapin, *L'Esprit des fortifications: Vaubin – Dufour – Les forts de Saint-Maurice* (Lausanne: Presses polytechniques et universitaire romandes, 2004), 89.

42 Friedrich Dürrenmatt, '"Ich kann mir eine Schweiz ohne Armee vorstellen": Eine Collage,' in *Unterwegs zu einer Schweiz ohne Armee: Der freie Gang aus der Festung*, ed. Roman Brodmann, Andreas Gross, and Marc Spescha (Basel: Z-Verlag, 1986), 28–47, at 46.

43 John McPhee, *La Place de la Concorde Suisse* (New York: Farrar Straus Giroux, 1983), 11.

the Swiss army. Not surprisingly, the leitmotif of Dürrenmatt's long-standing opposition to the concept of a Swiss military was the assertion, 'I can imagine a Switzerland without an army.' The very need for such a seemingly self-evident assertion testifies to the ideological force of Switzerland *as* an army and the country *as* a redoubt.

Such equations, arguably, were characteristic of the Second World War in general. This is not only because of the stark ideological divide between the Axis powers and the Allies (putting aside the vexed question of the Soviet Union) that facilitated a strong identification between civilian and armed forces. Even more so, this was the first large-scale 'total war' in the modern era, in which civilian populations were as much if not more of a target than the military forces on either side. In the aftermath of such a war, the concept of a national Redoubt came rather quickly to look like common sense as much as military necessity. The difference is where the bunker fantasy proper emerges from its parentage in what military historian Jean-Jacques Rapin terms the ancient 'spirit of fortifications'[44]: the threat of conventional invasion that had mobilized the Swiss to fortify their Alpine Redoubt soon became the threat of invasion from the air in general and of nuclear bombing by warplanes in particular. As the Cold War settled into the early 1960s, the central Redoubt was supplemented by legislation for a shelter and militia system diffused throughout the nation.[45] The Redoubt remained the focal point of the myth of national defense and a deterrent to any land invasion, whether or not accompanied by atomic, biological, or chemical weapons. At the same time, the broader goal of civil defense became survival wherever one was: the spirit of fortification was extended into the bunker fantasy. At the 1964 Swiss Expo in Lausanne, the Army pavilion, dedicated to the idea of 'Vigilant Switzerland' and molded of 3,300 cubic meters of concrete, was quickly nicknamed 'The Hedgehog' (*Le Hérisson*) (Figure 3.6).[46] In practice, the hedgehog defense could range from simple private shelters in individual homes (Figure 3.7) to the world's largest nuclear shelter, in the Sonnenberg Tunnel near Lucerne (now demolished), with a capacity of twenty thousand

44 Rapin, *L'Esprit des fortifications.*
45 The earliest legal basis for the shelters dates from 4 Oct. 1963; the apogee of construction was during the 1970s, when 300,000–400,000 new shelters were added each year (Mariani, 'A chacun son bunker'). The policy has been revisited a number of times since 1989, and although the pace of construction has slowed (as of 2009, Mariani cited about 50,000 annually), the regulation remained on the books as of 2023.
46 Adrien Fontanellaz, 'Compte-rendu V: La Suisse vigilante,' *militum Historia: Un regard helvétique sur l'histoire militaire* (5 Nov. 2014): http://web.archive.org/web/20211019012537/http://histoiresmilitaires.blogspot.com/2014/11/compte-rendu-v-la-suisse-vigilante.html#!http://web.archive.org/web/20211019012537/http://histoiresmilitaires.blogspot.com/.

Figure 3.6 'La Suisse Vigilante,' popularly known as *Le Hérisson* ('The Hedgehog'), the Swiss Army Pavilion at the National Exposition in Lausanne, 1964.

and fully equipped with sleeping quarters, five-foot-thick doors, sophisticated air filters, a prison, and everything the army would need to conduct the defense of the nation from within its confines.[47]

The possession of nuclear weapons established a qualitative distinction between great powers and lesser states. Switzerland debated and ultimately decided against acquiring such weapons if the opportunity presented itself. The consequent structural asymmetry with respect to the nuclear powers brought new types of comparison as Swiss military strategists sought to reconceive the army's function. Israel would be ruled out as a model once nuclear armament had been ruled out. As on Kinmen and Matsu, Vietnam was a touchstone, with two elements of its successful defiance of French and then US forces particularly relevant: the 'front-less' battle and the transformation of the countryside into a 'molehill' of tunnels. Summarizing

---

47 Imogen Foulkes, 'Swiss Still Braced for Nuclear War,' *BBC News* (10 Feb. 2007): http://web.archive.org/web/20220926020818/http://news.bbc.co.uk/2/hi/programmes/from_our_own_correspondent/6347519.stm. On the Sonnenberg facility, see also Ozorak, *Underground Shelters*, loc. 3508–14. For examples of individual Swiss shelters, see Ross, *Waiting*, 62–5, 116–21.

Figure 3.7 The 'proud owner' shows off his state-of-the-art shelter, 'Near Andelfingen, Switzerland, 2003.'

the findings of a 1966 report that was the first to confront directly the prospect of 'A-B-C' warfare, Commandant Alfred Ernst argued that the success of Israel in 1967 showed the need for better training and the positive outcome from defying conventional wisdom, while Vietnam demonstrated the effectiveness of hidden troops and 'Kleinkrieg,' or guerrilla warfare.[48] Like a number of military strategists, Ernst continued to argue for the acquisition of nuclear weapons. Addressing security issues at the end of the century, Bernard Wicht added to the now venerable example of Vietnam more recent conflicts in Beirut, Korramshar, Kabul, Panama City, Gaza, Vukovar, Sarajevo, Mogadishu, and Grozny, all successful combinations of old-fashioned armaments and fighting with 'a consummate art of digging in, of fortification and of making use of the underground,' itself partly reliant on the modern technology of subterranean urban construction.[49]

---

48 Alfred Ernst, Oberstkorpskomandant Z. D., *Die Konzeption der Schweizerischen Landesverteidigung 1815 bis 1966* (Frauenfeld: Verlag Huber, 1971), 416–18.
49 Bernard Wicht, *L'Art de la guerre au XXIe siècle* (Lausanne: L'Age d'Homme, 1998), 28, 37.

The hedgehog, the tortoise, and the world 109

There is an undeniable irony in a wealthy and secure western European nation that has flourished for centuries at the nexus of international trade and banking modeling its defense system on some of the most destabilized and insecure postcolonial cities in the world. This irony did not go unnoticed by those taking a more jaundiced view of the military-industrial complex and a more cynical stance toward Swiss neutrality and security. Until the end of the Cold War, attitudes towards the shelter system were starkly divided between a militaristic right and a pacifist left, with eminent writers such as Dürrenmatt and Max Frisch coming out strongly against the whole conception of a shelter society, and Igaal Niddam, Jean-Marc Lovay, and Claude Delarue similarly producing novels and films that used the idea of shelter as a conceptual framework for a satirical critique of Swiss society. 'The Swiss,' asserted Dürrenmatt in 1986, echoing sentiments he had been voicing since the late 1950s, 'are the most frightened people in the world.' It was not the Alpine Redoubt that had forestalled a Nazi invasion, he argued, but the fact that economic collaboration had eliminated any need for invasion. Even today, he went on, 'what really protects us is trade, not the army.'[50] Neutrality, Dürrenmatt insisted, was an illusion, and if there were ever to be war between NATO and the Soviet Union, Switzerland would not survive without the support of the former. Echoes of these sentiments can be found throughout the pacifist and oppositional literature, as when Jean-Gabriel Zufferey took on the 'hedgehog syndrome' in *Le syndrome du hérisson: la Suisse et son armée* (1989).[51] Already in 1966, Switzerland's other world-class postwar author, Max Frisch, was diagnosing the 'security-mentality' in terms of an inability to conceptualize the future: 'What do the Swiss want from their future: their past?'[52] The Alpine Redoubt and the hedgehog mentality, Frisch implied, were fundamentally conservative ideologies inimical to any conceptualization of radical change: 'Belief in the possibility of peace (and also in the survival of mankind) is a revolutionary belief.'[53]

We find this principle expressed negatively in Frisch's brief late novel, *Man in the Holocene* (1979), a portrait in indirect free style of the last days of an isolated old man living in an isolated alpine valley near the Italian border. Although written during the same years in which Frisch was actively speaking out against the hedgehog mentality and the Swiss military, it is

---

50 Dürrenmatt, 'Ich kann,' 42–4.
51 Jean-Gabriel Zufferey, *Le Syndrome du hérisson: la Suisse et son armée* [The hedgehog syndrome: Switzerland and its army] (Carouges-Genève, Switzerland: Editions Zoé, 1989).
52 Max Frisch, 'Mehr Fragemut vor dem Ernstfall' [1966], in Brodmann et al., *Unterwegs*, 13–27, at 14.
53 Frisch, 'Mehr Fragemut,' 23.

110 *After the end*

only the setting and the parable-like sparseness of the narration that indicate a nuclear threat nowhere mentioned explicitly. Instead, Frisch uses the clippings the widower Geiser cuts out from old reference books and fixes to the walls of his small house to allude to the terms of the critique of the Swiss mentality in his nonfiction. In a key passage reprinted from the sixteenth edition of the *Brockhaus* encyclopedia, Frisch suggests the postwar disjunction between Enlightenment definitions of 'human,' the long view of geological time in which homo sapiens is simply one among many other transient forms of animal life, and the possibility that the threat of nuclear warfare has cut short the utopian progress of humanism and could very likely cut short the life of the planet itself:

> That M. [Man] is a *historical being* is shown in the fact that he is shaped, both outwardly and inwardly, by inherited skills, arts, sciences, customs, standards of conduct, and value systems; toward these he adopts a critical attitude, which he then complements, improves, simplifies, complicates, modifies, and alters. Additionally, he is able to envisage different states of being and to plan these deliberately, to provide himself with purposes and aims, through the use of his productive imagination and will. The more highly developed animals display hopes and fears, but only M. works toward a 'future.'[54]

The only future toward which Geiser can work is the catastrophe he fears, whether coming from landslide, lightning, or flood. And even though his small house is possessed of a cellar, no doubt excavated as part of the national civil defense program, Geiser's imagination is limited exclusively to natural catastrophes. In one of the phrases that roll around in his mind as he nods off to sleep in the middle of an abortive and nearly fatal attempt to hike out of the valley, Frisch manages to remind us of the fallacy contained within his protagonist's formulation that 'only human beings can recognize catastrophes, provided they survive them; Nature recognizes no catastrophes.'[55]

The way Frisch restricts the surface of his narration to the cold abstractions of geological time gives the reader distance from Geiser's descent into a senility that encroaches on the melodramatic heights of madness. But it equally precludes the other human ability, to 'work towards a "future."' The stark parable of *Man in the Holocene* acidly diagnoses the cul-de-sac of catastrophe thinking, but that same starkness is unable itself to conceive of the utopian thought that persists in that same world only within the recesses of catastrophe. As with much of postwar European literature, the parable leads to an existential dead end. One token of a recent shift from

---

54 Max Frisch, *Man in the Holocene*, trans. Geoffrey Skelton (New York: Farrar Straus Giroux, 1980 [1979]), 53.
55 Frisch, *Man in the Holocene*, 79.

that perspective is that the Anthropocene, the epoch now held by many scientists to have superseded the Holocene of Frisch's novel, is indeed defined by the nuclear age, but in terms of a future scientist looking back at the geological record of radioactive particles in the soil rather than a contemporary one unable to imagine any future beyond that age.

Like Dürrenmatt, Frisch wrote out of the polarized terms of the Cold War, which divided all propositions into stark antinomies. What is so peculiar about the bunker fantasy, and one of the reasons all sides in the conflict had recourse to it, is that it did, in fact, imagine a different future than simply a return to the past, and was able to posit the survival of humanity in the same breath as its total destruction. And one of the reasons for the survival of the bunker fantasy beyond the Cold War that gave it form, and beyond the Cold War literature so much of which violently opposed it, is how aptly this spatial fantasy embodies the contradictions of the post-1989 world. In the past few decades, the unthinkable possibility of the instant destruction of the entire world seems to have receded into the background. However, it has been replaced by something perhaps more terrifying and more difficult to conceptualize: the slow march of climate crisis along that same path towards destruction, not instantaneously, but inexorably, and gaining momentum daily. The bunker fantasy affords thinking both moments at once, retaining, faintly but unmistakably, a belief in the possibility of survival and peace which seems able only to be expressed in the face of catastrophe. This fantasy has proven to be the mode of existence that best makes sense of a world which defines itself in terms of a constant, rather than an imminent, state of emergency.

Cold War absolutism thus tinges any Swiss writing that would be anything but unambiguously supportive of the Alpine Redoubt and civil defense measures, the stance taken by the vast majority of writing on civil defense, most of it authored by the officer corps and most of it written in German. In his 1973 novella *Dienstbüchlein* (the title refers to the 'little record book' in which each male citizen of Switzerland is required to record the history of his adult time of service in the militia), Frisch records with cutting irony his experience of the concept of the Redoubt at first hand while serving during World War II:

> The new concept: *reduit*. That's where they would get stuck with their panzer units. I remember how this concept relieved me. I don't remember its ever being discussed among enlisted men. ... On flat land – at that time sitting under the apple trees near Zurich – I could readily picture the German *Wehrmacht* (up to then known only from photos), swarms of armored cars, and so on. But not here. Here one almost forgot them. No question that our general staff took its own concept seriously. There was visible evidence: construction of dugouts in the mountains (for which I once had to draft blueprints in

112   *After the end*

a military office) and munitions magazines in the rock, bombproof at a glance.
How supply lines were supposed to function after the bridges had been blown
up, and, come to think of it, how the general staff imagined we could fight
after the loss of our industries and cities – such things, of course, they couldn't
explain to us.[56]

To be sure, Frisch's aging narrator here maintains a mocking distance from
the callow youth that was 'relieved' by the concept of the Redoubt, able to
'forget' the tanks once high up in the mountains, and happy to be permitted
not to worry about practical matters such as 'supply lines,' 'the loss of our
industries and cities,' or 'our families under German occupation while we
are in the mountains.'[57] Those were the terms of the Cold War, unable to
credit that, however immature, selfish, and impractical those feelings of
relief might have been, they were no less real or existent for being immature,
selfish, and impractical.

What the bunker fantasy did was to take the calculating rationality of
military strategy from which we are meant to be repelled in Frisch's texts
and place it in an apocalyptic setting. If the world is being destroyed, the
moral calculus changes, and hope for the future, anybody's future, comes
to be predicated on the loss of most of humanity, including 'our families.'
This principle, again, could easily be expressed satirically, as when Dr
Strangelove in the 1963 film assures the top brass that the pre-chosen
survivors will be taken down below in advance of the spectacle of destruction
that would otherwise traumatize them and prevent them from devoting
themselves to their appointed task of repopulating the world.[58] It could be
expressed tactically, as in the American debates during the early 1960s over
the ethical calculus between protecting one's own family in its private shelter
and admitting desperate individuals who had failed to look after their own.
And it could even be expressed positively, as in the literature that would
lead to 1980s survivalism.

Whether or not Frisch was consciously evoking it, there is an angry dose
of Christian apocalypticism in his formulation, as also of the Genesis figures
Lot and Noah. Not all shelter-builders, survivalists, or preppers are Christian,
but the imagery of Revelation and the many other depictions of the Last
Judgment in the Western tradition resonate powerfully within the idea of
a bunker sheltering those who thought to prepare ahead for the last days
and shutting out those who did not: the thresher separating the wheat and

---

56 Max Frisch, '*From* Military Service Record,' in *Novels, Plays, Essays*, ed. Rolf Kaiser
    (New York: Continuum, 1989), 137–9, at 139.
57 Frisch, 'Military Service Record,' 139.
58 *Dr Strangelove; or, How I Stopped Worrying and Learned to Love the Bomb* (1963,
    dir. Stanley Kubrick, dist. Columbia).

The hedgehog, the tortoise, and the world 113

the chaff of Jesus's harsh parable of nature's cycles in the Gospel of Matthew. That conception may have been secularized in warfare through to the end of the Second World War, but when the first bombs dropped, the only existent iconography even partly able to make sense of their results came from the religious imagination of apocalypse. Given that, very soon, the threat of nuclear war came to entail quite literally the end of the world, it starts to appear reasonable to take the 'fantasy' in the bunker fantasy as seriously in its positive valence as in the derogatory way in which Frisch, Kubrick, and many others on their side of the Cold War took it at the time.

One major artistic text emerged from Switzerland out of the first bunker age of the 1960s that directly engaged the meaning of survival in this context. In Igaal Niddam's film *Le Troisième Cri* (1974), the maintenance crew of an immense public fallout shelter is trapped inside. The crew members do not know if they are locked in because there has been a nuclear war of which they may be the only survivors, or if they have simply been sealed off from the outside world by a mechanical failure or an accident. The social cross section of characters inevitably suggests the national allegory for which the Swiss shelter system provides such a powerful ruling metaphor.[59] At the same time, as Freddy Buache notes in an analysis of the film, Niddam directed it in a sufficiently realistic style to prevent the allegory from dominating the viewer's experience of the film.[60] A good measure of the film's power, in other words, comes from its ability to present the events as if they were actually happening; however, what is happening also suggests a breakdown or liberation from social norms.[61] *Le Troisième Cri* is balanced between the eternal waiting in uncertainty characteristic of the nuclear age, the existentialist attitude towards life consonant with that age, and the everyday reality of life in a country ruled by the bunker fantasy, for better and for worse. As Buache persuasively argues, the allegorical reading wins out in the end when the bunker finally leads the crew members to an insight into the modern condition: 'Preserved from the apocalypse thanks to their luxuriously provisioned cocoon (pool, hospital and kitchen, neat hallways and armor-plated doors), they come to understand that their former values were twisted.'[62] Inevitably, at least for a pre-1989 European art film, the balance

---

59 Swiss fiction-writer Jean-Marc Lovay takes a similarly allegorical approach in 'Conférence de Stockholm,' a mordant philosophical dialogue depicting an imaginary writer's conference inside a military bunker, the '9th wonder of the world' (in *Conférences aux antipodes* (Genève: Editions Zoé, 1987), 9–29).

60 Freddy Buache, *Le Cinéma suisse 1898–1998* (Lausanne: L'Age d'Homme, 1998), 251.

61 Ziauddin, '(De)territorializing the Home,' 686.

62 Buache, *Le cinéma suisse*, 252.

114 *After the end*

resolves itself in death (the meaning of the 'third cry' of the title, following the 'first cry' of birth and the 'second cry' of love).

In the postwar Swiss context, it appears that the question of national identity can be raised only through the spatial medium of the bunker fantasy. It's the same medium whether expressed positively, as by supporters of the civilian military, or negatively, as by many writers, intellectuals, and left-leaning politicians. Seeking a local response to the events of May 1968, youths in Zurich founded the 'Autonomous Bunker Republic' in a public shelter, requiring 'passports' to enter a space of graffiti, music, drugs, and revolution; it lasted two months before the municipal council shut it down.[63] As the narrator of Jean-Marc Lovay's 'Stockholm Lecture' sardonically observes of the French-, German- and Italian-speaking authors assembled with a handful of foreign observers in a writer's union meeting deep in a mountain bunker, 'Never had I witnessed such a fraternal scene.'[64] How to think outside the bunker fantasy if that fantasy is the only glue holding together a federation of otherwise disparate peoples? How to account for difference or inequity within a form that defines identity by reduction to sameness? As the presence of foreign observers testifies, Lovay appears also to be suggesting that the same principle may apply to the world as a whole: all that unites it is the fact of existence under the specter of apocalypse. This is simultaneously an existential situation, in that it presents a compelling reflection of the human condition, and a sociopolitical one. Like Frisch before him, Lovay mocks the world's inability to think beyond the constraints of immediate survival. Unlike Frisch, he allows a glimmer of the possibility that even the most negatively formulated common ground might constitute the beginning of a pragmatic movement towards collective action.

Claude Delarue's award-winning novel *En attendant la guerre* (1989; *Waiting for War*), published just before the end of the Cold War, reaches a similarly bleak conclusion to its detailed and nuanced depiction of the Swiss bunker fantasy.[65] *Waiting* takes as its subject the legacy of one Samuel Leber, an architect who devoted his life to the design and production of fallout shelters, growing extremely wealthy in the process. It is the most sustained fictional meditation to date on the paradoxes of Switzerland's bunker fantasy, and it is unrelenting in its exploration of the principle that ethical motivations can lead to violent and often damaging actions. *Waiting* combines the abstract fatalism of a high modernist novel such as Thomas Mann's *The Magic Mountain* (1924, and mostly set in a Swiss alpine sanatorium)

63 Ziauddin, '(De)territorializing the Home,' 686.
64 Lovay, 'Conférence,' 25.
65 Claude Delarue, *En attendant la guerre* (Carouges-Genève: Editions Zoé, 2011 [1989]); *Waiting for War*, trans. Vivienne Menkes-Ivry (London: Minerva, 1992).

The hedgehog, the tortoise, and the world

with the stylized sex and violence of hard-boiled crime fiction. The bulk of Delarue's novel depicts the developing relationship between the protagonist, a monk and professional secretary cum wheelchair pusher, and his new employer, Leber's widow Olga Grekova-Leber, a former theater actor who was crippled in the bizarre 'accident' that killed her husband. The setting is her husband's alpine redoubt, a baroque melange of medieval fortifications, the modernist design of the mad architect's stronghold in Edgar Ulmer's horror movie classic of repressed wartime trauma, *The Black Cat* (1934), and the neo-medievalism of King Ludwig of Bavaria's concrete alpine folly Neuschwanstein. The surrounding grounds of the fortress are enclosed by 'the Great Wall,' a boundary fence tens of miles in circumference, built to prevent Leber's free-ranging menagerie of the region's formerly free-ranging predators (bears, wolves, wildcats) from terrorizing the nearby villages. Accessible only by the rickety funicular in which the architect met his death, via a treacherous mountain road, or by helicopter, the fortress shelters, along with the architect's writings and Olga's ever-expanding collection of newspaper clippings of tragic events around the world: a Colombian cook, a bevy of Tamil servants accompanied by their holy man, and the gamekeeper Tanguy, bastard son of the previous owner whose descent into madness drives the more lurid of the plot's events. Like the clippings and the local fauna, the global diversity of the supporting cast seems assembled expressly to be flattened under the apocalyptic weight of the central conceit.

Leber's fortress sits atop a vast multilevel fallout shelter designed to receive hundreds if not thousands of soldiers and local civilians in time of need. This shelter looms beneath the consciousness of the novel for most of its pages, but at the midpoint the secretary descends into its depths in the company of the engineer tasked with its maintenance. Delarue details the engineering genius involved in the creation of such a complex technological space, while devoting equal attention to the consequences of its inorganic isolation from the natural world. The condition of the bunker – that everything will be sacrificed to ensure survival – equally describes the contemporary world, where nature as such has ceased to exist, subsumed within human solipsism. As the secretary explains to the engineer, 'We're so far from God down here. We aren't anywhere, not even enduring ordeal by suffering. We can say anything, knowing it won't have any repercussions, yet still nothing eases the pain.'[66] Everything, Olga similarly argues at one point about her husband, was subordinated to his fear of death. 'War was merely a pretext, and he would have been quite happy to cover the whole planet with shelters just to protect himself and no one else.'[67] Delarue deftly limns the transition

66 Delarue, *Waiting*, 143.
67 Delarue, *Waiting*, 104.

116 *After the end*

from traditionally apocalyptic imagery to the even more disturbing vision of disaster that would come to dominate after the Cold War. 'We are living on a dead man's planet,' Olga maintains. 'We're dead too, fated to wither, not to be consumed by fire.'[68]

In their introduction to a collection of translations of Swiss writings on the United States, the volume's editors note the 'apparent preoccupation with the United States' in contemporary Swiss fiction. They cite the imperfect analogy between the 'Swiss dream' of a confederation of diverse peoples and the US 'melting pot,' and the contrast of a 'small, locked-in state' with the expansive openness of the United States. America, they suggest, has provided an important tool of 'self-critique' for postwar Swiss writers.[69] The editors do not mention civil defense or fallout shelters, and neither the concept nor the setting figures prominently in their selections. However, as Delarue makes evident in imagining Leber's dealings with the Americans in *Waiting*, the bunker fantasy constitutes both a profound common ground between the Swiss and the US and an accurate measure of the absolute distance between the two nations. Here is Olga on the ironic outcome of the business:

> Unfortunately, the Americans didn't know how to build hiding places where their missiles would be safe from attack. When Samuel went to the States to get hold of the necessary guarantees about setting up the Leber Foundation and to make sure that his shelters would be built on US soil, he met people from the army general staff, various politicians and engineers. The plan was given unanimous approval and within a few months several shelters were under construction, north of New York and Washington and south of Houston. Once he'd made sure of pulling off this victory, he came home. It was at this point that they dealt him the final blow. The Americans used the material he'd invented for his fallout shelters to build silos to house their missiles. When Samuel told me about this betrayal, I don't know what came over me, but I couldn't stop myself bursting out laughing – good and evil cast in the same concrete![70]

In a paradox analogous to being able to say anything without being consoled by doing so, the shelter designed to preserve life from thermonuclear missiles is appropriated to shelter the missiles themselves: 'good and evil cast in the same concrete.'

---

68 Delarue, *Waiting*, 103.
69 Cornelius Schnauber, Romey Sabalius, and Gene Stimpson, 'Introduction,' in *The Dream Never Becomes Reality: 24 Swiss Writers Challenge the United States*, ed. Schnauber, Sabalius, and Stimpson (Lanham, MD: University Press of America, 1995), vii–xiv.
70 Delarue, *Waiting*, 68–9.

The hedgehog, the tortoise, and the world 117

Olga's laughter is a mocking acknowledgment of her husband's idealistic ignorance of the world, of the ability of that world to distort good intentions, and of the fundamentally compromised target of her husband's idealism. But her concluding formulation also acknowledges a truth enacted elsewhere in Delarue's novel by the heat of the genre conventions that he imports into the detached abstractions of high modernism: whatever its evident and undeniable coldness, concrete is the twentieth-century residuum not only of the cold military calculations of mass destruction but of hot passions and warm ideals. Concrete may appear desiccated from the outside, but somehow penetrate within, and your embodied presence changes everything. As Army Captain Pierre Delévaux unironically asserted about a very similar space from a very different perspective, 'A work of fortification, however well placed, however well-conceived, however well-armed it may be, is worth nothing without the troop that occupies it, without its spirit of camaraderie, its will, its preparedness, and its pride to belong to this work.'[71] Because it poses the relationship between organic and inorganic nature in such stark opposition, the bunker has lent itself to expressing the hostility of shelter and the inhumanity of the war that necessitates such shelter. We tend to forget the lived experience that equally radiates from these spaces, in direct proportion to their appearance of inhospitableness.

Perhaps no writer has captured this paradox as well as John McPhee in his book-length essay on the Swiss military, *La Place de la Concorde Suisse*. '"About this we don't talk," a colonel on the general staff said to me one day. "Don't ask me about it. But keep your eyes open. You may see something"' (Figure 3.8).[72] In McPhee's rendering, Switzerland is a country torn between imperatives of openness and secrecy. On the one hand, it 'has so much to hide,' not just the identity of holders of its bank accounts but the militarization and fortification of the very natural beauty that drives its tourism industry: 'Thorn and rose, there is scarcely a scene in Switzerland that would not sell a calendar, and – valley after valley, mountain after mountain, village after village, page after page – there is scarcely a scene in Switzerland that is not ready to erupt in fire to repel an invasive war.'[73] The centuries of openness to visitors that have made the Swiss landscape one of the most intensively cultivated expanses of wildness in the world have also made it one of the most intensively fortified expanses of wildness in the world, ready in the blink of an eye to destroy itself to save itself (Figure 3.9).

---

71 Pierre Delévaux, *Fortifications de Saint-Maurice, Suisse: La Galerie du Scex 1911–2011* (Saint-Maurice: Fondation Forteresse historique Saint-Maurice & Association Saint-Maurice d'Etudes Militaires, 2011), 31.

72 McPhee, *La Place de la Concorde Suisse*, 21.

73 McPhee, *La Place de la Concorde Suisse*, 21.

Figure 3.8 'Keep your eyes open. You may see something': an entrance to the *gruyère* hidden in plain sight on public land not far from Saint-Maurice, Valais, Switzerland.

That McPhee was permitted to embed himself in a civilian militia unit in this secretive army is further evidence of the Swiss paradox, as is the choice by military authorities to embed him with a unit of French Swiss misfits rather than exemplary German Swiss. Here is how McPhee epitomized the memorable experience when writing about his onsite research some thirty years later:

> In 1982, I was walking around in the Alps with a patrol of Swiss soldiers. We had been together three weeks and were plenty compatible. Straying off limits, not for the first time, we went into a restaurant called Restaurant. Military exercises were going on involving mortars and artillery up and down the Rhone Valley, above which the cantilevered Restaurant was fourteen hundred feet high. The soldiers had a two-way radio with which to receive orders, be given information, or report intelligence to the Command Post. They stirred their fondue with its antenna. They sent coded messages to the Command Post: 'A PEASANT IN OBERWALD HAS SEEN FOUR ARMORED CARS COMING OUT OF ST. NIKLAUS AND HEADING FOR THE VALLEY.' More fondue, then this: 'TWO COMPANIES OF ENEMY MOTORIZED FUSILIERS HAVE REACHED RARON. ABOUT FIFTEEN ARMORED VEHICLES HAVE BEEN DESTROYED.' And later this: 'AN ATOMIC

The hedgehog, the tortoise, and the world

Figure 3.9 And they will also see you … Not long after taking these photos, the author was informed by a passerby that photos were not allowed. Close-up of entrance to tunnel deep into the mountain, informing of the presence of closed-circuit surveillance.

BOMB OF PETITE SIZE HAS BEEN DROPPED ON SIERRE. OUR BARRICADES AT VISP STILL HOLD. THE BRIDGES OF GRENGIOLS ARE SECURE. WE ARE IN CONTACT WITH THE ENEMY.' Setting down a pencil and returning to the fondue, I said to myself, 'There is my ending.' The petite A-bomb was a gift to structure. Ending pieces is difficult, and usable endings are difficult to come by. It's nice when they just appear in appropriate places and times.[74]

For all their 'straying off limits,' the civilian soldiers never reveal any actual secrets to the American reporter. Nor is there ever any doubt that, in a real emergency, they would do anything other than defend their homeland. In their giddy drunken joking, McPhee captures the sheer excess of the bunker fantasy, the way it gives the illusion of power over circumstances so far beyond one's control that they are impossible even to countenance. The counterfactuality of what the unit is reporting is what makes it such a good joke, even as the soldiers also take dead seriously the premise that counterfactuality is in fact the situation they are preparing to defend themselves against.

74 John McPhee, 'Structure,' *New Yorker* (6 Jan. 2013): www.newyorker.com/magazine/2013/01/14/structure.

120   *After the end*

As McPhee suggests, the only way perhaps to survive a nuclear war is constantly to live within its shadow, to devise a usable ending in order to ward off the specter of an impossible one. In a remarkable extended scene in the town of Brig, the townspeople continue to go about their daily business as soldiers fight, live ammunition flies, and shells explode around them in a complicated military exercise. 'Such a deep token of preparedness implies a deeper history of threat,' McPhee astutely observes.[75] There is no direct judgment made, nor any direct comparison with the bunker fantasy in the US. Nevertheless, given that McPhee began his career in journalism at the height of Cold War tensions in the early 1960s and chose an explicitly Cold War topic as an established author in the early 1980s of Reaganism, it is difficult not to read an American subtext into the essay. There is an undertone of shock over the way in which this extraordinary natural landscape has been seamed with human endeavor of the most technologized and destructive kind, such as when he realizes that it is possible to ascend an entire mountain by means of tunnels carved within it. Nevertheless, this shock expresses itself primarily as bemusement, as when the troop emerges from a steep climb 1400 feet up the Rhone valley only to happen 'with some surprise, as always … onto a curving mountain road' leading to the fondue restaurant where the essay will conclude.[76] If you are forced to live in a bunker fantasy and to go down in a nuclear war, McPhee seems to decide, you might as well do it in style, full of good food and drink and company, and with a sense of humor.

In contrast to McPhee's bon-vivant vintner guide Massy, the humorless Major Jaussi, whose family has been in the hotel business for generations, did, in fact, like many Swiss military officers, study in the US. That Jaussi's work experience abroad included a stint at the Greenbrier Resort in White Sulphur Springs, which for decades hid in plain sight within its walls a top-secret bunker designed for the protection of members of the US Congress (see Chapter 4), may merely be a delicious coincidence; this doesn't prevent it also from making a subtle yet effective comparison of two ways of dealing with the nuclear threat.[77] We may regard Switzerland as a country swallowed

---

75 McPhee, *La Place de la Concorde Suisse*, 108.
76 McPhee, *La Place de la Concorde Suisse*, 148.
77 McPhee, *La Place de la Concorde Suisse*, 85. For a history of Greenbrier, and the rumors about it that began circulating from the moment construction began on it in 1957, see chapter seven of Nathan Hodge and Sharon Weinberger, *A Nuclear Family Vacation: Travels in the World of Atomic Weaponry* (New York: Bloomsbury, 2011); Tom Vanderbilt, *Survival City: Adventures among the Ruins of Atomic America* (Chicago: University of Chicago Press, 2010 [2002]), 135–9; and chapter five of Pike, *Bunkered Decades*, 123–6. Ross includes several photos of Greenbrier in *Waiting*, 86–91; see also Figure 4.6.

The hedgehog, the tortoise, and the world

up by the security obsession that has never let it escape from Cold War paradigms or as a country that has successfully negotiated the democratic demand for openness with the secrecy required for equality of security. We may also note that its accumulated wealth and geopolitical situation contribute to the privilege of having a choice. But there is no question that the Swiss have come to terms with the open secrets of their past in a way in which the symbolic but impossible-to-countenance weight of Cold War culture suggests that few other nations, and certainly not the United States, have yet been able to do.

Albania and the principle of withdrawal

If the example of Switzerland pushes the degree to which the bunker fantasy can be deployed democratically, Albania raises the opposite question: can anything positive at all be rescued out of the ruins of the totalitarian application of that fantasy? The first major test came, in fact, fourteen years after the death of Albania's leader Enver Hoxha and eight years after the fall of his nearly fifteen-year-long regime. In 1999, at the height of the Kosovo War, the bunkers with which Hoxha had blanketed the country were actually put to use for the first time ever: as shelter for ethnic Albanian refugees, as shelter from Serbian shells for Albanian villagers living near the northern border, and, especially, as defensive fortifications for, at different times, the Kosovan Liberation Army and the Albanian army. As one villager put it, 'We blamed everything on Hoxha, but now his bunkers are saving our lives.'[78] However, when NATO forces mistakenly bombed Albanian bunkers instead of the Serbian ones a kilometer away, another myth about Hoxha's folly was exploded. They may not have been as useless as had always been thought, but neither were they as indestructible as advertised. Scattered among remnants of bombs bearing the telltale insignia of NATO were countless fragments of the bunkers' concrete and steel armature. Yes, they provided shelter against Serbian shells and sniper fire, but they were no match for the 'bunker-busting' firepower of the West. What is most striking about this episode is the fact that Hoxha's bunkers were for once experienced solely in terms of their function as shelter and fortification, momentarily shorn of the heavy ideological weight they had borne since construction on them had begun in the mid-1970s. Whether embodying the bunker mentality of an isolated nation feeling itself besieged on all sides, the ruinous folly of a paranoid leader, or the renewed energy of an irrepressible people, the

---

78 'KLA Takes Cover in Cold War Bunkers,' *The Times* [London] (25 May 1999): *Lexis-Nexis Academic*; accessed 7 July 2011.

122   *After the end*

bunkers had always been a metonym of the nation. For a brief moment, here they were: the functional infrastructure of a state at war.

Soon after this climactic moment of the Kosovo War, miniature bunkers began to appear for the first time around Albania: ashtrays and penholders in alabaster or clay, originally highly sought after by journalists and eventually to become a staple in souvenir stalls alongside figurines of Mother Teresa, artisanries, traditional peasant garb, and snow globes enclosing the figure of the Ottoman-bashing national hero, Skanderbeg. The bunkers had become part of the national myth. And, as befits any myth, there is much that is uncertain about them. For starters, nobody will ever know exactly how many were built; estimates range from around one hundred thousand to the full three-quarters of a million planned by Hoxha, about one for every four of the country's inhabitants in the late 1970s. They were designed by an engineer named Josef Zengali; however, it seems unlikely that, as legend has it, he was compelled to test their safety himself (more reliable accounts suggest that livestock was used). They came in three sizes: *Qander zjarri* or 'single fire,' colloquially known as 'tortoises' or 'concrete mushrooms,' pillbox bunkers just big enough for a single person with a gun, shaped like an igloo, and made of granite-full concrete reinforced with thirteen layers of steel (Plate 1); *Pike zjarri* or 'fire points,' colloquially known as 'oranges,' artillery bunkers large enough to hold maybe a dozen individuals and assembled out of concrete wedges gathered together into a dome (Plate 2); and larger, specialty bunkers in the mountains, used to store munitions and house larger numbers of forces, and often connected by tunnels (Plate 3). The latter bunkers include a hidden submarine base in the Porto Palermo bay, the 3,200 bunkers constructed on the island of Sazan after the Soviets occupied it in 1948,[79] and the Chinese-built airplane hangars with doors which slid open to allow planes to take off and land from within enormous tunnels, à la James Bond movies. These installations form a more spectacular but far less evident part of the physical and psychological landscape of the country than the nearly ubiquitous oranges and tortoises. All told, three billion dollars were spent, double the raw materials used in France's Maginot Line was consumed, factories around the country were devoted full-time to the project for over ten years, and the entire citizenry was charged with maintenance of the bunkers and required to train annually in their use.[80]

---

79 Kejsi Rama, 'Transforming a Former Military Island into an Eco-Resort: The Case of Sazan, Albania' (MA thesis, University of Strathclyde, 2016), 11–12.

80 Beyond agreement that the numbers are very large, there is no consensus on exact figures. I cite these numbers from Fabrizio Gallanti, Elian Stefa, and Gyler Mydyti, 'Concrete Mushrooms: Transformations of the Bunkers in Albania,' *Abitare* 502 (May 2010): www.abitare.it/en/architecture/2010/05/11/concrete-mushrooms-2/.

The hedgehog, the tortoise, and the world

It was a national project, modeled on Mao's Cultural Revolution and retaining the model's utter disregard for practical concerns or human cost. Nevertheless, despite Albania's ideological affinity with China, Hoxha's bunker fantasy more closely resembles the United States in the early 1960s, when every family in the country was urged to build a fallout shelter in its backyard. But while the US Congress chose against legislating construction and relied – with decidedly mixed results – on the persuasive power of ideology and market forces, Hoxha forcibly mobilized the entire country to carry out an equally implausible and in the end futile endeavor. While it seems likely that Albania's ruler was motivated by paranoia rather than a cynical manipulator of ideology, his country was never invaded either by the Soviet Union, by the US, or, for that matter, by its often hostile and far more proximate neighbors Yugoslavia and Greece. In 2005, a large store of chemical weapons was discovered stashed away in one of the more extensive systems in the mountains above Tirana, suggesting that Hoxha's obsession was for real. Like the Maginot Line, however, the bunkers were designed not for the present as much as for the conflict of a previous era. There was a strategy underlying their placement – all around the border regions; overlooking mountain passes and river crossings; guarding entrances to cities, towns, and villages – but that strategy was never going to protect Albania from either of the two superpowers. As philosopher Slavoj Žižek has argued, 'the role of these bunkers was neither real (as a means of military defense they were worthless) nor imaginary (they were certainly not built with the pleasurable experience of those trained to use them in mind), but for purely symbolic reasons: to serve as a sign of Albania's determination to defend itself at all costs.'[81] Žižek is certainly correct regarding the symbolic function played by the bunkers in Hoxha's regime. But I would argue that the afterlife of the bunkers has established that they *could* also play a 'real' role (as shown by the events of 1999) and that, while not built with 'the pleasurable experience of those trained to use them in mind,' the potential for pleasurable experience continues to figure powerfully if ambivalently in the bunkers' role, despite the devastating cost of building and maintaining them.

The 'bunker mentality' of Albania has roots within national mythology far deeper than Hoxha's era, and that same fantasy drives the fascination of every visitor to and writer about the country (including Žižek and this author), who cannot resist its temptations as they try to make sense of Albania's unique position within Europe. Moreover, this fantasy is not limited to expressing the symbolic qualities of a nation. The bunkers unite profound contradictions in a single space: the horrible spectacle of national

---

81 Slavoj Žižek, *Living in the End Times* (London: Verso, 2010), 247.

124 *After the end*

ideology gone haywire along with deeply satisfying if difficult to articulate and highly subjective associations with security and shelter, as well as the delightful kind of uselessness we tend to identify with childhood, leisure, and play. And it is the ability to express all of these associations at once, inextricably intertwined, that makes the bunker fantasy at once so powerful and so disturbing.

The bunkers do exert a compelling fascination on the viewer. And, although not a single Albanian with whom I spoke during my research there would outright admit to the fact, I remain unable to persuade myself that the fascination is limited to foreign visitors. There is a perverse pride evident even among Albanians in having succeeded in dotting the landscape with hundreds of thousands of turds, as one writer uncharitably if fairly accurately termed them. But, even more, there is the bizarre fact that these bunkers, as much as the ruggedly beautiful landscape that they blight – which would otherwise constitute some of the most unspoiled natural landscape remaining in Europe – form a common bond between Albanians and the outside world. They were built to communicate to the outside world and to the Albanian people a withdrawal from the world, the rejection of any other more direct form of interaction. Today, the bunkers continue to mediate the relationship with outsiders, except that now they stand in for the insurmountable gap in experience born of the country's decades-long isolation. They provide a blank but eloquent testimony to a formative experience unique to the country's inhabitants, and their gradual acceptance suggests that the gap is slowly closing.

The domed form of the bunker has deep roots in Albanian culture. The 'tortoise' nickname for the pillbox bunker derives from the iconic shape of the eastern Hermann's tortoise, a common sight in the scrubby fields of the high central valleys. The same shape features in the local style of icon painting which, following the Byzantine tradition, places the Christian nativity scene in a domed cave rather than a manger. Similarly, the dome echoes through contemporary spatial forms, especially the haystacks that dot the countryside, often alongside ruined bunkers being used for storage and livestock, but also in painted mosques, and even in the arches over a Tirana service station. The tortoise and the nativity cave, with their ancient symbolism of autonomy and shelter, synchronize perfectly with Hoxha's conception of the bunkers. The bunker mentality has equally deep roots in Albania's history, which recounts a nearly constant sequence of invasions and occupations, notably by the ancient Greeks, the ancient Romans, the Bulgarians, the Venetians, the Ottomans, and Mussolini's Italy. The very forms of the fortress architecture derive from constant invasion. Passes in the mountain ranges that crisscross the country from border to border in a roughly north–south direction offered a crucial trade route between

Europe and Asia. The mountain passes also concentrated populations and commerce in key strategic sites, reinforcing a sense of isolationism. Albania has been a country of castles and fortifications for millennia; the bunkers are only the latest manifestation of a fortress mentality dating back to the ancient Illyrians.

While the form and ideology of the bunker are indebted to an extensive local history, they were also informed by the global Cold War bunker fantasy both spatially and ideologically. This is directly related to Albania's deep ties first with the Soviet Union (Hoxha was a lifelong admirer of Stalin) and later with China. From the former came the containment strategy of the Iron Curtain, a bunker-fortified boundary line cutting across Europe, with the Berlin Wall its most visible symbol. The Soviets, too, wanted to leave their mark in Butrint, razing the ancient ruins to replace them with a submarine base just north of the border with Greece. When Hoxha refused, the base was shifted up the coast to Porto Palermo, near an ancient stronghold of the Ottoman administrator Ali Pasha, where the enormous hole of the tunnel entrance to the secret base can still be seen at sea level just off the coast road, and plans have been mooted to convert the site into a 'sort of Cold War museum' by an Italian architectural firm.[82] From the Chinese came the elimination of all army ranks and the basis of civil defense in civilian partisans, who were responsible for the upkeep of the bunkers, and were mobilized annually for training drills. The Chinese also left their physical mark on the system of fortifications when they blasted massive air force tunnels into the mountainsides, with camouflaged doorways able to swing back to allow their planes (hypothetically) to intercept NATO or Soviet bombers.

There are equally strong resemblances to the Swiss civil defense system as well as to the American campaign to build fallout shelters in the early 1960s. Albania shared near total participation in the shelter program with Switzerland, although the blatant visibility of its concrete mushrooms contrasted sharply with the invisibility of the Swiss gruyère. The American prototype never reached the point of legislation and, consequently, was never instituted on the same scale as in either Switzerland or Albania. Nevertheless, one could argue that America's postwar construction of the interstate highway system and a vast network of secret military installations, mountainside nuclear facilities, and buried missile silos demonstrates an investment in infrastructural security on an analogous scale. The difference is that the US model wholly separated the governmental system from private enterprise or collective endeavor. Still, they shared a national ideology of

---

82 Jeffrey Schnapp, 'Gjiri i panormes,' JeffreySchnapp.com (2011). Schnapp was a collaborator on the project.

126   *After the end*

the bunker fantasy: that participation in the security initiative would not only provide individual peace of mind but unite the nation on behalf of a single cause. And, while the material expression of that initiative in the US was predominantly the missile defense system, its ideological emblem was indubitably the individual shelter, which brilliantly melded the consumerist, nuclear family ideology of the 1950s with the Cold War rhetoric of total mobilization and constant alert, and a survivalist strand of classic American individualism.

The 1990s were understandably dominated by the negative deployment of the Hoxha bunker as the fulcrum of a savage critique of his long reign, in the allegorical novels of Ismail Kadaré and in filmmaker Kujtim Çashku's bleak satire, *Kolonel Bunker*. As Kadaré put it in his political fable *The Pyramid*, the construction of the Egyptian pyramids was an exercise in political domination, 'spawn[ing] not thousands, but hundreds of thousands of little [pyramids]. They were called bunkers, and each of them, however tiny it may have been in comparison, transmitted all the terror that the mother of all pyramids had inspired, and all the madness too.'[83] Çashku's 1996 film, nearly contemporaneous with Kadaré's novel, makes an equally grim argument without the allegorical displacement into the ancient past. Developed in consultation with Josef Zengali, the officer in charge of Hoxha's bunker project, *Kolonel Bunker* uses the genre of the historical drama to blast the dehumanizing effects of 'bunkerizing' the country. Played by Agim Qirjaki as a decent but blindly obedient career officer, Colonel 'Nuro Meto' learns at the beginning of the film that, rather than the anticipated promotion to general, he will be put in charge of the bunker project in an army newly shorn of the hierarchy of ranks.

Çashku's film documents the colonel's descent into the chaos of totalitarianism, as the bunker and all it stands for take over his life. In one scene, he brings a model of the bunker home to his wife Anna (Anna Nehrabecka), a classical pianist; it threatens to displace her beloved instrument (Figure 3.10). The colonel's response to nearly every situation is simple: 'bunker it.' Interspersed with this narrative of blind instrumentality in the service of national folly is an even darker vision of a state terrorism of purges, gulags, and random executions. By midway through the film, even the crazed productivity of the bunker scheme has been taken over by a country devolved into a stagnated prison-land, which then descends further into an orgy of capitalist greed after the fall of the communist government. In the words of Albanian political philosopher and memoirist Lea Ypi, 'We had spent decades preparing for assault, planning for nuclear war, designing bunkers, suppressing dissent, anticipating the words of counterrevolution, imagining

83 Ismail Kadaré, *The Pyramid* (New York: Vintage, 1996), 160.

Figure 3.10 'Bunkerizing' everyday life in Hoxha's Albania: Kujtim Çashku's *Kolonel Bunker*.

the contours of its face. ... But when the enemy eventually materialized, it looked too much like ourselves. We had no categories to describe what occurred, no definitions to capture what we had lost, and what we gained in its place.'[84]

Çashku's film suggests two traditional sources of resistance – love and music – the first of which is associated with the bunker and the second set up as its anathema. Music is embodied in the piano that follows Anna first to a swampy labor camp and then, at least metaphorically, to exile in her native Poland. Although the desire for music and aesthetic experience may persist, Çashku intimates, there was no longer any place for realizing that desire in contemporary Albania. Curiously, the bunker does provide a space of sexual desire, in the form of two young lovers who, evidently mirroring a common practice both under Hoxha and afterwards, use the shelter of the bunkers for private trysts. Even for Çashku, then, the space proffers the possibility of appropriation for individual desire. Moreover, by giving the young couple broadly philosophical dialogue in English, he associates that desire with a kind of freedom ostensibly available in the West. Certainly, the association of fallout shelters with sexuality ran through the American

---

84 Lea Ypi, *Free: A Child and a Country at the End of History* (New York: Norton, 2022 [2021]), 116–17.

128   *After the end*

imaginary for the duration of the Cold War.[85] Here, too, the possibility is intimated without being fully realized or enduring – the couple is summarily shot in their love nest during the height of the bunker madness, the executing officer arguing that bunkers and freedom are in fact incompatible. As opposed to the imported art of Anna's classical piano, the specific form of Hoxha's bunkers remains an implausibly local invention, and the film suggests that a local difference had the potential to emerge from that form. At the same time, the English idiom posits the hybrid nature of the bunker fantasy, simultaneously local and imported source of the bunkerization of the nation and glimpse of its possible relation to the world around it.

Sexual desire, aesthetic experience, and imported art also figure prominently in Kadaré's allegorical rendering of the post-communist era in *Spring Flowers, Spring Frost* (2000).[86] A peculiar but compelling combination of a mythico-traditional symbolic-allegorical armature with up-to-date details and plot events, *Spring Flowers* suggests the challenge of retrieving a viable national identity out of the landscape of totalitarianism. Kadaré draws a sharp line between traditional and 'Western' or global attitudes towards the body, especially in the explicitness of the sexuality and in various references to shaving pudenda. As the latter detail suggests, the two attitudes meet in the female body, which itself is mapped onto the landscape of Albania. The plot of the novel involves the journey of an urban, Tirana painter to investigate the mysterious death of his boss in a village in the north. This is the traditional locus of the blood feuds with which Albania was long associated in the outside world, and the area of the country conventionally portrayed as its most backwards and inward-looking, in contrast to the more Hellenized south. The core of the mystery appears to reside in a secret bunker purported to hold not only the dark secrets of the Hoxha dictatorship but also the more world-historical ones of Stalin, Tito, and other dictators/communist leaders. On the one hand a synecdoche for Albania itself, a locked box of the old regimes, the only place where they are still somehow visible as they were, the bunker is also likened to the cleft of a woman's sex. This sexualized landscape is simultaneously mythic and linked to the conventions of Western art, especially Gustave Courbet's infamous canvas *L'Origine du monde* – not an unlikely allusion given that the protagonist is an artist engaged throughout the book in a nude painting of his young lover. Significantly, the reader is never brought into the bunker, although seemingly meant to be persuaded of its existence, as if its necessity dwells in its existence rather than in any knowledge of its contents. An underlying tension persists between a national identity locked up in a totalitarian nightmare and a nightmare that remains

85 Pike, *Bunkered Decades*, chapters one and eight; see also Chapter 2 of this book.
86 Kadaré, *Spring Flowers, Spring Frost*, trans. David Bellos (New York: Arcade, 2012).

The *only* place where national identity can be found. This tension suggests a concatenation of the totalitarian space of the bunker with the archaic space of the wild mountains of the north and the location of the revival there of the blood feud, in contradistinction to the 'civilized' world of the capital Tirana or distant Spain, from which the painter is recently returned.

If the 1990s were dominated by the negative appropriation of the Hoxha bunker as the fulcrum of a savage critique of his long reign, there were already signs of the reuse that would equally characterize the bunker in the years to follow. Local appropriation was mostly limited to living in bunkers in the chaotic early 1990s following the fall of the communist regime, along with the still current livestock and storage functions (Plate 4). As tourists, reporters, and travel writers began to cross the newly opened frontier in the late 1990s, their fascination with the bunkers quickly gave rise to restaurant and bar conversions and to the soon ubiquitous bunker souvenirs. But it was not until the new millennium that the forward-looking projects discussed in Chapter 4 began to imagine the bunkers as a resource that could be put to use rather than merely a blight to be ignored whenever possible. The bunkers thus continue to mediate not only the Albanians' reckoning with their own past but also the encounter between Albanians and the long-separated world around them.

Haunted by the right to shelter

The contradictory emotions and motivations at play in any infrastructure conversion, newly visited ruin, or bunker converted into everyday use as a stables, cellar, dump, or bathroom find their most extreme expression in the bunker fantasy. This is simultaneously its strength and its weakness as an imaginary. Because it expresses a worldview in the starkest terms of apocalypse and survival, the bunker fantasy lends itself to extremism, exploitation, and stark opposition. Those same extremes make this fantasy well suited for utopianism and revolution as well – whence the enduring popularity in recent years of the *Matrix* or *Hunger Games* scenario of a postapocalyptic revolution that overturns the ostensibly entrenched totalitarian order to usher in a new age promising everything the prior order was not. Especially post-1945, the history of the twentieth century has done well to demonstrate how closely these extremes resembled one another in the forms they took and the kinds of thinking and images they afforded. As we saw in the survivalist narratives of Chapter 1, apocalyptic redemption seems likely to remain a lure to all extremes and the bunker fantasy to remain a primary site for imagining this redemption. To make the bunker fantasy do more simply than mirror those Cold War polarities, however, requires us to take seriously the alternatives that become available when those polarities are misplaced in space and time, and the powerfully flattening effect of these polarities on a difference-based vision of national or collective identity. While in many ways fully derivative of the specific forms of security afforded by the mainstream Cold War bunker fantasy, the examples of Switzerland, Albania, and other civil defense infrastructures are also deeply embedded in regional history and geography, in political exigencies, in fears and concerns specific to life on the peripheries rather than in the superpower centers of the war.

The strangely personal quality of Albania's mass construction of human-scaled bunkers reminds us of the affective element that dwells in even the most apparently inhuman environment. It has been a fairly straightforward process for the remains of industrial architecture of the nineteenth-century transport revolution to be repurposed as parks and museums; these tunnels, bridges, stations, viaducts, cuttings, and rolling stock had their aesthetic proponents already when they were being built. But the brutalist lines, raw power, and massive costs embedded in Cold War architecture raise the stakes of repurposing: how can something created out of a bankrupt ideology, driven by the fear of annihilation, and maintained by sheer force ever serve a positive or a pleasurable function? Given the demonstrable fact that they somehow *can* do so for many people, we would do well to take seriously the utopian impulse that persists even within the destructive extremes of the bunker fantasy. To do this requires recognizing two principles: that turning a built environment of abuse, suffering, and waste into something productive and useful in the present can be a more effective repudiation of the past than destroying or memorializing it; and that understanding the full range of emotions and desires that were folded into these extremes in the past is essential for understanding the ways they continue to work affectively on so many individuals and groups in the present.

Recent work on human-made catastrophes such as the Holocaust, the Nakba, the near-extermination of Native Americans, and the enslavement of Africans and their descendants in the Americas argues that forgetting can be as important as remembering in processing societal trauma. In the words of Holocaust survivor Ruth Kluger, 'A remembered massacre may serve as a deterrent, but it may also serve as a model for the next massacre ... We cannot impose the contents of our minds on our grandchildren.'[87] A Palestinian poet similarly 'called upon his elders and his own generation not to "forget" but to "forget about" the Nakba, in the sense that they should move on and focus instead on defeating the apartheid that governed

---

87 In Gavin Francis, 'The Dream of Forgetfulness,' *New York Review of Books* (9 March 2023): 31–4, at 34.

the lives of everyone living between the Mediterranean and the Jordan – a land de facto ruled by one power.'[88] The Cold War and its bunker fantasy bequeathed a powerful legacy of the choice between wholesale remembering and wholesale forgetting; a nuanced account of that legacy can help to balance this choice and reorient it toward the present day. This reorientation is especially pressing because the built environment of the Cold War is already doing conceptual work in the present just as it works to preserve inequities in the physical landscape of nation-states and their borders, as discussed in Chapter 6.

Writing about the principle of 'equality of survival' long after its blown cover had turned West Virginia's Greenbrier from a haven for the top brass into a destination for nuclear tourism, American moral philosopher Elaine Scarry could make explicit the comparison McPhee had only intimated in the earlier *La Place de la Concorde Suisse*. Scarry defines 'equality of survival' as 'universal access to the means of survival.'[89] She does so in the context of the legislation that created and maintains the Swiss shelter system, she claims it as a fundamental tenet of democratic governance, and she uses this system to explore the pressures placed on the right of exit since 1945. For Scarry, the Swiss shelter system is 'a feat of moral and civil engineering' that presents 'one of the few pieces of evidence we have that the right of exit (as well as the "right to exist") is still imaginable in the nuclear age.'[90] In contrast, she argues that the abandonment by most Western powers of the project, or even the principle, of sheltering the entirety of their population has profoundly compromised the basis of contractual democracy in these countries. Scarry goes on to contrast the Swiss refusal to acquire nuclear arms with the way that the broader populations of all eight of the current nuclear powers have ceded the control of nuclear weapons to a single individual or small group.

Scarry's argument is indicative of one way in which post–Cold War thinking about nuclear war and national security might be formulated outside of the polarized terms of Cold War debate. In her view, equality of survival is both a practical issue and a political one. In practical terms, she argues, we must take the security risk seriously because the US government continues to take it seriously. Why would the government spend billions of dollars on shelters for its members and for the military if it did not expect them

---

88 Francis, 'Dream of Forgetfulness,' 34.
89 Elaine Scarry, *Thinking in an Emergency* (New York: W. W. Norton, 2010), 50. With the exception of the preface, this short book was reprinted in its entirety within the capacious pages of Scarry, *Thermonuclear Monarchy: Choosing between Democracy and Doom* (New York: W. W. Norton, 2014).
90 Scarry, *Thinking in an Emergency*, 69.

to be necessary? The only distinction between US and Swiss spending on security is that in one case provision is made for a select elite and in the other case mandated for the entire population. Whether or not Scarry is a prepper – that is, whether she is making this argument rhetorically to emphasize the fundamental inequality of contemporary American democracy or whether she really believes in the need for or eventual utility of the shelters – is irrelevant. Only by taking shelters seriously, she suggests, can we come to grips with their meaning within the contemporary political process. Dismissing shelters exclusively as militaristic lunacy, as was typical of leftist thinking during the Cold War, can only, in the current context, obscure what is really at stake. Emergency preparedness, Scarry notes, is not in fact a Cold War invention but a fundamental component of organized society, actually predating democracy itself. Moreover, the US and the world more generally have, since the Cold War and especially since the terrorist attacks of 9/11 and after, been governed as if in an ongoing state of emergency. An analysis according to the terms of emergency preparedness may well afford the most accurate account available of the current political situation, including the rise of authoritarian governments and the pushback against civil rights and equity movements.

Consequently, Scarry introduces the premise that 'Nuclear weapons – their possession, threatened use, or use – reenact on a vast scale the structural features of torture.'[91] Because they permit no form of self-defense and because their use will not be authorized by the legislature or the general population, nuclear weapons nullify the requirements of contractual society and destroy the foundational concept of the law. What fundamentally separates Scarry's argument from traditional antinuclear arguments is her starting premise: that states of emergency have always existed and that 'habits of emergency preparedness' are essential to democracy rather than contrary to it. In other words, while she continues to argue that the existence of nuclear weapons undermines the principles of a functional democracy, she is mostly concerned with a more general application of the 'right of exit.' Implicit in Scarry's proposal is an awareness of contemporary theories of globalization such as Naomi Klein's account of 'disaster capitalism' that would identify the state of emergency as a defining characteristic of late capitalism and thus an enduring feature of modernity.[92] Put another way, Scarry's argument means that the bunker fantasy is fundamental to the recognition of the extreme juncture to which modernity has led the world – the coming end so readily recognized by anyone alive back during the Cold War. More importantly,

91 Scarry, *Thinking in an Emergency*, xv.
92 Naomi Klein, *The Shock Doctrine: The Rise of Disaster Capitalism* (New York: Knopf, 2007).

The hedgehog, the tortoise, and the world   133

it is fundamental to any mode of thinking that would take us beyond the dead-end polarities of the Cold War. Thinking after the end, she implies, must begin with a recognition of the democratic and even utopian principles wrought up within the apocalyptic reasoning that spurs the bunker fantasy. No wonder, then, that Scarry sees in Switzerland a prime example, not of the legacy of the prickly and insular hedgehog, the homogeneous nation-state, and the white patriarchal heteronormative global North but of the legacy of the Rousseauvian Enlightenment, the Geneva Convention, and the rule of law.

Misplaced from its fixed meanings within Cold War polarities, the bunker fantasy affords a powerful combination of ontology-weighted affect and epistemological openness. Such a combination is strongly evident, for instance, in Bong Joon-ho's award-winning 2019 Korean film *Gisaengchung* (*Parasite*). A Cold War-style fallout shelter beneath a high-end modernist home in Seoul raises the stakes of the film's critique of social inequality by introducing a third space to the verticalized polarities of familiar representations of urban poverty. The first half of the film drafts a savagely entertaining satire of class struggle and inequality based on the contrast between a wealthy family's coldly elegant and spacious home in the hills and a poor family's semi-basement infested with stinkbugs, prone to flooding, and open to the fluids and odors of the outside world. The second half swerves to a more complex presentation of the relationship between poverty and wealth, or low and high. Once the Kim family has insinuated itself into the showcase lives and home of the Parks as tutors, chauffeur, and maid, Bong introduces a forgotten sub-basement bunker that unbalances any easy understanding of the film's spatial metaphors and allegory of inequality. That the proletariat haunts the ruling class has been a truism since the *Communist Manifesto*; in recent years, the academic concept of spectrality has become an effective tool for describing the ways in which poverty and inequality are at once unseen, omnipresent, and, depending on one's politics, either subtly haunting or profoundly disturbing.

Bong's film literalizes Marx's metaphor through the figure of Geun-se (Park Myeong-hoon), the husband of Moon-gwang (Lee Jeong-eun), the longtime live-in maid who was displaced by the Kim family's infiltration of the house. Geun-se has been hiding in the bunker for years; he first manifests in a ghost story told from the perspective of the young Park boy: viewed from the kitchen table, the entrance to the basement stairs is a pitch-black vertical rectangle framed by a pair of showcases (Figure 3.11). In this telling, Geun-se slowly emerges from the blackness, eyes glowing like a specter. Geun-se belongs to a different genre than the rest of the characters, for he is introduced not as a member of the high/low satire of inequality but as a bunker survivor. Sealed in the fallout shelter to hide him from the enforcers

Figure 3.11 The foreboding entrance in the showpiece kitchen to the basement concealing a deep-level nuclear bunker in the modernist home in Seoul, South Korea, at the center of the action in Bong Joon-ho's 2019 film *Parasite*.

of a loan shark he had defaulted on, Geun-se, like his generic predecessors discussed in Chapter 2, has been bunkered for so long that he has lost his moorings in the world above. He sends signals in Morse code to the trio of ceiling bulbs illuminating the home's entrance and drinks milk from a baby's bottle. Bong's fallout shelter combines a utopian fantasy of security and insulation from the world and its problems analogous to the hermetically sealed home above it with the confinement and isolation of a prison cell.

Moon-gwang tells us that the bunker was built by the (fictional) architect Namgoong Hyeonja as part of the original design, a typical feature of homes of the wealthy as a retreat from potential attack by North Korea. This explanation provides a powerfully local meaning to the space, a meaning echoed in Moon-gwang's later comic performance of a TV announcer's dialogue of 'nuclear peace.' *Parasite* syncopates a history of privilege from the luxury home fallout shelters of the Cold War to their use by today's global elite to protect not so much against radioactive fallout as against ravaging hordes of have-nots. The bunker is formally complex because it mirrors *both* the semi-basement apartment of the Kims *and also* the starkly sumptuous mansion of the Parks. It is a space of conspicuous consumption and a shelter from the outside world – only the ultra-wealthy can afford to build one and have the luxury of planning for the contingent future rather than the immediate present. And it is a space of poverty and deprivation

The hedgehog, the tortoise, and the world 135

occupied as if a prison cell first by Geun-se and then, at film's end by Ki-taek (Kang-ho Song), the Kim family patriarch.

The bunker is also the origin of the house's haunting. This haunting is simultaneously literal, since Geun-se emerges at night from space unknown to the Parks to raid the refrigerator, and figurative, albeit in an inchoate yet affectively powerful way. Knowledge of the space binds first Moon-gwang and then Ki-taek's son to the house, compelling both to return. That it also binds them to internalizing the class warfare that identifies wealth as the only path to happiness is made clear by the son's concluding fantasy of a success so huge as to allow him to purchase the house and free his father, effectively uniting home and bunker and exorcising the ghosts of both. Bong briefly teases the audience that this fantasy is the film's 'happy ending,' only to return his camera once more to the semi-basement apartment, its segmented screens, and the son as a part-time pizza delivery boy to bracket the fantasy as just that – fantasy. In some ways, the bunker transforms *Parasite* into a retelling of SFF author Ursula K. Le Guin's well-known philosophical fable 'The Ones Who Walk Away from Omelas,' in which the happiness and comfort of a community is made possible only by the lifetime imprisonment of a child in a locked basement room. The ones who walk away are those that refuse the ontological bunker: the predication of the comfort of some upon the suffering of others. The son's knowledge of his father's imprisonment (which is also Ki-taek's protection from prosecution for murder) charges his pursuit of wealth with ethical purpose even as it binds him irrevocably to that pursuit. The bunker fantasy haunting the unequal world of late capitalism claims the right to shelter even as it limns the stark limitations imposed by the form in which that claim must be made.

The ongoing fascination of inhabitants of the twenty-first century with the material traces of the Cold War past is not simply a morbid and ironic distancing gesture or a neoliberal repackaging of the past into a vacuous simulacrum of its former meanings, although both positions certainly remain credible and available. This fascination also insists that dwelling in the recent past affords far more than to mock it or to submit meekly to its nostrums and inequities. In these traces, we can recognize beauty in horror and horror in beauty; we are able to look head-on and physically enter into something of that past; and we are able to see it not only for its original ideological purpose but also for the other potentialities hidden within that purpose and dwelling around and in opposition to it. Ruined, misplaced, adapted, and appropriated, these spaces and ideas are more readily available to read against the grain of their ideological impetus and also of their current functionality within the global neoliberalism of late capitalism. Such a reading helps us to feel the uncanny lure of the Parks' deceptively secure show-home and to understand the beauty, horror, and insanity of a life spent underground, whether in the Kims' semi-basement apartment or the Parks' sub-basement fallout shelter. And it helps us to grasp the willingness of local authorities to expose a 'a secret unmarked bunker built into the side of the Ecuadorean Andes' by a Chinese surveillance company for former leader Rafael Correa to enable its 'secretive intelligence agency' to spy on its citizens.[93] Similar to the Swiss military, these authorities are simultaneously desiring to maintain absolute control and also to distinguish their dedication to transparency. This is the contradictory duality of the bunker fantasy: not because these spaces exist in any way outside of that functionality or imaginary but because their participation is explicitly determined by their obliquity to it. The ruins of the global Cold War bunker fantasy indeed remain uncritically affirmative in making a visible space with which newly to contain the contradictions of the contemporary world; however, this remade space is also where those contradictions continue to remain most visible and thus most open to critique and appropriation.

93 Jonah M. Kessel, 'In a Secret Bunker in the Andes, a Wall That Was Really a Window,' *New York Times* (26 April 2019): www.nytimes.com/2019/04/26/reader-center/ecuador-china-surveillance-spying.html.

Plate 1 *Qander zjarri* or 'single fire' bunkers, colloquially known as 'tortoises,' in the mountain landscape of southeastern Albania. *Line of Bunkers, Edge of Ersekë, Albania, 2011.* Photo by Wayne Barrar.

Plate 2 *Pike zjarri* or 'fire point' bunkers, colloquially known as 'oranges.' *Bunker (slipping seaward), Durrës beach, Albania, 2011.* Photo by Wayne Barrar.

Plate 3 Large-scale bunker in the mountains outside Tirana. *Covered ammunition bunker, near Fushë-Krujë, Albania, 2011.* Photo by Wayne Barrar.

Plate 4 Practical sheltering in a disused large bunker. *Sheep in abandoned bunker, near Tirana, Albania, 2011.* Photo by Wayne Barrar.

Plate 5 A concrete mushroom gutted for raw materials and left overturned on the shore of Lake Ohrid. *Toppled bunker (near Macedonian border), Lake Ohrid, Albania, 2011.* Photo by Wayne Barrar.

Plate 6 Adaptive reuse on the Adriatic coast. *Seawall made from broken bunkers/ swimmers, Durrës, Albania, 2011.* Photo by Wayne Barrar.

Plate 7 Beach colors on a bunker converted for seaside tourism. *Painted bunker restaurant, Durrës beach, Albania, 2011.* Photo by Wayne Barrar.

Plate 8 A surviving bunker guards a remote mountain pass at the southeast border with Greece. *Roof of bunker, road to Elbasan, Albania, 2011.* Photo by Wayne Barrar.

Plate 9 Looking south. *Bunker Converted to a Bar, Bilisht, Albania, 2011*. Photo by Wayne Barrar.

Plate 10 Misplaced from their origins: bunker and Audi. *Front Yard Bunker / Car, Durrës, Albania, 2011*. Photo by Wayne Barrar.

Plate 11 At home in the bunker form. *Building over bunker (restaurant), Durrës beach Albania, 2011*. Photo by Wayne Barrar.

Plate 12 The iconography of apocalpyse in an everyday scene of biosecurity. *Rotenone pesticide application to Whitby Lake (removal of invasive fish), Porirua (NZ) 2007*. Photo by Wayne Barrar.

Plate 13 Imagining what it feels like to be an invasive species targeted for extinction. *Binned invasive koi at Koi Carp Classic (bowfishing event), Waikato (NZ) 2007.* Photo by Wayne Barrar.

Plate 14 The ambiguity of the laboratory setting: site for preservation or for elimination of the species pictured? *Biotron growth chamber, Bio-protection Research Centre, Lincoln (NZ) 2007.* Photo by Wayne Barrar.

Plate 15 The Santa Monica Wonderwall physically manifests the simultaneously massive and tenuous grip of future LA on the 'real' world in Brian K. Vaughan, Marcos Martín, and Muntsa Vicente's *Private Eye*.

Plate 16 The Wonderwall breached in Vaughan, Martín, and Vicente's *Private Eye*.

4

Life in the ontological bunker: Cold War continuance, appropriation, and repurposing from America to Taiwan

[For this epigraph, please read the lyrics of or listen to the bridge of the referenced song]

Def Leppard, 'Armageddon It' (1989)

The Cold War and its nuclear fortifications resemble any modern conflict in the deep physical and mental traces they left in the landscape on which they were fought; indeed, its signature forms emerged out of the concrete architecture of World War Two.[1] But like any modern war, they have their particularities as well. Classically, the traces of war slowly but fairly naturally become incorporated within the landscape around them to a degree that their presence must be sought out as often hard-to-see ruins; in memorials, historical sites and markers, and museums; and in the urban place and street names that may or may not trigger the search for ruins and markers, such as Paris's Place de la Bastille or Ho Chi Minh City's Venerable Thich Quảng Đức Monument, at the corner of Nguyễn Đình Chiểu and Cach Mạng Tháng Tám streets.[2] To be sure, this process of incorporation is nowhere near as smooth as the prior sentence implies: unexploded ordnance, leftover land mines, and toxic residue of chemical warfare unexpectedly surface, as do buried and unburied remains of the wars' many victims. Both forms of relic require proper disposal and momentarily disrupt the inexorable process whereby the traumas of war make an uneasy truce with the ongoing pressures of everyday life. But the nuclear condition presents a stiffer challenge to the always fraught negotiation between war as an exceptional condition and everyday life as its opposite and repudiation.

---

1 Paul Virilio, *Bunker Archéologie* (Paris: Editions du Demi-Cercle, 1991), trans. *Bunker Archeology* (Princeton: Princeton Architectural Press, 1997).
2 Thich Quảng Đức was the Buddhist monk who burned himself to death in protest against anti-Buddhist discrimination in 1963; the streets that form the corner where he did so have since been renamed after anticolonial poet Nguyễn Đình Chiểu and Cách mạng tháng Tám, the August Revolution of 1945 against French colonial rule.

138

After the end

If the total war that characterized the first half of the twentieth century was a challenge to the separation of life and war in its most viscerally physical sense, the Cold War of the second half was able to pull back from the existential breach of modernity at the expense of collapsing war into everyday life. This ontological bunker characterized life in the US or USSR as much as in the myriad of dictatorships nurtured by the conflict in the decolonizing global South or the looming threat of extinction that dominated life across the globe. The permanence of the built environment of the Cold War is a correlative for the relative evanescence of and failure to reckon fully with its human cost. In its formidable rise in use after World War Two, concrete proved simultaneously an inexpensive material 'beloved for its weight and endurance'; the 'foundation of modern development' and thus of great material and symbolic value to builders and governments across the globe; 'the world's dirtiest business' both literally and figuratively; and a force of antinature that currently 'outweighs the combined carbon mass of every tree, bush and shrub on the planet,' is 'said to be responsible for 4–8% of the world's CO_2,' and amplifies at least as many disasters and floods as it ameliorates.[3] Both literally and figuratively, the modern world is cast in concrete; the bunker is perhaps our most potent space for processing that fact.

In *Underland*, his 'deep time journey' through the world's subterranes, Robert Macfarlane suggests a powerful image for the contradictory permanence of the concrete bunker. 'In a dynamic I have seen so often in the underland that it has become a master trope,' he writes, 'troublesome history thought long since entombed is emerging again.'[4] In 1959, the US army engineering corps had built a 'hidden town' by tunneling deep into Greenland's permafrost: 'a two-mile network of passageways housing laboratories, a shop, a hospital, a cinema, a chapel, and accommodation for 200 soldiers, all powered by the world's first mobile nuclear generator.'[5] Abandoned in 1967 under the assumption that its infrastructure, its radioactive coolants, and its many pollutants would be 'preserved for eternity' under the ice, the toxic waste site was exposed by melt during the summer of 2016.[6] What troubles and compels about the built environment of the Cold War is its permanent embodiment of impermanence and its concrete mix of preservation and destruction, security and exposure, nature and antinature.

---

3 John Vidal, 'Concrete: The Most Destructive Material on Earth,' *Guardian* (25 Feb. 2019): www.theguardian.com/cities/2019/feb/25/concrete-the-most-destructive-material-on-earth.

4 Macfarlane, *Underland*, 329.

5 Macfarlane, *Underland*, 328–9.

6 Macfarlane, *Underland*, 328–9.

Fascination with this built environment has taken three primary forms since the end of the Cold War: the continuance of the bunker fantasy and its emblematic spaces in a putatively postwar world; the appropriation and adaptive reuse of already existing spaces; and the transference of the bunker fantasy to new and often oppositional modes of the postapocalyptic in the twenty-first century. Each form acknowledges in a different way that the world never emerged from the wartime footing of the Cold War or from the bunkers in which that footing imagined itself. Each form affords a different strategy for living with the world created by and unresolved through that war. In the ways they misplace the ontological bunker in the post–Cold War world, these different forms taken by the war's legacy together help to account for its continuing hold. By making visible similar forms existing already back within the confines of the Cold War, these misplaced spaces also open up alternate ways of thinking through the stark and unequal choices to which those confines continue to limit thought and action today. By showing how to read differently the spatial practices of the twenty-first century, the manifold legacies of the Cold War suggest the epistemological bunker can at times function as a critical and speculative tool rather than solely offering an ironic or nostalgic gaze into a simpler past.

The Cold War bunker fantasy misplaced in space

In 2011, the Swiss parliament voted to repeal the fallout shelter requirement for new construction that had been in place for nearly fifty years. Two days later, three reactors at the Fukushima Daiichi nuclear plant in Japan melted down. The repeal was quickly rescinded.[7] In 2017, after twenty years of stasis, and in response to 'Iran's nuclear program, the Fukushima accident, Russian military operations, North Korea's missile tests – and President Trump,' Sweden began looking to expand its network of sixty-five thousand nuclear fallout shelters to be able to protect the 30 percent of its population

---

7 Conseil des Etats, 'Loi sur les abris anti-atomiques sous toit,' *20 minutes* (8 June 2011): http://web.archive.org/web/20220207142459/https://www.20min.ch/fr/story/loi-sur-les-abris-anti-atomiques-sous-toit-841453096395; Jo Fahy, 'The Forgotten Underground World of Swiss Bunkers,' *swissinfo.ch* (1 Sept. 2016): http://web.archive.org/web/20230227141954/https://www.swissinfo.ch/eng/society/in-case-of-emergency_the-forgotten-underground-world-of-swiss-bunkers/42395820; 'Berne ne veut pas un 2e Fukushima en Suisse,' *Lematin.ch* (2 June 2017): http://web.archive.org/web/20190418073919/https://www.lematin.ch/suisse/berne-veut-2e-fukushima-suisse/story/10694228.

140 *After the end*

of ten million not currently covered.[8] On 13 January 2018, in Hawai'i, cellphones received an emergency alert informing the public of an incoming ballistic missile attack and instructing them to 'seek immediate shelter.'[9] 'As I sat there with my kids,' recalled one state representative, as visibly panicked as everyone else, 'I was going between *this doesn't really feel real* and *this is actually what it would feel like.*'[10] Three days later, citizens of Japan received a similar scare.[11] Both false alarms were attributed to human error; both spurred new discussion about existing provisions for shelter. As nuclear weapons historian Alex Wellerstein wrote in the *Washington Post*, 'We certainly have all the appearances of being in the grip of a "nuclear war scare" of the sort not yet seen since the Cold War.'[12] And this was before the Russian invasion of Ukraine that led in 2022 to renewed public fears of a tactical nuclear strike, of all-out war, or of a power plant meltdown. One headline hearkened back to Switzerland and its 'nuclear bunkers for all'; another summarized the situation, 'Putin's threats highlight the dangers of a new, riskier nuclear era.'[13] What moral philosopher Elaine Scarry terms 'equality of survival' and 'the right to shelter' had returned to the middle of conversations about what a democracy owes to its citizens.[14]

8 Rick Noack, 'Sweden Has 65,000 Nuclear Shelters. Now, in the Era of Trump, It Wants More,' *Washington Post* (3 Nov. 2017): www.washingtonpost.com/news/worldviews/wp/2017/11/03/sweden-has-65000-nuclear-bunkers-now-in-the-era-of-trump-it-wants-more/. For a detailed analysis of the public debate in Sweden around 2017, see Peter Bennesved, 'Shelter News: Affordance, Place and Proximity in News Media Representations of Civil Defence Artefacts,' *Critical Military Studies* (2023): 1–19, at 5–9. DOI: 10.1080/23337486.2023.2188004.

9 Adam Nagourney, David E. Sanger, and Johanna Barr, 'Hawaii Panics after Alert about Incoming Missile Is Sent in Error,' *New York Times* (13 Jan. 2018): www.nytimes.com/2018/01/13/us/hawaii-missile.html; accessed 17 April 2018.

10 Alia Wong, 'Pandemonium and Rage in Hawaii,' *Atlantic* (14 Jan. 2018): www.theatlantic.com/international/archive/2018/01/pandemonium-and-rage-in-hawaii/550529/; accessed 18 April 2018.

11 Kimiko de Freytas-Tamora, 'Days after Hawaii's False Missile Alarm, a New One in Japan,' *New York Times* (16 Jan. 2018): www.nytimes.com/2018/01/16/world/asia/japan-hawaii-alert.html; accessed 17 April 2018.

12 Alex Wellerstein, 'The Hawaii Alert Was an Accident. The Dread It Inspired Wasn't,' *Washington Post* (16 Jan. 2018): www.washingtonpost.com/news/posteverything/wp/2018/01/16/the-hawaii-alert-was-an-accident-the-dread-it-inspired-wasnt/; accessed 18 April 2018.

13 Charlotte Lam, 'Nuclear Bunkers for All: Switzerland Is Ready as International Tensions Mount,' *Euronews* (4 March 2022): http://web.archive.org/web/20230116081440/https://www.euronews.com/2022/04/03/nuclear-bunkers-for-all-switzerland-is-ready-as-international-tensions-mount; David E. Sanger and William J. Broad, 'Putin's Threats Highlight the Dangers of a New, Riskier Nuclear Era,' *New York Times* (1 June 2022): www.nytimes.com/2022/06/01/us/politics/nuclear-arms-treaties.html; accessed 20 Nov. 2022.

14 Scarry, *Thinking in an Emergency*, 69. For more on Scarry, see Chapter 3.

Life in the ontological bunker

What think-tanks and military strategists had never quite lost sight of was just as firmly back within public awareness. Honolulu's official webpage was soon updated to include instructions for 'shelter-in-place' that closely resemble the oft-ridiculed 'duck-and-cover' advice from the early Cold War decades; the webpage equally warns citizens to ignore 'The old yellow signs designating fallout shelters' because they 'are no longer current.'[15] Just six weeks prior to the false alarm, the state of Hawai'i had announced that, given the threat posed by North Korea, it would begin testing its nuclear warning system monthly.[16] The warning would be triggered, the article continued, 'from inside the 6-feet-thick concrete walls of a civil defense bunker nestled under the rock and dirt of the Diamond Head volcano crater, near Honolulu on the island of Oahu.'[17] Without a similar option for private citizens – even back in 1985 a list of shelters had offered scant provision for a much smaller population – inquiries about personal fallout shelters boomed as Hawai'i once again found itself the Pacific outpost most immediately vulnerable to the deadly consequences of American foreign policy.[18] Similar to Hawai'i although under radically different circumstances, Japan has no choice about whether to be militarized. Despite its strong support of nuclear disarmament and official refusal 'to manufacture, possess, or permit the introduction of nuclear weapons onto Japanese soil,' there has since the early 1950s been political tension between left and right over whether and how to remilitarize Japan. However, only in 2015 did the parliament pass a law permitting 'Japan's Self Defense Forces to engage in collective self-defense' and members of Shinzo Abe's hawkish government begin openly to speculate about the legality of acquiring nuclear weapons.[19]

---

15 City and County of Honolulu, Department of Emergency Management, 'FAQ': http://web.archive.org/web/20181025094849/http://www.honolulu.gov/dem/faq.html#NuclearThreat; accessed 31 Aug. 2023.

16 Doug Criss, 'For the First Time since the End of the Cold War, Hawaii Will Test Nuclear Sirens,' *CNN.com* (1 Dec. 2017): http://web.archive.org/web/20221104172331/https://www.cnn.com/2017/11/28/us/hawaii-nuclear-warning-trnd/index.html.

17 Criss, 'Hawaii Will Test Nuclear Sirens.'

18 Leila Fujimori, 'Taking Shelter: Nuclear Missile Alarm Snafu Spurs Interest in Backyard Bomb and Fallout Shelters,' *Honolulu Star-Advertiser* (19 Feb. 2018): A1.

19 Justin Jesty, 'Cold War Japan,' in 'Tokyo 1960: Days of Rage and Grief,' *MIT Visualizing Cultures* (2012): http://web.archive.org/web/20121110081744/http://ocw.mit.edu/ans7870/21f/21f.027/tokyo_1960/anp2_essay01.html; 'Japan: Nuclear,' *NTI: Nuclear Threat Initiative* (updated Oct. 2018): http://web.archive.org/web/20211016181359/https://www.nti.org/learn/countries/japan/nuclear/; Liubomir K. Topaloff, 'Japan's Nuclear Moment: Geopolitical Trends Have Combined to Open a Window of Opportunity for Japan to Become a Nuclear State,' *The Diplomat* (21 April 2017): http://web.archive.org/web/20221127044851/https://thediplomat.com/2017/04/japans-nuclear-moment/; accessed 31 Aug. 2023.

Not surprisingly, in Japan, a country 'where bunkers scarcely exist,' the fallout shelter business was booming.[20]

One legacy of the bunker fantasy is to afford recognition that the conditions that gave rise to it have not, in fact, gone away. Another is to afford recognition of the gap between Cold War fantasy and contemporary conditions. 'In recent months,' an academic colleague communicated to me in 2022, 'we have seen the limits of using old bunkers in the Ukrainian war, as those hiding there are often unsuccessful at surviving for any length of time. The war in Ukraine has been a tragic showpiece of how hiding places built during the Cold War are being retrofitted but are not providing safely for the civilian population. At the same time, the nuclear reactors of Ukraine do not provide shelter but only more danger as they are turned into weapons because of their high radioactivity. There is evidence that mobility rather than sheltering in place has emerged in this century as an alternative way of seeking safety.'[21] Attempting to evaluate multiple ways of seeking safety does not reduce anxiety – it may well increase it even, as the danger may well be inescapable – but it does at least hew more closely to material conditions than the bunker fantasy on its own.

These examples are thus related to but also distinct from the contemporary prepping movement discussed in Chapter 1 above. Preppers cite a wide variety of possible apocalypse scenarios and deploy the fallout shelter rhetorically to distance themselves from what they regard as a more lunatic fringe. In contrast, the sheltering responses by Switzerland, Hawai'i, Japan, and Ukraine and eastern Europe to specific fears widely accepted as credible establish a continuity with the bunkering consensus of early 1960s America or, at the very least, with the polarized debates of the 1980s. Similarly to Scarry's invocation of shelter as a fundamental citizen's right or Dan Zak's history of post–Cold War nuclear protesters and activists, these responses demonstrate that another legacy of the bunker since the Cold War is the continuing risk of accidental or intentional launching of nuclear missiles by one of the nine countries possessing them or another country that has since obtained them, or meltdown in one of the 439 nuclear reactors in operation worldwide, not to mention another fifty-three under construction as of May 2022.[22] In Seoul, South Korean artist Anna Lim has staged 'photographic

---

20 Yuta Yagishita, 'Japon: le boom des abris antiatomiques,' *Le Parisien* (7 Nov. 2017): www.leparisien.fr/international/japon-le-boom-des-abris-antiatomiques-07-11-2017-7377180.php; accessed 17 April 2018.

21 Email communication, 23 Sept. 2022.

22 Scarry, *Thinking in an Emergency*; Dan Zak, *Almighty: Courage, Resistance, and Existential Peril in the Nuclear Age* (New York: Blue Rider, 2016); 'Number of

metafictions' around what it means to be prepared for a nuclear strike or a terrorist attack; she calls the series 'Rehearsal of Anxiety.'[23] The case of Switzerland, like those of Sweden or Finland, reminds us that certain countries periodically evaluate risk and periodically elect to continue devoting a significant portion of their military budget to civil defense. The alarm in Hawai'i plays no differently than panic around the Cuban Missile Crisis or during the early Reagan years, when Americans were told in response to their justifiable fears that they were pretty much on their own, with a set of instructions provided by the government. And the case of Japan suggests that the direct experience of nuclear war is now far enough in the past that, for some at least, it has become possible to consider its costs and benefits in the way the rest of the nuclear powers apparently do: as an individual choice by a neoliberal citizen. The consequences of that framework are also imaginable from within the bunker imaginary.

Until quite recently, Japan had mostly declined to participate in the fantasy of choice. This fact is unsurprising, since the bunker fantasy has always been predicated on the ontological rather than the physical experience of the nuclear event, and has actively declined to acknowledge in particular the profound effects of the nuclear age on Native American populations in the southwest US, on Indigenous populations in the Marshall Islands, or on the citizens of Hiroshima and Nagasaki. As the novelist Ōe Kenzaburō wrote in 1995, 'In the A-bomb survivors' view,' there was a direct line to be drawn from 'Japan's rapid modernization' through waging war in Asia to the atomic bombing of its cities.[24] Ōe described his visit to Hiroshima and interviews with survivors in 1963 as a 'conversion' experience, a 'single week' that effected a 'complete turnabout' in his life and 'completely altered [his] literary work.'[25] He had traveled there to report on a 'large international rally to abolish nuclear weapons'; although nothing he saw altered his views, the focus of the book was, like the bunker fantasy, concerned with surviving nuclear war. Ōe struggled to balance familiar attention to the horrors of the bombs and the difficult endeavor, as one survivor put it in an essay quoted by

Operable Nuclear Power Reactors as of May 2022, by Country,' *statista*: www.statista.com/statistics/267158/number-of-nuclear-reactors-in-operation-by-country/; accessed 14 March 2023; 'Number of under construction nuclear reactors worldwide as of May 2022, by country,' *statista*: www.statista.com/statistics/513671/number-of-under-construction-nuclear-reactors-worldwide/; accessed 14 March 2023.

23 Brian Dillon, 'Anna Lim's Vision of Nuclear Anxiety in South Korea,' *New Yorker* (1 Dec. 2019): www.newyorker.com/culture/photo-booth/anna-lims-vision-of-nuclear-anxiety-in-south-korea.

24 Ōe Kenzaburō, '1995 Introduction,' in *Hiroshima Notes* (1965), trans. David L. Swain and Toshi Yonezawa (New York: Marion Boyars, 1995 [1981]), 7–11, at 9.

25 Ōe, '1995 Introduction,' 8.

Ōe, 'to be as optimistic as possible, so long as no further ill effects appeared.' For this reason, Mr Matsusaka continued, 'I have long wondered why virtually all of the "A-bomb literature" consists of stories of the miserable people who have not recovered their health, as well as of descriptions of radiation symptoms and the psychology of the A-bomb survivors. Why are there no stories, for example, of families who endured hard times but recovered their health and now live as normal human beings?'[26] Another survivor wrote a letter to Ōe protesting against the compulsion constantly to relive the experience. 'People in Hiroshima,' the doctor's son argued, 'do not like to display their misery for use as "data" in the movement against atomic bombs or in other political struggles. ... People who know firsthand the horror of atomic destruction choose to keep silent, or at most speak only a few words and leave their testimony for the historical record.'[27] Fully aware of the practical tension between these views, Ōe is careful in his essays to distinguish between the right of survivors to remain silent and the necessary refusal of the choice of silence about Hiroshima to those who possess and have wielded atomic weapons.[28] It's a similar distinction to the one Gavin Francis makes between 'true forgetting' and 'state-sanctioned insistence that victims on both sides "forget about" seeking reparations.'[29] Misplaced from a country that had never been invaded, that controlled the largest nuclear arsenal in the world, and that was the only nation ever to have actually used an atomic bomb, the bunker fantasy abroad took on alternate forms indeed.

Mr Matsusaka and the doctor's son, like Ōe himself, attest to the efficacy of the bunker fantasy. While both speakers fully support disarmament and oppose war, and while Ōe argues forcefully for war reparations rather than welfare payments for the survivors, their ontology precisely echoes the never-otherwise-achieved outcome of the bunker fantasy: to emerge on the other side of the bomb and survive again to live one's life. Hiroshima is necessary to the antinuclear movement as 'the prime example not of the power of atomic weapons but of the misery they cause.'[30] But Hiroshima also perversely demonstrates as nowhere else the utopian power inhering in being able to survive that misery, for the bunker fantasy not only posits apocalypse as necessary for putting everything into order with a clean slate but also imagines, as the interviewees quoted by Ōe suggest, regretfully,

---

26 Ōe, *Hiroshima Notes*, 21.
27 Ōe, *Hiroshima Notes*, 19–20.
28 Ōe, *Hiroshima Notes*, 108–10.
29 Francis, 'Dream of Forgetfulness,' 32.
30 Ōe, *Hiroshima Notes*, 109.

Life in the ontological bunker

that, like Hiroshima's Atomic Bomb Dome, some of us can in fact survive anything.

This paradox is also a subliminal message within French writer Marguerite Duras and director Alain Resnais's 1959 film *Hiroshima mon amour*, a film devoted primarily to the incommunicable and lasting trauma of war, both in Hiroshima and in occupied France: the fact that 'All one can do is talk about the impossibility of talking about Hiroshima.'[31] But that same trauma is also, according to Duras, the French Woman's (Emmanuelle Riva) 'most precious possession,' which she freely gives to her Japanese lover (Eiji Okada) in Hiroshima: 'her *survival*.'[32] As Ōe concedes in his conclusion, 'The most terrifying monster lurking in the darkness of Hiroshima is precisely the possibility that man might become no longer human.'[33] This 'incomparably larger abominable reality' is inseparable, however, from its converse, his 'first concrete insight into human authenticity' of 'people who refused to surrender to the worst despair or to incurable madness.'[34] Where the bunker fantasy failed, in its classic version within Cold War America, was in trying to separate survival from the horrors surrounding survival, to repress the reality of the latter from the fantasy of the former. However, that failure is also survival's promise and its authenticity; only in the imagination of surviving apocalypse is the fantasy also able to grant 'concrete insight into human authenticity.'

Writing postwar through 1989, there was no available space or form for articulating this paradox fully and publicly. The closest to such a moment might be Holocaust survivor Primo Levi's assertion in his memoir of Auschwitz that 'We are in fact convinced that no human experience is without meaning or unworthy of analysis, and that fundamental values, even if they are not positive, can be deduced from this particular world which we are describing.'[35] Ōe opens his own book by apologizing for the impropriety of 'a reference to one's personal experience' before going on to detail the 'utterly crushed' state of mind with which he and his editor made the 'exhausting, depressing, and suffocating' journey to Hiroshima, weighed down by the belief that his first son was dying in an incubator, by the editor's loss of his first daughter, and by the suicide of a mutual friend in Paris over despair at 'impending nuclear doom.'[36] The 'clue' they find to 'extricate' themselves from 'the

---

31 Marguerite Duras, *Hiroshima mon amour*, trans. Richard Seaver (New York: Grove, 1961 [1960]), 9.

32 Duras, *Hiroshima*, 112.

33 Ōe, *Hiroshima Notes*, 182.

34 Ōe, *Hiroshima Notes*, 181.

35 Primo Levi, *Survival in Auschwitz*, trans. of *Se questo è un uomo* (New York: Collier, 1959 [1947]), 79.

36 Ōe, *Hiroshima Notes*, 17.

146   *After the end*

deep gloom into which we had fallen' is the 'truly human character of the people of Hiroshima.'[37]

Ōe never found a way to unwind in print the relationship between his personal trauma and that of the people of Hiroshima and their resistance to being fodder for the global bunker fantasy; however, he did succeed in not smoothing over the contradictions. Looking back at this earlier moment in 1995 from the perspective of the Nobel Prize speech he had given the prior year and from the general opening-up of discourse after the end of the Cold War, Ōe was more explicit about the paradox of survival. 'In the lecture,' he explained,

> I recalled that my mentally impaired son Hikari became able to express in music what was not accessible to him in words, and that his earliest efforts were full of fresh splendor and delight. But gradually his music came to express something dark and sorrowful, like the voice of a crying and dark soul. Yet that voice is beautiful, and his ability to express it in music cures him of his dark sorrow in a process of recovery. Moreover, his music has been well received because it heals and restores his contemporary audiences as well. This gives me courage to believe in the wondrous healing power of art.[38]

The son that had lain dying during the Hiroshima visit had in fact survived; like the bombing victims, he was profoundly marked physically and psychologically by that experience. And like the Atomic Bomb Dome itself, the art that emerges from this kind of survival is truly dark, sorrowful, and beautiful. Ōe is not arguing that his son was better or worse off due to his trauma, or that the bombing of Hiroshima was somehow 'worth' the art and experience that survived it. Rather, he is dwelling in the bunker's fundamental promise of continuance, of survival, to make of that ontological state something transformative – *survivance* – rather than simply allowing it to be a static equation of bombers and victims, powerful states and powerless people.

We find a similar difficulty of representation in Abe Kōbō's 1984 novel *The Ark Sakura*, where the detail and strangeness of the particular world of the bunker the ironic title describes are, in reviewer Edmund White's words, so 'grim and impressive, sickening and memorable' that the reader cannot help but sense something more at stake than the surface satire the novel ostensibly mounts.[39] Abe's critique of the bunker fantasy is overt as only the 1980s could be – *sakura*, we are told, means 'shill'; the title could just as well have been translated as *The Bunco Ark*. When that critique is

---

37 Ōe, *Hiroshima Notes*, 18.
38 Ōe, *Hiroshima Notes*, 10.
39 Edmund White, 'Round and Round the Eupcaccia Goes,' *New York Times Book Review* (10 April 1988): 9.

Life in the ontological bunker

147

straightforwardly articulated – 'The important thing, after all, is not really survival, per se, but the ability to go on hoping, even in one's final moments'[40] – we are clearly meant to take the critique as an empty nostrum. Although main character Mole does finally leave his burrow at the novel's end, the characters are portrayed so unsympathetically that it is difficult to regard them as more than allegorical placeholders for this critique. And yet the space itself is as compelling as it is awful. It's a vast abandoned quarry that Mole has stocked with the gadgets and the traps of adolescent fantasy. Nevertheless, Abe gives voice here also to the burrower's pride and wonder:

> The last three years or so I've been living underground. Not in a cylindrical cave like a mole's burrow but in a former quarry for architectural stone, with vertical walls and level ceilings and floors. The place is a vast underground complex where thousands of people could live, with over seventy stone rooms piled up every which way, all interconnected by stone stairways and tunnels. In size the rooms range from great halls like indoor stadiums to tiny cubby-holes where they used to take test samples. Of course there are no amenities like piped water or drainage or power lines. No shops, no police stations, no post office. The sole inhabitant is me.[41]

Abe holds at arm's length the pulp imagery he conjures. The very materiality of the space distances the novel from the purely psychological underground of its nearest modernist models, Kafka's 'The Burrow' and Dostoyevsky's *Notes from Underground*. Indeed, Mole's inability to isolate himself suggests a different and more social set of circumstances than either of those earlier fictions. By describing the protagonist as fat, ugly, and psychologically damaged, and by making all the other characters outcasts, Abe keeps the vision at a distance from the reader. Nevertheless, he gives it just enough numinous mystery that we can imagine a positive version might yet come to be.

Spanish novelist Jorge Carrión's 2014 near-future satire *Los huérfanos* (The Orphans) similarly imagines a 'sickening and memorable' bunker, in this case a state-of-the-art group shelter in Beijing that ends up housing a multinational hodgepodge of friends, acquaintances, and lovers of the scientist Chang. The narrator Marcelo, a man of letters and erstwhile lover of Chang's deceased wife, gains some measure of insight into the atavistic and debased shelter he finds himself in after a slowly unrolling tactical nuclear war has destroyed or irradiated most of the world. What the bunker fantasy primarily affords Carrión, however, is a critique of the existential hell of the ontological

---

40 Abe Kōbō, *The Ark Sakura* (1984), trans. Juliet Winters Carpenter (New York: Knopf, 1988), 184.
41 Abe, *Ark Sakura*, 4.

148 *After the end*

bunker: a world of psychological torture, video surveillance, digital alienation, and sexual obsession. Misplacing a Western preoccupation dating to *Blade Runner* (1982) and the 1980s cyberpunk of William Gibson and others, Carrión's Chinese setting functions primarily to chart the pernicious spread of physical and digital bunkering the world over. Marcelo's online friend Mario – the Internet survives in isolated fits and starts – is similarly confined on a remote Pacific island. 'He is just as unable to leave his bunker. Or at least he believes he is unable to do it.'[42] Mario will eventually choose suicide; Marcelo appears resigned to whatever the *zulo* – as he calls the bunker in its Basque translation using a word also meaning 'negative space' – holds out for him in a future that promises to be nothing but infernal. 'We are living against nature,' he concludes. 'We are an aberration.'[43]

Whereas the global bunker fantasy affords Carrión a means to satirize a future irrevocably overtaken by the nuclear condition, in Vikram Chandra's *Sacred Games*, the same fantasy affords a meditation on India's seduction by and appropriation of Cold War modernity, while in Vietnamese American author Ocean Vuong's brief novel *On Earth We're Briefly Gorgeous* (2019), it charts the aftershocks of the Vietnam War. Rather than Abe's marginal dropouts in contemporary Japan or Carrión's academic elite in a near-future China, Chandra's novel revolves around the mystery of a high-end doomsday bunker on the periphery of a contemporary Mumbai that ostensibly knows nothing of bunkering (Figure 4.1). Like the yachts, drugs, and alcohol that fuel the decadent lifestyle of crime boss Ganesh Gaitonde, the bunker is an imported commodity so incongruous in its new setting that police inspector Sartaj Singh actually has to explain what it is to his less worldly partner. It perhaps goes without saying that Gaitonde's bunker does not protect him. Instead, it is the setting of his suicide and the space from which his voice issues to narrate the retrospective story of his life, a story that alternates with the account of Sartaj's present-day investigation. The novel's title alludes to the 'great game' of Cold War spycraft; along with Gaitonde's bunker and the rogue nuclear device he fears, it documents India's embrace of modernity and questions the consequences of that embrace for a postcolonial democracy with a history, priorities, and issues only tangentially related to that war. The bunker thus coalesces the incongruity of nuclear modernity in an India imbued with spirituality, metaphysics, and the situated ethics of everyday corruption. 'What use was it,' Sartaj wonders, 'to be concerned with the everyday matters of blackmail, thievery, murder, when this enormous fear billowed overhead? It was an abstracted danger, this grim notion of a

---

42 Jorge Carrión, *Los huérfanos* (Barcelona: Galaxia Gutenberg, 2014), 41.
43 Carrión, *Los huérfanos*, 179.

Life in the ontological bunker 149

Figure 4.1 The antinuclear bunker displaced to the periphery of Mumbai, India in the initial episode of *Sacred Games*.

sweeping fire, it was unreal. But with its cold drip of images, it crowded out the mundane.'[44] Could not we also argue, as the phrasing of Sartaj's question begs, that in India, as elsewhere in the global South or among marginalized populations of the global North, we are dealing rather with a question of the 'mundane ... crowd[ing] out ... the abstracted danger'?

While the plot on the ground traces the rise of a gangster and the petty corruptions of everyday survival that organized crime both enables and feeds on, the superstructure revolves around a high-concept plot by Gaitonde's guru to detonate a nuclear device to 'prepare the world for the coming cataclysm, the end of Kaliyug [the current age]' and the efforts of India's secret service to stop him without triggering mass hysteria in the process.[45] The dilemma faced by Gaitonde, and through him the reader, is to decide whether Guru is a charlatan solely interested in gain and partisan politics or, if we accept the idea of a metaphysical or sacred game, that the end of one world is necessary to usher in a new one. The reader must accept one of two incompatible contraries: either the situated ethics of a corrupted world or the full-bore bunker fantasy. Chandra uses the bunker to spatialize this choice and this dilemma as particular to Mumbai, imbricated within Cold War verities and also uncontained by them. Gaitonde is not alone in the bunker; indeed, he built it primarily to protect his dear friend Jojo, who refuses its confines, arguing that for many of its migrant citizens, their city

44 Chandra, *Sacred Games*, 584.
45 Chandra, *Sacred Games*, 580.

150   *After the end*

is already shelter enough. '"And if Bombay is gone, then where will I live anyway? I can't go back to my village." She laughed. ... "Listen, baba – if this city is gone, my office is gone, my home is gone, all my work is gone, what I know is gone. Then there's nothing to stay alive for anyway."'[46] As Sartaj muses later, wondering if there would even be a panicked evacuation were the threat to be revealed, 'Perhaps they would wait for the bomb in these tangled lanes, grown out of the earth without forethought or plan. People came here from gaon and vilayat, and they found a place to sit, they lay down on a dirty patch of land, which shifted and settled to take them in, and then they lived. And so they would stay.'[47] Sartaj will survive in this 'dirty patch of land'; like the families and victims of the shelter-obsessed and paternalistic survivalists in *The Nuclear Age*, *Take Shelter*, or *10 Cloverfield Lane* (see Chapter 2), Jojo will be abducted senseless into Gaitonde's bunker. Unlike the women and children in those texts, she will not survive the ordeal.

Rose, the mother of Little Dog, the epistolary narrator of *On Earth We're Briefly Gorgeous*, does survive her apocalyptic ordeal to settle as a nail salon worker in Hartford, CT. The daughter of a Vietnamese sex worker and an American soldier, Rose suffers from PTSD following a napalm attack on her school. Her trauma manifests itself in various ways, including as a bunker fantasy. In 2003, Little Dog remembers:

> Bush had already declared war on Iraq, citing weapons of mass destruction that never materialized ... It was the summer Tiger Woods would go on to receive the PGA Player of the Year for the fifth time in a row and the Marlins would upset the Yankees (not that I cared or understood), it was two years before Facebook and four before the first iPhone, Steve Jobs was still alive, and your nightmares had just started getting worse, and I'd find you at the kitchen table at some god-awful hour, butt naked, sweating, and counting your tips in order to buy 'a secret bunker' just in case, you said, a terrorist attack happened in Hartford. It was the year the Pioneer 10 spacecraft sent its last signal to NASA before losing contact forever 7.6 billion miles from Earth.[48]

Lacking the resources to carry out her folly, Rose simply suffers its lack. Rather than consoling, the fantasy of shelter demonstrates how out of place she is in relation to the world in which it persists: the world of Bush, of

---

46 Chandra, *Sacred Games*, 722.
47 Chandra, *Sacred Games*, 474. Gaon (Assam) and Vilayat (Gujarat) are villages in India.
48 Ocean Vuong, *On Earth We're Briefly Gorgeous* (New York: Penguin, 2021 [2019]), 86–7.

Life in the ontological bunker

American wars, of millionaire athletes with no relation to the everyday Black or Asian population, of Silicon Valley, and of distant spacecraft. 'Once, at a writing conference,' Little Dog tells his mother, 'a white man asked me if destruction was necessary for creation. His question was genuine … I regarded him the way I do every white veteran from the war, thinking he could be my grandfather, and I said no. "No, sir, destruction is not necessary for art." I said that, not because I was certain, but because I thought my saying it would help him believe me.'[49] The pull of the fantasy is well-nigh irresistible, for the connection and meaning, the 'belief' it promises.

Sacred Games similarly argues that the bunker fantasy is inseparable from modernity and that its presence changes everything. Chandra gives full credence to the bunker fantasy, but in post–Cold War Mumbai the bunker and its survivalist fantasies are shown not only to be inimical to everyday life; they are wholly alien to its practices. We see both elements in Sartaj's attempts to process the case, just as we see Gaitonde's embrace of the shelter as the latest effort in his neurotic quest for security:

> Sartaj had thought of this thing before, this device, he had encountered it in fictions and newspaper reports, but now that it was inside his city, in his home, he was unable to imagine it. He tried to see it, some sort of machine in the back of a truck, but all he could see was an absence, a hole in the world. What came out of this void was an avalanche of regret, a knifing pain in his gut for everything left undone and for all the memories of the past. …. Everything would be gone, not just loved ones and enemies. Everyone. This was the unbearable promise of this device, now made real. It was ridiculous but it was true.[50]

The fear and the fantasy are overwhelming and also intolerable. Deployed askance as a misplaced idea, the bunker affords Chandra a tool for transnational critique that avoids the old polarities of first world and the rest, of global North and global South. Mumbai is global and it has its own ontological bunker, but it does not work exactly the way it is supposed to.

The Cold War bunker fantasy misplaced in time

Ideas can be misplaced temporally as well as spatially. Only after the end of the Cold War would the validity of prior protest and dissent or the 'covert campaigns' of the CIA-funded 'cultural Cold War' be fully documented or

---

49 Vuong, *On Earth*, 177–8.
50 Chandra, *Sacred Games*, 738.

officially recognized.[51] Although workers had filed class action suits following the end of atmospheric testing in 1962, the Radiation Exposure Compensation Act (RECA) was not passed until 1990. RECA established specific compensation for uranium workers, '"on-site participants" at atmospheric nuclear weapons tests,' and 'downwinders,' or local inhabitants, including Native Americans.[52] The consequences of the fact that 'more nuclear bombs have been dropped on or have exploded in or above American soil than on that of any other country in the world'[53] can begin to be acknowledged and reckoned with. The first full account of American nuclear tests – a total of 1,054, with more than 200 of them exploded in the atmosphere or aboveground in the US – was not published until 1993.[54] The fact that Sedan Crater, at 1,280 feet in diameter and 330 feet deep the largest of the more than two hundred subsidence craters from underground tests scattered across Yucca Flat (Figure 4.2), was created in 1962 by 'Operation Plowshare' to 'develop peaceful uses for nuclear weapons'[55] cannot but chill the soul in its testimony to the degree to which the nuclear condition permeates not only war but peacetime. But it also tells us, however misguided or absurd the thought might seem, that the existence of nuclear weapons prompted visions of techno-utopia at the same time as fantasies of mass destruction.

Similarly, after 1989, histories and alternate American perspectives seldom if ever appearing in or recognized by the dominant discourse during the Cold War became newly or differently available. The Nevada Test Site Oral History Project, for example, which includes 335 hours of interviews with 'national laboratory scientists & engineers; labor trades and support personnel; cabinet-level officials, military personnel & corporate executives; Native American tribal & spiritual leaders; peace activists and protesters; Nevada ranchers, families & communities downwind of the test site,' was begun

51 On the 'wave of scholarship' uncovering details of the cultural warfare clandestinely funded by Western governments during the Cold War, see James Smith and Guy Woodward, 'Anglo-American Propaganda and the Transition from the Second World War to the Cultural Cold War,' in *The Bloomsbury Handbook to Cold War Literature Cultures*, ed. Greg Barnhisel (London: Bloomsbury Academic, 2022), 149–62; quoted from 149.

52 Andrew G. Kirk, *Doom Towns: The People and Landscapes of Atomic Testing* (New York: Oxford University Press, 2017), 254–8.

53 Emmet Gowin, *The Nevada Test Site* (Princeton: Princeton University Press, 2019), 145.

54 Gowin, *Nevada Test Site*, 148.

55 Gowin, *Nevada Test Site*, Plate 33.

Life in the ontological bunker 153

Figure 4.2 Sedan Crater, at 1,280 feet in diameter and 330 feet at its deepest, the largest of the hundreds of subsidence craters in Yucca Flat, created in 1962 by 'Operation Plowshare' to 'develop peaceful uses for nuclear weapons.'

only in 2003.[56] Leslie Marmon Silko introduced what would become a critique of nuclear colonialism based in the theft and poisoning of southwest Native lands in her award-winning 1977 novel *Ceremony*; she would expand it in the epic *Almanac of the Dead* (1991).[57] And something of this politico-historical process had started in the 1980s; however, as in Japan, the history

---

56 'Introduction,' *Nevada Test Site Oral History Project*, University of Nevada Las Vegas: http://digital.library.unlv.edu/ntsohp/; accessed 19 April 2018.
57 For more on *Ceremony* and *Almanac*, see Chapter 2 above. For more on this topic in the context of Silko, see Matsunaga, 'Leslie Marmon Silko and Nuclear Dissent.' As Matsunaga notes, environmental sociologist Valerie Kuletz coined the term nuclear colonialism in *The Tainted Desert: Environmental and Social Ruin in the American West* (New York: Routledge, 1998). See also Donald A. Grinde and Bruce E. Johansen, *Ecocide of Native America: Environmental Destruction on Indian Lands and Peoples* (Santa Fe: Clear Light, 1995), and Ward Churchill and Winona LaDuke, 'Native North America: The Political Economy of Radioactive Colonialism,' in *The State of Native America: Genocide, Colonization, and Resistance*, ed. M. Annette Jaimes (Boston: South End Press, 1992), 241–66.

154 *After the end*

was initially mobilized ontologically – almost solely in service of antinuclear arguments.[58] Like the scattered moments when the costs of the nuclear condition briefly surfaced in ways that necessitated some kind of American response – the images and experience of Hiroshima and Nagasaki and their aftermath; the Japanese fishing vessel some of whose crew were fatally contaminated by fallout from a 1954 nuclear weapons test on the Bikini Atoll – such arguments vividly documented the dangers of nuclear weapons and the ease with which the government could ignore those demands. They were able to address only effects rather than causes, however; there was no space in the Cold War discourse for mainstream confrontation with the mechanisms that allowed these incidents to happen or to understand the choices being made.

Part of the difficulty in getting the full picture, as Kirk acknowledges, is that, 'Despite, and at times because of, this extensive official coverage [of the tests], critical details of this globally significant history were shrouded in secrecy and misperception.'[59] Declassified sources remain full of blacked-out pages and phrases, the 'Cold War culture of secrecy' remains both formally and informally operative, and 'the hundreds of thousands of ordinary people who were neither protesters nor organizers of tests appeared usually only as statistics rather than three-dimensional people and historical actors with agency.'[60] Still today, anthropologist Joseph Masco argues, 'The U.S. nuclear complex is primarily visible ... only in moments of crisis, when the stakes of nuclear policy are framed by heightened anxiety, and thus, subject, not to reassessment and investigation, but to increased fortification.'[61] Writing in 1999, William Sanders in *Ballad of Billy Badass* would deploy the affordances of speculative fiction to link up the environmental racism inherent to uranium mining and nuclear testing in the vicinity of Indigenous populations

---

58 See, for instance, Howard Ball, *Justice Downwind: America's Atomic Testing Program in the 1950s* (New York: Oxford University Press, 1986); Philip I. Fradkin, *Fallout: An American Nuclear Tragedy* (Tucson: University of Arizona Press, 1989); Milton S. Katz, *Ban the Bomb: A History of SANE, the Committee for a Sane Nuclear Policy, 1957–1985* (New York: Greenwood, 1986); Richard Miller, *Under the Cloud: The Decades of Nuclear Testing* (New York: Free Press, 1986); Howard L. Rosenberg, *Atomic Soldiers: American Victims of Nuclear Experiments* (Boston: Beacon, 1980); Harvey Wasserman and Norman Solomon, *Killing Our Own: The Disaster of America's Experience with Atomic Radiation* (New York: Delacorte, 1982). Either directly or indirectly, these titles all demonstrate the stark arguments and high stakes of 1980s atomic historiography.

59 Kirk, *Doom Towns*, xix.

60 Kirk, *Doom Towns*, xix, xxi.

61 Joseph Masco, *The Nuclear Borderlands: The Manhattan Project in Post–Cold War New Mexico* (Princeton: Princeton University Press, 2013), 6.

Life in the ontological bunker 155

in Nevada, Kazakhstan, China, Australia, and the South Pacific.[62] But Sanders knew full well, as stated in the author's note, that 'the information … is factually correct according to the author's personal sources.'[63] As pop artist Sue Saad commented on the Las Vegas childhood that inspired her 1985 song 'Radioactive Dreams':

> We could feel the actual blasts of the atomic bomb tests out in the desert. … But day in and day out on Fremont Street, Vegas Vic would explode into color. Walking the streets you'd hear the deafening sounds of slot machines, vibrating and ringing endlessly. Waterfalls of coins falling to the ground. Loud grown-ups laughing, drinking and yelling to the early morning hours. Making their bets not even acknowledging the mushroom cloud that lingered in the city of lights. I played in the desert. It was pretty desolate and isolating.[64]

Dwelling in a world composed equally of apocalypse and anti-apocalypse clarified the real-life stakes of the bunker fantasy in ways a greater distance did not, and in ways that were difficult to articulate outside of a 'nonserious' cultural framework such as SFF or pop music.

Writer Kyle Higgins and artist Stephen Mooney found similar affordances in the comics form. Their six-issue miniseries *The Dead Hand* (2018) imagines an ongoing legacy of the Cold War in an isolated American mountain town that turns out to lie on a dead-end spur off the Trans-Siberian Railway peopled by a combination of innocent children and adult agents who continue to live life as if it were the 1980s (Figure 4.3).[65] American agent Carter and French mercenary Renae are both children of the 1960s: Carter was led to his career by superhero dreams born of silver-age comics; their daughter Harriet is a rebellious teenager impatient with the verities of her parents' generation. When Mountain View is beset by rogue agents, pretending to be tourists, intent on piercing the town's secret and seeking revenge, it falls to Harriet to resolve the puzzle of a still active 'dead hand' doomsday device of nuclear cataclysm embedded within an AI that manifests as a young, unstable boy named Roger. An 'old spy trying to do the impossible' in an 'impossible' town with an 'impossible boy' in 'the most unlikely of places,' Mountain View is a top-secret international conspiracy.[66] It conceals within its depths a bunkered relic of the Cold War that requires appropriation by a post–Cold War sensibility in order not to destroy the world (Figure 4.4).

62 Sanders, *Billy Badass*, 129–34.
63 Sanders, *Billy Badass*, 7.
64 Susan Boecker (née Saad), email communication, 18 February 2021.
65 Kyle Higgins (wr.) and Stephen Mooney (art), *The Dead Hand*, six issues (Portland, OR: Image Comics, 2018).
66 Higgins and Mooney, *Dead Hand #5* (Portland, OR: Aug. 2018), 18.

Figure 4.3 The dead-end spur leading to Mountain View, the 'impossible' American town in the middle of Siberia in Kyle Higgins and Stephen Mooney's *The Dead Hand*.

Life in the ontological bunker 157

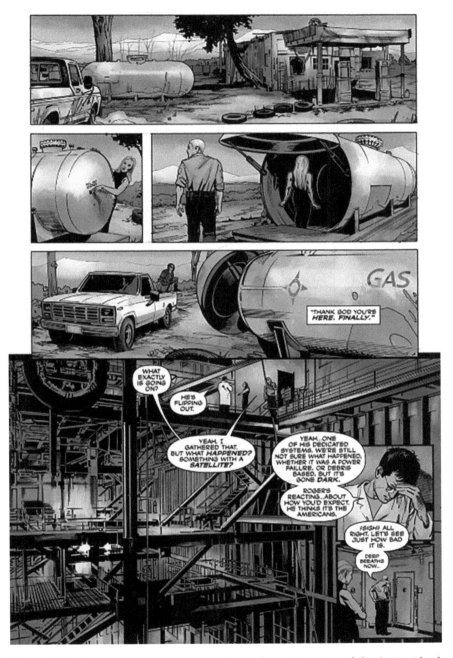

Figure 4.4 The retro-contemporary exterior and static interior of the Soviet 'dead hand' facility Mountain View was created to guard in *The Dead Hand*.

158 *After the end*

Whether well-meaning, unhinged, or bent on revenge, the adults in the room have never recognized, much less emerged from, the ontological bunker they continue to inhabit despite the deceptive appearance of an open-air mountain enclave.

Within the higher echelons of the military command, secrecy itself was secret. There were 'many levels of clearances, each more secret, more tightly held, and shared with fewer people than the last ... beyond Top Secret, the highest clearance known to exist by the general public.'[67] Faced with the knowledge of plans for nuclear war so 'closely held by planners and the Joint Chiefs of Staff ... that not even the secretary of defense or civilians in his office were ever shown or informed about the plan,' economist, military analyst, and eventual activist Daniel Ellsberg took it upon himself to inform President Kennedy and his Secretary of Defense Robert McNamara in the hope that 'they would be horrified by the details and would insist on changing the plan.'[68] In his review of Ellsberg's memoir about how he learned of and revealed secret plans for nuclear war, author and intelligence expert Thomas Powers also draws a telling separation between the Ellsberg from whom he heard these stories in detail at the late height of the Cold War in 1986, and the Ellsberg recounting those stories from the epistemological vantage point of the twenty-first century. While his goal remains what it had been most starkly in the 1980s – to do anything he could to diminish the threat of nuclear war – 'something important has been added,' a shift in attitude that Powers attributes both to new information and to 'an old man's warning, the fruit of long reflection and tinged with sorrow.' The new information is that Ellsberg was correct in his conviction that Khrushchev was not going to risk nuclear war and would back down, but that Kennedy's Executive Committee did not think so and 'had chosen a course of action that they believed risked a one in ten chance of a nuclear war that would kill hundreds of millions of people.' Moreover, because McNamara had told him that the missiles posed only 'a domestic political problem' rather than a military one, the President had taken this risk, 'just to help win the next election.'[69]

The conclusion that 'these weapons are too dangerous to have because they are too dangerous to lose,'[70] that no one can be trusted with the power because the fantasy they provide is too potent not militarily but politically,

---

67 Thomas Powers, 'The Nuclear Worrier, rev. of Daniel Ellsberg, *The Doomsday Machine: Confessions of a Nuclear War Planner,' New York Review of Books* (18 Jan. 2018): 13–15, at 13.
68 Powers, 'Nuclear Worrier,' 14.
69 Powers, 'Nuclear Worrier,' 15.
70 Powers, 'Nuclear Worrier,' 15.

would not surprise any peace activist or pacifist. But it is wholly different to grasp this truth in full possession of the facts and after decades spent within the bunkered circles of nuclear planners, as Ellsberg has, than from the outside looking in. The meaning of experiencing nuclear war has changed in Japan from the Cold War to the present, the American understanding of the ecology and everyday life of the Nevada Test Site has opened up from the stark public polarities of 1962, and the bunker fantasy affords a different vantage onto nuclearity from the middle of twenty-first-century Mumbai. In the same way, the continuance of nuclear weapons and the fantastic activity around them, without having substantively changed in form, nevertheless mean something different today than they did before. Moreover, the times when it did feel different now have been transformed, in retrospect as well, in unforeseen and variegated ways.

Continuance and repurposing for the nuclear tourist

Adaptive reuse of Cold War spaces always invokes explicitly or evokes implicitly the bunker fantasy; however, touristic repurposing functions somewhat differently than other kinds of reuse, such as for storage or habitation. Whereas the latter forms of reuse appropriate one or more of the space's affordances for a different function that may be wholly unrelated to the original design, touristic repurposing establishes an explicit conversation between the original function and the tourist's or visitor's own positionality. When the travel is motivated by the historical significance of the space and its practices – such as when mainland Chinese or Taiwanese tourists visit the tunnel fortifications on Kinmen and Matsu or when English and American tourists visit the Kelvedon Hatch 'Secret Nuclear Bunker' in Essex (Figure 4.5) or the Greenbrier congressional shelter in White Sulphur Springs (Figure 4.6) – this conversation is potentially a relatively straightforward reckoning with the past. Nevertheless, this reckoning remains mediated to a greater or lesser degree, by everything from plaques, dioramas, tour guides, souvenirs, and photo ops (one of the givens of an active military bunker is the strict prohibition of photography) to the opportunity for fantasy and cosplay. A shelter in Vitznau, Switzerland, for example, 'is outfitted for groups of tourists who pay to spend a weekend in a World War Two shelter';[71] according to the Greenbrier webpage, its 16,554 square foot Cold War–era 'Exhibit Hall … can be easily transformed for a variety of themed events, from a

---

71 Ross, *Waiting*, 62.

Figure 4.5 The ever-popular photo op of post–Cold War irony: a road sign for the Kelvedon Hatch Secret Nuclear Bunker, Brentwood, Essex, England.

50's Sock Hop to an elegant James Bond evening.'[72] Other times, when bunker spaces have been appropriated as tourism infrastructure – kiosks, bars, restaurants, hostels – the conversation is more oblique, although the choice of space still implies the value of the connection to a specific understanding of and interest in the past.

While seldom recognized or acknowledged as such at the time, the economics of nuclear tourism were in fact already an integral feature of the Kinmen fortifications, of atom bomb testing in Nevada, and of the postwar redevelopment of Hiroshima. In 1980, ROC president Chiang Ching-kuo boasted of the capacious new Hall of Welcoming Guests, a guesthouse dug out of the granite of Mount Taiwu at the heart of Kinmen Island. 'Compatriots at home and abroad,' he explained, 'and anti-Communists around the world, all wish to see this imposing maritime anti-communist Great Wall in person.'[73] Invoking emblematic walls in both China and Berlin, Ching-kuo deployed the bunker hotel as a spectacular site where local and global interests came

---

72 'Exhibit Hall at the Greenbrier,' *The Greenbrier: America's Resort*: http://web.archive.org/web/20160827134716/http://www.greenbrier.com/Meetings-Groups/Meeting-Rooms/Additional/Exhibit-Center.aspx; accessed 31 Aug. 2023.
73 Szonyi, *Cold War Island*, 101.

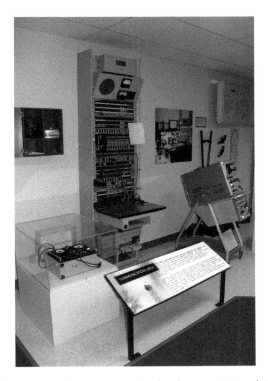

Figure 4.6 The communications room in the decommissioned Congressional fallout shelter, complete with explanatory panel, in the Greenbrier resort, White Sulphur Springs, West Virginia.

together in mutual self-protection. The cinematic spectacles around Kinmen discussed in Chapter 3 suggest the same convergence of interests. In a 2004 interview, Las Vegas News Bureau photographer Donald English similarly argued that because the tests put Las Vegas 'in the headlines almost every day' during the 1950s, 'it had to have had an effect on tourism.'[74] Because 'the newspapers were hungry for anything that had any kind of a different approach' than the standard 'mushroom cloud pictures,' English would instead take photos of shock wave effects in Las Vegas.[75] To encourage civil defense preparedness, 'every effort' was made 'to promote extensive and vivid coverage as possible by all media.'[76]

74 Kirk, *Doom Towns*, 195.
75 Kirk, *Doom Towns*, 193–4.
76 Kirk, *Doom Towns*, 71.

162   *After the end*

Especially in the 'Doom Town' tests of 1953 where model housing inhabited by mannequin families was blown to bits, the mediated spectacle of atomic testing experienced by most American spectators closely resembled the 'staged authenticity' Stefanie Schäfer identifies as central to the development of Hiroshima's ruins as a tourist site.[77] Schäfer argues that city officials consciously made atomic tourism a centerpiece of reconstruction and that tourism had been 'matched' with 'atomic memory culture' already at the first Peace ceremony in 1947.[78] Indeed, not only the admonitory power but also the tourism draw of the Atomic Bomb Dome was responsible for its preservation.[79] Schäfer argues that the 'silence' about tourism in historiography on Hiroshima speaks to the need, especially in the context of dark tourism, to maintain a separation between commemoration and commercialism.[80] Otherwise, as in a *Time* magazine article that invoked the word to criticize the city for '"advertis[ing] its past misery" ... Calling Hiroshima "touristic" with one stroke delegitimized Hiroshima and all it meant.'[81]

Indeed, this kind of delegitimation is just what occurs in the 1959 film *Hiroshima mon amour*, where the French Woman's futile effort not to forget is accompanied in the script by shots of '*Shops with hundreds of scale models of the Palace of Industry, the only monument whose twisted skeleton remained standing after the bomb – and was afterward preserved*' along with '*A busload of Japanese tourists. Tourists on Peace Square. A cat crossing Peace Square*' (Figures 4.7 & 4.8).[82] In retrospect, we can readily identify nuclear touristic practices dating back to the beginning of the Cold War. At the time, they could only be processed negatively, the taboo 'pleasure' of dark tourism kept at arm's length by conjuring the image of the debased Atomic Bomb Dome, even as that same pleasure was consciously invoked by a Hiroshima city chronicle of 1952 concerned about the risk that the bomb site was part of a visit that could 'provide real pleasure.'[83] The Cold War rhetoric that would absolutely separate serious and engaged analysis from frivolous or alienated spectacle persists to this day; however, that

---

77 Stefanie Schäfer, 'From Geisha Girls to the Atomic Bomb Dome: Dark Tourism and the Formation of Hiroshima Memory,' *Tourist Studies* 16.4 (2016): 351–66.
78 Schäfer, 'Atomic Bomb Dome,' 354.
79 Schäfer, 'Atomic Bomb Dome,' 355.
80 Schäfer, 'Atomic Bomb Dome,' 357.
81 Schäfer, 'Atomic Bomb Dome,' 358.
82 Duras, *Hiroshima*, 23. Curiously but perhaps unsurprisingly given Resnais's background in documentary, his film substituted Duras's image of plastic domes – doubtless one of Vizenor's sources for *Hiroshima Bugi* (see Chapter 2 above) – for a series of shots of the 'actual' ruined dome and a shot of an 'Atomic Tours' bus.
83 *Hiroshima shisei yōran, Overview of the Municipal Administration Hiroshima* (Hiroshima: Hiroshimashi, 1952), 256; qtd Schäfer, 'Atomic Bomb Dome,' 357.

Figure 4.7 The hidden face of nuclear tourism during the Cold War: 'Atomic Tour' bus in *Hiroshima mon amour*.

Figure 4.8 Nuclear tourists make their way to the Atomic Bomb Dome in the center background in *Hiroshima mon amour*.

164   *After the end*

rhetoric today is one among a number of available positionalities rather than the only one.

The more extreme form of dark tourism in both physiological and ethical terms is the visit to sites still dangerous for their radioactivity; such tourism is exemplified in the flourishing infrastructure that brings visitors into the Exclusion Zone around Chornobyl, which, like Hiroshima, features a unique nuclear dome. Popularized by genre movies, TV shows, and videogames, the sixty-kilometer-diameter Exclusion Zone is currently visited by tens of thousands of tourists a year, nearly all of them men.[84] Relentlessly scavenged by the local population but repurposed only to the degree of its preservation as a paradoxically pristine ruin and reliquary of nuclear disaster suitable as 'staged sets of the tragedy'[85] for disaster selfies and postapocalyptic spectacle, the Exclusion Zone has proved equally irresistible to chroniclers of nuclear tourism. Recounting his visit at the climax of his book *Notes from an Apocalypse*, O'Connell uses the occasion to attempt to parse what we could call the predictable ontological allure of the site for his fellow tourists as 'a spectacle of abandonment more vivid than anyplace on Earth' providing photo ops for 'the message ... I have been here, and I have felt the melancholy weight of this poisoned place. (#Chernobyl #amazing #melancholy #nucleardisaster).'[86] As urban explorer Bradley Garrett queries of his 'fellow trespassers' in the 'Coda' of his own book on *Building for the End Times* from 'the center of the doomed city of Pripyat ... "Is this what the world would look like after the apocalypse?"'[87] Belarusian oral historian Svetlana Alexievich concludes something similar at the end of her collection of interviews with Chornobyl survivors. 'These people had already seen what for everyone else is still unknown,' she explains. 'I felt like I was recording the future.'[88]

Although articulated solely in terms of commodified desires and expressed through the alienated form of the self-serving photo and the sensationalistic frame of the packaged tour, the impulse behind disaster tourism does not appear fundamentally different from Alexievich's response or Garrett's question. For Alexievich, dwelling on Chornobyl is both the logical conclusion of a life spent 'travel[ing] among other people's suffering' and something more intimate, because 'here I'm just as much a witness as the others. My

---

84 O'Connell, *Notes from an Apocalypse*, 192.
85 Bradley Garrett, *Bunker: Building for the End Times* (New York: Scribner, 2020), 275–6.
86 O'Connell, *Notes from an Apocalypse*, 195.
87 Garrett, *Building for the End Times*, 269–70.
88 Svetlana Alexievich, *Voices from Chernobyl: The Oral History of a Nuclear Disaster*, trans. Keith Gessen (Dallas, TX: Dalkey Archive Press, 2005 [1997]), 240.

Life in the ontological bunker

165

life is part of this event. I live here, with all of this.'[89] Garrett similarly marks Chornobyl as the experiential endpoint of an ethnographic investigation. Written with the goal of 'saturat[ing] myself in disaster,' Garrett's survey of doomsday prepping fittingly caps a globetrotting itinerary of apocalypse research with 'the most surreal experience I'd ever had. ... We'd survived traversing the ruins of the future.'[90] An ontological deep dive into the bunkered present, Garrett's visit to Chornobyl, as also his book, concludes with 'the later realization that ... the Exclusion Zone had trained me well for the future global disaster that awaited us: the COVID-19 pandemic. Radiation and viruses are cousins in disaster.'[91] As environmental historian Kate Brown insists in *Manual for Survival*, critical contemplation of the Chornobyl Zone is an essential 'Guide to the Future.'[92] Like Garrett, Brown finds a warning in her explorations and research. Rather than preppers or explorers, her subjects are individuals who 'soldiered on in contaminated territories' and those 'who refused to accept the assurances of the Soviet survival manuals' and studied on the ground the effects of radioactivity on human health; both experiences, Brown argues, constitute essential resources for the large proportion of the world's population who are 'exposed over their lifetimes to chronic doses of man-made radiation.'[93]

O'Connell's sense of Chornobyl as the culmination of his growing awareness of the stakes of his research project and his self-accusing conclusion that 'I myself am the apocalypse of which I speak' lead him to reflect on whether he is 'any less ethically compromised' in his Chornobyl tourism 'because I had come in search of poetic imagery, or of sociocultural insight?'[94] O'Connell implicitly contrasts his and his fellow tourists' experience of 'apocalyptic kitsch' with those of the deadpan tour guide Igor, who has led these tours seven days a week for eight years, calls himself 'a slave to money,' and sums up his life in one word as 'This'; with those of the '140 or so permanent residents ... who decided they would rather risk the consequences of returning to the only land they'd ever known than live healthy but miserable lives in the government-provided apartments in inner-city Kiev'; and with those of the pair of kestrels, 'spiraling ghosts of the sky' for which 'There was no division between human and nonhuman ... There was only nature. Only the

---

89 Alexievich, *Voices from Chernobyl*, 239.
90 Garrett, *Building for the End Times*, 10, 277.
91 Garrett, *Building for the End Times*, 277.
92 Kate Brown, *Manual for Survival: A Chernobyl Guide to the Future* (New York: Norton, 2019).
93 Brown, *Manual for Survival*, 301, 307–8, 312.
94 O'Connell, *Notes from an Apocalypse*, 9, 188.

Figure 4.9 Dwelling in a postapocalyptic landscape: one of the inhabitants who decided to return to their home in the Chornobyl Exclusion Zone.

world remained, and the things that were in it' (Figure 4.9).[95] In the end, the Exclusion Zone around Chornobyl proves no different from anywhere else in a world everywhere divided between the bunkered and the exposed. 'My discomfort in being here,' O'Connell concludes, 'had less to do with the risk of contamination than with the sense of myself as the contaminant.'[96]

The only truly anomalous structure in the Exclusion Zone – although evidently of less interest to most of the tourists than the abandoned Ferris Wheel, the photogenic ruins of the once model city of Prypiat, or the Elephant's Foot, 'the holy of holies, the most toxic object on the planet ... an accretion of fissile material that had burnt through the concrete floor of the reactor building to the basement beneath, cooled and hardened into a monstrous mass' – and also the only part of it postdating the accident is 'the immense dome of steel and concrete known as the "New Safe Confinement"' that

---

95 O'Connell, *Notes from an Apocalypse*, 204, 191, 208, 220. See also the sentiments expressed by Markiyan Kamysh in *Stalking the Atomic City*, trans. Hanna Leliv and Reilly Costigan Humes (London: Pushkin Press, 2022 [2015]) and by Igor Oprya, whose anarchist collective AVO organizes raves and modifies the landscape in protest against the corruption of official Zone tours (in Darmon Richter, *Chernobyl: A Stalker's Guide* (London: FUEL, 2020)).
96 O'Connell, *Notes from an Apocalypse*, 206.

Life in the ontological bunker 167

Figure 4.10 The 'New Safe Confinement' that covers Reactor Number 4 in the radioactive heart of the Chornobyl Exclusion Zone, viewed through the new growth of a once urban region.

covers Reactor Number 4 (Figure 4.10).[97] 'The result of a vast engineering project involving twenty-seven countries,' the dome, '360 feet tall at its apex' and 886 feet wide, is 'the largest movable object on the planet.'[98] As a collective, humanitarian effort and as a feat of engineering, the dome, while its shape was likely dictated by practical concerns, also embodies, like the Atomic Bomb Dome in Hiroshima, the principle of survivance that equally dwells in the ruins of the nuclear age even as it just as easily participates in the circulation of apocalyptic kitsch. It also, for Markiyan Kamysh, erstwhile stalker, current thrillseeker, and self-identified member of the generation the same age as the explosion, represents the apotheosis of Chornobyl's debasement.[99] 'The worst thing,' concludes Kamysh in his memoir, 'is that the new sarcophagus may become the next symbol of the Zone – this huge, ugly garage, and I feel sick at the thought that, in a decade, a new generation will grow up considering this barbarity a symbol of the Chornobyl meltdown.'[100]

97 O'Connell, *Notes from an Apocalypse*, 215–16.
98 O'Connell, *Notes from an Apocalypse*, 215.
99 Kamysh, *Stalking the Atomic City*, 4.
100 Kamysh, *Stalking the Atomic City*, 80.

168   *After the end*

Kinmen and Matsu revisited: retrofitting, repurposing, and appropriation

Although there is nothing of the dome in them, we find historical engagement and alienated spectacle in the civil defense networks of Taiwan, while the ongoing functionality of Switzerland's network militates against appropriation and Albania's hearty rejection of the historical associations of its 750,000 concrete bunkers was long signaled by an almost complete lack of memorialization. Bereft of typical urban amenities, the militarized and spartan form of urbanism practiced in the hand-excavated underground cities into which Kinmen (132 km²) and Matsu (12 km²) had been transformed during the Cold War echoes those in many speculative fictions of antinuclear bunkers and supershelters of the period. But today, fortresses and tunnels have been made over as parks and monuments, visited by busloads of ROC and PRC tourists, and supplemented with mannequins staging daily activities, explanatory maps and plaques, and activity rooms for younger visitors to color in tracings of wind lions, the local protective deity.[101] As in postwar Vietnam, the village tunnels have been 'widened and their walls smoothed out to make them safe for tourists' (Figures 3.4 & 3.5).[102] A 'Landmine Theme Park' on nearby Little Kinmen, or Lieyu, Island, complete with 'a tunnel filled with mines and warning signs' and 'a 'removal crew' of mannequins dressed in orange uniforms and protective gear,' has received thousands of visitors each month since opening in 2012.[103] The Siwei Tunnel is on a smaller scale than Jhaishan, but next to it, in the Jugon tunnel where an underground hospital used to be located, sits the high-design Lieyu/Kinmen National Park Visitors Center. The accomplished conversion artfully combines the roughhewn stone of the walls and arching ceiling with neatly presented information bytes about the islands and their geography, history, food, and culture (Figure 4.11).

Adaptive reuse of these enduring features of the landscape elucidates many of the meanings attached to these undergrounds. Other adaptations appropriate the literal stuff of war. The studio of Maestro Wu forges world-class kitchen knives from the high-grade steel used in the hundreds of thousands of propaganda shells launched from across the bay by PRC guns

---

101 According to a 'host' at the Jhaishan tunnel, a horseshoe-shaped passage large enough to shelter boats, the split between mainland and Taiwanese visitors at the time was about 50/50 (conversation with the author, 14 June 2012).

102 Szonyi, *Cold War Island*, 108.

103 Staff writer, 'Former Kinmen Minefield Now a Tourist Attraction,' *Taipei Times* (1 Jan. 2014): http://web.archive.org/web/20220817094649/http://www.taipeitimes.com/News/taiwan/archives/2014/01/01/2003580269.

Life in the ontological bunker 169

Figure 4.11 High-tech conversion in a low-tech space. Jugon tunnel, formerly an underground hospital for Republic of China forces on Little Kinmen Island; now the Lieyu/Kinmen National Park Visitors Center.

(Figure 4.12). Elsewhere, shell casings can be found incorporated into guardrails, perimeter fences, benches, and playgrounds, taking literally the antinuclear protest rallying cry 'swords into ploughshares' to assert that the deadly war of the past has been overcome and turned towards peaceful ends. While Kinmen continues to expand its newly legitimized role as a trading fulcrum between the PRC and the ROC, the residents of the more isolated Matsu archipelago voted in 2012 to allow a casino and resort to be developed on the two largest islands. No doubt, such a casino, too, would take advantage of the subterranean heritage of the island site as it designs its own artificial paradise.[104] Kinmen and Matsu are celebrated for their local *kaoliang* (sorghum) liquor, and distilleries on both islands have transformed nearby tunnels into cold storage – and branding – for their

---

104 At time of writing, the initiative remained stalled, awaiting authorization by Taiwan's Parliament ('The First Casino in Taiwan Is to Be Opened in 2019,' *Slots* (15 July 2018): http://web.archive.org/web/20220118051200/http://connexions-southcentral.org/the-first-casino-in-taiwan-is-to-be-opened-in-2019/).

Figure 4.12 A knifemaker converts spent shells from the PRC into kitchen implements in the Kinmen studio of Maestro Wu.

wares (Figure 4.13). Along with liquor, underground brothels were another traditional vice long indulged on the islands. Back in 1991, the Chinese artist Cai Guo-Qiang played on this history when he proposed transforming the still active Kinmen bunkers into 'love hotels'; the 2014 film drama *Paradise in Service* used the Jhaishan tunnel as one setting for its brothel-based plot (Figure 4.14; see also Chapter 3 and Figure 3.3).

Guo-Qiang was also responsible for the 2004 *Bunker Museum of Art*, an eighteen-artist installation in decommissioned Kinmen bunkers that displayed a combination of antiwar sentiments, historical reckoning, and ideas for making some kind of positive artistic, religious, or cultural meaning out of the inorganic relics of the Cold War.[105] Local filmmaker Dong Zhenliang had anticipated Guo-Qiang's multimedia exhibition when he held a small film festival in a bunker in the early 1990s.[106] One of the installations in

---

105 Cai Guo-Qiang, *Bunker Museum of Contemporary Art, Kinmen Island: A Permanent Sanctuary for Art in a Demilitarized Zone* (Kinmen, Taiwan: Kinmen County Government, 2006).
106 Wang, email communication.

Life in the ontological bunker

Figure 4.13 Marketing the vices of Tunnel 88: display window in the subterranean shop of the Matsu Distillery, in its present location on Nangan Island since 1970.

Figure 4.14 Tourists in Jhaishan Tunnel, Kinmen Island, where it opens to the sea.

172   *After the end*

Bunker Museum of Art, Wang Wen-Chih's *Dragon Dares Tiger Lair* in the Command Center and surrounding areas of the Nanshan Fortification No. 2 Bunker, extended the bunker with a bamboo and rattan network of tunnels and tower shaped like an artillery shell. The open weaving and exposure of the new spaces play with the spatial categories the bunker relies on. They are simultaneously light and dark, hidden and exposed, inside and outside. The use of natural fibers suggests a desire to integrate the former war zone into its natural environment and somehow to purify the site. Like the child pictured in the tunnel in an exhibition catalog photograph, the materials are resilient rather than hardened; like the child, they find the playful spirit in a space created for war. A similar spirit is invoked in contributions to the exhibition by local schoolchildren. Shikou Elementary School's *Bunker of the Wind Lion God* ambiguously invokes a traditional guardian spirit of the island; the invocation acknowledges the protective presence embodied by the military installations while also praying for protection from the fear elicited by that same presence. The bunker fantasy continues its dual and contradictory function, looking at once backwards and forwards.

Creative or commercial reuse of former fortifications remains highly contested on Kinmen, according to Ting-chi Wang, founder of Local Methodology, a nongovernmental organization dedicated to promoting Kinmen culture, who spent four months on a travel grant visiting former war sites in Europe. In comparison, Wang explained:

> The local govt is yet to figure out what to do with them besides turning them into museums or tourist centers. Private proprietor is one factor of the delay in more creative and open uses but lack of financially sustainable ideas from the govt is another. As far as I know, though, starting from this year a few will be released for private businesses. My prediction is that many will turn into cafes, restaurants, shops, or even artist studios not necessarily related to the history or memory of the structures themselves.[107]

On demilitarized Matsu, Wang noted, a 'grassroot museum' had recently opened, along with a café and a bed-and-breakfast inside decommissioned bunkers.

Switzerland revisited: retrofitting, repurposing, and appropriation

Because much of the system remains active, there has thus been less active redevelopment of the Swiss underground for tourism or creative reuse than in other once heavily fortified areas such as Albania, Germany, the United

---

107 Wang, email communication.

Figure 4.15 The forbidding entrance to Felsenhotel La Claustra, Airolo, Switzerland.

States, or the Kinmen and Matsu archipelagoes in the Taiwan Strait. A secret fortress in the St Gotthard mountain was declassified in 2001 when its location was exposed by an attempted break-in.[108] Since 2012, it has become a popular attraction, offering a ride on an underground cable car, massive crystals, and a tour of one of Switzerland's largest underground defensive fortifications.[109] A few minutes' drive away is the luxurious four-star Felsenhotel (lit. 'Rock-' or 'Rocky-Hotel') La Claustra, ensconced deep within another decommissioned bunker (Figures 4.15 & 4.16).[110] Opened in 2004 as 'a kind of meditative post-modern monastery' complete with restaurant and conference facilities, the hotel went bankrupt in 2010 for

---

108 Jennifer Nalewicki, 'Switzerland's Historic Bunkers Get a New Lease on Life,' *Smithsonian.com* (23 March 2016): http://web.archive.org/web/20221202134515/https://www.smithsonianmag.com/travel/switzerlands-bunkers-get-new-lease-life-180958233/.
109 'Sasso San Gotthardo': http://web.archive.org/web/20230309145901/https://www.sasso-sangottardo.ch/; accessed 31 Aug. 2023.
110 Nalewicki, 'Switzerland's Historic Bunkers.'

Figure 4.16 A banquet room inside the Felsenhotel La Claustra, Airolo, Switzerland.

lack of visitors, was sold at auction for $1000 two years later, and reopened to guests at the end of 2013.[111] 'Everything was perfect for a Hotel in a bunker,' reported one guest online, rather enigmatically, as if the idea went without saying.[112] At the low end of the hospitality spectrum, conceptual artists and entrepreneurs Frank and Patrik Riklin and Daniel Charbonnier opened the 29-euro-a-night 'Zero Star Hostel' in a former bunker in Teufen, in 2009.[113] After a year, it was converted into a museum, accessed through

---

111 Lyssandra Sears, 'Subterranean Hotel Sold for Rock Bottom Price,' *The Local.ch* (18 July 2012): http://web.archive.org/web/20220810193717/https://www.thelocal.ch/20120718/underground-hotel-almost-given-away-at-auction/; 'Felsenhotel La Claustra,' *Booking.com*: http://web.archive.org/web/20170330070254/http://www.booking.com/hotel/ch/felsenhotel-la-claustra.en-gb.html; accessed 31 Aug. 2023. As of April 2018, one night for two persons was going for €550.
112 'Felsenhotel La Claustra.'
113 'Null Stern Hotel – "The Only Star Is You,"' http://web.archive.org/web/20180121174424/http://nullsternhotel.ch/now.html; accessed 31 Aug. 2023

Life in the ontological bunker 175

the manhole cover that was its original emergency entrance.[114] The artists' later installation/enterprise turned the original conception on its head: an open-air 'room … [in] the majestic Swiss Alps in Saillon in the Valais,' complete with a butler ready to find the lodgers alternate accommodations in the case of inclement weather.[115] The tongue-in-cheek play between luxury and austerity, secrecy and openness suggests that Swiss fortifications since 1989 have retained an ongoing presence in everyday life and a productive function within the political process, even as a baseline of discomfort with the concept persists. As discussed in Chapter 3, while the built environment of the Redoubt remains among the most active in the world, its political underpinnings have been cited by philosopher Elaine Scarry as 'one of the few pieces of evidence we have that the right of exit (as well as the "right to exist") is still imaginable in the nuclear age.' Indeed, Scarry argues that emergency preparedness is, in fact, a fundamental component of organized society, even predating democracy.[116] Having outlived its Cold War identity, the Swiss underground suggests a different way to approach the ruins of bunker architecture that persist across the world.

Albania revisited: retrofitting, repurposing, and appropriation

In contrast with the Swiss model, whose imaginary is influential primarily in its persistent survival and ongoing utility, the Albanian model is striking in the ways it has managed to find new uses for a traumatically useless past as visually inescapable as Switzerland's continues to be out of sight. The faded and vandalized shells of the bunkers (in a struggling economy, the reinforcing iron is too valuable to ignore) testify to the evanescence of once mighty institutions (Plate 5). The more remote the location, the more pressing is the bunker's status as evidence of the presence of human labor throughout and as part of nature. The ruined bunker does not discard its message of human domination; rather, it reminds us that, while individual empires or regimes may fall to ruin, their meaningful traces persist. Closer to human habitation, the bunkers have been put to more diverse uses than as a dwindling supply of raw materials. Climate controlled and sheltered from the elements, the bunkers are useful to farmers as storage and as stabling for sheep and cows (Plate 4). Tipped into the sea, their solid mass makes for excellent

114 Nalewicki, 'Switzerland's Historic Bunkers.'
115 'Null Stern Hotel,' *uniqhotels.com*: http://web.archive.org/web/20230111140518/ https://www.uniqhotels.com/null-stern-hotel; accessed 14 March 2023.
116 Scarry, *Thinking in an Emergency*, 69.

jetties and breakwaters (Plate 6). Along the coast, bunkers have been painted with the bright colors and designs beloved by beach bums the world over (Plate 7). Along main roads, bunkers sport graffiti, painted advertisements, and stenciled political slogans.[117] While the steady flow of global capital into urban centers and resorts such as Tirana, Vlorë, and Durrës has brought enough financial incentive to remove most of the mushrooms from them, in the rest of the country, the slower and more uneven pace of development has made appropriation the rule of the day. What was always useful about the bunkers – their strength and durability, their domed shape, their shelter and security – is reincorporated into the contemporary lived space. Like much else about Albanian lives in a still-struggling economy, there may not be much beauty in them, but there is use.

Perhaps the most consistently aesthetic appropriations of the bunkers are found along the seaside. In his *Subterra* project, artist Wayne Barrar makes it clear that the act of photography is equally a form of intervention into the landscape. As he put it, 'imaging any landscape (including any space) is imaging a contested space in some way – all photography of land is essentially political!'[118] Barrar's Albanian photos are especially adept at capturing the ruined bunkers as mediating spaces between nature and technology.[119] In one photo, the shape of the foreground bunker echoes both the line of cloud-covered mountains rising behind it and the gas station down the road to the left. Half of the bunker roof sprouts clods of turf and shelters wildflowers, while the other half exposes crumbling cement akin to the scattered gravel of the road leading back into town. In another, the foregrounded iron buckles of a 'tortoise' so remote it has escaped vandalization effortlessly summon up the political history of a cleft in the distant mountains leading to the border with Greece (Plate 8). Terracotta tiling adds a southern Mediterranean flourish to a bar near that same border (Plate 9). Other photos testify to the quotidian presence of the bunkers. The rectangular headlights of a beat-up Audi (Albania is full of old-model luxury cars from northern Europe that mysteriously made their way southward during the height of political chaos and organized crime in the 1990s) repeat the empty gaze of the bunker to its right; both are wrapped in canvas, although the Audi sports the added comfort of a multicolored blanket (Plate 10).

---

117 For additional examples of the uses and adaptations discussed here and below, see especially the webpages of photographers Wayne Barrar (https://waynebarrar.com/other-projects/) and Robert Hackman (www.robhackman.com/Bunker-Albania/Statement—English/1/caption).

118 Julieanna Preston, '*Subterra*: Interior Economies of Underground Space. Conversations with Photographer Wayne Barrar,' *Idea Journal* (2011): 34–48, at 38.

119 Barrar, 'Hoxha's Bunkers' (2011), https://waynebarrar.com/other-projects/.

Exposed wires, a clothesline strung across the tiny patio, and a satellite dish complete the picture of a typically confused instance of global capitalism in a developing country. The bunker, as always, is perfectly at home and utterly out of place, reminding us about everything in this picture that we should not be taking for granted. Or there is the hard-working man on the seaside at Durrës, loading rubble into a wheelbarrow (Plate 11). The pile of rubble has itself settled, by the laws of physics and the zeal of the photographer's eye, into the temporary shape of a mushroom bunker. We can imagine its gradual disappearance from the scene as the worker transforms it into something new, offscreen. Meanwhile, the frame is dominated by a complex and labyrinthine construction which holds at its center, just visible, the shape of an artillery bunker that apparently has determined the form of the layers of blue-painted stucco and wood that have accreted around it as the result, presumably, of this same man's prior activity. A satellite dish tucked away in the corner suggests he is doing alright, while a tidy fence and well-tended flowering shrubs glow with pride in a home built around a bunker.

While these examples certainly appropriate Albania's history as part of their attempt to attract custom or otherwise make a living, there is nothing necessarily self-conscious or reflective about them. On the beaches as on the farm, the local inhabitants are making everyday use of what the world provides them, whether as a distinctive flourish or as a practical space. More recently, however, evidence began appearing that Albanians along with foreign visitors were also consciously appreciating the creative potential offered by the sheer number of remaining bunkers. The 'Concrete Mushrooms' project, devoted to 'The re-use of Albania's 750,000 inherited bunkers,' regards the bunkers and their physical visibility as a way of calling attention more broadly to questions of 'territorial transformations and development strategies' as Albania becomes ever more reincorporated into the rest of Europe and subject to the pressures of transnational capital.[120] Noting the preponderance of bunkers in locations favored by tourists – mountains, beaches, and urban perimeters – and the attraction they hold for those tourists, graduate students Elian Stefa and Gyler Mydyti proposed developing them into a nationwide infrastructure for promoting and supporting tourism. Depending on size and location, they could be readily and cheaply converted into everything from information points and news and souvenir kiosks to B&Bs, cafés, and even public toilets (effectively sanitizing an already ubiquitous practice). As the narrator in Martijn Payens's documentary *Mushrooms*

---

120 Stefa and Mydyti, *Concrete Mushrooms: Reusing Albania's 750,000 Abandoned Bunkers* (Barcelona: Actar, 2013). See also the project's Facebook page.

178   *After the end*

of Concrete (2010) puts it, over footage of a 'Bunkerfest' of music, food, and dancing around a rural artillery bunker repainted in psychedelic colors, 'We have to live with these bunkers, give them a new destination.'[121]

For a younger generation visiting from abroad – Payens made the documentary as a Dutch student studying at filmmaker Kujtim Çashku's Marubi Film & Multimedia School in Tirana – or for younger Albanians seeking ways to network with the rest of Europe through revitalizing and reinterpreting their own country's heritage, the bunkers are the perfect emblem of a new relationship between past and future. As designer Kejsi Rama argued in a thesis for the University of Strathclyde in Glasgow, Scotland, the decommissioned military base on the island of Sazan offers potential for development of a natural environment that became part of a Marine National Park in 2002, an archaeological history dating back to antiquity, and an abandoned built environment that includes an island-wide 'underground network of … reinforced concrete tunnels, spacious enough to comfortably shelter and protect 150 families [that] … offer[s] a peculiar, unexplored route for visitors into the dark secrets of the military past of Sazan.'[122] Bed & Bunker, a related venture of university architecture students in the northern resort town of Tale, was to be a hostel in a converted seaside bunker; it was abandoned just before its planned opening, citing too much pressure over money for a non-commercial enterprise.[123]

One venture that did get off the ground is the memorials and two museums established in a park and two former government shelters in Tirana by the capital city's artist-mayor and later prime minister Edi Rama. All three projects mediate between the country's past and present and the outside world in fraught and controversial ways that raise questions similar to the ones elicited by the Atomic Bomb Dome in Hiroshima. In March 2013, a memorial complex was created across from the prime minister's building by the critic Fatos Lubonja and artist Ardian Isufi. The Postbllok Memorial to Communist Isolation – the name plays on the Albanian word for 'checkpoint' and 'Blloku,' or 'the Block,' the name of the gated enclave of Hoxha's elite and now an upscale and trendy neighborhood – consists of three elements: 'a set of concrete pillars from the gallery of the Spaç forced labor mining camp; a piece of the Berlin Wall; and a concrete bunker that once

---

121 *Mushrooms of Concrete*, wr. and dir. Martijn Payens, 2010: http://web.archive.org/web/20221205233059/https://aeon.co/videos/albania-built-750000-bunkers-for-a-war-that-never-came-now-what.
122 Rama, 'Transforming a Former Military Island,' 11, 67–8.
123 Claus Hecking, 'Albanien: Im Land der 173.371 Bunker,' *Spiegel Online* (16 May 2017): http://web.archive.org/web/20220321162842/https://www.spiegel.de/reise/europa/albanien-im-land-der-173-371-bunker-a-1146477.html.

guarded the entrance to "the Block."'[124] Meanwhile Bunk'Art was opened in late 2014 in the vast continuance-of-government bunker secretly excavated for Hoxha and his top officials during the 1970s.[125] The supershelter had been built underground on five levels containing 106 rooms and a large assembly hall. The hall is now used for concerts; twenty-four of the rooms have been converted into a museum and art gallery, some containing 'authentic' reconstructions of the bunker's original spatial practices and others containing rotating exhibits inspired by the site; and entrance and exit tunnels were dug to supplement the original entrance through one of the ministry buildings.[126] Bunk'Art 2 opened two years later in the largest bunker in the city center, just off Skanderbeg Square, where it connected the various ministries beneath protective walls of '240 cm of rock, iron, and concrete, with five armored entrances.'[127] Like its predecessor, Bunk'Art 2 is dedicated both to reconstructive history and to contemporary art; in this case, it commemorates 'the victims of the communist terror.' Also like its predecessor, it has a newly built entrance, through a new street-level artillery bunker the underside of which is affixed with striations of photographs end to end of victims of the Hoxha regime alternating with the bare concrete, matching, like many bunker conversions, the segmented construction of the 'orange' bunkers.

The Bunk'Art conversions presented a natural target for opponents of Rama's government. In 2015, the new bunker construction was set on fire during demonstrations by the oppositional Democratic Party and holes were opened in its shell.[128] The damage was left unrepaired; one might argue that the vandalized surface brought the new bunker more in line with its Hoxhian legacy. Critics have written forcefully against the cultural politics embedded

---

124 Raino Isto, 'The Monument as Ruin: Natality, Spectrality, and the History of the Image in the Tirana Independence Monument,' *[sic]-A Journal of Literature, Culture, and Literary Translation* 2.6 (2016): http://web.archive.org/web/20220717065705/https://www.sic-journal.org/Article/Index/401.

125 Ministry of Defence, Republic of Albania, 'The museum exhibition "BUNK'ART" is opened,' *Newsroom* (4 Nov. 2014): http://web.archive.org/web/20150718192058/http://www.mod.gov.al/eng/index.php/newsroom/408-the-museum-exhibition-bunk-art-is-opened.

126 'Bunk'Art,' *Atlas Obscura* (30 March 2017): http://web.archive.org/web/20230225002106/https://www.atlasobscura.com/places/bunkart.

127 Vincent W. J. van Gerven Oei, 'A Response to Carlo Bollino's "Defense" of Bunk'Art 2,' *Exit.al* (6 Dec. 2016): http://web.archive.org/web/20200421031448/https://exit.al/en/2016/12/06/a-response-to-carlo-bollinos-defense-of-bunkart-2/.

128 Raino Isto, '"An Itinerary of the Creative Imagination": Bunk'Art and the Politics of Art and Tourism in Remembering Albania's Socialist Past,' *Cultures of History Forum* (2017): www.cultures-of-history.uni-jena.de/politics/albania/an-itinerary; accessed 14 March 2023.

180   *After the end*

in these spaces. Criticism has focused on the politicized and monetized elements of Bunk'Art: that the artistic practices allude to and reinforce Rama's public persona as politician/artist and that the branding, admission policy, and primary interpellation of a neoliberal tourist subject help line the pockets and further the interests of Italian journalist and entrepreneur Carlo Belloni.[129] Isto cites the 'touristic conception of historical experience' of the exhibitions in Bunk'Art, the ways they 'explicitly shap[e] memory as an aesthetic phenomenon,' and their primary address to the younger generation and visiting tourists as neoliberal citizens of the world rather than to survivors of Hoxha's regime working through its past traumas.[130] Van Gerven Oei's ad hominem attacks on the design and motivations of Bunk'Art 2 focus more directly on distortion, borrowing, and falsehoods. Van Gerven Oei takes issue, for example, with the claim that the shelter was intended as an antinuclear bunker when that language does not appear in the archive and when, despite its concrete reinforcements, it would not have survived a direct hit.[131]

Neither critique is incorrect nor is it inaccurate; they demonstrate the degree to which the bunkers remain a privileged site for political discourse within Albania. The critiques also clarify what is differently at stake in Rama's conversion of these spaces than in the earlier reckonings by Çashku and Kadaré discussed in Chapter 3, which used the bunkers as ontological spaces essentially to reverse the terms of their meaning. Isto and van Gerven Oei similarly treat the bunkers as an ontological record of the totalitarian regime that has not yet been resolved; their stance echoes the common critical focus on a single, if important, element of the bunker's complex legacy. In critic John Beck's formulation, 'A wrecked bunker is never safe since its very presence speaks to the continuation of its power elsewhere.'[132] We find an analogous response in the way the Democratic Party appropriated van Gerven Oei's essay to attack the 'fake bunker' of its political opponent. As Rama clearly recognized, the bunkers constitute a unique opportunity not only for global branding but for infrastructural development that allows the country to retain a different kind of autonomy than simply opening up its gates to the developers of global capitalism. To the media-savvy youth behind and interpellated by these projects, the bunkers can either present Albania to the world according to the bleak allegories of Kadaré and Çashku

---

129 Isto, 'Itinerary'; van Gerven Oei, 'Bunk'Art 2: A Nuclear Attack on Meaning, *Exit. al*, 21 November 2016: https://exit.al/en/bunkart-2-a-nuclear-attack-on-meaning/; accessed 14 March 2023; van Gerven Oei, 'Response.'
130 Isto, 'Itinerary.'
131 Van Gerven Oei, 'Nuclear Attack on Meaning' and 'Response.'
132 Beck, 'Concrete Ambivalence,' 87.

Life in the ontological bunker

or they can convert that allegory into the spatial production underpinning a different kind of infrastructure and a different kind of allegory for a new generation.

Like the inclusion of a piece of the Berlin Wall in the Postbllok Memorial, Rama's twin redevelopments explicitly position the Hoxha era within a global bunker fantasy, acknowledging the weird specificity that makes them such a powerful tourist attraction while arguing that the way to make sense of them moving forward is through dialogue rather than isolation. The two Bunk'Art projects stress that in the factual sense this dialogue is more aesthetic than historical. The overt acknowledgment of a hybridity of the authentic and the inauthentic challenges the illusion of 'staged authenticity' that Schäfer finds in the Atomic Bomb Dome in Hiroshima and argues is especially necessary to the mechanisms of dark tourism.[133] We find a similar negotiation at work in the Bunker Museum of Contemporary Art on Kinmen discussed above, where the different projects share a goal – the aesthetic renewal of a fixed and traumatic spatial meaning – with results ranging from scathingly critical to dreamily redemptive. Those installations would not exist without the fascination exerted by the strangeness of this subterranean past that equally drives more conventional tourism, nor are they distinct from monetization. The shell casings Maestro Wu hammers into knives on Kinmen are a potent symbol of renewal while also a saleable product and souvenir. Just as plastic domes proliferate in Hiroshima, so miniature bunker paperweights are for sale in gift shops around Albania.

Isto defines Bunk'Art in terms of the 'unique combination of the rhetoric of tourism and the logic of entrepreneurship it employs'; van Gerven Oei describes the absurdity of an entrance fee that is waived if the visitor deems she has been 'persecuted by the former regime,' no proof required.[134] The neoliberal model destabilizes the hardened categories and verities of Cold War history and offers in their place a world of unstable borders between economics, aesthetics, and politics. But at the same time, neoliberalism also affords a new and similarly unstable vision of the past. There is potential in the dissident temporality and ontological openness the bunker fantasy helps us to localize in the present through a new relationship to the past; there is also substantial risk. Stefa and Mydyti's project, like Rama's, is conceived as an economic pragmatist's negotiation with the past and with the neoliberal outside world that has transformed that past. They propose ingenious if at times disingenuous alliances between preservationist and

133 Schäfer, 'Atomic Bomb Dome.'
134 Isto, 'Itinerary'; van Gerven Oei, 'Nuclear Attack on Meaning'; van Gerven Oei, 'Response.'

commercial interests, arguing that a self-reflective, democratic, and creative reuse of the past is preferable to the exclusionary, predatory, and exclusively monetary motivations of most developers. Isto and van Gerven Oei correctly identify the process and its risks; however, by addressing those risks solely from within the categories to which they seek to return, both critics misrecognize ways the ground of the conversation has in fact irrevocably shifted.

Rama and his associates explicitly link their project of 'museumiz[ing] the entire remaining network of the memory of the dark underworld of the communist dictatorship' within a broader movement that has seen 'All such spaces located in the countries of the former Soviet Bloc ... along with similar spaces in Western Europe ... turned into incredibly important European tourist destinations.'[135] This development would delineate a border that is not only 'geographic' but also temporal and epistemological, a border that 'divides the mistakes and failures of the past from the future.'[136] The epistemological bunker, in this post-1989 sense, promises shelter from the traumas and categories of the past even as it reminds us that we continue to inhabit the world created by it. Rather than emerging from that world, we remain within its parameters and must find ways of reworking them rather than simply being able to escape from them at will. Where the ontological bunker imagined by J. G. Ballard back in 1964 (see the Introduction) naturalizes the nuclear condition in order fully to study its phenomenological range, the epistemological bunker makes visible the bunker fantasy as a system of knowledge production.

Bunker tourism and late capitalism

As Rama and his speechwriter Falma Fshazi recognized and as Cold War officials in Hiroshima, Kinmen, and Nevada equally knew, these spaces exert a fascination that exceeds even as it derives from their stark ideological function. Although not identified or labeled as such at the time, nuclear tourism was mobilized to reinforce and to combat that ideology already during the Cold War. Those same ideologies remain deeply embedded in these spaces, especially when reimagined by government officials, as in

135 Isto, 'Itinerary.' According to Isto, 'This statement appeared, accompanied by images of the newly opened House of Leaves museum, on the Prime Minister's Facebook and Twitter accounts in late January 2015.' This museum, another of Rama's projects, is 'housed at the site where surveillance and torture were conducted during the socialist years' (Isto, 'Itinerary').

136 Isto, 'Itinerary,' quoting an article about 'places such as Bunk'Art and the House of Leaves' by Rama's speechwriter Falma Fshazi published on 26 Jan. 2015.

Rama's Tirana museumifications or in the Chinese government's closure of the Underground City in Beijing in the run-up to the 2008 Olympics because its state of disrepair, support of non-sanctioned tourism, and mixed use by shopkeepers, squatters, and others poorly reflected the sense of controlled containment for which it would have been designed.[137] As Edward Geist has documented from now-available archives, such lack of control was part of Soviet civil defense from the end of the Second World War; since most civilian and public shelters were 'little more than fortified basements,' regular use as 'root cellars, coal cellars, and industrial equipment storage' was permitted, as long as the shelters could be 'available for occupancy within 24–72 hours.'[138] In Switzerland especially from the late 1980s, private and public bunkers were frequently converted for private use and borrowed for public functions.[139] The literature of nuclear tourism deploys a variety of devices to distance its own interest in ruins, exploration, and the past from the toxic fantasies of control and MAD embedded in those same spaces. Nevertheless, the growing prevalence of these practices and their ever-greater prominence within or even as impetus for 'conventional' tourism itineraries argues for a broader and more conflicted set of motivations.

Because they invoke self-conscious reflection on the space they inhabit and, indeed, often draw attention to their structures from the art they exhibit, museum conversions are some of the most fraught and also some of the most deeply considered examples of bunker conversion. In addition to Tirana's Bunk'Art conversions, large-scale German bunkers in Berlin and Mussolini's bunker in Rome are now art galleries.[140] Munich's Museum of Urban and Contemporary Art opened in 'Art Bunker' in 2021 in a World War II shelter next door that had previously been repurposed as a hotel and a nightclub.[141] Established in 1937 to exhibit Nazi-approved art, the Haus der Kunst began exhibiting contemporary art full-time in 2002, and the fourteen subterranean rooms of its $292\,m^2$ air-raid shelter were reopened in 2011; fittingly, the inaugural exhibition was entitled 'Aschemünder' (the world's

---

137 Ross, *Waiting*, 92. A 2009 piece by Alex Hoban for *Vice*, while sensationalistic in the extreme, establishes that while the tunnels were now sealed, they remained accessible illegally to urban explorers and local squatters ('Chairman Mao's Underground City,' *Vice* (17 Nov. 2009): http://web.archive.org/web/20220323110923/https://www.vice.com/en/article/nnmk8b/chairman-maos-underground-city).

138 Geist, 'Mineshaft Gap,' 9.

139 Ziauddin, '(De)territorializing the Home,' 687.

140 Beck, 'Concrete Ambivalence,' 96. On the Boros collection in Berlin, see Sascha Engelmann and Harriet Hawkins, 'Bunker Art: Christian and Karen Boros Collection, Berlin,' in *Global Undergrounds*, ed. Dobraszczyk et al., 91–5.

141 'MUCA Bunker,' http://web.archive.org/web/20201205143613/https://www.muca.eu/en/exhibitions/preview-4/muca-bunker/; accessed 31 Aug. 2023.

Figure 4.17 The separate entrance to the 292 m² space in the former air-raid shelter beneath the Haus der Kunst, Munich. The basement bunker was converted for exhibition in 2011 in collaboration with the Goetz Collection.

ashes), a selection of film and video pieces around the theme of 'the recurring atrocity of war and human oppression' (Figure 4.17).[142] Tito's $4.6 billion supershelter outside of Sarajevo, known as D-0 ARK (Atomic War Command) Underground, was reopened in 2011 as host to a biennial of contemporary art.[143] According to the organizers, the seventy-thousand-square-foot facility remains under the control of the Bosnia and Herzegovina Ministry of Defence and visitors are taken around by soldiers based at the still active complex.[144]

---

142 Sabine Brantler, 'The Air-Raid Shelter in the Haus der Kunst,' in *Aschemünder: Sammlung Goetz im Haus der Kunst*, ed. Ingvild Goetz, Suzanne Toew, and Stephan Urbaschek (Munich: Hatje Cantz Verlag, 2011), 16–17; Goetz, 'Aschemünder,' in *Aschemünder*, ed. Goetz et al., 6–8, at 6.
143 Ginanne Brownell, 'A Sarajevo Bunker Takes on New Life as an Art Museum,' *New York Times* (5 Aug. 2011): www.nytimes.com/2011/08/06/arts/06iht-scsarajevo06.html?_r=1&pagewanted=print; accessed 22 April 2018.
144 Brownell, 'Sarajevo Bunker'; Biennial Foundation: http://web.archive.org/web/20230307193903/https://biennialfoundation.org/biennials/d-0-ark-biennial-bosnia-and-herzegovina/; accessed 22 April 2018.

Life in the ontological bunker   185

Beck similarly notes the government funding of a volunteer-based endeavor 'to record nearly 20,000 twentieth century anti-invasion defense sites across the UK' and a number of 'institutionalized "interventions" into militarized space' that 'normalize the bunker-as-artwork.'[145]

This situation, not dissimilar to the intersection of art, tourism, and military operations on Kinmen and Matsu or the Albanian government's direct investment in Tirana's art installations, underlines Beck's warning that 'achieved cultural dominance' reinforces the totalitarian elements of the bunker fantasy and that 'the disturbingly invisible has been made safe for view.' It equally suggests newly available space for 'oblique critical interrogation and an expression of persistent and deep ambivalence.'[146] But this situation should also remind us that the bunker fantasy has since its inception incorporated art, tourism, and military operations into its spectacles in this way with similarly mixed motivations and mixed results, from Disney's movies about the atom to artistic photos at the Nevada Test Site to plastic models of the Hiroshima Atomic Bomb Dome. As Kirsty Bell writes of the underwhelming experience of visiting the 'Berlin Story Bunker,' there's nothing to be gleaned from the 'half-hearted exhibition in these chilly subterranean rooms which gives a rough potted history of Berlin but little information about this particular bunker, or bunkers in general, or even about the Second World War, beyond the most well-rehearsed points. But the bunker itself is fact enough. As is the graffiti on its exterior walls, daubed in huge black capital letters – *WER BUNKER BAUT WIRFT BOMBEN* – those who build bunkers drop bombs.'[147] We can grasp the oppositional power of this art only as we attend to the ways it has always also participated in the spectacles it opposes.

Individual installations and temporary shows run the gamut from ancillary rooms in museal tunnels and fortifications to pop-up art in converted urban spaces to graffiti around the world, and they invoke a range of responses from complicit to oppositional. French filmmaker Agnès Varda, whose career spanned the Cold War and the post–Cold War, incorporated a bunker art installation into the 2017 documentary she and former graffiti artist JR made about their travels around France photographing local citizens and affixing their enlarged photos on nearby buildings and ruins. JR found a Normandy beach fortification that had fallen off the cliff and was perched in the sand below like a monolithic sculpture. During an interview with the mayor of the nearby village, we learn that in fact it had been pushed over,

---

145 Beck, 'Concrete Ambivalence,' 94, 96.
146 Beck, 'Concrete Ambivalence,' 97–8, 95.
147 Kirsty Bell, *The Undercurrents* (London: Fitzcarraldo, 2022), 162.

Figure 4.18 Bunker art on a Normandy beach, displaced in space and time by JR and Agnès Varda in *Visages Villages (Faces Places)*.

out of concern it would some day fall. Varda provides JR with a photo taken on a beach nearby in 1954 of a now-deceased model and friend from her early days as a photographer. He blows it up and adapts it to the space of the fallen bunker where the placement combines with the subject's pose to recall simultaneously a lounger in a beach chair and a stretched body bent under the full weight of the past (Figure 4.18). They return the next day to discover that the tide has washed away the image from the bunker. The bunker is permanent; the people are not. It is both unnatural and of nature, a fittingly transient commemoration of the artists' own experiences along this beach. As elsewhere in the movie, Varda and JR are unconcerned with making explicitly political statements or intervening forcefully in historical arguments. At the same time, their gestures subtly challenge and transform the equation of power between public space and public citizens, arguing that the latter have always loomed larger in the former than we choose to believe. But they are also harder to see. The photos humanize and localize the usually anonymous architecture they are affixed to, while also reminding us of how evanescent that effect can be.

In its willful lack of seriousness, its epistemological play on the incongruities of scale and form, and its essentially vernacular mode, Varda and JR's collaborative artwork resembles in many ways the bunker conversions around

Figure 4.19 The bunker returned to its 'underground' identity at '"The Trendy Griboyedov Club," St. Petersburg, Russia.'

the world that often serve tourists but would not normally qualify as 'art' in a gallery or academic sense. Ross's photographs of the 'Trendy Griboyedov Club' in St Petersburg show the purple, blue, and green paint and decorative borders that signal a space for play without vitiating the spatial connotation of underground most strongly retained in the unaltered ventilation system intruding its alien concrete forms into the quiet neighborhood above (Figure 4.19).[148] Carlos López Galviz writes of 'The Shelter ... one of the highlights of Shanghai nightlife,' that its maze-like spaces, 'bare walls,' sparse lighting, and smoke give it 'all the ingredients of a "gritty" bar.'[149] As Beck observes of many gallery conversions, the space here 'gives a dubious ambient gravitas to even the most anodyne collection.'[150] Like conversions under arches, in old subterranean toilets, and in other forgotten or hidden urban spaces,

---

148 Ross, Waiting, 132–5.
149 Carlos López Galviz, 'Sheltered Lives: Shanghai Civil Defense Shelters,' in Global Undergrounds, ed. Dobraszczyk et al., 124–6, at 124.
150 Beck, 'Concrete Ambivalence,' 96.

bunker conversions sometimes play on their spatial resonance – wine cellars, bars, clubs, theaters, galleries – and other times simply look to be squeezing into somewhere available and cheap in a manner no different from a news-stand, shoe repair, barber, or florist in a subway arcade. Galviz notes that while 'The Shelter' has been developed in a never-used and long-abandoned bunker dating to the 1960s Chinese conflict with the USSR, elsewhere in the city and around China vast new civil defense tunnels are under construction.[151]

Larger-scale conversions equally range from overdetermined to oppor-tunistic. Beukes imagines both in her near-future novel *Afterland*. The narrator trolls two separate attempts of men to survive a gender-discriminating pandemic. There's an imagined 2021 sensationalist feature of armchair dark tourism in *Vice* on '"XY City," the controversial Ukrainian "manclave" ... set up in an old neofascist paramilitary compound with razor wire and bunkers in the forest hills. It's the kind of place where the ghosts of swastika graffiti seep through the white paint.'[152] And at another moment, there's Schadenfreude over 'a special report on the rise of deadmen tourism following morbid thrill-seekers making a pilgrimage to mass death sites, like Pionen, a Cold War bunker turned data center under Stockholm where 600 rich techbros, CEOs, government officials, and military higher-ups barricaded themselves away from the virus. And died anyway.'[153] A longform *New Yorker* feature on the conversion of a five-story deep, sixty-thousand-square-foot former West German army bunker into a 'bulletproof' website-hosting service called CyberBunker by an 'eccentric' Dutch IT expert obsessed with Nazi bunkers and science fiction played on the association between the site, the marginal character known as 'Xennt,' and the underground activities he was eventually arrested for, from cooking drugs to Dark Web activity including the storage and distribution of child pornography. The feature concludes with an unanswered question to an imprisoned Xennt:

> He told me about his childhood visits to the Second World War complex in Arnhem, and about how that space had bewitched him. ... He said that the first CyberBunker, in Goes, was the realization of 'a dream' to own 'one of these facilities and to renovate it to make it a modern hi-tech stronghold.' But he could go no deeper. Xennt wrote, 'I am unable to explain why I like bunkers. ... I cannot answer that. I just like bunkers. That is all.'[154]

151 Galviz, 'Sheltered Lives,' 124–5.
152 Beukes, *Afterland*, 207.
153 Beukes, *Afterland*, 124.
154 Ed Caesar, 'The Cold War Bunker That Became Home to a Dark-Web Empire,' *New Yorker* (3 & 10 Aug. 2020): www.newyorker.com/magazine/2020/08/03/the-cold-war-bunker-that-became-home-to-a-dark-web-empire.

Life in the ontological bunker   189

The bunker fantasy can be as much an ontological as a physical prison.

It is as easy to overdetermine as to underestimate the importance of a particular space. As a strange space and as the remnant of a once dominant spatial form, the bunker promises privileged information about the past and about the present; as an underground space, it similarly resonates with oppositional and clandestine power. But along with all that mystery and negation, the bunker's very quotidian and material nature as poured concrete with somebody's junk piled up inside it reminds us also that people made it, that people lived and died in relation to it, and that the apocalypse it was made to survive never happened, even as many other apocalyptic events did. Its existence, in other words, is as much a travesty, a miracle, and a banality as anything else we might look at in the world. One reason tourists flock to these sites is that it is a little bit easier to dwell on this fact inside a bunker, whether one is in it for the ontological frisson, the epistemological jolt, or – most of the time – some combination of the two. The effect is similar to what anthropologist Christina Schwenkel attributes to 'Obsolescent infrastructures [which], as sanctified ruins (and objects of touristic desire), can remain affectively charged long after the technological dreams attached to them have vanished, in this case linking life and death, and nature and city, while sustaining the social collectivity through memories of the infrastructural legacies of past futures.'[155] Especially in the limit-case of the bunker as networked in a potential rather than an active infrastructure, I would argue that the dreams with which it is affectively charged do not actually 'vanish'; rather, they dwell within and maintain the strength of the affective charge that remains.

In the United States, and in so many other parts of the world seamed with Cold War fortifications, the enduring symbolism of the built environment continues to outweigh the attempt to think them through or even simply to encounter them in a context distinct from that symbolism. Consequently, that history risks remaining a black hole of meaninglessness within American and global postwar history, meaningful neither on its own terms nor in relationship to the transformative social and cultural movements that occurred in everyday life during its decades in power: Civil Rights, Black Power, Indigenous Peoples' rights, disability rights, feminism, LGBTQ+ rights, animal liberation, the rise of drug culture and the counterculture, and rock 'n' roll, funk, punk, disco, rap, and hip hop in all their variations. As we might feel its presence in the everyday appropriations of these spaces, there are also hints of such a reading in literature and film: when *Bleeding Edge*, Thomas

---

155 Christina Schwenkel, 'The Current Never Stops: Intimacies of Energy Infrastructure in Vietnam,' in *The Promise of Infrastructure*, ed. Nikhil Anand, Akhil Gupta, and Hannah Appel (Durham: Duke University Press, 2018), 102–30, Kindle loc. 2748.

Pynchon's 2013 novel of 9/11 New York, bottoms out deep beneath the Atlantic Ocean beyond Montauk in the physical equivalent of the dark Internet, 'somebody's idea of Cold War salvation down there ... some faith in brute depth' that hides unconscionable Cold War secrets and threatens to unmoor our sense of time and space; when Don DeLillo's *Zero K* imagines a contemporary supershelter for the global one percent beneath a Central Asian wasteland; or when Colson Whitehead reimagines the Underground Railroad as a literally buried set of rails and hidden enclaves.[156] But our critical eyes, like those of fraud investigator Maxine Tarnow in *Bleeding Edge*, tend to be diverted from this ostensible zero point towards more immediate and more comprehensible catastrophes, never exactly to return to it. The next chapter examines some of those adjacent catastrophes and the ways in which the bunker fantasy has been appropriated by post–Cold War fictions for alternative apocalyptic scenarios.

156 Thomas Pynchon, *Bleeding Edge* (New York: Penguin, 2013), 194; DeLillo, *Zero K*; Colson Whitehead, *The Underground Railroad* (New York: Doubleday, 2016).

5

Writing from the epistemological bunker: fictions of postnuclear apocalypse

[For this epigraph, please read the lyrics of or listen to the first two lines of
Professor Griff's ad lib in the referenced song]
Public Enemy, 'Countdown to Armageddon' (1988)

In the midpoint episode of Cormac McCarthy's postapocalyptic novel *The Road* (2006), an aging father out of the old world and a son born into the new world stumble onto a pristine prepper's bunker buried in the yard of an abandoned house (Figure 5.1). Their divergent reactions neatly delineate the line between ontology and epistemology as also between two generations returning to the nuclear past as visitors from the future. The father knows what potential riches it contains; the son begs him not to open it. The boy has never really believed his father's stories of the wonders of the past, and his only prior experience with the bunker was a harrowing escape from the labyrinthine basement of a decrepit plantation mansion.[1] Lured there by the promise of the stuff of survival, they had found only the wrong stuff. The basement contains a store of human livestock and a baited trap to increase that store (Figure 5.2). The boy is traumatized not only by the immediate danger and the fact of cannibalism but also by their inability to save the other victims without being caught themselves.[2] It's an early vision of the zombie apocalypse that would take over pop culture soon thereafter; however, McCarthy's cannibalistic zombies are alive, still the recognizably human predators of 1980s survivalism and preppers' nightmares.

When the boy begs not to open the second bunker, the father reassures him that 'This door looks like the other door ... But it's not.'[3] The father retains a firm grasp of Cold War survivalism and bunker ethics; however, only his son is able to question the cost of those ethics and to recognize a deeper truth: the two 'doors' are, indeed, fundamentally inseparable from one another. The bunker fantasy always entails the bunker nightmare,

---

1 Cormac McCarthy, *The Road* (New York: Vintage, 2006), 108–11.
2 McCarthy, *The Road*, 127.
3 McCarthy, *The Road*, 137.

Figure 5.1 Studying the wonders of the past, preserved in a pristine front-yard bunker in *The Road*.

Figure 5.2 Trying to look away from the wrong stuff of the bunker fantasy in the dark basement of a former plantation in *The Road*.

McCarthy reminds us. But even though their sojourn in the bunker of plenty will be cut short by fear of being caught and trapped there, the narrator takes the time lovingly to dwell on the 'Crate upon crate of canned goods. Tomatoes, peaches, beans, apricots. Canned hams. Corned beef. Hundreds of gallons of water in ten gallon plastic jerry jugs. Paper towels, toilet paper, paper plates. Plastic trashbags stuffed with blankets.'[4] Certainly, one function of the scene is to stress ironically 'The richness of a vanished world,'[5] the futility of prepping, the tragedy of ruining a fecund and beautiful world, and the benighted priorities of the elder generation. But the degree to which

4 McCarthy, *The Road*, 138.
5 McCarthy, *The Road*, 139.

Writing from the epistemological bunker

the narrator attends to the pleasures of the bunker within an otherwise unremitting nightmare of a bleak survival forces an awareness that this respite, for the reader as for the boy, is a direct consequence of the experience of the bunker nightmare and material proof that something better is always somehow preserved within the nightmare. The dialectical image pairing dream with nightmare captures the doubleness characteristic of postapocalyptic fiction since the Cold War.

Postapocalyptic fictions of the twenty-first century, including McCarthy's novel, find in the legacy of the nuclear condition a way of thinking out of the rigid present, of questioning the fixed categories of that present, and of using the foreclosed future to imagine an alternate space and time from within the ontological bunker. Like dark tourism, these fictions require the staged authenticity of cataclysmic horror to validate the momentary glimpse of something unimaginably better. The dominant early twenty-first-century postapocalyptic genres of zombie fiction and future noir adapted the stark verities of Cold War nuclear fiction to reveal the horrors of life within the ontological bunker and to attempt at the same time to recover its pleasures. In contrast, Afrofuturist, Indigenous, and global South fictions from the 1970s through to the present misplace the epistemological bunker to open up dissident spacetimes within a centuries-old postapocalyptic ontology. Distant-future visions deploy the same fantasy to imagine radically different worlds enclaved however tenuously in the concerns of the present, preserved in the bunker that links divergent temporalities. Misplaced from their spatiotemporal home, these appropriations provide us with new tools for reading this same bunker fantasy at work within what looked like stark verities in the discourse of American Cold War culture.

Zombie apocalypse and the epistemological bunker

The zombie has a robust Cold War pedigree through the seminal films of George Romero. *Night of the Living Dead* (1968) – set mostly in a besieged home cellar – and *Day of the Dead* (1985) – set in a government supershelter – in particular speak to the dominant bunker fantasy of their respective epochs.[6] While the flesh-eating mutant originated from fantasies around the effects of nuclear radiation, the undead zombie's mindless – what Swanson terms 'desubjectized'[7] – threat emerged from a more inchoate fear of social conformity to which the 'new mutant' superheroes of early 1960s comic

---

6 Pike, *Bunkered Decades*, 67–9, 175–7.
7 Carl Joseph Swanson, '"The Only Metaphor Left": Colson Whitehead's *Zone One* and Zombie Narrative Form,' *Genre* 47.3 (2014): 379–405, at 385.

194 *After the end*

books were in fact also a response.[8] The bunker fantasy suggested both the necessary threat of the zombie and the means to survive its predations. One among many reasons the zombie apocalypse flourished as such a resonant pop cultural presence in the early twenty-first century was its ready adaptability to either a nuclear or a nonnuclear scenario. Mutants had featured as countless monsters in nuclear apocalypse fiction from the 1950s onward; they could equally be adapted to the vision of an earth where the zombie became the only threat in an otherwise unchanged world.

As with nuclear war survival fictions, the zombie apocalypse poses either a limited disaster to be survived and thwarted or an epic of perpetual survivalism in a neobarbarian future preserving scattered memories of a vanished world. By reducing etiology or causation to at best the narrative MacGuffin of a virus, zombie apocalypse sidesteps the implicit or explicit concern of the actuality of nuclear war that drives even the hardest-core survivalist fiction. Rather than invisible and speculative, the threat is physical and immediate. Where nuclear war poses a material and existential threat whose effects remain difficult to grasp outside of fiction, zombie apocalypse is an allegorical form collecting material fears and desires into a viscerally physical and reassuringly reductive menace. The epistemological bunker is the a priori condition that makes it possible to think, suffer, and enjoy the zombie apocalypse; scattered speculations on the potential for an actual zombie apocalypse only further demonstrate its quality as pure fantasy. There is nothing at stake but survival of a situation that always was beyond anyone's control and whatever ancillary ethical or speculative concerns might emerge are always subordinate to the fundamental imperative of survival.

Stripped of the ethical conundrums, political ideologies, or sheer uncertainties posed by the nuclear condition from which it mutated, the zombie apocalypse is ugly and unstable, a perfect distillation of the nightmare inequalities and predations of late capitalism. Survivors move through a barely ruined world testing out one shelter after another, only to discover that each is ultimately as vulnerable as the last, that every character is at risk of crossing over to the other side at any moment, and that bodies and lives have been permanently corrupted, disjointed, and profaned. One could argue that the form's brutal pleasure derives from recognizing in the degraded world of the zombie apocalypse the hypocritical verities of the global North stripped away to leave only the endlessly repeated gore and dismemberment of war severed from the ideologies that make it possible for most citizens daily to ignore them. Jessica Hurley similarly draws out the form's capacity both to hide racialized violence and to strip away the false veneer of racial

8 Pike, *Bunkered Decades*, 40–2.

Writing from the epistemological bunker

equality.[9] Black in folklore and in early Hollywood, then a white whose skin is 'cracked' and 'ruptured' and easily peeled away, the zombie figure, Hurley argues, is 'composed of the tension' between white and Black.[10]

Hurley's analysis focuses on Colson Whitehead's 2011 novel *Zone One*, where a volunteer soldier works clearing 'straggler' zombies out of the eponymous area of downtown Manhattan that has been reclaimed by the now-Buffalo-based government and sealed off with a massive wall at Canal Street. For Hurley, the novel's narrator, who is identified as Black only near the end of the novel, can survive as long as he 'passes' for white; once 'outed' for the reader, he is fated to be swallowed up by the horde of his kindred.[11] A number of critics similarly regard this late moment as a breakdown in the dominant zombie narrative of futurity in which a small group of survivors preserves civilization against a mindless horde. Forsberg argues that 'our protagonist can't help but rejoice once the skels make swiss cheese out of the Canal Street Wall and lay waste to the world once more.'[12] Hoberek cites 'the utopian ... breakdown of our categories of the individual human not as a tragedy but as a form of release.'[13] The barricade collapsing, as Swanson argues, is part of the core structure of the zombie narrative, which is composed of 'a flight from the zombies to a defensible shelter, a siege of that shelter that results in its eventual fall, and then a flight from the fallen defenses presumably to the next survival space.'[14] Whitehead cleaves to this generic structure, but the utopian moments flip its values in ways analogous to Langston Hughes's 1965 treatment of the bunker fantasy as anathema to the spatial practices of Black Harlem in the 'Simple Stories.' Rather than building a shelter and locking out those who failed to do so, Simple's wife pleads with her husband, 'If the bomb does come, let's just *all die* neighborly.'[15]

During the Cold War, the repudiation of the private shelter's bunker fantasy as white, male, suburban, and middle class was multivalent in function. Bob Dylan could use the refusal of the shelter to distinguish the neighborly working-class sentiments of white Minnesotans from the warmongering of

---

9 Jessica Hurley, 'History Is What Bites: Zombies, Race, and the Limits of Biopower in Colson Whitehead's *Zone One*,' *Extrapolation* 56.3 (2015): 311–33.
10 Hurley, 'History Is What Bites,' 318.
11 Hurley, 'History Is What Bites,' 325–6.
12 Soren Forsberg, 'Don't Believe Your Eyes,' *Transition* 109 (2012): 131–43, at 137.
13 Andrew Hoberek, 'Living with PASD,' *Contemporary Literature* 53.2 (2012): 406–13, at 412.
14 Swanson, 'Only Metaphor,' 388.
15 Langston Hughes, 'Bomb Shelters' (1965), in *The Collected Works of Langston Hughes, Vol. 8: The Later Simple Stories*, ed. Donna Akiba Sullivan Harper (Columbia, MO: University of Missouri Press, 2002), 175–7, at 176–7.

Figure 5.3 Leaving the bunker in a radical rejection of futurity and modernity as dictated by Brazil's military government in *Abrigo Nuclear*.

the military-industrial complex.[16] In his 1981 dystopian film *Abrigo Nuclear*, Brazilian antinuclear activist Roberto Pires could use the same flight from shelter to a blasted surface as repudiation of the modernity of military dictatorship (Figure 5.3).[17] In its radical rejection of character, futurity, and all categories that distinguish one human from another, the zombie as a figure for horror lends itself equally to the racialized reading Hurley traces and Whitehead cannily deploys or to the neoliberal reduction of all subjects to interchangeable passive nonentities to be picked off by the surviving humans. But it also lends itself to glimmers of utopianism in the inkling of a posthuman world of radical equality.

This utopianism is of a different order from the humanist claim that the united front against zombies resolves animosities and hatreds. The latter claim animates Max Brooks's vision of America reclaiming its lost values in *World War Z* (2006) and briefly appears in an oft-quoted passage from *Zone One*: 'There was a single Us now, reviling a single Them. Would the old bigotries be reborn as well, when they cleared out this Zone, and the next, and so on, and they were packed together again, tight and suffocating on top of each other?'[18] Like the ease with which nuclear mutants are killed off in Cold War postapocalyptic fiction, this melting-pot sentiment purports

---

16 Bob Dylan, *Chronicles: Volume 1* (New York: Simon & Schuster, 2004), 271.
17 *Abrigo Nuclear*, wr., dir., and feat. Roberto Pires, EMBRAFILME, 1981.
18 Colson Whitehead, *Zone One* (New York: Doubleday, 2011), 231.

Writing from the epistemological bunker 197

to cleanse the racialized colonial and imperial guilt of exterminating violence, making it available for viewing pleasure. In Jacqueline Druga's novel *The Last Woman*, a deadly pandemic causes victims to slip into comas that present as fatal; some do in fact die, but others eventually return to consciousness. When the survivors are mistaken for zombies, they are shot dead. 'They thought it was The Walking Dead. Ridiculous,' protests one character. 'I did too,' says another, 'When I woke up.'[19]

But it is not so easy to separate what is usually a guilty pleasure from that other pleasure that issues from the inevitable victory of the undead hordes, the surrender to the oceanic, as *Zone One*'s Mark Spitz articulates it: 'Fuck it, he thought. You have to learn how to swim sometime. He opened the door and walked into the sea of the dead.'[20] Spitz's decision is not a choice afforded by the nuclear bunker, where there is nothing heroic or subversive about exposing oneself to invisible radiation. And this decision can just as easily be – and always *also* is – played for tragedy, as in the movie *I Am Legend* (2007) when Neville (Will Smith) sacrifices himself to the ferals so that the woman and child he is sheltering can escape to a safe compound to the north of Manhattan. The bunker fantasy offers conventional shelter but also creates enclaves of dissident temporality. As opposed to Neville, there is no future in Spitz's gesture. But in the ambiguity of a fictional storyworld, there is an alternate reality powerfully asserted, an epistemological refusal to be bound by the ontological rules of sheltering that appear to be the only options this form will afford. A similar moment occurs at the end of the Cuban zombie movie *Juan de los Muertos* (2010), where the titular forty-year-old slacker antihero refuses to flee the island with his survivor group to seek new shelter; instead, he wades back onto the Malecón in Havana to take on the 'dissidents.' The gesture is perfectly balanced between defiance and assimilation; once the shelter is compromised, the fiction of zombie apocalypse at least briefly affords both stances, but only if both are invoked simultaneously.

In 'Apocalypse: What Disasters Reveal,' his outraged essay on the aftermath of the Haitian earthquake, Dominican American author Junot Díaz flips the allegory of 'zombie capitalism' on its head, detailing what the 'social disaster' of the earthquake reveals when, like any apocalypse, it slips off the veil we understand as 'normal life' to show the truth. In the devastation of Haiti wrought by centuries of intentional policies and human-created circumstances that stripped the earth bare, Díaz, like any prophet worth his salt, sees 'a sign of what is to come. ... a future out of a sci-fi fever

---

19 Jacqueline Druga, *The Last Woman* (n.p.: Vulpine Press, 2018 [2014]), Kindle loc. 2497.
20 Whitehead, *Zone One*, 259.

198   *After the end*

dream where the super-rich will live in walled-up plantations of impossible privilege and the rest of us will wallow in unimaginable extremity, staggering around the waste and being picked off by the hundreds of thousands by "natural disasters" – by "acts of god."'[21] The zombie hordes to which capitalist predation has reduced the surviving Haitian population become visible to us in their exposure as fodder for wanton murder by those possessing power. Díaz plays out the affordances of this flipped image in a litany of how to make a zombie that has in it nothing of the sui generis virus or natural disaster. He concludes, however, not, he says, with 'optimism' but with the 'hope' that emerges from this same walk with the zombie.[22] Hope in 'human solidarity' in response to disaster and in recognition of 'the legendary, divinely inspired endurance of the Haitian people'[23] does not mitigate the disaster or make it desirable. Nevertheless, Díaz argues, given the 'revelation' afforded by a disaster like this, given that such disasters have always occurred, given that such disasters will be occurring with ever greater frequency in years to come, and given that the alternative is to normalize them or ignore them from within our ontological bunkers, it behooves us to explain and to imagine their extremes; for the unimaginable extremes, both dystopian and utopian, are the epistemological opening afforded by the forms of apocalypse.

Future noir and the world to come

Like nuclear war fiction, the zombie genre tends to take place in either the present or the near future. The other dominant mode of twenty-first-century apocalypse thus far is set in a recognizable but distinctive future in which current conditions are the same but worse. Where the zombie apocalypse allegorizes the condition we already inhabit by stripping away the veneer of humanity and civilization, future apocalypse allegorizes the present by amplifying current conditions in a more or less science-fictional framework, typically as some kind of dystopia.[24] In future noir and other speculative

---

21 Junot Díaz, 'Apocalypse: What Disasters Reveal,' *Boston Review* (May/June 2011): 46–52, at 50.
22 Díaz, 'Apocalypse,' 50.
23 Díaz, 'Apocalypse,' 50.
24 Arguably, the Marvel and DC comics universes propose another, increasingly dominant, model of apocalypse, where superheroes and supervillains oppose each other in cosmic battles over the fate of the universe. Because this genre cleaves far more closely to the Cold War model of nuclear cataclysm in which it was conceived, with the threat always averted through specialized forces, I am leaving its ontologically static affordances aside here in favor of more misplaced versions of the bunker fantasy.

Writing from the epistemological bunker 199

dystopian fictions, there has either been an apocalyptic event in the past – the computer–human war that led to the harvesting of human batteries in the backstory of *The Matrix* trilogy (1999–2003) or the unspecified cataclysm that led to the formation of Panem and its surrounding districts in the Colorado Mountains in *The Hunger Games* trilogy (novels 2008–10, films 2012–15) – or a gradual deterioration of conditions until, as Díaz suggests of Haiti, they effectively have become apocalyptic. In the first three feature films of South African director Neill Blomkamp – *District 9* (2009), *Elysium* (2013), and *Chappie* (2015) – contemporary slum conditions are amplified by the incorporation of aliens, off-planet gated communities, and robot-policing in fortified ghettos, respectively. In *Ready Player One* (novel 2011, film 2018), climate-change-driven privation has forced everyday people into vertical slums of stacked trailer homes and storage containers and the elite into fortified vertical towers; they interface in virtual reality. Typically, the dystopian apocalyptic mode works from a doubly dysfunctional bunker fantasy based on entrenched inequality: the decadent power elite are sealed off both psychologically and physically in a luxurious and more or less utopian enclave and the rest of the world is locked up in urban or rural survivalist hell.

Both variants derive from the 1960s and 1970s: the post-nuclear-war imaginings of *The Planet of the Apes* movies (1968–73), *Zardoz* (1974), *Logan's Run* (1976), and many other films, and the urban blight extrapolations of *Soylent Green* (1973), *The Warriors* (1979), *Escape from New York* (1981), and others. Where the Cold War–era dystopia nearly always revealed that there is no escape from the dark bunker, no entry into the light bunker, and no resolution possible beyond recognition of this truth, the twenty-first-century dystopia nearly always ends with the walls, improbably and heroically, coming down. This shift in emphasis within the strict constraints afforded by this genre's form certainly testifies to the fondness in the early decades of the twenty-first century for something resembling happy endings; however, it also bespeaks a changed orientation towards temporality and possibility. The Cold War films of the 1970s are predicated on the only truly liberating option being an escape from the nuclear condition altogether, an escape deemed impossible. The bunker fantasy was untenable but inevitable and immovable. In the twenty-first century, the despair is gone, along with the negatively expressed hope that reality would somehow manage to escape the locked room of the fictions. Instead, the form was adapted for representing the gap between ontological and epistemological bunkers. The new dystopias are thus simultaneously wish-fulfilling and defeatist: Neo crashes the Matrix and defeats Agent Smith but when the system reboots discovers that he is himself part and parcel of the programming; at the end of the *Hunger Games* series the revolution has been exposed as corrupt and the games have been eliminated, but the political system has not fundamentally changed;

200   *After the end*

in *Ready Player One* the hero takes over OASIS but changes nothing in its fundamental model or in the world around it besides turning the game off once a week to force people to spend a few hours offline.

There is a tacit recognition here, to echo historian of technology Rosalind Williams, that 'We have always lived below the surface, beneath the atmospheric ocean, in a closed, sealed, finite environment, where everything is recycled and everything is limited,' the domed Earth that novelist J. M. Morgan terms 'Biosphere One.'[25] In other words, even though we truly do inhabit the ontological bunker of the planet Earth, the best way to imagine that fact is by treating it as if it were only epistemological, occurring in a not-yet-present future rather than already happening around us. Environmental degradation features powerfully in either the foreground or the background of pretty much all twenty-first-century dystopian fiction. Equally powerful is a recognition that the post-racial, posthuman, post-history, post–Cold War promises of the 1990s had led not to an emergence out of the bunker and into the sunlight, but to incremental progress and regression. The epistemological bunker affords the realization that 'there is no Planet B' as the protest banners put it, no world, whether pristine or wasted, waiting somewhere outside for us to return to; we must survive in what we have. The epistemological bunker affords the realization that we control and can perhaps change the world we actually live in without destroying it further. It affords the realization that these spaces enshrine inequality and spatially segregate populations in unfair and unequal ways. It does not afford the dream of steady progress, of a tabula rasa or a new start; indeed, in its stress on continuance, the dystopian bunker discredits the very possibility. But in its survivalist reduction and the restrictive clarity of its vision, the dystopian bunker does afford a potent thought-puzzle for a problematic present.

Where *Matrix*, *Hunger Games*, and *Ready Player One* appropriate the bunker fantasy into dystopian fiction in ways strongly embedded in American history and culture and incorporate global motifs into the forcefield of that history and culture, Blomkamp's two Johannesburg films, *District 9* and *Chappie*, misplace the global American model into a local setting in meaningful ways. Despite their narrative incongruities and the vexed racial dynamics for which they were rightly criticized, these films gain power from the incisive anger with which they eviscerate the hypocritical nostrums of neoliberalism.[26] They deploy the pulp tropes of science fiction to stack

25 Rosalind Williams, *Notes on the Underground* (Cambridge, MA: MIT Press, 2008 [1990]), 212; J[ill] M[eredith] Morgan, *Desert Eden* (New York: Pinnacle, 1991), 14.

26 For an elaboration of this reading, see Pike, 'Future Slums: Problems of Urban Space in Science Fiction Cinema,' *The Apollonian* 5 (2018): 51–69.

Writing from the epistemological bunker

audience sympathy fully on the side of the aliens, urban poor, and even gangsters who have been bunkered in by the explicitly multinational forces ranged against them. The exclusions built into the bunker fantasy but seldom effectively articulated until after the Cold War find new utility in the powerful visual shorthand they provide for dwelling on contemporary inequality. Because the bunker as a form has for so long afforded both positive feelings of shelter and negative feelings of fear and containment, this shorthand also expresses profound ambivalence and contradiction in its sheer presence. The reader or viewer is readily positioned on both sides of the barricade, uneasy with the comforts offered by the neoliberal bunker while appalled and entranced by the human emotions of suffering and compassion currently imaginable only in the ghetto.

Afrofuturism and dissident spacetime

Certain Afrofuturist fictions similarly suggest ways of appropriating the bunker fantasy to address questions of uneven development, destabilizing spatiotemporal relationships in order to question local and transnational power structures. As Katherine McKittrick writes of the protagonist of Octavia Butler's historical time-travel fantasy *Kindred*, '[B]y stepping into what might be considered unknown or inaccessible spaces and places (the past, underacknowledged black geographies, time-space reversal), [she] respatializes the potential of black femininity and black subjectivity in general. Blackness becomes a site of radical possibility, supernatural travels, and difficult epistemological returns to the past and the present.'[27] As 'imaginary enclaves' (to borrow Jameson's language) from the threatened apocalypse of nuclear war in the 'real social spaces' of the historical apocalypse survived by Black Americans, the dissident geographies in Afrofuturist postapocalyptic writing by Butler, Nalo Hopkinson, Nnedi Okorafor, and others uncover 'radical possibility' in the ossified structures of the nuclear condition.

These texts mobilize the ontological force of the bunker fantasy to capture viscerally its doubleness and contradictions. In *Kindred*, for instance, a young Black woman is caught in a time-jumping loop between her modern life as a 'wage-slave' in 1976 LA and her enslaved ancestors' world on a middling plantation in 1816 Maryland. Both spaces find Dana trapped in a world over which she has little control; both also find her affectively entwined in that world. In 1976, she lives with her lover, a white writer named Kevin who will gradually come himself to know firsthand what his whiteness means in both spacetimes. And in 1816, she must both ensure

27 McKittrick, *Demonic Grounds*, 1.

202   *After the end*

the survival of her own family line, born of rape and enslavement, and process her own troubling identification with the perverse security of the past: 'I could recall feeling relief at seeing the house, feeling that I had come home. And having to stop and correct myself, remind myself that I was in an alien, dangerous place. I could recall being surprised that I would come to think of such a place as home. ... Rufus's time was a sharper, stronger reality.'[28] Butler captured the classic SFF theme of longing for a simpler, more immediate, less alienated world that the bunker fantasy and survivalism project into the future; however, by lodging it in the past, she neatly undercut the gendered and raced assumption of that longing but without thereby dismissing the affective power, the lived reality, of the past. That doubleness, which the bunker fantasy eschews, distinguishes what time-travel and other forms of alternate history afford from what the postapocalyptic offers as a form. The potential for mobility, of movement from one spacetime to the other, permits a more ambiguous weighing and opens up alternate ways of thinking about the relationship between the two. *Kindred* summons the full weight of an unacknowledged persistence of the past in the present. Rather than dwelling in the bunkered past, Butler's novel opens up the intricate dynamics of its ontological fantasy.

In the postapocalyptic near future of Nalo Hopkinson's *Brown Girl in the Ring* (1998), urban Toronto has been sealed off for twelve years following rioting, white flight, and urban blight; as in *Chappie*'s Johannesburg, the city is ruled by a crime lord ensconced in an iconic citadel of capital, in this case the CN Tower. Hopkinson's 'Muddy York' is at once dystopian and utopian: drug-filled and dangerous, it nevertheless celebrates the village-like barter economy to which it has reverted.[29] Muddy York is distinguished from the typical feudalism of American and British postapocalyptic neo-barbarianism in the inhabitants' constant awareness of the technologically advanced world beyond the confines of their ghetto and in the distinctly Caribbean inflection of their own culture, from the dialect in which Jamaican-born Canadian author Hopkinson renders the thoughts and words of the principal characters to the fearful and transformative magic performed by them. Similar to the dreamlike false ending of *Parasite* discussed in Chapter 3, *Brown Girl*'s comic resolution following a gruesome middle section intimates a potential bunker emergence sequel: the grandmother's heart, cut out by the villainous crime lord (who is also her son-in-law), ends up transplanted into the body of the corrupt and power-hungry mayor, leading the latter to a new understanding of the conditions in Muddy York and

28 Butler, *Kindred* (Boston: Beacon, 1988 [1979]), 191.
29 Nalo Hopkinson, *Brown Girl in the Ring* (New York: Warner, 1998).

Writing from the epistemological bunker   203

new plans to transform it for the better, change truly driven from within epistemology rendered as a new ontology.

Bunkered spaces, shelters, and survivalism run through Butler's post-apocalyptic fictions from the first volume in the Patternist series in 1976 to the short story 'Amnesty' in 2003. There is nothing so straightforward in her fiction as an emergence narrative, but then none of the captivity scenarios plays out conventionally, either. Like Hopkinson and Okorafor after her, Butler approached the postapocalyptic imaginary as an epistemological tool for a critical opening of our understanding of the present and a spatiotemporal misplacing of the stories we tell about the past and the future. Motifs of captivity and refractions of the forms and history of chattel slavery permeate her fictions to the degree that, for Butler scholar Gerry Canavan, 'neoslavery fantasy ... of one sort or another can be found in every single one of her novels, and in most of her short stories as well.'[30] What Thomas Foster argues of the 'area of intersection ... between speculative alien contact scenarios and the history of slavery, between future and past' holds equally true for the intersection between the spaces of confinement and modes of future and past apocalyptic. Meaning, insight, and survival arise from 'the ambivalent space of cultural exchange they both produce, and the way in which Butler represents alien contact as neither clearly utopian nor dystopian.'[31]

Survivalist figures clinging to a conventional human identity tend to come into conflict with the alternate, pre- and posthuman ontologies in which alien races – the Oankali in the Xenogenesis trilogy; the Patternists, Clayarks, and Kohn in the Patternist series; the Communities in 'Amnesty' – interact and interbreed with human survivors. Similarly, conflicting human groups – Earthseed and President Andrew Steele Jarret's Church of Christian America in the Parable series; the slave-owning Weylin family and the enslaved Greenwood family in *Kindred* – are simultaneously necessary and inimical to each other. The need to be a survivalist is always a given with Butler's protagonists, with no resolution in sight. Instead, the question is what they make of themselves in the process of surviving, and what surviving makes of them. As Donna Haraway puts it, 'This is survival fiction rather than salvation fiction.'[32]

---

30 Gerry Canavan, *Octavia E. Butler* (Champaign: University of Illinois Press, 2016), 47.

31 Thomas Foster, '"We Get to Live, and So Do They": Octavia Butler's Contact Zones,' *Strange Matings: Science Fiction, Feminism, African American Voices, and Octavia E. Butler*, ed. Rebecca J. Holden and Nisi Shawl (Seattle: Aqueduct Press, 2013), Kindle loc. 3069.

32 Donna Haraway, *Primate Visions: Gender, Race, and Nature in the World of Modern Science* (New York: Routledge, 1989), 378.

204   *After the end*

Written in the aftermath of but inspired from within the Cold War and its Reagan years, *Parable of the Sower* (1993) and *Parable of the Talents* (1998) most directly engage the postapocalyptic as genre and survivalism as practice. A key lesson of Reaganism, Butler wrote in 1990, was that 'People will pay any price for praise, reassurance, and an illusion of security.'[33] The fascistic, fundamentalist President Jarret, who reigns over postapocalyptic America with an iron hand, she noted in her journal, was 'Reagan, young, vigorous, and utterly unencumbered by conscience.'[34] *Sower* opens with the violent invasion of a bunkered enclave in LA that thrusts seventeen-year-old protagonist Lauren Oya Olamina into a neobarbarian postapocalypse, which will require of her both a judicious deployment of survivalist skills and a practico-spiritual vision of a new society that can emerge from the ruins. *Talents* documents the establishment of a new utopian enclave in northern California, its brutal suppression by forces of white reactionary Christian fundamentalism, and its final transformation into the 'substance' of a starship loaded with 'frozen human and animal embryos, plant seeds, tools, equipment, memories, dreams, and hopes [and] the libraries of Earth' to seed a better future (although, according to Butler's plan for the series, the new planet they were going to find would 'make them wish they'd never left Earth in the first place'[35]). Rather than a revolution, the space flight is a negotiated compromise, named 'the *Christopher Columbus*' despite the fact that it was not about 'riches and empire ... slaves and gold ... and some European monarch. ... One must know which battle to fight,' Lauren concludes her diary in 2090, 'The name is nothing.'[36]

The 'Pox,' explains Olamina's companion Bankolé in retrospect, was not simply the term historians used to refer to a fifteen-year period of 'chaos' between 2015 and 2030. Rather, it was 'an installment-plan World War III,' the status quo of late capitalist inequality and traceable back to the decades Butler had been writing in:

> It began ... perhaps even before the turn of the millennium. It has not ended. I have also read that the Pox was caused by accidentally coinciding climatic, economic, and sociological crises. It would be more honest to say that the Pox was caused by our own refusal to deal with obvious problems in those areas. We caused the problems: then we sat and watched as they grew into crises. I have heard people deny this, but I was born in 1970. I have seen enough to know that it is true.[37]

33 In Canavan, *Butler*, 140.
34 In Canavan, *Butler*, 140.
35 In Canavan, *Butler*, 179.
36 Butler, *Parable of the Talents* (New York: Seven Stories Press, 1998), 363.
37 Butler, *Talents*, 14.

For Butler, the nuclear threat was so incidental in relation to everyday inequity that she shrugged it off within the novel as a briefly mentioned and quickly disregarded tactical exchange in 2029 between Iran and Iraq.[38] The threat on the ground was not so much nuclear war as the bunker ontology that had accompanied it.

The Parable series rings changes on types of bunkering and survivalism: the middle- and upper-class walled urban enclave as shelter and as cage, the postapocalyptic slum and squatter settlement indistinguishable from the ones Butler knew, the survivalist trek, the hidden rural compound, the brutalizing reeducation camp, the cave shelter, the starship ark. As in other aspects of her work, Butler appears more invested in comparing and weighing the potential affordances of each mode of imagining than in ranking or judging them. Significantly, the ten-odd years covered by the two novels unroll not so much in the absence of governance as in its capitalistic, predatory, and at times murderous presence. In the walled, middle-class, self-policed enclave twenty miles outside of LA where *Sower* opens in 2024, city police and fire departments are available, but only on a pay-as-you-go basis for the rich while preying on the poor and vulnerable. Professionals telecommute or travel physically to their jobs; the Pox is doubly terrifying because it feels postapocalyptic and because it feels just like the unequal world we already inhabit: 'The family has spent money it could not afford to get the police involved to try to find the killer. I suspect that the only good this will do will be to chase away the people who live on the sidewalks and streets nearest to our wall. Is that good? The street poor will be back, and they won't love us for sicking the cops on them.'[39] Olamina is a prepper avant la lettre, responding to obsessive visions of 'the day a big gang of those hungry, desperate, crazy people outside decide to come in ... [to] this cul-de-sac with a wall around it. ... I'm talking about what we've got to do before that happens so that we can survive and rebuild – or at least survive and escape to be something other than beggars.'[40] Both fearful of survivalists and a survivalist herself, Olamina reads everything she can find 'that would help me survive out there.'[41] In the end, she is right on both counts: the Robledo enclave is soon sacked and looted, its inhabitants raped and murdered, and Olamina flees on her own, a survivor with a grab bag essential to her survival.

38 Butler, *Talents*, 79.
39 Butler, *Parable of the Sower* (New York: Seven Stories Press, 1993), 48.
40 Butler, *Sower*, 52.
41 Butler, *Sower*, 54.

206 *After the end*

'Even some fiction might be useful,' Olamina concedes.[42] And it is tempting to want to separate Olamina's admirable survival skills from the religious vision of interplanetary travel and credo that 'God is Change' that she calls Earthseed, that she records in the sayings Butler reproduces from *The Books of the Living*, and that she insists her community of travelers and, later, members in the hidden northern California community Acorn share in order also to share in her survival. As if to underline the tenuous, if not counterfactual, path Olamina takes, Butler parallels it with the path of her older brother Marcus, lost to her in the attack on the enclave and not recovered until the middle of the following novel when Olamina purchases him from a slaver in Eureka. For Marcus, the walled enclave of his childhood was 'a cage,' but in the world he survived into at the age of fourteen he was

> part of the trash that the new mayor, the city council, and the business community wanted to sweep out. It seemed to them that all the trouble of the past few years was our fault – poor people's fault, I mean. Homeless people's fault. Squatters' fault. So they sent an army of cops to drive out everyone who couldn't prove they had a right to be where they were. ... They drove us all out – poor squatters, drug dealers, junkies, crazies, gangs, whores, you name it.[43]

Rather than Olamina's choice to found a new religion of escape, Marcus retrenches as a fundamentalist preacher and ideologue for the fascistic government to whom Olamina is a 'charismatic, dangerous, heathen cult leader.'[44] But Marcus will also raise Olamina's daughter as his own, both preserving and repudiating his family. 'Forgiveness,' as Noah Cannon explains in 'Amnesty' of her relationship to the aliens that abducted her when she was an eleven-year-old girl, experimented on her, and kept her captive for twelve years, is irrelevant; the ability for both parties to 'get to live' would suffice.[45] That Noah finds more reciprocity and space to live with the Community than with the fellow captives who had raped her or the government officials who would later imprison and torture her is equally clear.

Amidst the vexed family dramas by which Butler throughout her fiction actualized the intersection of the personal and the political, the body and the ideology, Black and white, contained and opened spatiality, and human and alien, there are few truly one-dimensional villains beyond the predatory rapists and murderers who haunt the fringes of the enclaves of *Clay's Ark*, *Sower* and *Talents*, and *Adulthood Rites* and *Imago*. Even here, as in *Kindred*, Butler takes us inside the minds of those working violence against her main characters and imagines what makes them tick. Jarret's Crusaders invade

42 Butler, *Sower*, 55.
43 Butler, *Talents*, 101, 112.
44 Butler, *Talents*, 354.
45 Butler, 'Amnesty' (2003), *Callaloo* 27.3 (2004): 597–615, at 602, 613.

Writing from the epistemological bunker 207

Acorn – as all enclaves in the Parable series are eventually invaded – to take away the children for 'reeducation' and to enslave the adults in an ostensibly legal process. Like Blacks in the post-Reconstruction era, vagrants are legally 'indentured' to the Church of Christian America, 'collared,' and brutalized.[46] Butler displaces the white masculinist violence of survivalism onto the Church but translates its lifesaving practices to the escaped survivors of the reeducation camp, who are able to 'dig out' one of Acorn's prepping caches in a small mountain cave, 'the supplies that we had stored in heavy, heat-sealed plastic sacks and stored there. That gave us all packets of dried foods – fruit, nuts, beans, eggs, and milk – plus blankets and ammunition.'[47] Rather than the civilized savagery of the organized future state, the provisioned cave furnishes the 'animal comforts' that were 'all we could afford.'[48]

Survivalism, especially in the Parable series, is not an ideology or a creed; it is simply a necessary practice. And it never strays too far from historical memory. Remembering the cave, Olamina writes, 'My ancestors in this hemisphere were, by law, chattel slaves. In the U.S., they were chattel slaves for two and a half centuries – at least 10 generations. I used to think I knew what that meant. Now I realize that I can't begin to imagine the many terrible things that it must have done to them. How did they survive it all and keep their humanity? Certainly, they were never intended to keep it just as we weren't.'[49] Only those for whom survival was a generations-long necessity and for whom the postapocalypse was their everyday reality can understand survivalism apart from its fantasies. In Haraway's formulation, 'Butler's communities are assembled out of the genocides of history, not rooted in the fantasies of natural roots and recoverable origins.'[50] Only from within the experience of those same generations could one begin to imagine the answer to Butler's essential conundrum: 'How did they survive it all and keep their humanity?' The possible answers to that question are best afforded, she argued, through speculative fiction; however, she did not thereby suggest that slavery itself is speculative. Just as, in *Kindred*, Dana refers to her present-day life as 'wage-slavery,' so does Olamina imagine her small band illegally walking north on I-5 along with 'a heterogeneous mass – black and white, Asian and Latin, whole families … on the move with babies on backs or perched atop loads in carts, wagons or bicycle baskets, sometimes along with an old or handicapped person' as 'the crew of a modern underground railroad … Slavery again – even worse than my

46 Butler, *Talents*, 208, 282.
47 Butler, *Talents*, 539.
48 Butler, *Talents*, 243.
49 Butler, *Talents*, 244.
50 Haraway, *Primate Visions*, 379.

208   *After the end*

father thought, or at least sooner.'[51] 'None of this is new,' Bankolé responds, describing modern practices of debt slavery that obtained back in the 1990s.[52] Speculative fiction is required not because postapocalyptic and survivalist conditions are unreal in the present day, but because they are unimaginable within the available forms of the world as it is. 'The problem with Earthseed,' Olamina explains at one point, 'has always been that it isn't a very comforting belief system.'[53] Butler's fictions enact the ontological lure of the bunker fantasy at the same time as they transmute its comforts into something far less alluring but perhaps more effective for a nation that has never yet confronted the fact that the postapocalyptic mode is historical just as much as it is future-gazing.

In *Who Fears Death* (2010), Nigerian American writer Okorafor similarly interweaves alternate realities into a sealed-off postapocalyptic community; however, her novel withholds its bunker fantasy core until a crucial moment, taking place for the rest of its narrative in a flat barren plain that looks for all the world like a timeless African desert spotted with villages struggling for survival. Beyond a few oblique references to the fact that the story is being dictated to a laptop and to electronic devices that resemble but are not named as smartphones, the story of the rite-of-passage quest of Onyewonsu (the novel's title is an English translation of her name) to discover her full powers and lift the curse on her Okeke people reads, intentionally, like an oft-told tale of the emergence of a deity. Okorafor plants the key to this mystery in a terrifying cave in which Onyewonsu and her companions are forced to shelter from a massive dust storm. The cave is simultaneously mythic – two bodies have been hanging at the entrance for ten years, are impossible to take down, and are swarming with sentient white spiders – and historicizing – packed with 'old and amazingly ancient things' such as 'monitors, portables, e-books. ... The Great Book spoke of such places, caves full of computers. They were put here by terrified Okekes trying to escape Ani's wrath when she turned back to the world and saw the havoc the Okeke had created. ... We were in a tomb of humans, machines, and ideas.'[54] Part of a dream world beyond history but also repository of the secrets of how that world became what it is, simultaneously natural cave and manmade bunker, this space both repudiates the bunker fantasy in its conventional formulation and demonstrates its utility for giving shape to everything that exceeds its form. The Wilderness, an alternate dimension or universe to which Onyewonsu and other sorcerers travel, is both a time

---

51 Butler, *Sower*, 161, 268.
52 Butler, *Sower*, 268.
53 Butler, *Talents*, 235.
54 Nnedi Okorafor, *Who Fears Death* (New York: DAW, 2010), 329.

Writing from the epistemological bunker

before the apocalypse and an alternate plane accessed through their powers. The Indigenous belief system of which sorcery is the foundation is afforded no natural place by the bunker. Yet it is not outside of the form either; the apocalypse that has put a curse on the Okeke and wasted the land has been self-inflicted by a technologically advanced people. The bunker fantasy per se requires linearity, a before and an after, but it also enables the insinuation of a nonlinear, dissident temporality into the linearity of modernity.

Within linearity, Onyewonsu's actions simply cause further destruction. In the process of defeating Daib, whose rape of her mother to create a powerful son in his image had created her instead, she kills the menfolk of his village; the story we are reading is narrated by her while awaiting execution for this deed. But in a different time, her rewriting of the Great Book essentially changes the past so that the Okeke are no longer cursed. Nor will she die when executed; in 'Chapter 1: Rewritten,' which concludes the novel, Onyewonsu refuses martyrdom and instead flies off to an island in the Wilderness to meet her lover Mwiti. Meanwhile, the Epilogue, narrated by the young woman recording the story on the laptop, concludes with a spatial marker that inserts the novel within the future of a very real history: 'It was the most we could do for the woman who saved the people of the Seven Rivers Kingdom, this place that used to be part of the Kingdom of Sudan.'[55] Okorafor never spells out whether the apocalypse that has beset the Seven Rivers Kingdom was local or global. The implicit argument is that for those inside its boundaries it really does not matter, just as it likely made no difference to the Haitians in 2010 how much of the world outside their immediate knowledge had also been destroyed by the earthquake that had devastated theirs.

This is only a partially true argument, however; in its identity as enclosure, the bunker always signals or remembers the existence of an outside world where something might be different. For this reason, the cave of future relics destabilizes any assumption of exclusively mythic time by introducing a conception of history. The reference to the Kingdom of Sudan has a similar effect: Okorafor is arguing simultaneously, from within the novel, that the Sudanese are responsible for their own fate, an apocalypse caused by genocidal madness enabled by advanced technology, and, from the reader's knowledge, that the rest of the world did little to stop this apocalypse, essentially sealing it off in its own destruction. Life in the epistemological bunker means accepting the ongoing threat and actual occurrence of apocalypse as a normal, everyday experience. But it also affords recognition of this fact. And it enables the conception of alternate ways of working with and responding to it.

---

55 Okorafor, *Who Fears Death*, 381.

Distant-future speculation in speculative time

Butler had originally planned anywhere from one to four additional Parable novels, describing what happens to the Earthseed settlers on the distant planet they reach in a distant future. She explained in an interview that, in *The Parable of the Trickster* and other potential sequels, she would not, as in her earlier distant-future novels, 'confront ... them with natives. ... What I'm going to confront them with is just a nasty world. It's not violent, just nasty and dull and awful, and what they're going to have to deal with is themselves. There's no going home. ... The real problem is dealing with themselves, surviving their promised land.'[56] Despite the essential pessimism that contributed to the writer's block that kept her from getting beyond 'dozens upon dozens of false starts,' Butler's investment in distant-future speculation remained essentially hopeful in the assertion embedded in its very form that there was something in humanity worth preserving and that this something could somehow best be grasped when tested against a world that would be both profoundly alien and intimately familiar. What Canavan terms Butler's 'sense of constrained hope ... is ... a hope made possible *by* constraints. ... "We can't afford to go someplace else and make the mistakes we make here, here in the nest."'[57] Distant-future thinking afforded Butler simultaneously a radical critique of present-day society, the opportunity to choose what might remain in the prepper's grab bag from that society, and the realism to know that the grab bag would also bring with it exactly what the prepper would have preferred to have left behind. Distant-future thinking allowed her to imagine the very limits of the mistakes that could be made without extinction, and the very limits of how to remedy those mistakes without ceasing to be human altogether. That she was never able to finish *Trickster* suggests how difficult that task proved to be.

Distant-future speculation is perhaps the most radical challenge to linear spacetime afforded by the bunker fantasy. Since the beginning of the nuclear age, science fiction has mobilized the device of nuclear war to explore and to narrate deep time. Most distant-future nuclear fictions use this temporal affordance to stage a neobarbarian world with bunker-buried traces of the lost world, often sealed off not just physically but with taboos against exploration or excavation, such as the 'Time Vault,' in Poul Anderson's *Vault of the Ages* (1952) or the 'Forbidden Zone' in the *Planet of the Apes*

---

56 Qtd in Canavan, '"There's Nothing New / Under The Sun, / But There Are New Suns": Recovering Octavia E. Butler's Lost Parables,' *Los Angeles Review of Books* (9 June 2014): https://lareviewofbooks.org/article/theres-nothing-new-sun-new-suns-recovering-octavia-e-butlers-lost-parables. See also Canavan, *Butler*, 179–88.

57 Canavan, 'Octavia E. Butler's Lost Parables.'

Writing from the epistemological bunker

series, which hides the forgotten past of nuclear war. Walter M. Miller's seminal novel *Canticle for Leibowitz* (1955–60) satirized the motif, imagining an entire cult of worship developed around the boring minutiae of everyday life rendered holy relics when excavated centuries after the fact from buried ruins of the titular nobody's fallout shelter. This tenuous historical link poses a threat as much as a continuity: in *Apes* and *Leibowitz*, as elsewhere, the rediscovery of the bunkered past issues in an endless recurrence of redevelopment and further Armageddons.

The two distant-future series that Butler did finish – the Patternist series (1976–84) and the Xenogenesis trilogy (1987–89) – imagine a humanity able to survive its own mistakes only by interbreeding with alien lifeforms to create something new, hybrid, and persistently but no longer fatally flawed. 'Amnesty,' one of the last stories Butler wrote, reimagined the Xenogenesis scenario but with hive-mind aliens stranded on Earth in thirty-seven 'bubbles' scattered like impermeable biodomes across the world's desert terrains, and addicted to human contact as if to drugs. The apocalypse they have brought has been purely economic; however, we learn from Noah, a Translator in the Mojave Bubble, that there was 'a short, quiet war ... We lost.' And it was a nuclear war:

> I have no idea how that attack was repelled, but I do know this, and my military captors confirmed it with their lines of questioning: the missiles fired at the bubbles never detonated. They should have, but they didn't. And sometime later, exactly half of the missiles that had been fired were returned. They were discovered armed and intact, scattered around Washington DC in the White House – one in the Oval Office – in the capitol, in the Pentagon. In China, half of the missiles fired at the Gobi Bubbles were found scattered around Beijing. London and Paris got one half of their missiles back from the Sahara and Australia. There was panic, confusion, fury. ... Apparently, the Communities still have the other half – along with whatever weapons they brought with them and any they've built since they've been here.[58]

Instead of a cataclysmic conflict propelling the scenario into the distant future, Butler simply rooted the kernel of the bunker fantasy in the speculative present, doubling down on what McKittrick terms 'difficult epistemological returns to the past and the present.'

The two extended series keep the springboard into the distant future but link it explicitly with an alternate understanding of the past and the present similar to 'Amnesty,' in which, in Foster's words, 'the most basic ontological categories defining "our" existence, including words like "our," are negotiated, not given.'[59] A linked series of five novels published out of chronological

---

58 Butler, 'Amnesty,' 614–15.
59 Foster, 'We Get to Live,' loc. 3056.

order and telling an alternate history from 1690 into a distant future of human-like telepaths, mute enslaved humans, and alien Clayarks born of humans mutated by an alien microorganism, the Patternist series opens embedded within the transatlantic slave trade and ends in a neofeudal future of enclaves inhabited by feuding Patternists and their 'mute,' or normal human slaves, besieged by Clayark predations. In *Clay's Ark* (1984), the hinge volume of the series and the final one she wrote, a densely concentrated survivalist narrative recounts the onset of an apocalyptic pandemic as a sequence of conflicting survivalist scenarios, flawed individuals fighting for control over their own emotions and bodies. In these fictions, comments Andrea Hairston, 'The only hope for humanity is assimilation.'[60] The most sympathetically rendered characters are Keira, a kidnapped young woman dying of cancer for whom alien possession promises survival and who wants to join the enclave that has kidnapped her, and younger child Jacob, a four-legged mutant offspring, or Clayark, who is not human enough to pass. *Survivor* (1979), the fourth volume chronologically, narrates the story of the Missionaries of Verrick Colony, sent to a distant planet in a Patternist ship 'to preserve and to spread the sacred God-image of humankind.'[61] What they find, however, is a fully established society of semi-human clans on a more or less neobarbarian model, but far more advanced and adapted than the bare survival means of the Missionaries. Instead, they must risk indentured servitude if not extinction; the dilemma is resolved by the feral child Alanna, who had been adopted into a walled Missionary town by its leading couple. Like Keira's choice in *Clay's Ark*, the survival Alanna will offer to the Missionaries is predicated not only on alliance with a Kohn clan but on giving up their ideology of racial purity. Married to the Tehkohn leader and pregnant with their child, Alanna's offering of survival and shelter will necessitate interspecies hybridization with the clan the Missionaries perceive as their mortal enemy.

In Butler's fiction, apocalypse, everyday life, and species-level change are inextricably interwoven in a fabric of form that affords a narrative reckoning in particular with apparently intractable differences of race and gender in the context of inequality. 'The core at which all comes together in Butler's universe,' argues Sandra Y. Govan, 'is the delineation of power. "I began writing about power," Butler has said, "because I had so little."'[62]

---

60 Andrea Hairston, 'Octavia Butler – Praise Song to a Prophetic Artist' (2006), in *Luminescent Threads: Connections to Octavia E. Butler*, ed. Alexandra Pierce and Mimi Mondal (Yokine, WA: Twelfth Planet Press, 2017), Kindle loc. 1239.

61 Butler, *Survivor* (New York: Signet, 1979), 28.

62 Sandra Y. Govan, 'Connections, Links, and Extended Networks: Patterns in Octavia Butler's Science Fiction' (1984), in *Luminescent Threads*, loc. 2658.

Writing from the epistemological bunker 213

Not only do these fictions pry apart and challenge basic assumptions about race, identity, and ethnicity, but they do so without thereby dissolving their differences, what Rebecca Holden calls the characters' 'lived realities.'[63] For Butler, as Gregory Hampton writes, 'ambiguity is both empowering and necessary for the survival of humanity. The notions of racial purity and cultural commonality are written as detriments to humanities' history and future.'[64] The distant and alien futures she imagines thus remain intimately resonant in the known world even as they challenge basic assumptions about that world. *Dawn*, for instance, charts Lilith Iyapo's ambivalent journey from awakening as a captive in an alien spacecraft 250 years after the world has been devastated by a nuclear war, to accepting an intimate relationship with a tentacled ooloi known as Jdhaya (later Nikanj), to training and leading a band of artificially sustained human survivors to a new colonization of a regrown earth. The spaceship, which we come to know eventually as a sentient entity named Chkahichdahk, functions as a nurturing, all-sustaining, organic bunker able to construct anything they might need from the genetic code provided it.

Butler briefly but memorably distinguishes the spaceship as ambiguous shelter from the dead end of bunker survivalism. 'Some of the people we picked up,' Jdhaya tells her, 'had been hiding deep underground. They had created much of the destruction.' And although informed that she resembles those warmongers in some ways, she is also informed that she will be returned to Earth. Asked if those others will be joining her, Lilith receives a curt 'No.'[65] In its larval stage, Lo, another of these entities, will shelter them on Earth in what had once been the Brazilian rainforest. While the Oankali travel the galaxy seeking to 'trade' with the inhabitants of each planet and take with them whatever they deem worth preserving, 'Anything to do with Humans,' Nikanj decides, 'always seems to involve contradictions.'[66] This 'lethal genetic conflict' between 'intelligence' and 'hierarchical tendencies,' the Oankali have determined, will eventually lead them again to world destruction even if they are permitted to settle a new planet.[67] And this lethal contradiction, imagined through a distant future that was equally an apocalyptic present, is the form that affords Butler's 'giving us what sometimes seems like contradictory and multiple truths.'[68]

---

63 Rebecca Holden, '"Let's Dwell a Little": The Trickster within Octavia E. Butler,' in *Luminescent Threads*, loc. 900.

64 Gregory Hampton, *Changing Bodies in the Fiction of Octavia Butler: Slaves, Aliens, and Vampires* (Lanham, MD: Lexington, 2010), 67.

65 Butler, *Dawn* (New York: Warner, 1988 [1987]), 14, 16.

66 Butler, *Adulthood Rites* (New York: Warner, 1988), 182.

67 Butler, *Imago* (New York: Warner, 1989), 10.

68 Holden, 'Let's Dwell a Little,' loc. 900.

214   *After the end*

Butler never explicitly reduces humanity's 'hierarchical tendencies' to cis-gendered white men and fully explores an 'unconscious will to survive' that is equally strong in her male and female characters but whose violence, selfishness, and rigidity are far less tempered by other concerns.[69] Nevertheless, there is no question that these men offer the least and pose the greatest threat to the hybrid and miscegenated futures Butler imagined for what she once called the 'Lost Races of Science Fiction.'[70] We find a similar if less fully articulated vision of a mongrel future imagined out of an alternate past in Susan Torian Olan's distant-future novel *The Earth Remembers* (1989). Although set in a Texas at least one thousand years following a nuclear cataclysm that transformed its coastline and sent its technology and political structures into a neobarbarian Dark Age, *Earth Remembers* reads like a spaghetti Western mashup set in a mythic present. The novel's central conflict pits a brutally expansionist Tesharka Confederation dominated by white men against a motley alliance of marginalized populations. The conflict involves the Confederation's resident astrologer priest Zumarraga Apocalypse's obsession to unleash the Fire God (a thermonuclear device) from the remote and unmapped San Cris mountains.[71] A Pecos cowboy and righthand man of the Mexican bandit general Diego Laredo is joined by a mercenary refugee from Lagos and three magical figures out of premodernity: a Toltec *curandera*, or healer, the 'daughter of Quetzelcoatl' whose cloud forest mountain city survived as an island enclave separated by war from Guatemala; the last surviving giant from the prehistoric race of Paleoricans or 'People of the Earth'; and a female *itzaur*, whose race and whose secret subterranean city of Itzamma date back forty million years to the age of dinosaurs. A version of the Lemurians, the lizard men reputed to have fought cosmic nuclear battles in a cycle of civilization and destruction since the dawn of time, the *itzaurs* are survivors of their own 'Holocaust, when a meteor and the Earth burned.'[72] Among their allies are Comanche warriors, a ferocious band of orphaned children living in abandoned mine tunnels, and the survivors of the now-conquered Republic of Pecos, a futuristic refraction of 'Old World Texas.' Their leader, whom Angelina is being brought to cure, is Falling Eagle, 'the last Aztec *Uey-Tlateoni*, or Revered Speaker, reborn.'[73] They are

---

69 Butler, *Clay's Ark*, 470.
70 Butler, 'Lost Races of Science Fiction,' *Transmission* (Summer 1980): 17–18; rpt in Canavan, *Butler*, 181–6.
71 Susan Torian Olan, *Earth Remembers* (Lake Geneva, WI: TSR, 1989), 91.
72 Olan, *Earth Remembers*, 133, 140. On the Lemurians and nuclear war, see Pike, 'Haunted Mountains, Supershelters and the Afterlives of Cold War Infrastructure,' *Journal for the Study of Religion, Nature and Culture* 13.2 (2019): 208–29.
73 Olan, *Earth Remembers*, 171.

Figure 5.4 Worshipping the bomb: mutant priests reveal their 'true selves' to their thermonuclear god in *Beneath the Planet of the Apes*.

even aided in the final battle by a Sasquatch, 'the oldest of the races' and once sole possessors of the land.[74]

While its pulp adventure yarn is overstuffed and its rendering of Indigenous characters highly romanticized, *Earth Remembers* shares with Butler's Afrofuturist fictions a spatiotemporal imaginary. This imaginary affords a transhistorical rewriting of American history as the deep-time myth of a multiply peopled region spanning geological epochs and shrinking the form of humanity embodied as white America to a brief but deadly blip in the second half of the second millennium in a land to which it never had any legitimate claim. In the end, this underdog alliance composed of 'people of every known nation or tribe on the continent' will be trapped in its hidden mountain redoubt of Epitaph, where Falling Eagle will detonate the 'Fire God' and decimate the Confederation army of armored 'Clankers' along with nearly all the ragtag survivors of the defeated rebels.[75] Like the H-bomb worshipped by a mutant priesthood in the buried ruins of Manhattan's St Patrick's Cathedral in *Beneath the Planet of the Apes* (1970; Figure 5.4), Epitaph's nuclear device is embedded within the sacred space of a deeply subterranean *kiva*. Olan renders its technology mythopoetically: 'The Ancient Ones believed their ancestors had emerged into the world through these holes called *kivas*. They believed the *kiva* led to the underground where the gods lived. Many of the gods were not pleasant characters, the one that dwells here most especially.'[76] At the same time, she renders it futuristically:

74 Olan, *Earth Remembers*, 240.
75 Olan, *Earth Remembers*, 253.
76 Olan, *Earth Remembers*, 251.

216 *After the end*

a 'safety mechanism' activated by Falling Eagle releases a controlled underground explosion that swallows up Epitaph in a blast crater without permanently 'burning' the land or releasing toxic fallout into the air.[77] In Olan's fantasy, the 'War God' itself is repurposed against the oppressive forces descended from the warmongers of her day who had been responsible for burning the world in the first place. And while she sacrifices a good portion of her characters, a chosen few are able to escape through a long, deep tunnel leading out from the *kiva* to emerge safe and sound on the other side of the mountains. Olan's denouement explicitly echoes origin myths of Indigenous Peoples of the Southwest; a novel that begins with the clandestine crossing of the fortified Rio Bravo ends with a tale of emergence echoing those of the original inhabitants of this land: '[O]ur Elder Brother brought us across, his name was I'itio. On our setting out from the other side, he turned us into ants. He brought us through narrow darkness and out at Baboquivari Peak into this land. Here we became human again, and our Elder Brother rested in a cave on Baboquivari, and there he rests till this day, helping us.'[78] The mythic time afforded by distant-future speculation respatializes presentist fixity within the broader imaginary of the bunker fantasy.

Rather than politically focused on the 'cold warrior' policies of 1980s Reaganism, prolific SFF author Robert Silverberg's projected far-future trilogy considers survival and identity as philosophical questions. In *At Winter's End* (1988) and *The Queen of Springtime* (1990), the two published volumes, the 'People' emerge to reinhabit the world from the 'cocoon' where they have survived a seven-hundred-thousand-year Ice Age. Silverberg explores the qualities that might permit humans to survive so long in a sealed-off bunker space, including an excursion into the 'hive-mind' of the *hjjk* people, for whom the bunker fantasy ('the Nest') is their natural state: 'Whether the Nest is a place of good or evil, one thing is true of it: while you're in it you feel utterly secure. You know that you live in a place where uncertainty and pain are unknown. I surrendered myself completely to it, and gladly, as who wouldn't?'[79] For Silverberg, too, the bunker fantasy permits deep-time speculation that concludes in a cyclical vision of advanced beings 'seeding' new species that will be adequate to the next postapocalyptic world. For these Cold War fictions, the threat of war is both an opportunity for thought and a recognition that the bunker would fundamentally transform those

---

77 Olan, *Earth Remembers*, 313.

78 As recounted in Teju Cole, 'A Piece of the Wall,' in *Known and Strange Things* (New York: Random House, 2016 [2014]), 363–76, at 367.

79 Robert Silverberg, *The Queen of Springtime* (Lincoln: University of Nebraska Press, 2005 [1990]), 245.

Writing from the epistemological bunker 217

who sheltered within it. Deployed in the changed circumstances of the world created in the ontological bunker, fictions such as those of Butler, Hopkinson, Okorafor, or Olan find that the misplaced fantasy can lead even to the secrets and pasts it appeared to have shut out.

The long view, argues science and SFF writer Annalee Newitz, informs about apocalypse that 'the world has been almost completely destroyed at least half a dozen times already in Earth's 4.5-billion-year history, and every single time there have been survivors. ... [L]iving creatures carried on, adapting to survive under the harshest of conditions. ... If we want to survive for another million years, we should look to our history to find strategies that already worked.'[80] SFF, they continue, is how we imagine survival: 'Fiction about tomorrow can provide a symbolic map that tells us where we want to go.'[81] Newitz's pragmatic survivalism is simultaneously chilling and refreshing. 'If survival means that our species will evolve into creatures like ourselves, but with new abilities – like, say, flight – that's not so bad,' they conclude. 'Some would even call it an improvement. Survival may be far weirder, and better, than we ever imagined.'[82] It would be easy to dismiss Newitz's approach as starry-eyed techno-utopianism, except that they draw many of their examples of survival strategies from at-risk and oppressed groups over the last few centuries – from the Indigenous Peoples, enslaved and colonized populations, and impoverished or imperiled migrants for whom apocalypse is an ongoing and intimately familiar condition; from those who in different ways 'are connected to their cultural traditions, but also living them dynamically, reshaping them to suit life in a world forever changed by colonial contact';[83] from those who are practicing survivance, as Vizenor described it in *Hiroshima Bugi: Atomu 57* (see Chapter 2). The dissident temporality enabled by the deep-time long view can also be accessed by an epistemological shift that uncovers dissident temporality within the world we currently inhabit.

Distant-future speculation in real time

The deep-time thinking enabled by the bunker fantasy in fact affords dissident temporality within the present. And as Newitz suggests, distant-future speculation is not only the SFF writer's purview; the Clock of the Long Now, buried deep inside mountains in Texas and Nevada, ticks once every

80 Newitz, *Scatter, Adapt, and Remember*, 1–2.
81 Newitz, *Scatter, Adapt, and Remember*, 9.
82 Newitz, *Scatter, Adapt, and Remember*, 102.
83 Newitz, *Scatter, Adapt, and Remember*, 55.

218 *After the end*

decade, has a century hand, chimes once a millennium, and is designed to run for ten thousand years.[84] Its goal is 'to promote long-term thinking.'[85] In stark opposition to the Doomsday Clock of the *Bulletin of the Atomic Scientists*, set at its earliest (seventeen minutes to midnight) in 1991 and its latest (ninety seconds to midnight) in 2023, the Clock of the Long Now asks us to think beyond the effects of nuclear war and other cataclysms rather than exclusively address their imminent threat. Thinking from within the ontological bunker does give up the possibility of forestalling the end; like all survivalist thinking, it embraces cataclysmic change while seeking to consider what may still be saved or most worth saving. Similar deep-underground projects also promote long-term thinking; at the same time, they remind us that clock-time is not the only way to think long term.

It is not surprising that the branch of moral philosophy known as 'population ethics' emerged in the early 1980s as an attempt to address the question: how 'to act when the consequences of our actions will affect not only the well-being of future people but their very existence?'[86] In Derek Parfit's population ethics and his student Toby Ord's philosophical analysis of present-day responsibility for ensuring the long-term survival of the human race, we find also embedded a highly political question, a cost–benefit analysis of the Anthropocene and its threats to humanity. As Jim Holt phrases it, 'How much should we be willing to sacrifice today in order to ensure humanity's long-term future?'[87] This premise takes for granted in some ways an affirmative answer to the more fundamental question asked by Mark O'Connell, 'Was it so unacceptable that humanity should eventually run its course?', and asserted more bleakly to him in conversation, by a woman echoing the AI avatar Agent Smith in *The Matrix*, that 'on some level we are a cancer, and the world will cure itself of us.'[88] Ord's calculations of risk suggest the Anthropocene should be regarded not only as the acknowledgment of nuclearity in the geological record. They also accept that 'anthropogenic risk' of extinction for the first time far exceeds 'natural risk ... a new age of unsustainably heightened risk, what Ord calls "the Precipice."'[89] While Ord estimates that nuclear war would cause devastation rather than extinction, he views other threats – AI and human-amplified pandemic – as

---

84 Galviz, 'Time Underground: The Clock of the Long Now,' in *Global Undergrounds*, ed. Dobraszczyk et al., 245–7.
85 Galviz, 'Time Underground,' 247.
86 Jim Holt, 'The Power of Catastrophic Thinking,' *New York Review of Books* (25 Feb. 2021): www.nybooks.com/articles/2021/02/25/power-catastrophic-thinking-toby -ord-precipice/.
87 Holt, 'Catastrophic Thinking.'
88 O'Connell, *Notes from an Apocalypse*, 123, 154.
89 Holt, 'Catastrophic Thinking.'

Writing from the epistemological bunker

219

far more likely contributors to the one-in-six chance of the extinction of the human race in the current century. Ord's endeavor is laudable in seeking to parse what we owe to the present versus what we owe to the future, and to shift our imagination and resources towards considering greater versus lesser threats. But the abstractness of his calculations suggests the difficulty in appreciating the practical difference between, as Parfit phrased it in 1984, 'A nuclear war that kills 99 percent of the world's population' and one that kills 100 percent.[90] Preppers, of course, view that difference solely in terms of ensuring that they can be part of the surviving one percent; distant-future SFF imagines not so much the philosophy as the practical questions raised by survival, and, as Newitz suggests, what survival would look like and what would be worth saving. But all, as also Parfit and Ord, use deep-time thinking primarily as a way to understand and act on the world we live in now.

The Future Library, for instance, commissions new work from eminent contemporary writers 'that will remain unread until 2114, when they will be opened and printed on 1,000 trees currently growing just outside Oslo.'[91] According to Vietnamese American poet and novelist Ocean Vuong, the decision to participate came down to thinking beyond the present: 'So many of our problems have to do with this Yolo approach – you only live once, use all the resources, forget about the next generation, destroy the world to get what you want. This is something antithetical to that.'[92] Vuong imagined a story that would echo his own attitude towards the future: 'I could write a story about a group of folks who have heard of the wonderful literature of the past and are trekking through a Norwegian forest in a postapocalyptic world, thinking they'll find some great tablets – and only finding some poems about being sad.'[93] In return, the Scottish artist Katie Paterson, who came up with the concept, commented of Vuong, 'His poetry and prose is raw and fearless, capturing the essence of survival.'[94]

Other deep-time planners are concerned with more directly practical aspects of future survival. Both nuclear waste deposits and seed banks attempt to calculate the effects of millennia on the contents they desire to safeguard. These calculations, too, invoke ontologies and epistemologies that exceed humanity or rationality and enter realms the developed world previously entrusted to myth. Writing of *Into Eternity*, Danish filmmaker

90 Holt, 'Catastrophic Thinking.'
91 Sian Cain, '"You'll have to die to get these texts": Ocean Vuong's Next Manuscript to Be Unveiled in 2114,' *Guardian* (19 Aug. 2020): www.theguardian.com/books/2020/aug/19/ocean-vuong-2114-book-future-library-norway.
92 Cain, 'You'll have to die.'
93 Cain, 'You'll have to die.'
94 Cain, 'You'll have to die.'

Figure 5.5 Excavating for the distant future: the Onkalo spent nuclear fuel repository, Finland.

Michael Madsen's documentary about the Finnish design of a five-hundred-meter-deep bunker for keeping the surface of the earth free from contamination by nuclear waste for one hundred thousand years, critic Peter Bradshaw concluded that 'This is nothing less than post-human architecture we are talking about' (Figure 5.5).[95] Plans for the similarly deep Yucca Mountain Nuclear Storage, first proposed in 1987 and ultimately losing its federal funding in 2010, equally involved complex speculation and passionate debate about the best way to signal its contents without tempting the curious to open it up in search of treasure or knowledge.[96] As A. O. Scott mused in his review of *Into Eternity*, 'If it lasts as long as it is supposed to … this enormous feat of engineering may well be the only thing that survives us.

---

95 Peter Bradshaw, '*Into Eternity* – Review,' *Guardian* (11 Nov. 2010): www.theguardian.com/film/2010/nov/11/into-eternity-film-review; accessed 25 April 2018.
96 On the various technical issues involved in deep underground waste storage and its necessity to deal long term with the tens of thousands of tons of waste generated by nuclear power plants, see Chris G. Whipple, 'Can Nuclear Waste Be Stored Safely at Yucca Mountain?' *Scientific American* 274.6 (1996): 72–9. On the question of avoiding attention and excavation in the far-distant future, see Douglas Cruickshank, 'How Do You Design a 'Keep Out!' Sign to Last 10,000 Years?' *Salon* (10 May 2002): https://web.archive.org/web/20230217125418/https://www.salon.com/2002/05/10/yucca_mountain/; and Bradley L. Garrett, 'Burying Incomprehensible Horror: Yucca Mountain Nuclear Storage,' in *Global Undergrounds*, ed. Dobraszczyk et al., 85–7.

Writing from the epistemological bunker

It may, in other words, constitute the whole of the human legacy for a long, post-human time to come. And this will be especially true, and especially fitting, if the place is forgotten and never found.'[97] Unsurprisingly, the prospect of the 'extension of the timescales of law and risk governance one million years into the future' caused as much alarm in practice as the metaphysical questions fascinated.[98]

At Yucca Mountain, alarm centered on the failure truly to think long term: on the impermanence of the site, and on the short-term political motivations behind the decision-making. For instance, it was clear to many scientists involved in the process that the ten-thousand-year time span determined for planning the site, if barely comprehensible in relation to human time, was absurdly short compared with the tens of millions of years that would need to pass before the more than 77,000 tons of nuclear waste to be stored would actually cease emitting fatal radiation.[99] Similarly, what appeared immutable mountain rock in the geological short term was anything but: satellite surveillance studies led to estimates that 'the entire mountain was likely to move almost fifty full feet over the next 1,000 years'; that an earthquake zone crisscrossed by the Sundance and Ghost Dance faults ran directly beneath the site; that the mountain itself was porous; and that any metal that might be used to seal the waste from water seepage would be corroded within a proportionately brief period of time.[100] In the words of a Nevadan waste consultant, the whole project was 'an exercise in planning for a nuclear catastrophe that is fundamentally rhetorical. It's theatrical security, because the preparations that are being made by the Department of Energy have no real chance of succeeding.'[101] The Yucca Mountain Project, in other words, was a new variation of the classic bunker fantasy; rather than hiding in a bunker to reemerge after the nuclear danger was gone, it proposed hiding the nuclear danger in a bunker and trying to forget about it. But the fantasy of protection was just as dubious as it had been in the fallout shelters of the past.

Yucca Mountain also raised another sort of question. What could be understood as the colonization of deep time by 'law and risk governance' came directly into conflict with beliefs and claims by Indigenous Peoples whose worldview had in fact always included the capacity to encompass

---

97 A. O. Scott, 'Humans, Who Once Buried Their Treasures, Now Bury Their Dangers,' *New York Times* (1 Feb. 2011): www.nytimes.com/2011/02/02/movies/02into.html.

98 Vincent F. Ialenti, 'Adjudicating Deep Time: Revisiting the United States' High-Level Nuclear Waste Repository Project at Yucca Mountain,' *Science & Technology Studies* 27.2 (2014): 27–48, at 29.

99 John D'Agata, *About a Mountain* (New York: W. W. Norton, 2010), 67.

100 D'Agata, *About a Mountain*, 60, 54–7.

101 Bob Halstead, qtd D'Agata, *About a Mountain*, 67.

222   *After the end*

deep time. As Danielle Endres argues, the 'nuclear colonialism' of the Yucca Mountain site abrogated both treaty claims and 'spiritual rights' to the land by American Indian tribes: 'Members of the Las Vegas Paiute, the Lone Pine Paiute Shoshone, the Big Pine Paiute, the Western Shoshone National Council, Western Shoshone, and the Utah Paiute all comment that Yucca Mountain has been part of their homeland since "time immemorial."'[102] The epistemological approaches mandated by the unforeseen consequences of the nuclear condition offer the terrifying prospect of poisoning the earth and dealing death to the planet's inhabitants hundreds of thousands of years hence. Planning for such a contingency raises the specter, as Ialenti argues, of projecting the already outdated and oppressive categories of personhood enshrined in American law as created facts into a modeled future they would essentially colonize.[103] The dispute around what we could term the polar opposite of dissident temporality thus equally affords the realization that science and the law must be opened up to alternate ways of thinking space and time – alternate ways of thinking in fact also available to us, as the SFF writers discussed above let us know, from 'time immemorial.'

The natural correlative to the horrible yet necessary prospect of rendering a supershelter impermeable and impenetrable for up to a million years is the Svalbard Global Seed Vault. A far less costly but no less ambitious endeavor, this 'Doomsday Vault' or 'Noah's Ark' holds more than a million packets of seeds representing crops from around the world.[104] '[T]unnelled 125 metres (410 ft) into the side of a mountain, 130 metres (430 ft) above sea level in a region of permafrost untroubled by seismic activity ... [it] boasts 1-metre-thick (3 ft) reinforced-concrete tunnel walls, and is designed to withstand even nuclear attack.'[105] As Alexander Moss observes, the 'global central vault' was established at a time when 'seed banks in Afghanistan and Iraq were being destroyed by warfare and those in the Philippines by flood damage.'[106] Equally likely is a response to controversy over biodiversity,

102 Danielle Endres, 'The Rhetoric of Nuclear Colonialism: Rhetorical Exclusion of American Indian Arguments in the Yucca Mountain Nuclear Waste Siting Decision,' *Communication and Critical/Cultural Studies* 6.1 (2009): 39–60, DOI: 10.1080/14791420802632103, at 48.
103 Ialenti, 'Adjudicating Deep Time,' 36.
104 Damian Carrington, 'Arctic Stronghold of World's Seeds Flooded after Permafrost Melts,' *Guardian* (19 May 2017): www.theguardian.com/environment/2017/may/19/arctic-stronghold-of-worlds-seeds-flooded-after-permafrost-melts.
105 Alexander Moss, 'After the End: Svalbard Global Seed Vault,' in *Global Undergrounds*, Dobraszczyk et al., 247–9, at 248.
106 Moss, 'After the End,' 247–8. For a summary of the issues related to genetically modified seeds, see Anna Lappé, 'The Battle for Biodiversity: Monsanto and Farmers Clash,' *Atlantic* (28 March 2011): www.theatlantic.com/health/archive/2011/03/the-battle-for-biodiversity-monsanto-and-farmers-clash/73117/.

Writing from the epistemological bunker

the privatization of seeds, the forced planting of nonrenewable genetically modified seeds, and other ways in which multinational corporations were gaining control over stores of seeds and knowledge that had been passed down for millennia.

Just as the bunker form has been appropriated as the most effective means both to store nuclear waste and to imagine the process of that storage, so the seed bunker used the same form to capture a specific imagination and to brand a high-tech infrastructure project with a potent symbol of cyclical, natural time. Less than ten years after its opening, however, reports already circulated that the vault had been breached by flooding from melting permafrost; global warming had accelerated at a rate unforeseen at the time of construction.[107] Whereas the vault had been designed to operate free of any human oversight, it now required twenty-four-hour supervision to prevent any permanent damage. A follow-up article attempted to dampen the panic, insisting that the water seepage had only made it into the entry tunnel and that a number of further barriers would need to be breached before any threat would be posed to the seed bank itself.[108] Both the seepage and the panic over the seepage are salutary reminders that, just as it shelters the dystopian and utopian extremes seldom able to survive exposure in the normal world outside, the bunker fantasy equally always envisions its own failure as part of its imaginary. The global appropriations studied in Chapters 4 and 5 suggest the potential afforded by this fantasy to the critical analysis of contemporary society, its pasts, and its futures; they equally suggest the degree to which the bunker – whether epistemological or ontological – dominates contemporary modes of thinking and being. The book's final chapter moves from these self-evident appropriations to less frequently recognized ways in which the bunker organizes twenty-first-century space in the form of borders and security, and what happens when we think about these phenomena through the bunker fantasy.

107 Carrington, 'Arctic Stronghold.'
108 Mary Beth Griggs, 'Turns Out the Svalbard Seed Vault Is Probably Fine,' *Popular Science* (22 May 2017): https://web.archive.org/web/20221205012621/https://www.popsci.com/seed-vault-flooding/.

6

Wall and tunnel: security, containment, and subversion

> Mother, do you think they'll drop the bomb?
> Mother, do you think they'll like this song?
> Mother, do you think they'll try to break my balls?
> Ooh ah ... Mother, should I build the wall?
> Pink Floyd / Roger Waters, 'Mother' (1979)

The story of walls is not quite the same as the story of bunkers, but they are closely related forms whose meanings have been tightly associated since the Cold War. The difference between them is one of perspective, and that changed perspective suggests why the bunker is more visible in today's past imagination around security, while the wall dominates its present imaginary. Bunkers treat the space they enclose as underground, sheltered, and inaccessible. Walls can either divide or enclose; the verticality of their barrier affords the same protection as the bunker but their visibly horizontal sprawl stresses paratactic segmentation of similar aboveground spaces rather than a vertically stacked hierarchization. In their ancient tendency to create inequality in their division and in their modern propensity towards opacity and impermeability, walls tend more and more to echo the security and containment features of the bunker. For all their negative affordances, bunkers nevertheless resonate with what Elaine Scarry terms the 'equality of survival' and the 'right to shelter' of all. Walls, in contrast, exist in order to exclude; especially since 1989, their form exudes inequity and separation.

Walls and bunkers thus afford different qualities and potentialities despite their formal convergence. Walls are more effectively narrated from the outside and shelters more effectively from within; so, wall-jumpers tend to be sympathetic if not outright heroic, while bunker-busters are more easily suspect. Moreover, it is assumed that a wall will eventually come down, like the Berlin Wall; become a historic spectacle for tourists, like the Great Wall of China; or be itself enclosed, like the rings of city walls that mark the growth of older, once fortified metropolises such as Paris. Walls exist in and for present threats; bunkers exist in and for future threats. Considered another way, barrier walls short-circuit the bunker's fantasy to create an endlessly deferred present that shelters 'us' from the threat of 'them' or prevents 'us' from getting at the shelter and survival we need on the other side. Both literally and figuratively, the twenty-first century has come much closer to realizing the 1962 American dream of a shelter society than at any time during the Cold War culture that first dreamed it.

Boundary walls and bunkered living

The conceit of a bunker is that it is permanent; the conceit of a wall, especially a border or boundary wall, is that sooner or later it will be gone. Curiously, this fact makes the wall appear more mendacious as a structure than the bunker which, true to its brutalist form, is what it is. Walls, as Octavia Butler understood already in 1993, were more likely than bunkers to define space and survival in a post–Cold War apocalypse. Set in 2024 near the end of the fifteen-year-long 'Pox,' *Parable of the Sower* opens in a relatively secure and relatively privileged walled middle-class enclave set among a variety of less prosperous and less secure urban neighborhoods. The gradation is defined by the state of the enclosing barrier wall:

> A lot of our ride was along one neighborhood wall after another; some a block long, some two blocks, some five. ... Up toward the hills there were walled estates – one big house and a lot of shacky little dependencies where the servants lived. We didn't pass anything like that today. In fact we passed a couple of neighborhoods so poor that their walls were made up of unmortared rocks, chunks of concrete, and trash. Then there were the pitiful, unwalled residential areas. A lot of the houses were trashed – burned, vandalized, infested with drunks or druggies or squatted-in by homeless families with their filthy, gaunt, half-naked children.[1]

Rather than the way that boundary walls typically divide experiences into incommensurable halves, Butler's young narrator is characteristically able to share in something of each perspective; indeed, the medical condition of 'hyperempathy' from which she suffers both threatens and enables her survival. 'If they couldn't see our guns,' she muses, 'We could wind up like that naked woman. ... I wish we could have given her something. My stepmother says she and my father stopped to help an injured woman once, and the guys who had injured her jumped out from behind a wall and almost killed them. ... Crazy to live without a wall to protect you.'[2] Humanity

---

1 Butler, *Sower*, 9.
2 Butler, *Sower*, 9–10.

226 *After the end*

depends on ignoring the function of walls; survival depends on respecting it. Olamina will soon lose her protective wall when her enclave is sacked, her family and neighbors are raped and murdered, and she is cast out into the 'unwalled' life where the rest of the novel takes place.

Unlike Olamina's plain speaking, those who support walls in the present day, as Marcello Di Cintio notes, seldom call them walls; instead, they give them more ideologically palatable if less sonorous names such as 'anti-fascist protection bulwark' (*'antifaschistischer Schutzwall*,' Berlin); 'seam-line obstacle,' 'separation fence,' 'anti-terrorist fence' (West Bank); or 'border fence' (US–Mexico border).[3] In John Lanchester's eponymous satirical novel, the official name for the ten-thousand-kilometer structure that encircles an island much like Britain is 'National Coastal Defense Structure.' Naturally, to the foot soldiers tasked with defending it to the death from encroaching 'Others,' it's simply 'The Wall.'[4] Similarly, when opponents labeled the Berlin Wall the *Schandmauer* (Wall of Shame) or call the West Bank barrier an 'Apartheid Wall'[5] or American opponents to immigration shout the slogan 'Build the Wall,' they remind us that 'Wall' is as much a symbolic term as a descriptor for an architectural form. The fantasy of security and containment afforded by that term and the stark and unbreachable division it equally conjures reveal its formal debt to the Cold War bunker (Figure 6.1).

At the same time, the mendacious identity of the border wall affords the illusion of security in ways that the ambivalent form of the nuclear bunker never quite did. In this respect, the wall resembles the dome that arose as a utopian expression of the bunker fantasy in the late 1960s; however, in its qualities as covered and as maintaining a strong identity of inside and outside, and in its focus on the experience of being enclosed rather than shut out, the dome leans towards the bunker. Whereas the bunker form affords an enclave sheltering both dystopian and utopian extremes of the Cold War waged around it, the dome tends toward the utopian while the boundary wall delineates a divide only to maintain it. Consequently, the wall's dystopia looms in self-evidence and its opposite extreme can be realized only through subversion: a wall can be scaled, torn down, punched through, or tunneled under, but in its capacity as wall, it powerfully resists pleasure or redemption. As the American novelist Fletcher Knebel cynically

---

3 Marcello Di Cintio, *Walls: Travels along the Barricades* (Berkeley: Soft Skull Press, 2013), 14, 102; Eyal Weizman, *Hollow Land: Israel's Architecture of Occupation* (London: Verso, 2017 [2007]), 145.
4 John Lanchester, *The Wall: A Novel* (New York: Norton, 2019), 21, 129.
5 David L. Pike, 'Wall and Tunnel: The Spatial Metaphorics of Cold War Berlin,' *New German Critique* 110 (2010): 73–94, at 74; Di Cintio, *Walls*, 104.

Figure 6.1 Lovers separated by the grim reality of a separation wall: the original incarnation of the Berlin Wall, as reimagined in the German historical drama *Der Tunnel*.

but accurately put it in his espionage novel *Crossing in Berlin* (1981), at the end of a long list of the reasons the Wall was a useful construct: '[T]he mass of voters in the Western democracies love it unconsciously because it hides the complexities of international politics and makes everything quite simple .... It's a prison wall, ... and over there are all the bad prisoners and their keepers, and over here we are all the good chaps.'[6] W. L. Goodwater's 2018 'atompunk' fantasy novel *Breach* deployed Knebel's premise as the basis for an alternate-history plot: why would the Allies be so desperate to keep the Soviets from breaching the Wall? The Wall, it turns out here, is not only a barrier; it's a magicked container for a world-destroying evil unleashed into the world by Nazi magicians and coveted by the current enemy. Magic in this misplaced version of the Cold War 'was like the fear of the atomic bomb or of God: too terrifying to be anything other than abstract.'[7] Freed from the overdetermined ideological weight of its singular meaning, the Wall expresses the full contradictions of terrifying technologies and practices – what Cameroonian political theorist Achille Mbembe terms the 'necropolitics' or sovereign wielding of death-dealing power[8] – unpinned from the constraints of human scale or embodied experience.

---

6 Fletcher Knebel, *Crossing in Berlin* (Garden City, NY: Doubleday, 1981), 119; qtd Ernst Schirer, Manfred Keune, and Philip Jenkins, ed., *The Berlin Wall: Representations and Perspectives* (New York: Lang, 1996), 58.
7 W. L. Goodwater, *Breach* (New York: Ace, 2018), 84.
8 Achille Mbembe, *Necropolitics*, trans. Steve Corcoran (Durham: Duke University Press, 2019 [2016]).

228   *After the end*

Around 1989, in this sense, was a brief opening when tearing down the Wall promised as its straightforward consequence to allow the world's populations to emerge from their respective bunkers and to heal the traumas consequent to their confinement. The signature moment of the end of the Cold War did not involve any of the more hidden and more enduring bunker spaces; rather, it entailed the spectacularly visible breaching and destruction of the 'anti-fascist protection bulwark' dividing West from East, summed up in the pop apotheosis of that symbolism: Roger Waters performing Pink Floyd's late–Cold War concept album *The Wall* live in 1990 from a stage erected in the no-man's-land where the Berlin Wall had been, preserving one section as a security fence behind the stage. What in the 1979 of the album's release had taken the Cold War division as a metaphor for psychological isolation implying political stasis – 'Mother, should I build the wall?' – had inverted the gesture ten years after into an image of political liberation implying individual release. And presumably, the anxiety that had been condensed into the song's opening line – 'Mother, do you think they'll drop the bomb?' – would be, after 1989, no longer operative. In three incarnations – its startlingly sudden appearance overnight on 13 August 1961 and rapid construction thereafter; its startlingly sudden downfall once opened up in November 1989; and the dissemination of its graffitied fragments as thousands of relics large and small throughout the post–Cold War 'free' world and across the Internet – the Berlin Wall shadows the trajectory of the bunker fantasy, suggesting how the two forms converge and differ as emblematic spaces of the Cold War.

This chapter studies the legacy of the bunker fantasy within the wall's proliferation as the emblem of security and containment for the twenty-first-century nation-state and the inevitable pairing of wall with its spatial counterpart, the tunnel. These discussions draw on fiction, nonfiction, and journalism, and on material practices; the former suggest the underlying potentialities of the latter in the twenty-first century while simultaneously addressing their actual and potential pathologies. The argument stresses the legacy of the bunker fantasy within wall and tunnel imaginaries and the consequences of that legacy for a global society ever more obsessed with security and boundaries, whether from an insider or an outsider perspective, or an ambivalent combination of the two.

Wall and tunnel in Berlin

Like bunkers and fortifications, border walls and fences have been around as long as wars over territory have occurred; nevertheless, more separation barriers were initiated in the first two decades of the twenty-first century than during the more than forty years of the Cold War.[9] As of 2023, barriers – primarily walls or fences – occupied or were under construction along more than sixty borders covering a total of more than twenty-five thousand kilometers.[10] Since 9/11, not only have physical barriers been 'hardened,' writes journalist Joshua Jelly-Shapiro, but there has also been an 'unprecedented' rise in 'cross-border collaboration in the name of surveillance,' in 'co-bordering' from both sides, and in 'thick' borders.[11] These heightened barriers, both physical and administrative, are more likely to be built against poorer populations and against Muslim populations.[12] Lanchester's fictional vision of a near-future UK bunkered against 'Others' desperately seeking refuge from the effects of climate crisis known as 'The Change' starkly captures this dynamic. Five meters high and three meters thick, the island wall is a totalized concretization of the forces behind Brexit. Narrated like Orwell's *1984* and like the 1959 nuclear supershelter fable *Level 7* by a callow young cog chewed up and spit out by the system's merciless wheels, *The Wall* makes abundantly clear the symbolic emptiness of the barrier wall. Because of population decline, any invading Other that makes it past the two hundred thousand shoot-to-kill 'Defenders' stationed in rotating shifts atop the Wall is allowed to remain in indentured servitude, their children assimilated as citizens. At the same time, for every Other allowed in, one Defender is put out to sea, essentially trading places; to the system as defined by the Wall, Defenders and Others may be ideologically opposed, but they are also fundamentally interchangeable. Even 'Elites,' Lanchester suggests, have no individual power over this bunkered social structure.

While barrier walls, like the nuclear condition at their foundation, lend themselves to such an ontological dead end, the physically stark asymmetry

9 Uri Friedman, 'A World of Walls: Donald Trump's Proposal for the U.S.-Mexico Border Isn't Outdated. It's a Sign of the Times,' *Atlantic* (19 May 2016): www.theatlantic.com/international/archive/2016/05/donald-trump-wall-mexico/483156/.

10 Ron E. Hassner and Jason Wittenberg, 'Barriers to Entry: Who Builds Fortified Boundaries and Why?' *International Security* 40.1 (2015): 157–90; Wikipedia contributors, 'List of Current Barriers,' in 'Border Barriers,' *Wikipedia*: https://en.wikipedia.org/wiki/Border_barrier; accessed 8 March 2021. Hassner and Wittenberg omit numbers for length in many of their entries; nevertheless, even their more conservative data show that, 'Moreover, at least since the 1990s the barriers have become significantly more ambitious in terms of their length' (165).

11 Joshua Jelly-Shapiro, 'What Are Borders For?' *New Yorker* (27 Nov. 2019): www.newyorker.com/books/under-review/what-are-borders-for; see also Matthew Longo, *The Politics of Borders: Sovereignty, Security, and the Citizen after 9/11* (Cambridge: Cambridge University Press, 2017).

12 Hassner and Wittenberg, 'Barriers to Entry,' 173–5.

Figure 6.2 The tunnel as ideological spectacle: a cameraman films the construction of an escape tunnel funded in 1962 by NBC in violation of international law in a 2001 recreation of a Cold War media frenzy.

that walls, like bunkers, maintain between included and excluded populations helps to explain writer and artist Bryan Finoki's claim that '[J]ust as every wall casts a shadow, so too does each inspire its own mechanism of subversion. Each wall invariably serves as the instrument of its own undoing, its own intrinsic failure.'[13] Finoki's formulation accurately characterizes the boundary wall imaginary and well describes the form typically taken by attempts at subverting its spatial blockage; however, in practice, 'undoing' and 'intrinsic failure' tend to remain more partial and aspirational than fully realized. And while there is any number of more or less dramatic, effective, and dangerous ways to cross boundary walls – over, under, through, or around – the tunnel most effectively fulfills the imaginative role of spatial counterpart to the Wall (Figures 6.2 & 6.3). No wall manages to serve its dreamed function uncontested or as designed, but no wall fails utterly and immediately to do so, either. The Wall imaginary, like the bunker fantasy, captures in its range the insider ideal of security and impermeability, the outsider ideal of openness and mobility, and the many unpredictable contingencies, some happy and many miserable, surrounding the actual experience of a wall in space and time. Wall and tunnel, in other words, belong together because together they express the range of extremes we are otherwise hard pressed to imagine about the contested space marked and produced by them.

13 Bryan Finoki, 'Tunnelling Borders,' *openDemocracy* (26 Nov. 2013): https://web.archive.org/web/20200422042150/https://www.opendemocracy.net/en/opensecurity/tunnelling-borders/.

Figure 6.3 The tunnel as ideological spectacle: a 2001 studio recreation of a 1962 facsimile of the Berlin Wall on a Berlin film set for the Hollywood docudrama *Tunnel 28* (1962, dir. Robert Siodmak).

Wall and tunnel split the dystopian and utopian extremes united in the bunker fantasy into distinct but dependent spaces. The wall assumes the bunker's affordances of technologized security and shelter; the tunnel assumes its affordances of animal freedom, existential reduction, and repudiation of the status quo. Depending on the perspective, each space can figure either extreme, but never at the same time. From the internal perspective of bunkered security, the boundary wall is a necessary protection criminally undermined by attackers from without; from the external perspective, the wall is a stark assertion of inequity and exclusion, to which the tunnel is a resourceful and justified response. In contrast to the bunker fantasy, neither threat is universally accepted; consequently, there is no common ground for argument. One reason the Berlin Wall was able to become such a potent symbol of Cold War divisions, despite the proportionately small number of fatalities produced by it, is that in one sense it transformed the German Democratic Republic (GDR) and the empire behind it into an underworld – the nine circles, to adapt Aleksandr Solzhenitsyn's contemporaneous gulag metaphor, of a modern hell.[14] Or, expressed from the other side, a socialist paradise opposed to a devil's realm of empty illusions. The ideological split between the borders was so stark that it could be represented only in terms of two opposed worlds, and only death, it was suggested, could allow one to cross over (Figure 6.1). The Berlin Wall asserted the absolute separation and the

---

14 Alexander Solzhenitsyn, *In the First Circle* (New York: Harper, 2009 [1968]).

232   *After the end*

blockage of any passage between worlds; however, the thirty-odd escape tunnels dug (partly or completely) beneath it in the ten years following its construction maintained instead that relations were more fluid than they appeared, that common ground continued between the two spaces, and that it was impossible to seal them off completely from one another. The tunnel opposed a praxis of connections to a metaphysics of divisions. This is a consequence of so expressly spatializing ideology: the contradictions in that ideology also become able to manifest physically.

The tunnel, in fact, had a meaning within the Cold War prior to its identity as escape route. After the war, espionage tunnels had been widely used by both sides for eavesdropping purposes in occupied cities. As would later be the case in the twin Mexico–US border cities of Nogales, subterranean infrastructure connected European metropolises such as Vienna and Berlin irrespective of clearly delineated political divisions aboveground. A former imperial center, Vienna was still a switchboard for communications across Europe. Realizing the strategic potential in tapping these cables, the British Secret Intelligence Service (SIS) began work on the Vienna espionage tunnel in 1948; tunnels remained in operation when British and Russian forces left the city in 1950.[15] Historical writing about these tunnels stresses their technical expertise; however, fictional depictions stress their organic associations with natural underground space. Due to novelist and screenwriter Graham Greene's intimate knowledge of British intelligence activity and of the political topography of postwar Vienna, the spy tunnel found its way into the imaginary of Carol Reed's 1949 film, *The Third Man*, where the racketeer Harry Lime (Orson Welles) is able to travel the city irrespective of political divisions by using the sewer tunnels. Greene drew on the sewer's organic connotations of animal materiality and sullied morality to express existential ambivalence about the fallen postwar world. British writer Ian McEwan would use the CIA's Berlin espionage tunnels to similar effect in his 1990 historical novel, *The Innocent*. In this space of 'earth, and a lurid dampness, and shit not quite neutralised by chemicals,' a callow American radio technician will secrete the chopped-up remains of his local lover's murdered husband.[16]

The Berlin initiative known as Operation Gold (aka Operation Stopwatch), which began in the early 1950s as a rare collaboration between the SIS and the Berlin Operations Base of the Central Intelligence Agency (CIA), was far more ambitious, expensive, and technically sophisticated than the Vienna scheme, tunneling some eighteen hundred meters beneath the border and

---

15 David Stafford, *Spies beneath Berlin* (Woodstock, NY: Overlook, 2003), 24–5. For further detail on the imaginaries around these tunnels, see Pike, 'Wall and Tunnel,' 76–81.

16 Ian McEwan, *The Innocent* (New York: Anchor, 1999 [1990]), 21.

Wall and tunnel   233

far into the Russian sector, once again to tap phone lines.[17] Completed in early 1955, the tunnel remained in operation for just over eleven months, although it did produce so much material that it took until 1958 to process all of it. Cold War historians and participants still debate the utility of the information obtained, especially after it emerged in 1961 that the double agent George Blake had betrayed the tunnel's existence to the Kremlin even before CIA head Allen Dulles had given the final approval for its construction.[18] The Kremlin eventually decided to expose the tunnel in a carefully staged reality show, acted by unsuspecting utility workers and Vopos (*Volkspolizei*) and filmed for posterity by the local news. GDR authorities would subsequently claim that later escape tunnels were funded by and dug for the CIA to introduce spies surreptitiously into the East.[19] There may have been some grounds for this assertion; certainly, the sealing of the border and erection of the Wall had in fact turned the espionage world upside down by severely limiting cross-border communications. The presence of espionage within the tunnel imaginary troubles the stark divisions of the Wall not in terms of freedom and mobility but in terms of ethical murkiness and epistemological uncertainty.

Like the bunker captivity fictions discussed in Chapter 2, where the psychopathic or mentally unstable survivalist holds his victims in a doomsday bunker, the tunnel escape drama places moral certainty, personal heroism, and belief in autonomy and freedom above all other values. Unlike the bunker escape, where the captor occupies the same space as the captive, the tunnel escape contrasts its values to the space of the Wall it passes beneath. Espionage is present in every tunnel fiction I have encountered from both during and after the Cold War; there is always at least one tunnel digger or potential escapee being blackmailed by the Stasi or suspected of betrayal; there is nearly always a need to double-cross the border police and the Stasi to complete the escape, usually just under their noses.[20]

---

17 Between the extensive excavations and the sophisticated listening, amplification, and recording equipment, the tunnel cost between six million and thirty million dollars, notwithstanding that it was built under the assumption that it would remain secret only a short time. Stafford gives the conservative number (*Spies*, 79); David C. Martin proffers the high estimate in *Wilderness of Mirrors* (New York: Harper and Row, 1980), 89.

18 See Joseph C. Evans, 'Berlin Tunnel Intelligence: A Bumbling KGB,' *International Journal of Intelligence and Counterintelligence* 9 (1996): 43–50; David E. Murphy, Sergei A. Kondrashev, and George Bailey, *Battleground Berlin: CIA vs. KGB in the Cold War* (New Haven, CT: Yale University Press, 1997), 205–37; Stafford, *Spies*; and George Feifer, 'The Berlin Tunnel,' in *The Cold War: A Military History*, ed. Robert Cowley (New York: Random House, 2005), 189–208.

19 See, for example, 'Berlin Tunnel Plot Brings Red Arrests,' *New York Times* (25 Feb. 1962): ProQuest Historical Newspapers: *The New York Times*, 1851–2003.

20 For specific examples, see Pike, 'Wall and Tunnel,' 81–92.

234 *After the end*

Consistent in the Western imaginary of the Berlin tunnels, and even in East German fictions of tunnels as vehicles for thwarting Western spies and enabling Eastern espionage, is the identification of the tunnels with freedom, broadly construed and appropriating the tunnel's primary identity as a locus of opposition and subversion, of everything that contradicted or no longer existed in the capitalist world above. This valorization of the tunnel and debasing of the barrier wall complicates spatial imaginaries in the post–Cold War period, especially as the enduring symbolic power of the Berlin Wall stands in tension with the reversed dynamics of wall and tunnel pairings on the West Bank, the Mexico–US border, and elsewhere. Political scientists Hassner and Wittenberg's conclusion to their analysis of the striking rise in border wall construction since the year 2000 echoes the persistence of this imaginary: 'For this practice to spread, it would have to tip the balance against the prior enthusiasm for globalization and permeable borders that has characterized the post–Cold War world and the stigma attached to barriers as symbols of oppression, such as the Berlin Wall.'[21]

In February 2009, English playwright David Hare sat in a chair on the stage of the Lyttelton auditorium of the National Theatre, London, at the concrete heart of the Cold War–era brutalist arts complex known as the South Bank Centre, and read his dramatic monologue *Berlin*, about what it means to a city when its 'most famous landmark has gone.'[22] In Berlin as author of the screenplay for the motion-picture adaptation of Bernhard Schlink's novel *The Reader*, which revisited one of Hitler's accomplished goals – 'to kill the Jews' – Hare sees a city rapidly accomplishing another of the Führer's dreams – 'to rebuild Berlin.'[23] The 'radical city which had always hated him' had been destroyed by Allied bombs at the end of the war; since 1989, 'key parts of what was once Soviet Berlin have vanished as well, torn down … in a fit of righteous horror at past sufferings.'[24] As emblem of what has taken their place, Hare singles out 'Fort Knox at the Brandenburg Gate,' the new American Embassy, 'an undistinguished lump of Cold War blah, a post-9/11 bunker of over-reach and paranoia' built as 'a piece of deliberate symbolism … where the Wall once ran.'[25] After the missed opportunity 'between the ending of one Cold War and the beginning of another,' Berlin was transformed from 'the city of polarity, of East and West, of democracy and communism, of fascism and resistance, the twentieth-century battleground of art and resistance.' Theater and other culture, he

---

21 Hassner and Wittenberg, 'Barriers to Entry,' 188; qtd Friedman, 'World of Walls.'
22 David Hare, *Berlin/Wall* (London: Faber and Faber, 2009), 4.
23 Hare, *Berlin/Wall*, 8–10.
24 Hare, *Berlin/Wall*, 10.
25 Hare, *Berlin/Wall*, 11.

Wall and tunnel 235

concludes of this new neoliberal space, is nothing but 'a redoubt of worthiness in a blaze of consumerism.'[26] From deep within the ontological bunker of Cold War leftism, Hare mourns the Wall for its tunnels. Or at least he needs their memory to be present enough, their spaces to be memorialized enough to be able to be missed rather than simply repeated, blindly.

Wall and tunnel around Palestine

'The Berlin Wall was built to keep people in,' says David Hare in his performance of *Wall*, which premiered the month after *Berlin* in 2009. 'This one, they say is being built to keep people out.'[27] Begun in 1994, twice as high as the Berlin wall, planned to be more than thirty times as long, just as deadly, and judged illegal by the International Court of Justice in 2004, the West Bank Wall, writes Marcello Di Cintio, 'erased any ambiguity between Here and There. ... [Its] impressive height, its concrete severity, and the clarity with which it drew its line astonished me.'[28] The wall instituted, so argued then-Prime Minister Yitzhak Rabin, 'something ... radical, something existential. "We have to decide on separation as a philosophy"' (Figure 6.4).[29] An ontological wall, for a bunkered people for whom separation had become a way of life, a creed: such is the barrier wall in the twenty-first century.

Di Cintio records his 'Travels along the Barricades' primarily as a journalist, but he regularly slips into the role of dark tourist, as if emphasizing that an outsider's interest in boundary walls is spectacular as well as political. 'The international media,' he continues, 'had derided the barrier ever since construction began in 2002. By the time I saw it, the West Bank Wall had already joined the Western Wall – Judaism's holiest site – and the ancient

---

26 Hare, *Berlin/Wall*, 21.

27 Hare, *Berlin/Wall*, 29.

28 Di Cintio, *Walls*, 9–10, 102. On the dimensions of the wall and its political context, see M. Alaa Mandour, 'Inside-Outside: The Making of the West Bank Security Wall,' in *Building Walls and Dissolving Borders: The Challenges of Alterity, Community and Securitizing Space*, ed. Max O. Stephenson, Jr, and Laura Zanotti (Burlington, VT: Ashgate, 2013), 99–113. Israel built its first separation barrier along the Gaza Strip in 1994. Initially improved in 2002 and planned to extend 450 miles, the West Bank barrier was 62 percent completed in 2014, with little apparent further progress since (Hassner and Wittenberg, 'Barriers to Entry,' 178–9). A 150-mile steel fence was erected on the border between Israel and Egypt between 2011 and 2012 (Harriet Sherwood, 'Israeli Fence Construction Cuts Off Migration from Egypt,' *Guardian* (31 Dec. 2012): www.theguardian.com/world/2012/dec/31/israeli-fence-cuts-migration-egypt; accessed 1 May 2018).

29 Hare, *Berlin/Wall*, 29.

Figure 6.4 The physical manifestation of an ontological wall: *Route 60, Beit Jala, Bethlehem area, Israel-Palestine, 2011*.

stone ramparts around the Old City to form the trinity of walls that travellers to Jerusalem visit and photograph.'[30] The same media with which local and global activists contest the Wall – reportage, protests, and graffiti – feed a network of NGOs, tours, and travelers fascinated and appalled by this phenomenon in equal measure: 'A man in Jayyous told me that before the Wall, the only place he'd see a European was on television: now the Jayyousi were used to foreigners.'[31] Di Cintio similarly describes the daily ritual of confrontation between rock-slinging Palestinians and tear-gas, sound grenade, and rubber-bullet-wielding Israeli soldiers, which, despite resulting in destruction, injuries, and fatalities on both sides, is primarily a performance of defiance: '"Stones are the only way for us to show power. To show anger. To show togetherness." The sling boys were icons of resistance.'[32]

The Wall towers over and defines the conflict to such a degree that Basel Abbas, one of Di Cintio's local interviewees, actively voices his 'distrust' of its symbolic function:

> Though he understands the draw of the Wall, and concedes the barrier has inspired sympathy for the Palestinians, he fears the barrier is being commodified. 'The Wall is not central to the Palestinian experience,' he insists. The artists who come to paint the Wall don't always understand that everything the barrier represents – apartheid, injustice, racism – existed long before the Wall itself. 'I've never been allowed to cross the Green Line into Jerusalem,' Basel said. 'Not before the Wall and not now.' The Wall is a stark and sudden manifestation of the occupation. The barrier provides a potent symbol to rally around, a theatre for outsiders to stage their solidarity dramas, and a surface to both spray with paint and pound with fists. But only the physicality is new. 'The Wall is not the point,' he insisted. 'It is not all about the Wall.'[33]

30 Di Cintio, *Walls*, 9–10.
31 Di Cintio, *Walls*, 105.
32 Di Cintio, *Walls*, 109.
33 Di Cintio, *Walls*, 112.

The argument is stunning in its simplicity: the Wall makes no difference. Not because it is constantly undermined but because it is merely the physical expression of an exclusion and inequity that extend far beyond physical barriers: 'I've never been allowed to cross. ... Not before the Wall and not now.' The sheer visibility of the boundary wall draws stones, graffiti, tourists. and global attention to its looming monumentality, making it what British street artist Banksy called, tongue only partly in cheek, 'the ultimate activity holiday destination for graffiti writers.' He backed up the claim in 2017 by creating the 'Walled Off Hotel': 'a genuine art hotel with fully functioning en suite facilities ... fully open to tourists from across the world' and '500 metres from the checkpoint to Jerusalem,' and featuring 'Wall Mart ... Your one-stop shop for decorating the wall.'[34] As Banksy's expansive engagement with the Wall suggests, boundary fences project outwards, unlike the defensive posture claimed for the bunker by its proponents. As a screen for projecting symbolic meanings, the barrier wall affords an international audience, even as its most deleterious effects are profoundly local.

Those effects are everywhere visible in the Occupied Territories or along the US–Mexico border, and for those waiting along them the end of the world has already long since arrived. Even as it draws what legitimacy it has from the promise of security inherited from the bunker fantasy, the boundary wall cynically rejects the speculative and hopeful kernel of survival into a better world sheltered in the shadows of that equally brutal fantasy. While the asymmetric performance of resistance goes on aboveground, the stuff of everyday survival passes in and out of the Occupied Territories through the tunnels excavated and destroyed in an equally ritualistic pattern with far greater material consequences. The tunnels preserve a trace of hope that the wall is not absolute or permanent; however, the power of that imaginary is compromised by its easy assimilation into the narratives of criminality, violence, and clandestineness to which smuggling tunnels have always lent themselves. Geographer Stephen Graham argues that digging underground in the asymmetric conflict typical of the post–Cold War era provides 'nonstate adversaries' a low-tech way to evade surveillance and attack by the 'drones, aircraft and – especially – satellites circling and loitering at various heights overhead.'[35] According to Graham, 'The US Department of Defense estimates that there are 10,000 "deeply buried faculties" in existence globally.'[36] Although Graham rightly questions whether that number is inflated, the belief or desire to publicize such a high number nevertheless

---

34 Banksy, 'The Walled Off Hotel,' https://web.archive.org/web/20230214233314/https://walledoffhotel.com/; accessed 8 March 2023.

35 Stephen Graham, *Vertical: The City from Satellites to Bunkers* (London: Verso, 2016), Kindle loc. 5379–80.

36 Graham, *Vertical*, loc. 5393–4.

238   *After the end*

testifies to the polarized form taken by the bunker fantasy since 1989. Like the nuclear weapons from which they were conceived as protection, Cold War bunkers and shelters meant the same whether attributed to oneself or to one's enemy. The ideology differed but the hope for survival was acknowledged to be a shared value in the great game; that the two sides precisely mirrored one another in a MAD arms race expressed both the fundamental absurdity of the Cold War and what at odd and usually imagined moments became the strangely liberating sense that everyone was in it together, equally.

When Graham's language equates bunker and tunneling, this is an accurate assessment in terms of sheltering only. But it belies the different affordance of the tunnel form within which most of these 'deeply buried faculties' can be categorized. Like the tunnels with which North Vietnamese forces successfully resisted carpet bombing by American planes in the interregnum of the Cold War, twenty-first-century smuggling tunnels and Al-Qaeda caves are predicated on resistance rather than survival. They are temporary passages rather than permanent dwellings; consequently, they retain nothing of the positive affordances of the bunker as shelter. Instead, they accrete the powerfully subversive affordances long associated with the organic underground: dirt, decay, criminality, animality, terrorism, and anarchy.[37] Such qualities can take on positive and even utopian associations, but only in resistance and never on their own terms. To borrow Slavoj Žižek's language, their ontology is closed rather than open.

Eyal Weizman attributes Rafah's saturation with tunnels to its location at the Egyptian and Israeli borders, to its dry and easily excavated sandstone geology, and to the socioeconomic necessity for a flow of supplies.[38] Consequently, we find grumbling by the local population about the smuggling tunnels dating back to 1982 under the hundred-meter buffer zone of the Egypt–Rafah border in Joe Sacco's 2003 graphic reportage, 'The Underground War in Gaza.'[39] Without touching on the potential use of tunnels as a lifeline for bringing in supplies, Sacco's interviewees focus solely on their use for smuggling weapons or drugs and the excuse they provide for the Israeli Defense Forces (IDF) to bulldoze property and extend their control of the border. As one Palestinian militant interviewed by Sacco

---

37 Pike, 'The Cinematic Sewer,' in *Dirt: New Geographies of Cleanliness and Contamination*, ed. Ben Campkin and Rosie Cox (London: I. B. Tauris, 2007), 138–50; Pike, 'Sewage Treatments: Vertical Space and the Discourse of Waste in 19th-Century Paris and London,' in *Filth: Dirt, Disgust, and Modern Life*, ed. William Cohen and Ryan Thompson (Minneapolis: University of Minnesota Press, 2004), 51–77.

38 Eyal Weizman, *Forensic Architecture: Violence at the Threshold of Detectability* (New York: Zone, 2017), 197.

39 Joe Sacco, 'The Underground War in Gaza,' *New York Times Magazine* (6 July 2003): 24–7.

Wall and tunnel 239

Figure 6.5 The practical and the ideological functions of tunneling: frames from Joe Sacco, 'The Underground War in Gaza.'

argued at that time (Figure 6.5), the symbolic function of the tunnels had long outlasted their practical utility. Following the Israeli withdrawal in 2005, however, the tunnels became 'essentially a regulated port of entry for the Hamas-administered Gaza government, through which 80% of the enclave's imports arrive.'[40] According to the mayor of Rafah at the time, 'The municipality supplies electricity and levies $2,500 in taxes' for each of the 'nearly 400 tunnels ... employing 15,000 people and bringing in $1 million in goods a day.'[41] In 2009, the Egyptian government responded with a nearly seven-mile-long steel wall designed by American army engineers to extend up to eighteen meters underground in order to collapse and block the hundreds of tunnels beneath the border.[42] The plan proved ineffective and was abandoned in 2012.[43]

Two years later, Egypt revived the Israeli practice, razing three thousand houses to extend the buffer zone and then, in 2015, flooding the tunnels

40 Charles Levinson, 'Egypt Tightens Gaza Barrier to Close Tunnels,' *Wall Street Journal* (22 Feb. 2010): https://web.archive.org/web/20220301181415/https://www.wsj.com/articles/SB10001424052748703787304575075524152161044.
41 Associated Press, 'New Egypt-Gaza Steel Fence Angers Hamas,' *NBC News.com* (5 Jan. 2010): www.nbcnews.com/id/34699874/ns/world_news-mideast_n_africa/t/new-egypt-gaza-steel-barrier-angers-hamas/; accessed 1 May 2018.
42 Christian Fraser, 'Egypt starts building steel wall on Gaza Strip border,' *BBC News* (9 Dec. 2009): https://web.archive.org/web/20221221180903/http://news.bbc.co.uk/2/hi/8405020.stm.
43 Lucas Winter, 'Egypt and Israel: Tunnel Neutralization Efforts in Gaza,' *Engineer* (Sept.–Dec. 2017): 30–4, at 31.

240 *After the end*

with seawater; these measures reduced the smugglers' network to a meager twenty tunnels.[44] Nevertheless, as military analyst Lucas Winter concluded, 'These interdiction methods have all had political costs, and tunnel diggers have found relatively simple ways of circumventing them. As a result, tunnels are likely to remain a persistent feature of this and similar operational environments.'[45] Weizman reports that tunneling has been 'reoriented' toward narrow 'attack' tunnels under the fence at the Israeli border; similar tunnels in the West Bank and under the barrier wall have also been found and destroyed.[46] Supported by a besieged government in asymmetrical relationship to two powerful neighbors, the Gaza tunnels are both ideologically and economically vital to Hamas; however, what they afford is resistance rather than long-term potential for change or survival. Weizman's forensic architecture project, for example, is able to track and explicate the Israeli military practice of dropping ground-penetrating bombs to destroy suspected but unsurveillable tunnels and the directive of killing hostages underground in order to avoid prisoner exchanges; however, he also concedes that 'the line between winning and losing is often unclear' and that his team members must 'brace ourselves for a political struggle in the long haul.'[47] The tunnels shelter both subversive actions and violent reprisals; exposing their workings to the open air does not change the fundamental asymmetry of the political situation they dramatize (Figures 6.6 & 6.7).

Žižek worked hard at the time of the flooding to renovate the imaginary function of these tunnels, to reopen their closed underground ontology. Beginning a 2014 piece on Palestinian tunnels, he recounts a legend 'based on the double-meaning of the Hebrew word *mechilot*: "underground tunnels" and "forgiveness" ... that righteous Jews murdered in exile will roll in underground tunnels in order to be forgiven and resurrected on the Mount of Olives when the Messiah comes.'[48] Zionism, he continues, 'inverted the symbolic tunnel into a concrete settling (*aaliyah*).'[49] Žižek alludes to but

44 Diaa Hadid and Wissam Nassar, 'As Egypt Floods Gaza Tunnels, Smugglers Fear an End to Their Trade,' *New York Times* (7 Oct. 2015).
45 Winter, 'Egypt and Israel,' 34.
46 Weizman, *Forensic Architecture*, 198; Yoav Zitun, 'Dozens of Terror Tunnels Discovered in West Bank,' *Ynetnews.com* (22 June 2014): https://web.archive.org/web/20230220142027/https://www.ynetnews.com/articles/0,7340,L-4533293,00.html; TOI Staff, 'IDF Seals Off 10 Tunnels under West Bank Security Fence,' *Times of Israel* (28 Oct. 2017): https://web.archive.org/web/20210916215922/https://www.timesofisrael.com/idf-seals-off-10-tunnels-under-west-bank-security-fence/.
47 Weizman, *Forensic Architecture*, 213.
48 Slavoj Žižek, 'Rolling in Underground Tunnels,' *Mondoweiss* (24 Aug. 2014): https://web.archive.org/web/20221206131132/https://mondoweiss.net/2014/08/rolling-underground-tunnels.
49 Žižek, 'Rolling.'

Figure 6.6 The Gaza tunnel as photo op: 'U.S. Senator Lindsey Graham inspects a recently found cross-border Hamas tunnel during a visit to the Israel-Gaza border area March 10, 2019 in Golan, Israel.'

elides that other 'concrete settling' of modern Israel – its extensive sheltering system – in order to focus on the polysemous meanings of the current tunnels:

> When they are used to smuggle food, tools, or a bride and a groom, the tunnels can function as a manifestation of life. Or, when armed militants emerge from them, they can be conduits for death. They can be tunnels of salvation here on earth, salvation of life as such. Or they may become apocalyptic salvation, salvation by weapons and destruction. We can help to define the future meanings of the tunnels. We can help determine whether through their gates will come the messiah of peace and justice, or the angel of death. They are very heavy on us, the gates of Gaza. Maybe if we open them together to life, the *mechilot* (underground tunnels) will become *mechilot* (forgiveness).[50]

Despite the desire for reconciliation, the metaphor remains mixed. To be fully reconciled, the concluding conversion of the underground tunnel into a bunker fantasy reuniting them with the utopian openness of 'forgiveness'

---

50 Žižek, 'Rolling.'

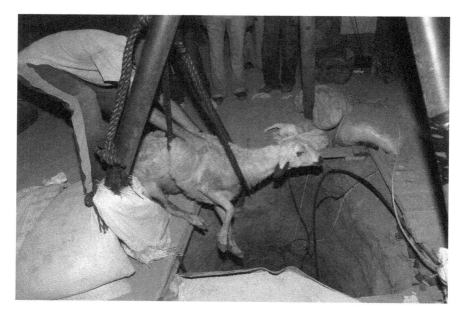

Figure 6.7 The Gaza tunnel as lifeline: 'Palestinian smugglers bring a goat to the Gaza Strip through an underground smuggling tunnel between Egypt and the Palestinian territory. Rafah, Palestine – 29.10.08.'

would also somehow have to restore to the same space the 'concrete settling' and the wall surrounding and enabling that settling.

The yearning of the language for positive ambiguity out of a blocked situation has natural recourse to the most recent moment when underground metaphorics held together the apocalypse as both destruction and rebirth. But the twenty-first-century underground imaginary does not currently afford that range. The physical tunnel remains locked beneath the physical wall. As an Israeli friend of Hare's explains to him in exasperation in *Wall*, 'The wall is a symbol we cannot live together. ... The wall tells the world we no longer wish to be normal. ... It's an admission of failure. ... I mean, who in their right mind wants to make a metaphor concrete? You might as well dig a big pit in the middle of your country, light a fire at the bottom and call it hell.'[51]

The Israeli friend would likely not see it this way, but the path leading inevitably from that wall to the pit of hell suggests that the subversive qualities of the tunnel are equally available to the wall builder. Because the West Bank Wall, rather than following the Green Line (the internationally accepted

---

51 Hare, *Berlin/Wall*, 45.

border drawn in the 1949 armistice agreement), loops and tucks to incorporate seventy Israeli-established settlements and to exclude Palestinian villages, a winding barrier has resulted that is projected to be more than twice as long as the Green Line it ostensibly follows (Figure 6.4).[52] To connect West Bank settlements with Jewish Jerusalem, Prime Minister Ariel Sharon and then-Minister of National Infrastructure Benjamin Netanyahu devised a 'Tunnel Road' of officially Israeli territory that bridges a valley cultivated by Palestinians and passes beneath the town of Beit Jala.[53] A related scheme that calls for parallel West Bank roads includes thirty-five 'vertical interchanges of bridges and tunnels' to 'facilitate the possibility of contiguous walled-out Palestinian territories without the need to evacuate the Israeli settlements.'[54] As Weizman concludes his spatial analysis, '[T]he physical arrangements deny even the possibility of a cognitive encounter.'[55] The tunnel subverts the Wall's fundamental affordance of physical separation, but in the service of a more insidious separation. Little wonder that SFF writer China Miéville used Jerusalem as one of the models for his 2009 novel *The City & the City*, in which a web of laws, behaviors, and traditions allows two cities to occupy simultaneously the same urban space without either population ever 'seeing' the other: 'You would have a single urban space in which different citizens are covered by completely different juridical relations and social relations, and in which you would have two overlapping authorities.'[56]

In this way, wall and tunnel can be made irrationally to support each other; however, they can equally undercut one another conceptually. Experienced together, they afford a bunker epistemology able briefly to expose the knowledge production underpinning the wall's or the tunnel's closed ontology. 'The wittiest graffiti by far' – opines Hare – 'the instruction scrawled across six cement blocks, just the letters: CTL-ALT-DEL as if at the press of three computer keys, the wall might disappear. Not a wall, just a drawing of a wall.'[57] The 'wit' of the graffito, as Hare implies but does not spell out, is the recognition that the wall itself, certainly, will never simply reset into something fluid and functional at the click of a button (Figure 6.8). But 'separation as a philosophy,' the epistemology made ontology by the metaphoric and imaginative weight and bulk and authority of the Wall, still

---

52 Josef Koudelka, *Wall: Israeli & Palestinian Landscape 2008–2012* (New York: Aperture, 2013), 1.
53 Weizman, *Hollow Land*, 179–80.
54 Weizman, *Hollow Land*, 181.
55 Weizman, *Hollow Land*, 181
56 'Unsolving the City: An Interview with China Miéville,' by Geoff Manaugh, *BLDG-BLOG* (1 March 2011): https://web.archive.org/web/20221203132229/https://bldgblog.com/2011/03/unsolving-the-city-an-interview-with-china-mieville/.
57 Hare, *Berlin/Wall*, 45.

Figure 6.8 'CTRL+ALT+DELETE': the epistemological wall made material. 'Graffiti on the Separation Wall, Ramallah, Palestine, 5 November 2008.'

could, at least for an imagined moment, if we could find the right buttons to press and the right persons to press them.

Perhaps the most iconic images from Banksy's West Bank sojourn in 2005 are variations on openings in the Wall: virtual tunneling. One pictures two children playing with sand buckets, a cracked hole in the wall leading to a beach scene with palm trees above them (Figure 6.9).[58] Another shows a boy with a bucket standing on a painted rock above a pile of (actual) rocks in the foreground, silhouetted by a trompe l'oeil blue sky reaching almost to the top of the wall.[59] Two more show an impossibly stretched horse peering out a window high up on the wall and a pair of stenciled armchairs with a curtained window looking out on a photo of a mountain landscape.[60] Later derivations include a rhinoceros coming through the wall, a sledgehammer opening cracks, a hole with cracks showing the Dome of the Rock mosque, a door opening into a stencil of Disney's Bambi with her friends, a door opening onto a blue desert sky, a helicopter blasting the wall with bombs (Figure 6.10).[61] Artwork by New York street artist Swoon

58 Nigel Parry, 'Well-known UK Graffiti Artist Banksy Hacks the Wall,' *The Electronic Intifada* (2 Sept. 2005): https://web.archive.org/web/20221208194820/https://electronicintifada.net/content/well-known-uk-graffiti-artist-banksy-hacks-wall/5733.
59 Parry, 'Banksy Hacks the Wall.'
60 Parry, 'Banksy Hacks the Wall.'
61 William Parry, *Against the Wall: The Art of Resistance in Palestine* (Chicago: Lawrence Hill, 2010), 24, 174, 175, 44–5, 55.

Wall and tunnel

Figure 6.9 An epistemological hole in the wall. Banksy's wall painting with additional graffiti, Bethlehem, 2008.

Figure 6.10 Still standing in 2018: blasting a virtual tunnel in the Wall, paired with signs pointing to the commercial side of Banksy's Bethlehem endeavor. 'Graffiti at Palestine-Israel border wall in Bethlehem, Palestine, West Bank, 15 April 2018.'

246 *After the end*

glued 'all kinds of pockets all over the Wall,' into a figure of a woman's skirts, containing inspirational quotes – another way of opening up the monolithic space.[62] Other powerful images of escape include an escalator moving a dozen people up over the Wall and a girl releasing a bundle of balloons.[63] But it is the trompe l'oeil of the opening in the wall, simultaneously obvious and impossible, that seems best to capture the twenty-first-century contradictions of separation walls and of the art opposing them.

One initial response to this activity led with the associative title, 'Banksy Hacks the Wall.'[64] In those early days of the anarchist 'hacktivist' group Anonymous, the verb was still full of subversive resonance with an Internet that 'wanted' to be free from firewalls and barriers. Blogger and web designer Nigel Parry, who lived in Palestine for several years during the 1990s, accurately identified the goal of Banksy's art to be 'reclaiming public spaces as a space for public imagination and enlightenment where they have become propagandistic barriers to thought and awareness'; however, the conclusion conceded that aesthetic imagery of tunneling through the Wall might speak eloquently to the global imagination but left the local situation unchanged. Parry ends his piece with an oft-quoted anecdote from Banksy's webpage recording an exchange between the artist and an old man: '*Old man:* You paint the wall, you make it look beautiful. *Me:* Thanks. *Old man:* We don't want it to be beautiful, we hate this wall, go home.'[65] A conceptual tunnel hacks a concrete Wall; like wormholes in spacetime, the early twenty-first-century imaginary was full of imagery of ideas crashing 'reality.' But unlike the absent-present materiality of underground bunkers, the visibility of barrier walls is essential to their form: we cannot but see clearly how the walls serve their function, and they remain standing. Later photos of Banksy's pieces show the blue sky and beach have been whitewashed and the mountain landscape bricked over, rendering the illusion less vibrant, the idea more abstract, and the wall less beautiful.[66]

Each sharply 'debeautified' large-format black-and-white image in Moravian photographer Josef Koudelka's 2013 collection, *Wall*, is stretched across a pair of 10.5 x 14-inch pages, emphasizing the construction's horizontal sprawl.[67] Koudelka includes only a few examples of wall art, always directly

---

62 Parry, *Against the Wall*, 42–3.
63 Parry, *Against the Wall*, 68, 143.
64 Parry, 'Banksy Hacks the Wall.'
65 Parry, 'Banksy Hacks the Wall.'
66 Parry, *Against the Wall*, 174, 29.
67 I borrow the term 'debeautified' from William Parry's description of the fate of Banksy's living-room graffiti (*Against the Wall*, 29).

Figure 6.11 Another kind of hole in the wall. *Crusader map mural, Kalia Junction, Dead Sea area, ISRAEL- PALESTINE, 2009.*

political in content.[68] The only hole he shows, in what looks and feels like a direct response to Banksy's, is a physical opening, torn in a wall through a mural of mountains and hill-towns (Figure 6.11). Through the hole, we see mostly open sky with flat land below, and a barrier fence winding its way, camouflaged by the framing, just beneath the skyline. A window on the facing page shows more sky, flat land, and fence. One caption tells us what we are seeing: 'Crusader map mural, Kalia Junction, Dead Sea area,' and another explains that 'Structures from the British Mandate (1922–48) and Jordanian era (1948–67) remain in the West Bank.'[69] Rather than hope for the future, the only opening in Koudelka's bleak vision shows us how little has changed and argues that the only openings available to us lie firmly in the past.

'The wall is a perfect crime,' asserts Professor Sari Nusseibeh of Al-Quds University. 'It creates the violence it was ostensibly built to prevent.'[70] Palestinian American author Thaer Husien's novel *Beside the Sickle Moon* speculates on what the world created by the Wall would look like if that crime were perpetuated through to 2060 – a scenario that seems both eminently plausible and impossible to imagine. The story of a young Palestinian man caught between rival factions, family loyalties, and the despair that comes from full awareness of the slow-motion apocalypse he is caught in the middle of, *Sickle Moon* is balanced between Laeth's conviction that 'If the future doesn't exist, what good's the present?' and the historical truth he is reluctant to recognize: 'You shame the plight of your ancestors by not believing in

68 Koudelka, *Wall*, 15, 21, 31, 34.
69 Koudelka, *Wall*, 51.
70 Hare, *Berlin/Wall*, 33.

248   *After the end*

your future.'[71] Renting out the cellar of his father's village food shop to Hamas, Laeth's ontological prison rejects the escape embedded in the extensive tunnel network opening out beneath his feet when he becomes unwitting accomplice to a bombing that destroys the subterranean command center. The Wall, in contrast, never appears on the scene; instead, it looms over even the future, the perfect crime. 'Occupation, curfew, settlements, closed military zone, administrative detention, siege, preventive strike, terrorist infrastructure, transfer,' writes the American poet-activist and Palestinian refugee Suheir Hammad, in words Husien quotes in the 2060 present of *Sickle Moon*. 'Their war destroys language. ... Occupation means that every day you die, and the world watches in silence. As if your death was nothing, as if you were a stone falling in the earth, water falling over water.'[72]

Crossing America's Great Wall

A similar fatalism persists on the ground in the American Southwest, despite the fond hopes of Wall proponents, the staunch activism of immigrant support groups, and the persistent humanity and will to survive of the migrants themselves. The trompe l'oeil illusions on this Wall are less idealistic and more rooted in regional and national politics. As on the West Bank Wall, the art is permitted (or allowed to remain) only on the side with no control over the barrier's existence. Several depict a hand pulling another hand through a gaping hole in the Wall. In Figure 6.12, one brown hand pulls another against an abstract backdrop. Elsewhere, a lighter-skinned hand pulls a darker one, against the backdrop of a Mexican flag, and a photo pictures a physical hand reaching through the Wall to join a pair of painted handprints on metal (Figure 6.13).[73] As opposed to the ontological force of the separation established by the West Bank Wall, this border is a reality accepted at least to some degree by all concerned; the tunnel here simply imagines some kind of an opening to pass through. Such openings exist all along the lengthy border, where the most common barrier continues to be formed of rib-like sections that once permitted people to squeeze

71 Thaer Husien, 'Beside the Sickle Moon,' unpublished manuscript in the author's possession. Permission of the author.
72 Husien, *Sickle Moon*. Permission of the author.
73 File photo showing a view of a graffiti on the border fence that divides the state of Mexicali, Mexico and Calexico, United States on 26 January 2017. EFE/ Juan Barak: https://web.archive.org/web/20210917162809/https://aldianews.com/articles/editors-picks/mexican-firm-bidding-help-build-trump-s-wall-it-s-not-betrayal/46640; accessed 31 Aug. 2023.

Figure 6.12 A hand through the Wall: 'Agua Prieta, Sonora, Mexico – Painting on the U.S.-Mexico border fence, 13 Oct. 2016.'

through and still permit objects and hands to pass. Four overlapping but also somewhat contradictory motifs recur throughout the imaginary of the Wall, or *la linea*, as it is known to the Spanish-speaking population that is its primary target. The first motif, common to nearly all Wall imaginaries, is that the Wall will always be incomplete and permeable despite any protestations to the contrary. The other three motifs are particular to this Wall. One is that the incompleteness – which channels border crossings away from urban agglomerations and towards desert and wilderness where conditions are harsher and concealment more difficult – is an intentional strategy. Another is that the Wall is more important as a symbol than as a physical barrier. And a third, more frequently implicit than explicit, is that this symbolism has deep roots in the history of the region. There has not always been a border, but as Teju Cole writes of the Tohono O'odham origin myth, 'The land is a maze. You have to be guided through, right from the beginning you had to be guided. The first story in the world is about safe passage.'[74]

The myriad of ways this border is simultaneously open and closed is intricately connected to the ongoing crisis that the Wall simplifies and the

---

74 Cole, 'A Piece of the Wall,' 367.

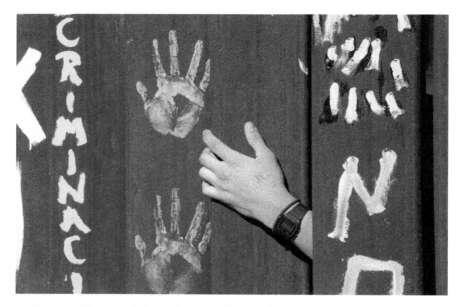

Figure 6.13 A hand through the Wall: 'Nogales, Arizona USA and Nogales, Sonora Mexico – 11 November 2017 – A hand reaches through the border fence as rallies were held on both sides of the fence calling for more open immigration. The events were organized by the School of the Americas Watch, a group of religious and community activists.'

Wall's gaps and tunnels complicate anew. For the Tohono O'odham (lit. 'Desert People') Nation, the wall bisects a territory 'known as the Papagueria' that had once extended south into Sonora, Mexico, north beyond what is now Phoenix, some four hundred kilometers from the Gulf of California in the west to the San Pedro River, and where the Tohono O'odham had lived for thousands of years.[75] The straight lines that form the border from the Pacific Ocean to El Paso, Texas, in disregard of topography, environment, and local history, were drawn by treaty terms dictated by the United States in 1848 and slightly modified in 1853 in a deal to acquire railroad land.[76] The Tohono O'odham's Arizona reservation follows the border for 120 kilometers west of Nogales; nine 'reserves of lands for indigenous peoples'

---

75 'History & Culture,' *Official Website of the Tohono O'odham Nation*: https://web.archive.org/web/20230203194144/http://www.tonation-nsn.gov/history-culture/; accessed 23 Feb. 2021.
76 Edward S. Casey and Mary Watkins, *Up Against the Wall: Re-Imagining the U.S.-Mexico Border* (Austin: University of Texas Press, 2014), 15–16; Mohammed Chaichian, *Empires and Walls: Globalization, Migration, and Colonial Domination* (Leiden: Brill, 2014), 207.

Wall and tunnel 251

were established on the Mexican side in 1927.[77] Because they were 'not informed that a purchase of their land had been made' and because the border was not strictly enforced, the Tohono O'odham were unaffected by it for decades; however, in recent years, it has come to present 'an artificial barrier to the freedom ... to traverse their lands, impairing their ability to collect foods and materials needed to sustain their culture and to visit family members and traditional sacred sites.'[78] This has led to the detention and deportation of Tohono O'odham 'who were simply traveling through their own traditional lands, practicing migratory traditions essential to their religion, economy and culture.'[79] The tension and conflict between divergent understandings of migration marks this account as it does those of immigrants seeking 'safe passage' to a new life north of the border. The dissident spatiality of the Tohono O'odham and other Indigenous understandings of this region and the mythic temporality afforded by alternate understandings of border crossing permeate responses to the Wall as barrier.

As a Yaqui Indian character in Leslie Marmon Silko's *Almanac of the Dead* explains,

> We don't believe in boundaries. Borders. Nothing like that. We are here thousands of years before the first whites. ... We know where we belong on this earth. We have always moved freely. North-south. East-west. We pay no attention to what isn't real. Imaginary lines. Imaginary minutes and hours. Written law. We recognize none of that. And we carry a great many things back and forth. We don't see any border.[80]

Counterbalanced against Calabazas's absolute rejection of 'what isn't real' is poet and critical theorist Gloria Anzaldúa's nearly contemporaneous formulation of the 'Borderlands' that exist anywhere that asymmetric cultures 'edge each other':

> The actual physical borderland that I'm dealing with ... is the Texas-U.S. Southwest/Mexican border. The psychological borderlands, the sexual borderlands and the spiritual borderlands are not particular to the Southwest. In fact, the Borderlands are physically present wherever two or more cultures edge each other, where people of different races occupy the same territory, where under, lower, middle and upper classes touch, where the space between two individuals shrinks with intimacy.[81]

---

77 Di Cintio, *Walls*, 173; 'History & Culture,' *Official Website of the Tohono O'odham Nation*.
78 'History & Culture.'
79 'History & Culture.'
80 Silko, *Almanac of the Dead*, 216.
81 Gloria Anzaldúa, *Borderlands / La Frontera: The New Mestiza*, 4th ed. (San Francisco: Aunt Lute Books, 2012 [1987], 19.

252   *After the end*

The refusal to acknowledge the border altogether and the radical expansion of the Borderlands into a global grid of inequity use different approaches to open up the same closed ontology.

The border wall symbolizes the border as a place that is fixed, immutable, and impermeable, an epistemology made ontological. Calabazas rejects that ontology as an epistemology his culture pre-exists and need not recognize. In contrast, Anzaldúa's poetic language repurposes the wall's affordances to assert an unstable ontology seamed with open wounds, 'in a constant state of transition.' She influentially described this border as '*una herida abierta* where the Third World grates against the first and bleeds. And before a scab forms it hemorrhages again, the lifeblood of two worlds merging to form a third country – a border culture.'[82] Anzaldúa's language of trauma refuses permanence even as it acknowledges that, within this epistemology, the wounds are opened only in '*Los atravesados* [that] live here: the squint-eyed, the perverse, the queer, the troublesome, the mongrel, the mulato, the half-breed, the half dead; in short, those who cross over, pass over, or go through the confines of the "normal."'[83] As ethnographer Anna Lowenhaupt Tsing argues, 'friction reminds us that heterogeneous and unequal encounters can lead to new arrangements of culture and power.'[84]

One way friction does this is by making visible the very literal violence enabled by the bunkered imagination of a neutral and static wall. As anthropologist Jason De Léon argues,

> The terrible things that this mass of migrating people experience en route are neither random nor senseless, but rather part of a strategic federal plan that has rarely been publicly illuminated and exposed for what it is: a killing machine that simultaneously uses and hides behind the viciousness of the Sonoran Desert. The Border Patrol disguises the impact of its current enforcement policy by mobilizing a combination of sterilized discourse, redirected blame, and 'natural' environmental processes that erase evidence of what happens in the most remote parts of southern Arizona. The goal is to render invisible the innumerable consequences this sociopolitical phenomenon has for the lives and bodies of undocumented people.[85]

The bunker fantasy affords recognition of the ontological violence of exclusion in the moral calculus that a 1959 novel summed up in its title as 'the rest must die' and that persists in the visible spectacle of mass death that haunts

---

82 Anzaldúa, *Borderlands / La Frontera*, 25.
83 Anzaldúa, *Borderlands / La Frontera*, 25.
84 Anna Lowenhaupt Tsing, *Friction: An Ethnography of Global Connection* (Princeton: Princeton University Press, 2005), 5.
85 Jason De Léon, *The Land of Open Graves: Living and Dying on the Migrant Trail* (Berkeley: University of California Press, 2015), 3–4.

Wall and tunnel 253

zombie fictions, future noir, Afrofuturism, and related postapocalyptic forms. In contrast, the wall affords epistemological 'disguise' and 'erasure' of what De Léon terms the 'necroviolence'[86] it concentrates and deploys against outsiders granted neither the right to shelter nor even the lost agency and humanity of the zombie or the oppressed. 'This invisibility,' writes De Léon, 'is a crucial part of both the suffering and the necroviolence that emerge from the hybrid collectif.'[87]

Through the friction they expose, border tunnels and other forms of crossing refigure borders as consisting of far more than the simple barriers or lines on a map to which they are so often reduced. When walls are understood more in terms of friction than in terms of stasis, borders become sites of friction rather than stations of mobility and their ontological claims are made visible as deadly but unstable epistemologies. 'Friction refuses the lie that global power operates as a well-oiled machine,' writes Tsing.[88] This dynamic has long been visible not just in the Arizona desert but also at the border crossing at San Ysidro, between San Diego and Tijuana, one of the world's busiest. Except during the COVID-19 pandemic, hundreds of thousands of documented crossings occur daily and, for a long time, many thousands more that were not documented.[89] Since the institution of the North American Free Trade Agreement (NAFTA) in 1994, border crossing has been criminalized at the same time that material commodities flow more freely than ever and NAFTA's (since 2020, USMCA) neoliberalist economic policies have created and exacerbated the unstable conditions that motivate migration.[90] Meanwhile, the closure of the border blocks the seasonal flux that typifies contemporary patterns of migratory labor, whether documented or undocumented.[91]

In the parts of Texas where the Wall has been constructed alongside the Rio Grande (or Rio Bravo, as it is known in Mexico), a no-man's-land has been created akin to the Seam Zone enclosed by the West Bank Wall.[92]

86 De Léon, *Land of Open Graves*, 69–70.
87 De Léon, *Land of Open Graves*, 214.
88 Tsing, *Friction*, 6.
89 Sebastian Rotella, *Twilight on the Line* (New York: W. W. Norton, 1998), 21.
90 Chaichian, *Empires and Walls*, 210–13, 16; Cole, 'A Piece of the Wall,' 371–2; De Léon, *Land of Open Graves*, 6. Although replaced in 2020 by the United States–Mexico–Canada Agreement, consensus was that, as a report from the Brookings Institute suggested, the biggest change was the name itself (Geoffrey Gertz, '5 Things to Know about USMCA, the New NAFTA,' *Brookings* (2 Oct. 2018): https://web.archive.org/web/20230117071627/https://www.brookings.edu/blog/up-front/2018/10/02/5-things-to-know-about-usmca-the-new-nafta/).
91 Mike Davis, 'The Great Wall of Capital,' *Socialist Review* (5 Feb. 2004): https://socialistworker.co.uk/socialist-review-archive/great-wall-capital/.
92 Chaichian, *Empires and Walls*, 233.

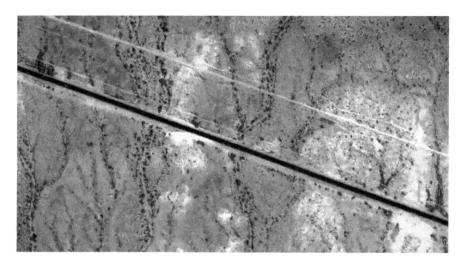

Figure 6.14 Part of the mostly straight-line border that runs from the Pacific coast to El Paso, Texas.

Artist Josh Begley's six-minute video *Best of Luck with the Wall*, composed of two hundred thousand satellite images downloaded from Google Maps, gives a powerful sense of the vast extent of the Wall and the stark contrast between the straight-line and river-based parts of the border (Figures 6.14 & 6.15).[93] The aerial perspective of the satellite photos simultaneously conjures the vast and mostly uninhabited expanse of the border and also the enormous scale of any project to wall it off. In what Mohammed Chaichian deems a 'land grab' disproportionately targeting poorer Latinx landowners along the border and Denise Gilman argues constitutes a violation of guaranteed private property rights, the Wall effectively blocks landowners from their own land.[94]

While initial calls for a barrier at the border came in the 1970s and the first legislation towards comprehensive border control dates to the early 1990s, only after the terrorist attacks of 9/11, the creation of the Department of Homeland Security, and the 2003 passage of House Bill 4437 was border crossing made a felony crime and a mandate created for a fence covering

---

93 Josh Begley, *Best of Luck with the Wall*, Field of Vision (2016): https://vimeo.com/189015526; accessed 14 March 2023.

94 Chaichian, *Empires and Walls*, 233; Denise Gilman, 'Seeking Breaches in the Wall: An International Human Rights Law Challenge to the Texas-Mexico Border Wall,' *Texas International Law Journal* 46 (2011): 257–93, at 275–6.

Figure 6.15 Part of the border that follows the Rio Grande to the Gulf of Mexico.

seven hundred miles of the border. As Tohono O'odham elder Ofelia, founder of O'odham Voice Against the Wall, put it, 'We didn't realize it was a border, really, until 9/11.'[95] The Secure Fence Act of 2006 repeated the instruction to secure existing barriers and complete construction of the planned seven hundred miles of physical fencing, with uncovered border, especially along the Rio Grande, secured by the Virtual Fence, a multibillion-dollar electronic surveillance scheme contracted out to the Boeing Corporation.[96] Virtual Fence was canceled in 2011 when proven ineffective in covering an initial target of fifty-four miles, at a cost of over one billion dollars.[97] The incomplete coverage is a concern both to supporters and to opponents of the Wall. The former, especially when campaigning, are enabled to make claims that if elected they will wall off the border up to the last inch (Michelle Bachmann, 2011); electrify it and put an alligator-filled moat in the middle (Herman Cain, 2011); or make it over fifty-feet high, 'big, beautiful, tall and strong,' and paid for by Mexico (Donald Trump, 2016); or that they already have

95 Di Cintio, *Walls*, 176,
96 Chaichian, *Empires and Walls*, 222; Di Cintio, *Walls*, 169.
97 Danielle Ivory and Julie Creswell, 'One Certainty of Trump's Wall: Big Money,' *New York Times* (18 Jan. 2017): www.nytimes.com/2017/01/28/business/mexico-border-wall-trump.html; accessed 8 March 2021; Chaichian, *Empires and Walls*, 222–5.

256   *After the end*

completed it (Donald Trump, 2020).[98] Such claims have invited comparison to the overtly militarized barriers and shoot-to-kill policies of the Berlin Wall, as did the hiring of Israeli security firm Elbit to provide electronics and drone technology already in use on the West Bank Wall.[99]

Few expect the full two thousand-plus miles of the border ever to be fully covered by fence or wall and others cite statistics showing that unauthorized border crossing for most of the 2010s was at its lowest level since the 1970s.[100] At the time of writing, President Biden had pledged 'not to add another foot' to the Wall, and fact-checking on Trump's claims had counted a total of 452 miles of border fencing, with a maximum of 'about 80 miles of primary and secondary barriers ... built in areas where there were previously no structures,' and elsewhere a question of replacing 'existing barriers ... or added secondary or tertiary barriers of security.'[101] In a criminalized and militarized border, those still attempting to cross illegally are channeled to the gaps, which has led to an ongoing humanitarian crisis as thousands of migrants die in sparsely populated land on the US side that is deadly to those unaccustomed to its harsh conditions.[102] As a former Border Patrol agent recalls his mother telling him about a conversation with a rancher:

> It's inhumane what the government does, he told her. Border Patrol doesn't stop these people at the line, they let them cross and they chase them on the north side – thirty, forty, fifty miles or more north of the border. They let these

98 Costica Bradatan, 'Scaling "The Wall in the Head,"' *New York Times* (27 Nov. 2011): https://archive.nytimes.com/opinionator.blogs.nytimes.com/2011/11/27/scaling-the-wall-in-the-head/; Chaichian, *Empires and Walls*, 243; Julia Preston, Alan Rappeport, and Matt Richtel, 'Donald Trump's Immigration Plan: Big Promises, Bigger Doubts,' *New York Times* (19 May 2016).

99 Di Cintio, *Walls*, 169.

100 There are unsurprisingly no precise numbers; however, CBP statistics of annual arrests at the border show a steady rise from 1960 to a plateau of around 700,000 from the mid-1970s to the early 1980s, and a much higher plateau between around 900,000 and 1.6 million from 1986 through 2007. Between FY 2008 and 2018, apprehensions plummeted to an average of around 400,000 (United States Border Patrol Southwest Border Sectors, 'Total Illegal Alien Apprehensions by Fiscal Year (Oct. 1st through Sept. 30th),' www.cbp.gov/sites/default/files/assets/documents/2019-Mar/bp-southwest-border-sector-apps-fy1960-fy2018.pdf). There was a rebound in 2020 (Kirk Semple, 'After a Lull, the Number of Migrants Trying to Enter the U.S. Has Soared,' *New York Times* (10 Aug. 2020): www.nytimes.com/2020/08/06/world/americas/mexico-immigration-usa.html.

101 Lauren Giella, 'Fact Check: Did President Trump Build the "Big, Beautiful" Border Wall He Promised?' *Newsweek* (12 Jan. 2021): www.newsweek.com/fact-check-did-president-trump-build-big-beautiful-border-wall-he-promised-1560942.

102 De Léon, *Land of Open Graves*, 7–8. According to Francisco Cantú, over 6,000 deaths were recorded by the Border Patrol between 2000 and 2016 (*The Line Becomes a River: Dispatches from the Border* (New York: Penguin, 2018), 106).

people wreak havoc on ranchers' land, they let them die in the desert. My mother narrowed her eyes and looked at me. Is it true? she asked. I think it's a little more complicated than that, I said. I'd call it an unintended consequence. My mother tilted her head and stared at me unbelievingly. I glared back at her. What do you want me to say? I snapped. That agents are purposely driving people to their deaths? Field agents don't write border policy. We just show up and patrol where we're assigned.[103]

The Wall is a physical barrier that poses significant risk and often fatal consequences to all those that live, work, or pass near the borderlands it creates (to some, of course, more than to others): wildlife, ranchers, Indigenous Peoples, Border Patrol and other law enforcement agents, militia and vigilante groups, criminals, migrants, and the American and Mexican organizations that attempt to help them. That this physical presence and the ideologies and policies surrounding it also contribute to a *Mauer im Kopf* akin to the 'Wall in the Head' that infected East and West Germans during the Cold War or that continues to infect Palestinians and Israelis today does not mitigate the physical impact; rather, the one feeds off the other.[104]

The *Mauer im Kopf* may characterize especially those north of the border who unthinkingly accept its premise as they accept its permanence; however, for those most in danger from the crossing, it is simply another obstacle in a long journey toward a potential livelihood. 'Children run and flee,' writes Mexican American author Valeria Luiselli of her experience helping asylum-seeking children fill out the necessary application forms. 'They have an instinct for survival, perhaps, that allows them to endure almost anything just to make it to the other side of horror, whatever may be waiting there for them.'[105] In Luiselli's telling, as in the movie *Sin Nombre* (discussed below), that horror is embodied in *la bestia* (Figures 6.16 & 6.17), the mythically named train that long carried around half a million Central Americans every year across Mexico to *la linea*, killing many along the way, and the setting for the abuse of many of the women and girl migrants, 80 percent of whom are sexually assaulted somewhere along the journey.[106] 'And once you're here,' she concludes, 'And once you're here, you're ready

---

103 Cantú, *Line Becomes a River*, 90–1.

104 In 'Scaling "The Wall in the Head,"' Bradatan makes the analogy between the German *Mauer im Kopf* and the US–Mexico Wall; however, in pressing hard on the way the wall creates 'a sense of security' rather than security, and that walls are built primarily for those included in rather than excluded from, Bradatan downplays the feedback between material and symbolic and between inside and outside that constitute the bunkered condition of the Wall.

105 Valeria Luiselli, *Tell Me How It Ends: An Essay in 40 Questions* (Minneapolis: Coffee House Press, 2017), 19.

106 Luiselli, *Tell Me How It Ends*, 19, 25.

Figure 6.16 Iconography of *la bestia*: Sayra and her family on their dark way from San Pedro Sula, Honduras to the US border in *Sin Nombre*.

Figure 6.17 Iconography of *la bestia*: Oscar riding *la bestia* from San Pedro Sula to the US border through the brightly colored world of Brian K. Vaughan, Marcos Martín, and Muntsa Vicente's *Barrier*.

to give everything, or almost everything, to stay and play a part in the great theater of belonging.'[107] Luiselli would address the theater of belonging in greater detail in her 2019 novel *Lost Children Archive*, where she doubles the episode of refugee children refused asylum being deported by plane with the disappearance of the narrator's own children at the end of a cross-country

107 Luiselli, *Tell Me How It Ends*, 98.

car journey to the Arizona border in search of the children of her immigrant friend Manuela in New York City. In the 'Sixteenth Elegy' for these 'lost children,' *la bestia* and the border fence merge in a calque of T. S. Eliot's poetic revision of a scene of crossing in Dante's *Inferno*: 'Unreal desert. Under the brown fog of a desert dawn, a crowd flows over the iron wall, so many. None thought the trains would bring so many. Bodies flow up the ladder and down onto the desert floor. It all happens too quickly after that.'[108] The novel ends badly for Manuela's children, and equivocally for the narrator and her own family. Of the story it tells, however, we can echo the narrator's comment that 'children's imaginations destabilize our adult sense of reality and force us to question the very grounds of that reality. The more time one spends surrounded by children, disconnected from other adults, the more their imaginations leak through the cracks of our own fragile structures.'[109] Luiselli does not find a solution for balancing the friction of the loss of these children with the affordances of essays and stories; however, neither appears able to move forward without those free to stay having our 'adult sense of reality' destabilized by the borderlands experience of those who are not. After watching the plane fly off with the rejected children, the boy imagines the different possibilities:

> I asked Ma what she thought was going to happen to the children in the airplane. She said she didn't know, but said that if those lost children hadn't got caught the way they got caught, they would all have spread out across the country, and she was showing the big map from her seat like always, and moving her finger around it like she was drawing with her fingertip. All of them would have found a place to go, she said.[110]

Crossing is a fraught spatiotemporal moment in any journey, and both fictional and nonfictional journeys participate in an imaginary that conjoins physical danger from the environment and from human actors, an occulting effect that makes the moment of migration simultaneously a passage into unknown hardship and an emergence into possibility, and the mythopoetic weight of an otherworld passage for 'those who cross over, pass over, or go through the confines of the "normal."'[111] Mexican writer Yuri Herrera captures the range of this imaginary in his 2009 novella *Signs Preceding the End of the World*. *Signs* is narrated exclusively through the fragmented but razor-sharp mind of young Makina, who agrees to courier a local crime boss's package across the border in order to deliver a paper from her mother

---

108 Luiselli, *Lost Children Archive* (New York: Knopf, 2019), 315.
109 Luiselli, *Lost Children Archive*, 160.
110 Luiselli, *Lost Children Archive*, 193.
111 Anzaldúa, *Borderlands / La Frontera*, 25.

260   *After the end*

to her brother, missing in action since he followed a dubious promise of inherited land across the border. 'You're going to cross,' 'Mr Q' tells her, 'You're going to cross and you're going to get your feet wet and you're going to be up against real roughnecks; you'll get desperate, of course, but you'll see wonders and in the end you'll find your brother, and even if you're sad, you'll wind up where you need to be.'[112] Not much of what Mr Q promises about the crossing comes to pass; the truth is closer to one of Makina's 'rules' for survival: 'You are the door, not the one who walks through it.'[113]

Because Makina is neither coyote nor migrant, Herrera is able to shift in and out of the familiar tropes of migration. Makina's attention flows seamlessly between fine observation of the contents of the rucksacks of her fellow travelers; profane analysis of the world around her and its sexual, racial, and migratory politics ('Slippery bitch of a city, she said to herself. Always about to sink back into the cellar'[114]); viscerally physical moments such as when she falls in the river, unable to swim; and moments of dreamspace, such as the underworld in which the novella concludes:

> Makina caught a glimpse of the last rays of sun. Then she went on down. After four spiral turns she came to another door, which was answered by a handsome old woman with very long white fingernails and a powdered face, wearing a butterfly pin that held back the folds of her dress. Over the door was a sign that said Verse. She tried to remember how to say verse in any of her tongues but couldn't. This was the only word that came to her lips. Verse. The woman drew two cigarettes from a black case, lit them both and held one out. Makina took it and stepped through. The place was like a sleepwalker's bedroom: specific yet inexact, somehow unreal and yet vivid; there were lots of people, very calm, all smoking, and though she saw no ventilation shafts nor felt any currents the air didn't smell.[115]

'Specific yet inexact, somehow unreal and yet vivid': this is Herrera's rendering of the experience of border crossing, an experience that stretches thousands of miles both north and south of the actual *linea*.

'Verse,' as the translator Lisa Dillman explains, is an English rendering of 'the novel's most talked-about neologism: *jarchar*. Yuri himself has discussed this verb in multiple places. Within *Signs*, it means, essentially, "to leave."'[116] Derived from the Arabic word '*kharja*, meaning exit,' coined

---

112 Yuri Herrera, *Signs Preceding the End of the World*, trans. Lisa Dillman (Sheffield: And Other Stories, 2015 [2009]), 13.
113 Herrera, *Signs*, 12.
114 Herrera, *Signs*, 8.
115 Herrera, *Signs*, 61.
116 Dillman, 'Translator's Note,' in Herrera, *Signs*, loc. 850.

Wall and tunnel

261

to describe 'short Mozarabic verses or couplets tacked on to the end of longer Arabic or Hebrew poems written in Al-Andalus, the region we now call Spain,' Herrera's 'verse' is an active verb, not a noun or passive experience. It brings together border crossing, cultural hybridity, and the creative dream of 'exit' as an extraterritorial door in the same way they are conjoined in Mohsin Hamid's 2017 novel *Exit West* (see Conclusion). Its etymology identifies this borderland as a place of friction, crossings, and exits as generative and as violent and oppressive as the Christians, Jews, and Arabs in the Muslim kingdom of Al-Andalus. Although the elemental physicality as which Makina experiences her journey strongly evokes the animal imagery of Indigenous belief-systems, she lives within rather than explicitly articulating any specific deities, spirits or animals; instead, the experience of such a spacetime imbues her own rendering of the journey. Like Olan's postapocalyptic novel *Earth Remembers* (see Chapter 5), comics such as *Coyotes* and *Border Town* explicitly invoke Aztec underworld figures and *curanderas* or *brujas*, appropriating these figures both as spectacle and as earnest attempts to open up the locked-down space of the Wall. We explore these, and other modes of dwelling on life at and beneath the border, in the next section.

Dwelling beneath the border

There are two distinct communities directly blocked by the wall: immigrants and drug smugglers. These populations overlap in the political imaginary and at times their paths cross. The *coyotes* who specialize in human smuggling are often related to other forms of organized crime; migrants making the crossing may also agree or be compelled to work as drug mules. In Lawrence Taylor and Maeve Hickey's ethnography of the children and teenagers who haunt the drainage tunnels linking Nogales, Sonora, and Nogales, Arizona, the 'tunnel kids' at times smuggle drugs under the border and at other times people; they periodically travel to '*el otro lado*' for 'jobs' and to purchase sneakers and clothes with the money they take from the border-crossing migrants they ambush in the tunnels. In other contexts, they are described as '*bajadores*, roving gangsters who prowl the tunnels and smuggler routes for migrants to rob, abduct, or assault. The *bajadores* are the pirates of the borderlands.'[117] At once 'dangerous street thug[s]' in the eyes of the authorities and many townspeople, 'solid citizen[s] of Barrio Libre' in their own eyes, and kids possessing a 'complex humanity,' they 'dwell in [the] ambiguity,

117 Di Cintio, *Walls*, 188.

262   *After the end*

irony, contradictions, and subversions' of life around and beneath the Wall.[118] In this multiplicity, the kids of Barrio Libre capture the impossibility of fully disentangling the different elements of borderlands culture individual to individual. At the same time, Taylor and Hickey are clear-eyed about the larger forces of inequity, insecurity, and intolerance whose damage is evident for all to see. From their shack in a *colonia*, or slum, in the hills high above Nogales, young Boston explains, 'You can see everything from here. Everything.'[119]

Taylor and Hickey's ethnography discovers confused loyalties, disregard of the law and jurisdictions, and ethical conflicts unacknowledged by the stark and easy division of the walled border, striving to restore complex humanity to 'tunnel kids' typically assimilated in the border imaginary to the rats that inhabit the same tunnels. Fictional texts such as *Coyotes* and *Border Town* seek to incorporate similar figures into alternate border mythologies. In the eight-issue series *Coyotes* (2017–18), writer Sean Lewis and artist Caitlin Yarsky conjure a border world that phantasmagorically renders the trauma of the border situation and the specific vulnerability of women, while creating a transhistorical spacetime in which they can exert agency over this terror and trauma (Figure 6.18). In the border town known as the City of Lost Girls, a young girl, abused and abandoned in the desert mountains, is taken in by the *abuelas*, vigilante warrior witches who live in a train in an abandoned subway tunnel called Victoria Station. The coyotes in this border town are not ambiguous paid guides; they are were-creatures, created by a drug, that drape themselves in coyote hides to prey on the girls and women. The violence is constant and visceral, from both sides. There is a positively rendered border control detective, but the more cosmic struggle is between the female force of Gaia and the masculine Wolves. The first story arc ends when the girl and the *abuelas* persuade the coyotes that they have been manipulated; the second ends with the defeat of the Wolf. In their attempt to use comics as 'a way to create new myths in the traditional sense' about 'the most confusing, upsetting and terrifying aspects of … our lives,'[120] Lewis and Yarsky conclude an ultraviolent ongoing apocalypse with an image of emergence from a dark and narrow canyon underworld into a 'safe' place, a 'home.' It is a fitting image for an alternate borderlands.

---

118 Lawrence J. Taylor and Maeve Hickey, *Tunnel Kids* (Tucson: University of Arizona Press, 2001), 5, xvi.
119 Taylor and Hickey, *Tunnel Kids*, 36.
120 Sean Lewis (wr.) and Caitlin Yarsky (art), *Coyotes* 8 (Portland, OR: Image Comics, 2018), 28.

Figure 6.18 A women's sanctuary in a phantasmagoric border setting in Sean Lewis and Caitlin Yarsky's revenge fantasy, *Coyotes*.

264 *After the end*

The horror-fantasy YA comic *Border Town* (2018–19) mined a different mythic vision out of the border imaginary.[121] A typically diverse hodgepodge of marginalized YA schoolkids in Devil's Fork, Arizona, discovers that their border fence is also 'the door between two worlds' leading to the 'subterrestrial nightmare realm of Mictlan,' the Aztec underworld populated by several particularly grizzly members of the pantheon, led by their king Mictlāntēcutli.[122] Predictably, the invasion from the otherworld is mistaken by the town sheriff for 'a god-damn full-blown Mexican invasion.'[123] He is of course right, but for all the wrong reasons. The fence itself has enabled the invasion; the way to close one door is to open the other. *Border Town* riffs on fear and xenophobia: 'Reports are conflicted,' we hear on the news, 'and run the gamut from sightings of political protesters, to religious terrorists, to little green men. All that's clear is that something dangerous has crossed the border between the United States and Mexico.'[124] The racist classmate is possessed by a demon from hell, and the danger from outside turns out to come from long before the settler-colonialists had even arrived. Similar to *Coyotes*, a *curandera* who runs a *botánica* in Devil's Fork schools the four teenagers in the history of Mictlān, its relationship to the world above, and the ways of *brujería*. And, as in *Coyotes*, certain genders and individuals may be more readily possessed by it, but evil arises not from individuals so much as from the landscapes of injustice they create and perpetuate.

Although they afford different meanings when treated as ethnography rather than as fantasy or as dramatic realism, the landscapes of injustice at the border partake of the same tunnel imaginary. Realistic dramas set around the border and its tunnels afford a starker, if no less mythic experience. In Gregory Nava's film *El Norte* (1983), the traumatic passage through a drainage pipe includes flooding, swarming rats, and hours of crawling on corrugated metal. The tunnel encapsulates the difficulties and trauma of the young pair's journey from rural Guatemala to San Diego; their emerging glimpse of the starry sky of California is the only respite before descending into the film's equally terrible second half of the migrant's life. Di Cintio

---

121 Eric M. Esquivel (story), Ramon Villalobos (art), Tamra Bonvillain (coloring), *Border Town* (Burbank, CA: DC Comics, 2018–19). Originally planned as a six-issue run for DC's Vertigo imprint, the comic was canceled after four issues when Villalobos and Bonvillain pulled out following allegations of sexual abuse against Esquivel (Graeme McMillan, 'DC Cancels Hit Comic Book Series "Border Town" after Abuse Claims,' *Hollywood Reporter* (14 Dec. 2018): http://web.archive.org/web/20230218220841/https://www.hollywoodreporter.com/news/general-news/dc-cancels-border-town-comic-abuse-claims-1169513/).

122 *Border Town* #4 (Feb. 2019), 16; #2 (Dec. 2018), 8.

123 *Border Town* #4, 22.

124 *Border Town* #2, 15.

Wall and tunnel   265

narrates a similar passage through the Nogales drainage tunnel, in fear of rats, flooding, and *bajadores*, before an equally difficult life to come for those who cross.[125] De Léon bids farewell at a Nogales tunnel to two of his ethnographic subjects, veteran border crossers Lucho and Memo. As Memo explains their 'system' for evading rattlesnakes and *bajadores* and cracks tension-relieving jokes, De Léon questions his academic motivations that will process their stories as 'data for a publication that will benefit me and do little to help them survive' and tries to repress the 'waves of apocalyptic visions' of the necroviolence awaiting them.[126] The drug tunnel undermines easy assumptions about the Wall's effectiveness and ideological efficacy; the immigrant's drainage tunnel emphasizes the dehumanizing effect of the process and the identity the Wall fixes on what it regards as the waste flowing beneath it. In the harrowing tunnel scene in Québécois filmmaker Denis Villeneuve's border crime drama *Sicario* (2015), when FBI agent Kate Macer (Emily Blunt) follows an extralegal government task force under the border near Nogales and attempts to arrest assassin Alejandro Gillick (Benicio del Toro) for the murders he has just committed in the tunnel passage, she is shot for her pains.

Since 1990, well over a hundred tunnels have been discovered in the Tucson Sector that includes Nogales, around half of all the tunnels found beneath the US–Mexico border; the most recent to reach news outlets at the time of writing was in 2020.[127] Like the sewers that ran freely beneath the Allied and Soviet zones of occupied Vienna or divided Berlin, the original Nogales tunnels, large enough to drive a car through, long predate strict border control; they were designed to contain flooding in the region by draining runoff from the higher Sonoran side to the lower Arizonan side. Miles long with side tunnels branching off, the twin drainage tunnels first came to light in the 1990s, through an AP story and a feature on 'tunnel rats' for the news show *20/20*; the tunnels were gated off and the epithet would eventually pass on to the Border Patrol authorities charged with policing them.[128] The association with vermin, dirt, and disease is apt in

125 Di Cintio, *Walls*, 188–9.
126 De Léon, *Land of Open Graves*, 153–4.
127 'Cross-Border Drug Tunnel Found beneath Streets of Nogales,' *abc15.com* (27 Feb. 2020): http://web.archive.org/web/20211128173647/https://www.abc15.com/news/region-central-southern-az/nogales/cross-border-drug-tunnel-found-beneath-streets-of-nogales; Kevin Sieff, 'Under the U.S.-Mexico Border, Miles of Tunnels Worth Millions of Dollars – to Traffickers,' *Washington Post* (13 Oct. 2020): www.washingtonpost.com/world/the_americas/mexico-border-tunnels-drugs/2020/10/09/0f4dafe8-0438-11eb-897d-3a6201d6643f_story.html.
128 Associated Press, 'Tunnel Children Irk Border City,' *New York Times* (27 March 1994): section 1, p. 24: www.nytimes.com/1994/03/27/us/tunnel-children-irk-border-city.html; Taylor and Hickey, *Tunnel Kids*, xiv.

266

After the end

some ways even as it is sensationalized in often mythic terms. As Taylor and Hickey observe, 'Nobody was paying attention to the homeless Mexican children all over the country or even to those of the border region. The tunnel kids, however, were a story ... a kind of *Les Miserables* of the border.'[129] The story of Victor Hugo's *Les Misérables* was not only of misery. It was also a tale of persistent subversion, climaxing with a sewer escape during the July Revolution of 1830. 'Difference can disrupt,' writes Tsing, 'causing everyday malfunctions as well as unexpected cataclysms. ... Furthermore, difference sometimes inspires insurrection.'[130]

As so often occurs beneath borders, tunneling continued to subvert the Arizona barrier. 'We'd weld the gates shut, and then five minutes after we'd weld them, they'd break the welds,' explained one Border Patrol officer.[131] When the US Customs and Border Protection agency (CBP) posted officers at the main opening, 'migrants and smugglers began appearing from the scores of storm drains and manhole covers across the city – carrying their shoes in plastic bags to keep them dry, disappearing into downtown stores in the hope of mingling with shoppers.'[132] In 2007, the CBP finally installed a set of iron gates that passed the test of permanence; smugglers opened crude tunnels that detoured around the gates, emerging instead nearby, out of sight.[133] Despite the awareness and vigilance of the authorities, and despite their short lifespan before detection, tunnels are such a lucrative proposition for the border economy that they continue regularly to be made.[134]

As border control tightened in the twenty-first century, the crossing has become more expensive for migrants and more profitable for those controlling the routes, and organized crime has asserted greater control. Brian K. Vaughan and Marcos Martín amplify this confusion in the five-issue miniseries *Barrier* (2015–17; Figure 6.17), which begins with rancher Liddy finding an eviscerated horse on her property near the border, for which she blames drug gangs. She next finds the cowering Oscar, a reformed Honduran gang member and lone survivor of a trip through Mexico on *la bestia*, whom she assumes to be the culprit. Both are then kidnapped by 'real' aliens, themselves apparently lost in transit and unable to communicate with either of their captives. Like Esquivel, Villalobos, and Bonvillain in *Border Town*, Vaughan

129 Taylor and Hickey, *Tunnel Kids*, xiv.
130 Tsing, *Friction*, 6.
131 Adam Higginbotham, 'The Narco Tunnels of Nogales,' *Bloomberg Businessweek* (6 Aug. 2012): http://web.archive.org/web/20221207185822/http://adamhigginbotham.com/Archive/Writing.html.
133 Higginbotham, 'Narco Tunnels.'
132 Higginbotham, 'Narco Tunnels.'
134 Sieff, 'Under the U.S.-Mexico Border.'

and Martín play on the multiple meanings of 'alien' and 'border' to open up the affordances of the migration story. Oscar had swum across the border, as does young Sayra at the end of *Sin Nombre*, Corey Fukiyama's 2009 drama about a similar flight to the border from gang violence in Honduras (Figure 6.16); the crossing through water figures often in fiction, as in Herrera's *Signs*, associating the migrants with a femininized animal underground. This association stresses their helplessness, their assimilation in the colonial imagination with vermin, and their own sense of degradation from the experience; it equally dissociates them from the drug gangs, whose tunnels are often figured dirt and dry, still animal but dangerous and masculine, as in *Sicario*. In reality, as we see in *Tunnel Kids*, they are at different times both; there's no fixed identity to a physical space.

Bryan Finoki eloquently summarizes the basic spatial relationship between Wall and tunnel in discussing the discovery that the more the border was physically closed, the more tunnels were excavated under it: 'This is intimately curious to me, the relationship the fence and tunnel share, where the spatial dynamics of territorial authority are built up and broken down again, are constantly uprooted and re-challenged, where the limits of power are undone by the primordial urge to human ingenuity persistent in its crudest form, in its naked right to move freely beyond all constraints and survive, snoop, escape, evade, profit.'[135] Verticalizing power is an effective yet reductive rhetorical technique. Migrants use available conduits, especially drainage tunnels that testify to the ecological connections denied by the Wall; organized crime builds its own. Many migrants enter legally as refugees; until the policies were changed during the Trump administration, children would cross the border intending to turn themselves in on the other side; the fences are breached thousands of times every year; coyotes have all manner of equipment designed or jury-rigged rapidly to pass over or through the barriers. The Wall and tunnel imaginary visualizes the contested border space as an endless cycle opposing the forces of order, biopower, and state and nonstate authorities against the forces of disorder, criminality, and individual 'ingenuity': the status quo versus the underground. This time-honored and highly effective form affords a visual schema placing all the complex moving parts around the border in relation to one another; however, in its fixed verticalization, it is also a highly reductive form that affords no possibility for change beyond apocalyptic revolutionary overturning of one system by its inverse.

135 Bryan Finoki, 'Tunnelizing Migration I: The Border Tunnel Capital of North America,' *Subtopia: A Field Guide to Military Urbanism* (5 March 2009): http://web.archive. org/web/20230307093832/http://subtopia.blogspot.com/2009/03/tunnelizing-migration-1-border-tunnel.html.

Figure 6.19 The view from across the border of JR's gentle giant, San Diego, California, 7 Sept. 2017.

As in Berlin, in Palestine, and elsewhere, artists have endeavored to create alternate models to the bunker fantasy of the Wall. Rather than the materialized imaginary of Wall and tunnel, overtly artistic or fantastic forms exchange the affordance of a claim to 'real world' relevance for the affordance of imagining alternate spatial practices. The trompe l'oeil graffiti discussed above is utopian not only in its visual imagination of a breached barrier but also in its wager that we will suspend our disbelief long enough to enjoy the illusion of 'an imaginary enclave within real social space'[136] and to imagine in turn how such a breach might actually occur, not so much in the Wall itself as in the policies underpinning its existence. To recall the words of Palestinian Basel Abbas in the West Bank: 'It is not all about the Wall. ... I've never been allowed to cross the Green Line into Jerusalem ... Not before the Wall and not now.'[137]

In a temporary installation late in 2017 at the border fence in Tecate, Mexico, near San Diego, French street artist JR mounted a double trompe l'oeil of Kikito, a one-year-old Mexican boy, peering over the wall like a curious, gentle giant. Seen from the California side (Figure 6.19), it echoed on a vast scale utopian graffiti of children opening, scaling, or playing along the West Bank Wall. Seen from the Tecate side (Figure 6.20), near the boy's home, the viewer realizes that what appeared through the fence as emerging

136 Jameson, *Archaeologies of the Future*, 15.
137 Di Cintio, *Walls*, 112.

Wall and tunnel

Figure 6.20 The view from behind the scenes, San Diego, California, 7 Sept. 2017.

directly out of and over the fence's vertical slats was in fact mounted on a giant billboard-like scaffolding, set many yards back from the wall, firmly ensconced within home soil. Seen from one side, this was a harmless refugee; seen from the other, this was merely a curious resident of the local *colonia*. As JR explained to the boy's mother, 'He lives here, he overlooks the wall every day, but he doesn't know what it is.' She responded, having seen the rendering, 'I hope this will help people see us differently than what they hear in the media, that they will stop taking us like criminals or rapists. ... I hope in that image they won't only see my kid. They will see us all.'[138] That act of seeing would not end necropolitics, restore lost children, or bring down the Wall; however, it could contribute to the work of shifting future policy.[139]

---

138 Alexandra Schwartz, 'The Artist JR Lifts a Mexican Child over the Border Wall,' *New Yorker* (11 Sept. 2017): www.newyorker.com/news/as-told-to/the-artist-jr-lifts-a-mexican-child-over-the-border-wall.
139 As of late 2020, the parents of many hundreds of children separated at the border had still not been located (Priscilla Alvarez, 'Parents of 628 Migrant Children Separated at Border Still Have Not Been Found, Court Filing Says,' *CNN.com* (2 Dec. 2020): http://web.archive.org/web/20220927000822/http://edition.cnn.com/2020/12/02/politics/family-separation-us-border-children/index.html).

270   *After the end*

Conceived at the time of the tragic US government policy to separate children from their parents at the border, JR's piece was a direct intervention into the debate; he uploaded a photo of two border guards looking up at the installation to an Instagram account with over a million followers and added a pin on Google Maps to facilitate onsite viewing. And although he dismissed any direct political effect ('It didn't bring a political conversation, but a human conversation. "What is this kid thinking?" It was really just a love message. No hate debate.'[140]), it is equally unlikely that the response to JR's 'love message' was not also motivated by the political imaginary in which it was participating and whose terms it was striving to open up. A more direct but similarly imaginative intervention at the border from a European artist was made a few months later by Christoph Büchel, 'an artist of Swiss-Finnish parentage who now lives in Iceland,' regarding eight prototypes for then-President Trump's Great Wall, erected near the current separation barrier. Büchel, according to essayist Malise Ruthven,

> has cheekily proposed that the prototypes be designated a US national monument and protected from demolition as objects of 'significant cultural value' under the 1906 Antiquities Act. 'This is a collective sculpture,' he says. The prototypes are, as *The New York Times* paraphrased his view, 'an unintended sculpture garden willed into existence by the president and his supporters.' Even if the border wall is never built, says Büchel, the sample sections 'need to be preserved because they can signify and change meaning through time.'[141]

Just as Begley's video *Best of Luck with the Wall* repurposed the satellite mapping of tech giant Google to chart an alternate spatiality and different perspective on the southern border, so Büchel's conceptual artwork imagines a productive afterlife to then-President Trump's Wall prototypes. Not only, he hoped, would they become testimonials to a security imagination that never came to fruition but, in their fragmentary substance, they would also testify to the necessary incompleteness of any barrier wall, whether a material one or a *Mauer im Kopf*.

Alex Rivera's transnational border science fiction film, *Sleep Dealer* (2008), imagines the *Mauer im Kopf* as an ontological phenomenon in the factories of 'Tijuana del Futuro.'[142] Their bodies no longer required or admitted within the US, migrants instead work in factories on the Mexican side, remotely operating robot agricultural, domestic, and construction workers through metal nodes that plug directly into their nervous systems (Figure 6.21). This virtual-reality labor in twelve-hour shifts drains their energy

140 Schwartz, 'Mexican Child.'
141 Malise Ruthven, 'Physical Graffiti on the Border,' *New York Review of Books* (9 April 2018): www.nybooks.com/daily/2018/04/09/physical-graffiti-on-the-border/.
142 *Sleep Dealer*, dir. Alex Rivera, dist. Maya Entertainment, 2008.

Figure 6.21 'The American Dream': ontologically bunkered in a *maquiladora* in *Sleep Dealer*'s Tijuana while laboring virtually in southern California.

and vitality as surely as we are warned today that Internet and gaming addictions will do. To recharge, they use the same nodes for virtual drinking, sex, drugs, and other escapism. The only difference, in other words, from present-day labor practices is that they are exploited virtually and at arm's length rather than in person. As Villazana notes, the setting marks the paradoxical migration: 'the urban landscape becomes a transnational virtual mobile city; a sort of bridge between Mexico and the United States.'[143] At the same time, multinational companies have grabbed water rights and deploy their own remote guardians from their side of the border to police the seized territory from water thieves and 'Aqua-Terrorists' via remote drones and warplanes. The portentously named protagonist Memo has migrated from his Oaxacan village of Santa Elena del Río to support his mother and brother after his house has been destroyed and his father killed by drones putatively protecting the water in the dammed river that used to belong to the villagers and which it now sells back to them. Memo travels to Tijuana del Futuro, where he obtains black-market 'nodes' from a 'coyoteka' who is herself milking him for a life story of memories she downloads through her nodes and sells online. Rivera's primary interest shows in the complex speculative geography he invented with co-writer David Riker,

---

143 Libia Villazana, 'Transnational Virtual Mobility as a Reification of Deployment of Power: Exploring Transnational Processes in the Film *Sleep Dealer*,' *Transnational Cinemas* 4.2 (2013): 217–30, at 224.

Figure 6.22 Imagining the end of the wall at a future border in *Sleep Dealer* that looks a lot like today's.

visualizing for the viewer the nexus of stolen resources, exploitative transactions, and digital frontiers that molds transnational networks. Rather than a simple movement from south to north, Rivera argues, these worlds are linked through natural resources, through human resources, and through innumerable digital connections, with goods and information constantly moving in both directions. Twice, Memo visits the wall that runs down into the Pacific Ocean south of San Diego, an ongoing barrier to corporeal but not sensorial crossing (Figure 6.22). And several times Rivera cuts away to a perspective shot of an enormous white metal pipeline receding into the frame as it crosses the desert: in real life, probably a water pipe; in the language of *Sleep Dealer*, it contains the wires transmitting thousands of neural signals; in our imaginary, it is the infrastructure of late capitalism that is buried in the middle-class world but always exposed along the border. Rivera thus momentarily visualizes the imaginary of Wall and tunnel in order to dwell on the intricate networks surrounding them. The occulting spatiality of artworks and fictions on and around separation walls does not seek to replace or explain away the physical and mental barrier they constitute; like the physical and conceptual tunnels excavated beneath them, they seek to subvert their foundations and open up their affordances to the friction of unforeseen possibilities.

Conclusion
Biosecurity, siloing, and the legacies of a shelter society

[For this epigraph, please read the lyrics of or listen to the first verse of the referenced song. Or all of it, and really dance this mess around.]

The B-52s, 'Private Idaho' (1980)

This survey of Cold War culture since the Cold War opened with the utopian image of the dome, a new form of sheltering that broached the possibility of security joined with transparency to the world above and outside. We conclude with the dome's literal and figurative correlatives in biomes and biosecurity, respectively, and its sealed-off counterimage in the tubular silos that function as physical and metaphorical self-enclosures, walled-in from and blind to anything beyond their windowless confines. These final spatial variations on the bunker fantasy are a logical culmination of the shelter society initiated by the way the Second World War ended and developed through the Cold War. The shelter society that coalesced around 1962 has, in the many ways encompassed by dystopian visions of biosecurity and siloing, been realized ontologically in the twenty-first century. Security constitutes, dominates, and segregates the American and many other ways of life to a degree that it perhaps has not done since prehistoric times. But even prophets of doom are never wholly bereft of hope; along with the requisite despair, the act of speaking out emerges from a place of hope and offers an epistemology able to grasp the knowledge production afforded by the ontological bunker as well as to understand what emerging from that bunker would mean. The primary goal of this book has been to open up what McKittrick terms 'a site of radical possibility' in the spaces of hope from which the apocalyptic visions of the bunker fantasy issue.

Throughout this book, I have interwoven four methodological decenterings: to attend carefully and openly to the full range of meaning behind the spatial forms encompassed by what I call the bunker fantasy; to trace the ways later forms of this fantasy build on and rework earlier ones, from the period around 1962 through the early 1980s to the twenty-first century; to account for the different affordances of the bunker fantasy within genre enclaves in the popular cultures of SFF, cinema, comics, music, and

274   *After the end*

vernacular architecture; and to focus on effects of peripheral and marginalized misplacements prior to, within, and external to the dominant American model, which appropriate or transform that model into alternate modalities within the bunker fantasy. Applying these methodological decenterings to biosecurity and siloing, I attempt to bring this argument into the present day of the bunker imaginary as it has emerged during the fifteen years since the book's inception. The first section of the conclusion examines the bunker fantasy in figurative applications of the wall's Cold War form: walls against climate crisis and unpredictable nature imagined by biosecurity, seed vaults and sea walls. The second section takes a concluding glance at the physical and metaphorical self-enclosures of siloing, the vertical pilings enabling and enabled by the horizontal spread of the wall.

Walls against change: sea walls and biosecurity

Separation walls work to make imaginary islands of geographically contiguous spaces; islands, by contrast, are geographically separated from their neighbors while at the same time, and often especially, vulnerable to the global forces circulating around them. And just as island nations were particularly exposed during the Cold War to the dominant nations' preparations for the apocalypse, so their identity and survival as nations or peoples are under imminent threat from invasive species and climate crisis. At the time of writing, these threats were just beginning to register broadly in the nations of the global North whose walls would soon be actively working to exclude and to punish refugees from the flooded global South, and the sea itself from coastal cities like New York. This is nothing new. During the fifty years between 1946 and 1996 in which 'more than 315 atmospheric, underground and underwater nuclear tests were conducted in the region by Britain, France and the United States,' entire populations were deemed inconsequential as nations, forcibly relocated from test sites such as Enewetak and Bikini Atolls in the Marshall Islands and subjected without warning to the short- and long-term effects of fallout.[1] The geographic isolation and small footprint that had assured

---

1 Stewart Firth, *Nuclear Playground* (New York: Routledge, 2021 [1987]); Nic Maclellan, *Grappling with the Bomb: Britain's Pacific H-Bomb Tests* (Acton, Australia: ANU Press, 2017), 1. See also United States Congress, House Committee on Foreign Affairs, Subcommittee on Asia, the Pacific, and the Global Environment, *Oversight on the Compact of Free Association with the Republic of the Marshall Islands (RMI)* (Washington: U.S. G.P.O., 2010): www.govinfo.gov/content/pkg/CHRG-111hhrg56559/pdf/CHRG-111hhrg56559.pdf; Giff Johnson, 'Exposing the US Nuclear Test Legacy in the Marshall Islands,' *Pacific Journalism Review* 12.2 (2006): 188–91; Tilman A. Russ, 'The Humanitarian Impact and Implications of Nuclear Test Explosions in the

the original settlers' security made these archipelagoes especially vulnerable to the politics and physics of nuclear colonialism.

Referenced by news sources and activists and obliquely registered in fictions like Ballard's short story 'Terminal Beach' or the Australian setting of *On the Beach*, the Pacific island imaginary served speculative notice that the nuclear condition was more than a mindset of the superpowers; it entailed an ontological transformation on a global scale. Nor has that ontology disappeared in the twenty-first century. During the Cold War, Pacific Islanders found themselves displaced and left unprotected from the ravages of the global North as 'nuclear nomads.'[2] Currently, they face the same kind of threat from rising sea levels as they did from windblown radiation and the same inadequate options: forced evacuation or helpless waiting. Where a more secure allied nation like New Zealand once worried about the fallout from a nuclear war they wanted no part of, now its government worries about biosecurity, painstakingly vetting each new arrival to the island for alien matter, waging exterminating war against invasive species, creating secure habitats to permit nature to revert to an imagined pre-invasive state. Back in the global North, wealthy doomsday preppers rush to buy into the survivalist potential of a biosecure New Zealand, while seed bunkers and sea walls promise infrastructure to preserve a threatened way of life into an uncertain future.

The Indian Ocean tsunami of 2004 that killed at least 225,000 people in a dozen countries coalesced in a single traumatic instant the inexorable threat of rising sea levels that has generally proved resistant to direct representation. The earthquake and tsunami seven years later that killed over 15,000 people and caused multiple meltdowns at the Fukushima Daiichi Nuclear Power Plant complex in Japan reminded a post–Cold War world that it still indubitably inhabited a nuclear age. Despite that reminder and despite even their return to consciousness through the Russian war of aggression in Ukraine, the many different dangers posed by nuclear power and nuclear weapons similarly remain strongly resistant to direct representation. Despite its market dominance, twenty-first-century postapocalyptic and speculative fiction is infrequently nuclear, addressing its dangers obliquely and in terms of the currently dominant security imaginary rather than the bunkered world from which that imaginary emerged. The postapocalyptic mode easily affords a reckoning of the social and personal costs of our

---

Pacific Region,' *International Review of the Red Cross* 97.899 (2015), 775–813, DOI: 10.1017/S1816383116000163; Martha Smith-Norris, *Domination and Resistance: The United States and the Marshall Islands during the Cold War* (Honolulu: University of Hawai'i Press, 2016).

2 Johnson, 'US Nuclear Test Legacy,' 191.

276 *After the end*

current inaction but affords little in the way of practical measures for change or spurs to put those measures into action. Nevertheless, it does more on this front than much of current political discourse, especially when it misplaces the spatiotemporal setting of postapocalypse from its typical location firmly within a hopefully avoidable future to a credible alternate path already or soon to be taken.

As we saw in the fiction of Octavia Butler, Nalo Hopkinson, Nnedi Okorafor, and others, or in Junot Díaz's analysis of Haiti (see Chapter 5), the dissident spacetime of the bunker fantasy is especially effective as a critical tool when displaced to a Black or Indigenous American spatiality or to a global South that was seldom invested in Cold War verities and their imperial fantasies to begin with. The slow apocalypse epitomized in the natural world by climate crisis and in the human world by chattel slavery, colonialism, and social inequality is plausibly represented in the bunker fantasy's stark divisions between those with shelter and those without it. Displaced from its proper spacetime after a nuclear apocalypse, it offers a tool for visualizing inequity and disaster in everyday life. In this, the bunker as imaginary can work both to fortify and to undermine the stark division discussed in Chapter 6 and embodied in the metaphor deployed by cultural critic Mike Davis to describe the inequities of late capitalism:

> This Great Wall of Capital, which separates a few dozen rich countries from the earth's poor majority, completely dwarfs the old Iron Curtain. It girds half the earth, cordons off at least 12,000 kilometres of terrestrial borderline, and is comparably more deadly to desperate trespassers. ... Although it includes traditional ramparts (the Mexican border of the United States) and barbed wire-fenced minefields (between Greece and Turkey), much of globalised immigration enforcement today takes place at sea or in the air. Moreover, borders are now digital as well as geographical.[3]

True to Davis's classically Marxist formulation, a Great Wall of Capital is built or imagined only so as to be undermined by revolution. The metaphor affords a dominant image of the status quo and no way around it except by elimination. The bunker, on the other hand, paradoxically acknowledges a collective danger *and* articulates a collective need for shelter. No one inside a bunker has ever argued against the principle that everyone *needs* shelter; arguments about exclusion from a particular shelter are always contingent rather than necessary. By imagining a world in which everyone would need shelter, the bunker fantasy affords a critical purchase on a world that would not provide them or would provide them inequitably; at the same time, it also affords affective justification for shirking that responsibility.

---

3 Davis, 'Great Wall.'

Biosecurity, siloing, and shelter society   277

Both a motivation for and consequence of the widespread embrace of SFF by twenty-first-century writers in the global South, the bunker fantasy affords a critical stance on the fixed verities of the global North, what Argentinian novelist Betina González calls, in her recent novel *American Delirium*, 'that door hidden behind the system.'[4] In *Exit West*, for example, Pakistani diasporic novelist Mohsin Hamid uses the fantastic motif of doors between cities to imagine migration not so much as a question of separation barriers and border crossings but of personal narratives and psychic adjustments. As an old woman in California reflects near the end of the novel, '[I]t seemed to her that she too had migrated, that everyone migrates, even if we stay in the same houses our whole lives, because we can't help it. We are all migrants through time.'[5] The door is a powerful contemporary variation on the tunnel's relationship to the barrier wall, respatializing the ostensibly stable distinction between sheltering in place, being locked down or in, and moving freely through the world. The deceptive promise of gates in the West Bank Wall to provide access to Palestinian-owned lands in the Seam Zone or the ninety thousand Indians who reports claimed 'resided between the border [with Bangladesh] and the new fences' figures the mendacious spatiality of the wall as a whole.[6] Conversely, the Manhattan-based nonprofit The Door 'offers services and support for young migrants that extend beyond the immigration process'; as the name implies, they aim to open up and ease passage into 'the other side of the door.'[7] Like the openings figured in Banksy's West Bank Wall graffiti and elsewhere (Figures 6.9, 6.10, 6.12, 6.13), the novel's conceit preserves the trauma, fear, and persecution that drive migration, the shock of arrival, dangers and indignities in transit, and the long and difficult adjustment. At the same time, Hamid displaces trauma from the long physical journey to the contours of a relationship created and maintained under the conditions of migration and the ontological force of the experience from the structure to the individuals. This displacement renders the experience as a politically engaged love story of hope and suffering rather than a predetermined fate stripped of agency or subjectivity. By interjecting the fantastic into the reality of migration, Hamid displaces the reader's expectations and opens space for alternate ways to experience and understand its workings.

---

4 Betina González, *American Delirium*, trans. Heather Cleary (New York: Henry Holt, 2021 [2016]), 63.
5 Mohsin Hamid, *Exit West* (New York: Riverhead, 2017), 209–10.
6 Di Cintio, *Walls*, 85, 88–9; see also Koudelka, 'Lexicon,' in *Wall*; Parry, *Against the Wall*, 113; Weizman, *Hollow Land*, 145.
7 Luiselli, *Tell Me How It Ends*, 36, 113–14.

In her 2014 novel *The Girl in the Road*, white American author Monica Byrne imagines what the world might look like if its center were the Arabian Sea and its dominant power a repressively neoliberal Indian empire locked in a cold war with China. The novel's center of gravity is the Trail, an energy-generating pontoon bridge stretching from Mumbai to Djibouti. Byrne explicitly denies the label 'postapocalyptic' ('The world described therein is very much like ours, just displaced a few decades in the future'[8]); instead, her language and thematics make clear that in her imagination the apocalypse is already occurring daily around the inhabitants of both her and our worlds. The novel is structured around two alternating journeys, one of a West African girl escaping enslavement and abuse when she stows away in a truck convoy traveling cross-country to Ethiopia (Addis Ababa is this future's 'flagship city of Africa'[9]) carrying the metallic hydrogen (highly toxic, unlike Wakanda's fantastic vibranium and much like Niger's uranium deposits, the world's largest) that enables the sophisticated technology of the Trail. The other journey follows a troubled woman suffering from paranoia on a walkabout across the Indian Ocean on the Trail. This journey, especially near the end, when she jettisons her equipment, starts drinking seawater, and suffers vivid hallucinations, reads like an homage to 'Terminal Beach.' In this language and the way the novel resolves its densely circular plotting as a parable of guilt and responsibility, Byrne not only renders the Trail into some kind of contemporary monument to technology gone wrong but links it back to the earlier Cold War history of an equally powerful and equally fatal technology also displaced from its typical setting in the American empire.

Brian K. Vaughan and Marcos Martín's ten-issue miniseries *The Private Eye* (2013–15) equally imagines an unconventional apocalypse in order to reframe familiar questions of shelter. *Private Eye* takes place in a 2076 Los Angeles following a digital apocalypse that has eliminated the Internet and partially materialized the practices of social media into the physical world. When hackers make public the sum total of online secrets from the cloud, a suddenly exposed population responds by donning masks, trying on personae, and giving themselves license to explore their every fantasy IRL ('in real life') rather than online. Needless to say, it's a stratified society; public disguise is authorized only for legal adults and available in proportion to the level of one's income. The villains of the comic are a media mogul (future LA continues to be dominated by mendacious and omnipresent

---

8 Monica Byrne, 'A Conversation with Monica Byrne,' in Byrne, *The Girl in the Road* (New York: Broadway, 2015 [2014]), 324.
9 Byrne, *Girl in the Road*, 106.

'teevee') and a retro-tech genius for whom electronic devices serve as bunkers holding the promise and lost data of a vanished world. Because invention, resource, and development are devoted to material rather than electronic technology, physical infrastructure has boomed in ambition and sophistication, embodied in the Wonderwall, a massive sea wall centered in Santa Monica and protecting the metropolis from the rising sea (Plate 15). The villains have built and primed a massive missile that is intended either to reestablish the Internet and reconnect the masses or to blow a hole in the Wonderwall. When the latter occurs, by intention or accident, a tidal wave pours in through the breached wall (Plate 16); however, the comic ends with the city apparently undaunted and unchanged. Like Byrne's everyday apocalypse of human trafficking, toxic freight, and personal betrayal, Vaughan and Martín's near future is more concerned with the ways fantasies of security transform everyday life than in the clear-cut before and after of the conventional apocalypse.

Like *Private Eye*'s Wonderwall, the African-led Great Green Wall (GGW) movement imagines a protective wall against the consequences of the climate crisis. Like Byrne's narrative of trans-African trafficking, the GGW will span the continent across the Sahel region. Unlike either of those speculative imaginations, this real-life eco-speculation will establish a bulwark against desertification, 'by creating a mosaic of green and productive landscapes across 11 countries (Senegal, Mauritania, Mali, Burkina Faso, Niger, Nigeria, Chad, Sudan, Ethiopia, Eritrea, Djibouti).'[10] First conceived in the 1980s and officially established by the African Union in 2007, the GGW boasted in 2021 of 'almost 18 million hectares of degraded lands restored and 350.000 jobs created across the Sahel and the Great Green Wall countries,' while acknowledging challenges in organization, implementation, and coordination in reaching the goal of completion by 2030. The webpage estimates that this goal will require upwards of US$33 billion to realize its goals of 'restor[ing] 100 million hectares of degraded land'; 'sequester[ing] 250 million tons of carbon'; and 'creating 10 million green jobs in rural areas.'[11] The speculative imagination can drive ambitious progressive policy just as much as it drives regressive bunkering fantasies.

There are many modes in the twenty-first century that were unavailable to survivors of the Cold War to capture the phenomenality of the need for security that defines the contemporary world. Biosecurity similarly grounds the experience of apocalypse within the present by imagining the extinction of one species by the misplaced predations of another. Wayne Barrar's *Imaging*

10 'Great Green Wall Accelerator,' http://web.archive.org/web/20220913210522/https://www.greatgreenwall.org/great-green-wall-accelerator; accessed 22 April 2021.
11 'Great Green Wall Accelerator.'

280 *After the end*

Biosecurity project (2007–9) 'considers efforts to prevent, monitor or address the introduction and spread of invasive species in New Zealand and to minimize their ecological effects. It includes two extended case studies, focusing on the invasive alga, didymo, and the pest fish, the koi carp.'[12] Barrar's photographs capture the exterminating violence entailed in expurgating invasive species, the complex and ideologically unstable means of defining 'invasive,' and the sensible and often necessary motivations underlying both of these questionable practices. In Plate 12, two figures in biohazard suits spray a manmade lake to kill invasive fish species. The distant framing, windblown evergreen, lowering sky, and red-brick institutional building create a strong association with the iconography of apocalypse. In Plate 13, the tight framing through a thicket of naked flesh intimately captures the koi's-eye-view as it hopelessly gasps for air, prompting the viewer to imagine what it might feel like to be a member of the invasive species being exterminated. Finally, Plate 14 pictures an antiseptic interior used to 'model' how plants cope with predicted ecosystems of 'elevated CO2.' As Barrar notes, the pictured pines are themselves a ubiquitous and often invasive species, while the biotron, or controlled environment, is itself a form of bunkering aimed at containing 'high risk organisms' (i.e. pests) or 'climate change.'[13]

Where Barrar's art documents practices of biosecurity in the present day, the postapocalyptic mode extrapolates present risk into future cataclysms. Airports around the world are awash with warnings about infectious diseases; travelers returning to the global North are vetted for symptoms of invasive diseases including parasite-borne diseases like Zika that threaten to infect not only adult subjects but their unborn children, raising the deeply rooted specter of atomic mutation. At times such as the Ebola epidemic of 2013–16 or the height of the COVID-19 pandemic in 2020–21, travelers and citizens are actively quarantined. Concerns about biosecurity underlie the most prevalent plot device for disaster in twenty-first-century speculative fiction: viral infection. A virus, in this sense, is also an invasive species; in the postapocalyptic scenario, its invasion threatens to make the human species extinct – as in Tom Sweterlitsch's 1985-rooted time-travel horror fantasy *The Gone World* (2018) – or to create a new, hybrid species altogether – as with the imagined alien microorganism in Butler's *Clay's Ark* (see Chapter 5).[14]

Short-term protection in biosecurity SFF resides nearly always in walls, separation barriers, biodomes, and sealed environments; resolution, when possible, comes from a miraculous technological solution without specific

12 Barrar, *Imaging Biosecurity* (2007–9), https://waynebarrar.com/imaging-biosecurity/.
13 Barrar, communication with the author, 27 Oct. 2022.
14 Tom Sweterlitsch, *The Gone World* (New York: G. P. Putnam's Sons, 2018).

location. J. M. Morgan's Eden trilogy (1991–92) imagined a gene-manipulated virus, secretly and illegally financed by a Texas multimillionaire in Siberia's Biosphere Four, killing off the world's population.[15] A handful of survivors remain sheltered in two of the original six transparent Biospheres, a few of them in England but most hermetically sealed in Biosphere Seven, also known as 'the Crystal Kingdom': a 'beehive dome' enclosing 'six distinct ecologies' over five hundred acres and three hundred feet at its highest point.[16] Morgan's plot revolves around the difficult desire to reunite those inside with a handful of immune survivors in the wilderness outside, and the environmental dangers posed by each form of 'Eden.' When bone-marrow transplants allow the survivors to leave the failing Biosphere Seven after a twenty-three-year confinement, they emerge in May 2021 simultaneously 'released from' and 'allowed into Eden. ... The Earth is a biosphere, isn't it?'[17] The typical barrier in pandemic and other varieties of postapocalyptic, however, is a class of separation wall. But because the wall form is so familiar in its conventions, writers can readily adapt its affordances to explore alternate permutations. The plague survivors featured in Emily St. John Mandel's 2014 novel *Station Eleven*, for instance, are clustered in two utopian but vulnerable enclaves, one an airport and the other a traveling caravan of performers.[18] The perilous openness of these communities, like the narrative's unusual alternation between the pre- and postapocalyptic world, imparts a powerful but threatened sense of ongoing potentiality in the present day.

Peter Heller's 2012 novel *The Dog Stars* imagines an uneasy but eventually fulfilling relationship between educated liberal outdoorsman Hig and dyed-in-the-wool veteran survivalist Bangley in their fortified compound.[19] The ability of pilot Hig to make short hops for supplies and reconnaissance and his ongoing aid to an ostracized settlement of the infected leave the compound vulnerable but argue by the end for the necessary inclusion of imagination, contingency, and compassion in the calculus of long-term security even in a survivalist future. Like Butler's *Parable of the Sower* and many other novels, Edan Lepucki's 2014 novel *California* extrapolates a world split between luxurious gated compounds and survivalists struggling in a neobarbarian wilderness.[20] Lepucki's attention focuses on The Land, an

---

15 Morgan, *Desert Eden* (1991); *Beyond Eden* (New York: Pinnacle, 1992); and *Future Eden* (New York: Pinnacle, 1992).
16 Morgan, *Desert Eden*, 13.
17 Morgan, *Future Eden*, 314, 317–18.
18 Emily St. John Mandel, *Station Eleven* (New York: Knopf, 2014).
19 Peter Heller, *The Dog Stars* (New York: Knopf, 2012).
20 Edan Lepucki, *California* (New York: Little, Brown, 2014).

282

After the end

ambiguously situated door between these two extremes that locates traces of Californian utopianism – communes, anarchist politics, and outsider art – in dialogue with corruption, collaboration, and totalitarianism. Rather than the original counterculture's domes (see Chapter 1), however, the novel's dominant image is the Spikes, the beautiful, uncanny, and at times deadly labyrinth of Watts Tower–like assemblages that constitutes The Land's densely layered wall and doors, with pathways known to insiders and nearly impossible for outsiders to navigate. All three novels deploy the familiar spatial forms of the bunker fantasy to open up fissures and alliances within present-day polarities. The variations signal a greater investment in thinking alternately through the fixed categories of the present day.

Holly Goddard Jones's 2017 novel *The Salt Line* unfolds a similar strategy by visualizing and problematizing the very nature of the vehicle of the apocalypse into the banal yet terrifying miner tick. This shift allows Jones effectively to spatialize the shelter imaginary around biosecurity to make a partially apocalyptic near future resonate strongly with a partially apocalyptic present. Set in an eastern United States where a plague of the voracious ticks carries a 100 percent fatal disease and causes immense suffering with any bite, *The Salt Line* occurs mostly outside of the safe zones created by the titular wall that seals off various autonomous zones from a wilderness abandoned to the deadly arachnids. Erected along 'borders where, during the eradication, controlled chemical burnings had taken place, and so the earth was "salted" in the symbolic sense of having been purified, rendered uninhabitable,' the Wall eventually becomes further fortified, in the protagonist's zone, by 'TerraVibra … emanating its pulse fifty kilometers eastward, a layer of protection that no other zone, even New England, could boast.'[21] In the flesh, so to speak, the Wall turns out to be underwhelming for the protagonist who lives within its safe confines: 'the Wall was a wasteland of garbage – a seemingly endless mountain of trash that emitted a sulfurous odor that she realized now she had been smelling for kilometers.'[22] Dissatisfied in a world without enough physical risk, the superrich pay for luxurious but challenging and dangerous camping expeditions beyond the salt line. Cleverly, Jones slowly reveals the threat of the ticks to be both as fatal as advertised and also not so much of a risk except to a class unwilling to accept any risk at all. Survivalist communities have found different ways to inhabit the wilderness in despite of the ticks. Their primary risk, unsurprisingly, comes from their own corruptions and those, especially, of the contacts they have with powerful interests back within the salt line. The apocalypse

---

21 Holly Goddard Jones, *The Salt Line* (New York: G. P. Putnam's Sons, 2017), 73.
22 Jones, *Salt Line*, 73–4.

Biosecurity, siloing, and shelter society 283

is real, the risk is real, the suffering is real; however, these vagaries of a typical everyday life pose nothing like the existential threat of the extralegal structures that operate with impunity and in disregard of the boundaries between security and danger we began the novel assuming to be fixed and immutable.

In its imagination of a natural world mostly freed from human occupation and mostly unaffected by the developed zones sealed off from it, *Salt Line* operates a willful refusal of the ways environmental depredation ignores walls and boundaries as much as multinationals and extralegal networks do. At the same time, this refusal affords Jones the space to meditate on the vexed question of parks and conservation as bunker fantasies and to compare the touristic impulse of the wilderness expedition with the back-to-the-land sentiments of the settlers in Ruby City. Reversion to nature is an implicit side effect in the neobarbarian postapocalyptic form, which typically affords fear of the wild unknown, loss of the goods of civilization, and recovery of rudimentary techniques of survival as its consequences. Nature preserves exist de facto in restricted nuclear areas such as the Chornobyl Exclusion Zone and the Nevada Test Site and de jure on the five-thousand-acre Rocky Flats National Wildlife Refuge opened in 2018 near Denver, Colorado, on the former site of a nuclear weapons facility and, later, of a $7 billion cleanup.[23] Similarly, the no-man's-land between border walls has the potential to create isolated pockets of 'wilding' or 'rewilding,' a conservationist practice dating back to the 1980s to describe, 'the active return of land once used for farming, ranching, and other human purposes to a more "natural," pre-industrial state.'[24] Di Cintio describes the 'unintended wildlife preserve' created over fifty years in the Demilitarized Zone between North and South Korea, 'four kilometres wide, 250 kilometres long, and edged by barbed wire fences and watchtowers' (Figure C.1), and 'a narrow biosphere teeming with nearly six hundred endangered animal and plant species' in the *Grünes Band*, the 1,400-kilometer former border

---

23 Dan Boyce, 'A New Wildlife Refuge on the Grounds around an Old Nuclear Weapons Plant,' *NPR* (15 Sept. 2018): http://web.archive.org/web/20221206111649/https://www.npr.org/2018/09/15/647878022/a-new-wildlife-refuge-on-the-grounds-around-an-old-nuclear-weapons-plant. According to Boyce, there remained, evidently, concern over the safety of the refuge for human visitors, especially schoolchildren.

24 'Explorer's Club Roundtable: "Rewilding" America,' *rewilding.org* (28 April 2018): http://web.archive.org/web/20221004031059/https://rewilding.org/explorers-club-roundtable-rewilding-america/; accessed 31 Aug. 2023. British farmer Isabella Tree takes issue with the 'idealistic' assumption implicit in 'rewilding' that a return to a state of nature is possible, especially in isolated enclaves like her farm; she prefers the more practical goal of 'wilding' (*Wilding: The Return of Nature to a British Farm* (London: Picador, 2018), 153).

Figure C.1 Symbolic rewilding in the DMZ: 'Fence with barbed wire in green nature, trees and bushes with painted deer on the fence along the DMZ, the third tunnel, South Korea, at Korean Demilitarized Zone, 8 Sept. 2017.'

between East and West Germany that has been officially preserved as the 'Green Belt.'[25]

Like the possibility afforded by imagined nuclear war of 'rewilding' the Earth in the absence of a surfeit of human life, border walls offer sparks of radically alternate visions wholly unrelated to their primary function or threat. Especially short term, the environmental impact of separation barriers and the infrastructure necessary to build and support them take a high toll on local plant and animal life. The 'Seam Zone,' as the area between the Green Line and the West Bank Wall is called by the Israeli military, has expropriated and cut off Palestinians from water, olive groves, and grazing land; the infrastructure of the Wall has damaged those same resources.[26] As Di Cintio notes about the US–Mexico wall, thirty-three environmental protection laws and regulations that prohibited the construction of the border wall were waived by the Department of Homeland Security to carry out the 2006 Secure Fence Act; the same thing happened again during the presidency of Donald Trump.[27]

---

25 Di Cintio, *Walls*, 191–2.
26 Parry, *Against the Wall*, 99.
27 Di Cintio, *Walls*, 192–4.

Biosecurity, siloing, and shelter society

All walls are territorial and asymmetrical in form, but despite the political polarization around most contemporary barrier walls, others are differently polarized, even though they employ similar strategies and a similar language. Since the late 1970s, the UNESCO Biosphere Reserve program has supported the creation of 'areas comprising terrestrial, marine and coastal ecosystems' in three parts radiating out from 'a strictly protected' core, 'that contributes to the conservation of landscapes, ecosystems, species and genetic variation.'[28] Although some have been withdrawn, in 2021 the UNESCO webpage listed 738 land and marine biosphere reserves around the world.[29] National, local, or private endeavors like the one described in the Swiss mountains of Claude Delarue's bunkering novel *Waiting for War* (Chapter 3) aim literally or figuratively to wall off natural ecosystems from the depredations of humans and other invasive species.[30] Predator Free 2050, a joint venture led by the New Zealand government, aims 'to save the country's birds by completely eradicating its invasive predators. … rats, possums, and stoats (a large weasel)' by using conventional means like poison and traps, along with a 'gene drive' to prevent them from reproducing.[31] PF2050's call to 'return our forests, farms and cities to life' and its motto 'Kia uru ora, return to life'[32] for New Zealand's endangered birds is laudable and persuasive. But it is difficult to ignore the self-evident contradiction that 'return to life' for some lifeforms entails mass death for others. This was the mantra of 1960s bunker ethics: 'the rest must die' so that the sheltered may live. That a reasonable risk exists that an 'unstoppable wave of gene-drive rodents'[33] might intentionally or accidentally spread around the world only heightens the apocalyptic tenor of this modern-day bunker dilemma.

Managed by the community-led NGO Karori Sanctuary Trust, the 500-acre enclave of Wellington's Zealandia 'ecosanctuary' boasts of being 'the world's first fully-fenced urban ecosanctuary … that has reintroduced 18 species of native wildlife back into the area.'[34] As its history reads, 'drastic measures'

---

28 UNESCO, 'What Are Biosphere Reserves?' (2021): http://web.archive.org/web/20230306184206/https://en.unesco.org/biosphere/about; accessed 31 Aug. 2023.

29 UNESCO, 'World Network of Biosphere Reserves' (2021): http://web.archive.org/web/20230314193028/https://en.unesco.org/biosphere/wnbr; accessed 31 Aug. 2023.

30 Pike, 'Cold War Reduction: The Principle of the Swiss Bunker Fantasy,' *Space and Culture* 20.1 (2017): 94–106; see also Chapter 3 above.

31 Ed Yong, 'New Zealand's War on Rats Could Change the World,' *The Atlantic* (16 Nov. 2017): www.theatlantic.com/science/archive/2017/11/new-zealand-predator-free-2050-rats-gene-drive-ruh-roh/546011/.

32 Predator Free 2050 official webpage (2023): http://web.archive.org/web/20230313120837/https://pf2050.co.nz/; accessed 31 Aug. 2023.

33 Yong, 'New Zealand's War.'

34 'As Nature Intended,' *Zealandia / Te Māra a Tāne*: http://web.archive.org/web/20230315074014/https://www.visitzealandia.com/; accessed 15 March 2023.

Figure C.2 Zealandia excludes unwanted invasive species and warns off the canine invaders who remain welcome: 'Poison sign on Predator exclusion fence at Zealandia eco attraction park Wellington, New Zealand, 3 Feb. 2015.'

were required in the 1990s to preserve endangered bird and reptile species from extinction in the face of the 'multitude of mammalian pests' that had arrived on the mammal-free island with British settlers.[35] Zealandia provides a stark version of the natural preserve as an ecosystem walled off from the world around it. The prototypical 'pest mammal exclusion fence' with tightly woven mesh, top curved outward, and a metal skirt expansive enough underground to prevent entry to mice and other burrowing or climbing mammals, has been widely copied (Figure C.2). Tours are available, and, in a reversal of the wildlife habitats that have emerged in other wall buffer zones, a nine-kilometer running path dedicated to humans follows the perimeter. Biosecurity is strictly maintained through a 'monitoring programme [that] includes ongoing pest auditing, regular use of the Sanctuary's specially trained detector dog, bag and vehicle checks, and fence monitoring,' along

---

35 'History,' *Zealandia / Te Māra a Tāne*: http://web.archive.org/web/20230307095156/ https://www.visitzealandia.com/About; accessed 15 March 2023.

Biosecurity, siloing, and shelter society   287

with 'tracking tunnels' to detect the presence of small mammals.[36] Even if 100 percent success may continue to elude it – mice infestations and interloping weasels and rats have been reported – response has been enthusiastic.[37]

In terms of non-island nations, a biosecurity limit-case such as Zealandia underlines both the fascination and the impossibility of a 'pure' nature preserve and the difficult negotiations between use and conservation that drive disputes about protected land and animal species the world over. The charged quality of the discourse comes partly from the often life-and-death stakes involved (for humans as well as for other animals); partly from the growing shortage of resources and space; and partly from competing claims for land rights, ranging from conservationists to Indigenous Peoples to farmers and hunters to corporate entities seeking profit from mining and other forms of exploitation. The imaginary of this discourse nearly always involves a naturalized form of walled enclave, bunker, and dome fantasy: walled because of the necessity of security and protection in the present; bunkered because required to preserve the contents of the enclave from a future cataclysm that is already long underway; domed when the goal of preservation is more utopian and speculative than directly practical. Counterarguments to these measures seek to breach the wall and break down the enclave to a greater or lesser degree and with wildly divergent motivations. The bunker fantasy embedded within these ongoing disputes sets the stakes quickly and sharply; at the same time, the more starkly the divisions are drawn by wall and bunker, the more strictly the options afforded for negotiated solutions are thereby delimited.

Sheltered and siloed in the twenty-first century

That citizens of the global North inhabit siloed enclaves in self-selecting, firewall-protected social-media cocoons while safely ensconced in gated communities they leave only in hermetically sealed, self-driving, and armored automobiles or to travel the world in the artificial environment of flying machines from one sanitized no-place airport to another while distracting themselves with multimedia spectacles of the universe ending or barely being

---

36 'Karori Wildlife Sanctuary Biosecurity Programme Detects Weasel,' *Sanctuary.org* (9 July 2004): http://web.archive.org/web/20080509061919/http://www.sanctuary.org. nz/whatsnew/news/news79.html; accessed 3 May 2018. 'Karori Wildlife Sanctuary' was the former name of Zealandia.

37 'Biosecurity Programme Detects Weasel'; Wikipedia contributors, 'Zealandia (Wildlife Sanctuary),' *Wikipedia*: https://en.wikipedia.org/wiki/Zealandia_(wildlife_sanctuary); accessed 3 May. 2018.

288   *After the end*

saved from ending has been a commonplace pronouncement of doomsaying prophets of modern life for decades now. These doomsayers are not wholly wrong in their vision – prophets seldom are *wholly* wrong. There is no question that the bunker fantasies that remain deeply entrenched in the global North and circulate South and North alike powerfully constrain the ways we may dwell in the world. 'Silo' is the neologism deployed in recent years to describe the ontological bunker in which much of the world – and nearly all of the fraction of the world that holds most of its wealth – dwells, always in the literal sense, and at times in the 'affective and structural dimensions' Lily Wong identifies in the 'actively inactive' process of dwelling 'that repoliticizes our relationship to cultural and historical formations in the contemporary.'[38] Dwelling on silos in the context of bunkering suggests that the silo constitutes, in many ways, an individual, circular wall: biosecurity for the individual.

The word *silo* originally referred to an underground grain storage facility: a food bunker. The familiar American form of a domed cylinder rising aboveground dates to the late nineteenth century; it has appeared as a climactic fictional setting in which the life-giving foodstuff stored in it works to thwart external evil in films from Danish director Carl-Theodor Dreyer's *Vampyr* (1932) through Australian émigré Peter Weir's standoff between American urban corruption and premodern Amish values in *Witness* (1985) to the postapocalyptic horror-thriller *A Quiet Place* (2018). The more recent and equally American missile silos were built rapidly and extensively underground during the late 1950s and early 1960s Cold War epoch; by the 1980s, there were about 40 'wings,' or clusters of around 150 silos, scattered from California to upstate New York, with the majority located in the plains states of Colorado, Kansas, Missouri, Montana, Nebraska, North and South Dakota, and Wyoming.[39] Decommissioned missile silos have since been adapted as private homes, apartment buildings, and – in one sensational story – shelter for the world's primary source of the hallucinogen LSD; they are now commonly used for data storage.[40]

38 Wong, 'Dwelling over China,' 721.
39 Bill Ganzel, 'Planting Fields of ICBMs,' *Living History Farm* (2007): http://web.archive.org/web/20220129172004/https://livinghistoryfarm.org/farminginthe50s/life_06.html; accessed 31 Aug. 2023.
40 For residential conversions, see Chapter 1 above. On the pair of decommissioned Atlas Missile Silos in Wamego, Kansas in which a hidden lab at one point in the 1990s was producing an estimated 90 percent of the LSD in the US, see 'Wamego LSD Missile Silo,' *Atlas Obscura* (2013): http://web.archive.org/web/20221207165216/https://www.atlasobscura.com/places/wamego-lsd-missile-silo; Dennis McDougal, *Operation White Rabbit: LSD, the DEA, and the Fate of the Acid King* (New York: Skyhorse, 2020); and Ed Prideaux, 'The 'Acid King' Convicted of Running the Biggest LSD Ring in History,' *Vice* (12 Oct. 2020): http://web.archive.org/web/20211128100801/https://www.vice.com/en/article/wxqmwz/william-leonard-pickard-acid-king-book.

Biosecurity, siloing, and shelter society

289

While the figurative usage to refer to an individual or community sheltered from any opinions or beliefs but their own is somewhat aptly applied to the image of a windowless grain storage tower, it seems far more resonant of the buried and impossibly fortified missile launch facilities emblematic of the Cold War. A Google Ngram shows a rapid uptick in usage of the verb 'siloed' since the turn of the millennium. To be siloed in the twenty-first century implies being secured from the outside world, sealed off from everyday alterity in a farmland container redolent both of stored-away resources and of buried weapons of mass destruction. The silo is a life-preserving storehouse and a site of intense concentration on preexistent knowledge. What siloing affords even less than other permutations of the bunker fantasy is any look outside. Its mode of dwelling is invariably inward-looking.

Between 2011 and 2012, writer Hugh Howey self-published the five-volume *Wool* series, set in a post-nuclear-war 144-level underground silo-shelter. The series became a bestseller and was eventually issued in print, adapted as a graphic novel, optioned for film, and amplified with a three-volume prequel and a final ninth volume. In its verticality, Howey's scheme is highly derivative of Fritz Lang's class-stratified parable in the SFF movie *Metropolis* (1926). In the way it pits the deeper-down manual laborers and engineers against the mendacious IT experts higher up, and in its stress on the deceptive workings of authority and visual media, Howey's series shows a debt to novels by Philip K. Dick such as *The Penultimate Truth* (1964), where cynical Yance-Men rule over an irradiated surface world supported by the labor of workers sealed into 'Ant Tanks' deep underground under the illusion that World War III had not ended years before, and the Wachowski sisters' 1999 film *The Matrix*, where the illusion of 'real life' is created by computers powered by human batteries stacked like grains in massive corn-cob towers in a postapocalyptic wasteland. The spatial conceit, however, comes more directly than in either of those sources from the missile silo wing: there are fifty silos clustered near enough to each other that lateral digging is forbidden. Each silo is built around an enormous spiral staircase. The series' title refers both to the 'wool' with which the silo inhabitants clean the lenses which show the uninhabitable world outside and to the 'wool' pulled over their eyes by the IT folk, who not only control communications with the other silos but also hide the existence of a government silo-shelter. Especially in the ways the plotting negatively incorporates electronic communications technology, Howey seems also to be thinking about siloing as a social problem; as in *Metropolis*, a worker's revolution restores the head, hands, and heart to their properly productive working relationship. Howey's is not a complex or original formulation, and the everyday functioning of technology for which insufficient power-sources seem to exist within the silos is never well explained, but these pulp qualities and the novels' popularity suggest a resonance in its unfamiliar setting of familiar themes. The bunker fantasy,

290 *After the end*

as always, affords more space for digging in than for looking out; however, in the enclaves, tunnels, and doors it imagines within the world as it is, even its most siloed visions can be opened out in directions otherwise invisible to the 'real' world.

The more we recognize the twenty-first-century proliferation of the bunker fantasy and dwell in its siloed extremes, the more it behooves us to do more than simply decry its undeniably deleterious consequences or laugh cringingly at its naive absurdities. Journalist Mark O'Connell gleans two essential insights from his book-length exploration of the relationship between his own anxiety over the end of the world and the anxieties of the world around him. First, as he realizes watching a fighter jet speed off on a bombing run to Syria from the heart of a solo wilderness retreat in the remote Scottish Highlands, 'It was already the end of the world for the people that fighter jet was likely headed toward. They were experiencing all the things by which I, in my remote and abstract fashion, was preoccupied: the fragility of political orders, the collapse of civilization. Five million of them, fleeing the terror and chaos of their ruined country, meeting the cruel machinery of Europe and its borders. It was always the end of the world for someone, somewhere.'[41] O'Connell thus necessarily extends into the present moment the now familiar insight that apocalypse as an existential condition has long been the experience of oppressed, enslaved, or colonized populations. Then he makes a less familiar move, a move that also suggests why the ontological bunker is far more comfortable of a position to occupy than its epistemological counterpart. 'There is no way of contemplating the catastrophe of our way of life from the outside,' he concludes, reflecting on his own complicity in the consumption and exploitation that he recognizes is driving his known world to its end. 'There is no outside. Here, too, I myself am the contaminant. I myself am the apocalypse of which I speak.'[42]

On the one hand, O'Connell's insight is no different from Pogo Possum's conclusion when confronted with the fact that his own garbage is what is polluting his beloved Okefenokee Swamp: 'We have met the enemy and he is us.'[43] On the other hand, O'Connell has updated cartoonist Walt Kelly's early environmentalist consciousness into a global condition encompassing late capitalism, rampant inequality, climate crisis, and the paradoxical optimism of reproductive futurity. Like Green initiatives in the twenty-first century, Pogo's self-accusation in 1972 presumed that he might still be able

41 O'Connell, *Notes from an Apocalypse*, 182.
42 O'Connell, *Notes from an Apocalypse*, 239.
43 Walt Kelly, *We Have Met the Enemy and He Is Us* (New York: Simon and Schuster, 1972), 25–39.

Biosecurity, siloing, and shelter society 291

to change his habits enough to preserve something of nature outside the bunkered modernity into which the Earth was rapidly being transformed physically and imaginatively. O'Connell argues, conversely, that siloing is itself an apocalyptic act, in that the ways so many in the global North process their anxiety – from recycling to consuming to knowledge production – themselves participate in the processes driving our apocalypse-in-progress. *Notes from an Apocalypse* offers no resolution to this conundrum beyond the attempt more accurately and clear-sightedly to dwell on the epistemology producing the siloed ontology he has come to understand that he inhabits. His book ends when his anxiety over a report of the looming extinction of insects is dispelled by an exchange of noisy 'raspberries' with his 'impish' baby daughter.[44] *We Have Met the Enemy and He Is Us* similarly concludes on a bad pun in the back of a garbage cart generated by a nonsensical song lyric: 'Snoo? What's snoo?' 'I dunno … What's new with you?'[45]

Apocalypse is never funny but it is always absurd. It is absurd because it is nearly always preventable. It is absurd because it is unfair in more ways than can be calculated. It is absurd because there is nothing to do about it and there is no way out from it. A clear-eyed analysis, embrace, and appropriation of that absurdity into something irrevocably one's own has always been an essential survival strategy of those for whom the world is already postapocalyptic; it is available imaginatively, epistemologically, and affectively even to those to whom siloing is second nature if not an accidental birthright or assumed privilege. Rebecca Makkai argues that 'the exercise of freedom is a de facto defense of that same freedom. … And no, it's not always political art we fight for. H. A. and Margaret Rey fled Paris in 1940 on bicycles they'd made themselves, carrying with them the manuscript of *Curious George*.'[46] The more exigent, the more apocalyptic the circumstances, the more dearly the free exercise of the imagination has always been treasured. It is often, if not always and not everywhere, the best tool we have; it is certainly the most universal, the most collective tool we have. And while it may not quite be itself the 'real world,' the imagination affords insight and alternatives even when they are not available as such in the more perfectly siloed – but not yet fully apocalyptic or extinguished – real.

As economist Peter Fleming similarly argues in *The Worst Is Yet to Come*, 'You can only write about this devastating future if you are already living

---

44 O'Connell, *Notes from an Apocalypse*, 250–2.
45 Kelly, *We Have Met the Enemy*, 127.
46 Rebecca Makkai, 'The World's on Fire. Can We Still Talk about Books?' *Electric Literature* (6 Dec. 2018): http://web.archive.org/web/20221128083532/https://electricliterature.com/the-worlds-on-fire-can-we-still-talk-about-books/.

it.'[47] And the more that the walled-in features of physical siloing – through streaming rather than cinemas or even family television; through climate-controlled interiors and too-hot-to-handle exteriors; through ever-more-targeted personalization in lieu of necessary interaction with alien perspectives – become prevalent in the lives of those of the world's inhabitants who aren't dying outside the silos, the more understanding that process for what it is can help to disentangle what is physically necessary from what is driven by a bunkered imaginary. As philosopher Bruno Latour asserts, 'The most basic right of all is to feel safe and protected, especially at a moment when the old protections are disappearing.'[48] We need to know how the bunker fantasy and other core imaginaries work in order to use that knowledge to open up more space in our practices to encourage the few liberatory or even utopian affordances that are wrought into its mostly regressive forms. For example, once we recognize what journalist Stephen Buranyi calls the 'air conditioning trap' – 'warmer temperatures lead to more air conditioning; more air conditioning leads to warmer temperatures' – as a form of increased bunkering, we can recognize not only, as he argues, that 'the problem posed by air conditioning resembles, in miniature, the problem we face in tackling the climate crisis.'[49] We can also recognize why 'the global dominance of air conditioning was not inevitable,' we can parse out the affects and desires that were mobilized in the drive to air-condition, and we can divert that knowledge into counternarratives away from such deadly but increasingly vital forms of Anthropocene bunkering.

The modes of realism that have dominated cultural production since the nineteenth century powerfully reflect and critique the worlds from which they emerged; out of them they produced a singular world that, until the middle of the twentieth century, stood for what was broadly accepted as real. Because the premise of the nuclear condition is counterfactual, not only did realist modes prove inadequate for capturing its workings, but 'reality' as defined by the enslaving, imperial, colonialist, and capitalist West was inadequate as a description of reality. The speculative, fantastic, and unreal fictions that capture the bunker fantasy afford a broader spectrum of understanding, even as that spectrum ranges wildly from the worst

---

47 Peter Fleming, 'Has the New Dark Age Begun Yet?' *Literary Hub* (4 March 2019): http://web.archive.org/web/20221206080957/https://lithub.com/has-the-new-dark-age-begun-yet/.

48 Bruno Latour, *Down to Earth: Politics in the New Climatic Regime* (Medford, MA: Polity, 2018), 11.

49 Stephen Buranyi, 'The Air Conditioning Trap: How Cold Air Is Heating the World,' *Guardian* (29 Aug. 2019): www.theguardian.com/environment/2019/aug/29/the-air-conditioning-trap-how-cold-air-is-heating-the-world.

Biosecurity, siloing, and shelter society 293

nightmares of 'reality' to utopian imaginings beyond its wildest dreams. This book, along with its companion volume, *The Bunkered Decades*, has traced the movement of these new forms of fiction based on the bunker fantasy, from the emergence of the new mutants around 1962 to the survivalists who defined the 1980s as the mutated decade to the twenty-first century, siloed deeply within the bunkered world inherited from the 1980s. This is not the only way to tell the story of the last seventy-five years, but as its moment recedes from the horizon of the recent past, our moment is a propitious one for this story and the openings it creates beyond that horizon.

Select Bibliography

Abbey, Edward. 'Home Is Where the Hearth Is.' Review of *Shelter* (1973): http://theshelterblog.com/shelter/_shelter/abbey.html; accessed 6 April 2018.

Abe Kōbō. *The Ark Sakura*. Trans. Juliet Winters Carpenter. New York: Knopf, 1988 [1984].

Abdurraqib, Hanif. *They Can't Kill Us Until They Kill Us*. Columbus, OH: Two Dollar Radio, 2017.

Ahern, Jerry. *The Survivalist #9, Earth Fire*. New York: Zebra, 1984.

Ahern, Jerry. *The Survivalist #10, The Awakening*. New York: Zebra, 1984.

Alexievich, Svetlana. *Voices from Chernobyl: The Oral History of a Nuclear Disaster*. Trans. Keith Gessen. Dallas, TX: Dalkey Archive Press, 2005 [1997].

Alter, Alexandra. '"We've Already Survived an Apocalypse": Indigenous Writers Are Changing Sci-Fi.' *New York Times* (14 Aug. 2020): http://web.archive.org/web/20230311130649/http://www.nytimes.com/2020/08/14/books/indigenous-native-american-sci-fi-horror.html.

Anzaldúa, Gloria. *Borderlands / La Frontera: The New Mestiza*. Fourth ed. San Francisco: Aunt Lute Books, 2012 [1987].

Asher, Marty. *Shelter*. New York: Arbor House, 1986.

Baldwin, James. 'The Black Boy Looks at the White Boy.' *Esquire* (1 May 1961). In *Collected Essays*, edited by Toni Morrison. New York: Library of America, 1998. 269–85.

Ballard, J. G. 'The Terminal Beach' (1964). In *The Complete Stories of J. G. Ballard*. New York: W. W. Norton, 2009. 589–604.

Barkun, Michael. *Religion and the Racist Right: The Origins of the Christian Identity Movement*. Chapel Hill: University of North Carolina Press, 1997.

Beck, John. 'Concrete Ambivalence: Inside the Bunker Complex.' *Cultural Politics* 7.1 (2011): 79–102.

Begley, Josh. *Best of Luck with the Wall*. Field of Vision, 2016: https://vimeo.com/189015526; accessed 14 March 2023.

Bell, Kirsty. *The Undercurrents*. London: Fitzcarraldo, 2022.

Benjamin, Walter 'On the Concept of History.' In *Selected Writings, Vol. 4, 1938–1940*, edited by Howard Eiland and Michael W. Jennings. Cambridge, MA: Harvard University Press, 2003. 389–97.

Bennesved, Peter. 'Shelter News: Affordance, Place and Proximity in News Media Representations of Civil Defence Artefacts.' *Critical Military Studies* (2023): 1–19. DOI: 10.1080/23337486.2023.2188004.

Bibliography

Berger, J. M. 'The Turner Legacy: The Storied Origins and Enduring Impact of White Nationalism's Deadly Bible.' International Centre for Counter-Terrorism Research Paper (2016): 6. http://web.archive.org/web/20230106164845/https://icct.nl/publication/the-turner-legacy-the-storied-origins-and-enduring-impact-of-white-nationalisms-deadly-bible/.

Berlant, Lauren, and Jordan Greenwald. 'Affect in the End Times: A Conversation with Lauren Berlant.' *Qui Parle* 20.2 (2012): 71–89.

Best, John. 'Translator's Preface.' In *Black Rain* by Masuji Ibuse. Bunkyo-ku, Tokyo: Kodansha International, 1979 [1969]. 5–8.

Beukes, Lauren. *Afterland*. New York: Little, Brown, 2020.

Boyce, Dan. 'A New Wildlife Refuge on the Grounds around an Old Nuclear Weapons Plant.' *NPR* (15 Sept. 2018): http://web.archive.org/web/20221206111649/https://www.npr.org/2018/09/15/647878022/a-new-wildlife-refuge-on-the-grounds-around-an-old-nuclear-weapons-plant.

Bradatan, Costica. 'Scaling "The Wall in the Head."' *New York Times* (27 Nov. 2011): https://archive.nytimes.com/opinionator.blogs.nytimes.com/2011/11/27/scaling-the-wall-in-the-head/.

Bradshaw, Peter. '*Into Eternity* – Review,' *Guardian* (11 Nov. 2010): www.theguardian.com/film/2010/nov/11/into-eternity-film-review.

Brand, Stewart. *Whole Earth Catalog: Access to Tools*. San Rafael, CA: Point Foundation, 1998 [1968].

Brantler, Sabine. 'The Air-Raid Shelter in the Haus der Kunst.' In *Aschemünder: Sammlung Goetz im Haus der Kunst*, edited by Ingvild Goetz, Suzanne Toew, and Stephan Urbaschek. Munich: Hatje Cantz Verlag, 2011. 16–17.

Brody, Richard. 'The Silently Regressive Politics of *A Quiet Place*.' *New Yorker* (10 April 2018): www.newyorker.com/culture/richard-brody/the-silently-regressive-politics-of-a-quiet-place.

Brown, Kate. *Manual for Survival: A Chernobyl Guide to the Future*. New York: Norton, 2019.

Brownell, Ginanne. 'A Sarajevo Bunker Takes on New Life as an Art Museum.' *New York Times* (5 Aug. 2011): www.nytimes.com/2011/08/06/arts/06iht-scsarajevo06.html?_r=1&pagewanted=print.

Buache, Freddy. *Le Cinéma suisse 1898–1998*. Lausanne: L'Age d'Homme, 1998.

Buranyi, Stephen. 'The Air Conditioning Trap: How Cold Air Is Heating the World.' *Guardian* (29 Aug. 2019): www.theguardian.com/environment/2019/aug/29/the-air-conditioning-trap-how-cold-air-is-heating-the-world.

Butler, Octavia. *Adulthood Rites*. New York: Warner, 1988.

Butler, Octavia. 'Amnesty' (2003). *Callaloo* 27.3 (2004): 597–615.

Butler, Octavia. *Clay's Ark*. In *Seed to Harvest*. New York: Grand Central, 2007 [1984]. 453–624.

Butler, Octavia. *Dawn*. New York: Warner, 1988 [1987].

Butler, Octavia. *Imago*. New York: Warner, 1989.

Butler, Octavia. *Kindred*. Boston: Beacon, 1988 [1979].

Butler, Octavia. 'Lost Races of Science Fiction.' *Transmission* (Summer 1980): 17–18. Rpt in Canavan. *Butler*. 181–6.

Bibliography

Butler, Octavia. *Parable of the Sower*. New York: Seven Stories Press, 1993.

Butler, Octavia. *Parable of the Talents*. New York: Seven Stories Press, 1998.

Butler, Octavia. *Survivor*. New York: Signet, 1979.

Byrne, Monica. *The Girl in the Road*. New York: Broadway, 2015 [2014].

Caesar, Ed. 'The Cold War Bunker That Became Home to a Dark-Web Empire.' *New Yorker* (3 & 10 Aug. 2020): www.newyorker.com/magazine/2020/08/03/the-cold-war-bunker-that-became-home-to-a-dark-web-empire.

Cai Guo-Qiang. *Bunker Museum of Contemporary Art, Kinmen Island: A Permanent Sanctuary for Art in a Demilitarized Zone*. Kinmen, Taiwan: Kinmen County Government, 2006.

Cain, Sian. '"You'll have to die to get these texts": Ocean Vuong's Next Manuscript to Be Unveiled in 2114.' *Guardian* (19 Aug. 2020): www.theguardian.com/books/2020/aug/19/ocean-vuong-2114-book-future-library-norway.

Canavan, Gerry. *Octavia E. Butler*. Champaign: University of Illinois Press, 2016.

Canavan, Gerry. '"There's Nothing New / Under The Sun, / But There Are New Suns": Recovering Octavia E. Butler's Lost Parables.' *Los Angeles Review of Books* (9 June 2014): https://lareviewofbooks.org/article/theres-nothing-new-sun-new-suns-recovering-octavia-e-butlers-lost-parables.

Cantú, Francisco. *The Line Becomes a River: Dispatches from the Border*. New York: Penguin, 2018.

Carrington, Damian. 'Arctic Stronghold of World's Seeds Flooded after Permafrost Melts.' *Guardian* (19 May 2017): www.theguardian.com/environment/2017/may/19/arctic-stronghold-of-worlds-seeds-flooded-after-permafrost-melts.

Carrión, Jorge. *Los huérfanos*. Barcelona: Galaxia Gutenberg, 2014.

Casey, Edward S., and Mary Watkins. *Up Against the Wall: Re-Imagining the U.S.-Mexico Border*. Austin: University of Texas Press, 2014.

Chaichian, Mohammed. *Empires and Walls: Globalization, Migration, and Colonial Domination*. Leiden: Brill, 2014.

Chandra, Vikram. *Sacred Games*. London: Faber & Faber, 2006.

Chi, Robert. 'The New Taiwanese Documentary.' *Modern Chinese Literature and Culture* 15.1 (2003): 146–96.

Cole, Teju. 'A Piece of the Wall.' In *Known and Strange Things*. New York: Random House, 2016 [2014]. 363–76.

Cordle, Daniel. *States of Suspense: The Nuclear Age, Postmodernism and United States Fiction and Prose*. Manchester: Manchester University Press, 2008.

Criss, Doug. 'For the First Time since the End of the Cold War, Hawaii Will Test Nuclear Sirens.' *CNN.com* (1 Dec. 2017): http://web.archive.org/web/20221104172331/https://www.cnn.com/2017/11/28/us/hawaii-nuclear-warning-trnd/index.html.

Cruickshank, Douglas. 'How Do You Design a "Keep Out!" Sign to Last 10,000 Years?' *Salon* (10 May 2002): https://web.archive.org/web/20230217125418/https://www.salon.com/2002/05/10/yucca_mountain/.

D'Agata, John. *About a Mountain*. New York: W. W. Norton, 2010.

Davis, Mike. 'The Great Wall of Capital.' *Socialist Review* (5 Feb. 2004): https://socialistworker.co.uk/socialist-review-archive/great-wall-capital/.

Delarue, Claude. *En attendant la guerre*. Carouges-Genève: Editions Zoé, 2011 [1989].

Bibliography

Delarue, Claude. *Waiting for War*. Trans. Vivienne Menkes-Ivry. London: Minerva, 1992.

De Léon, Jason. *The Land of Open Graves: Living and Dying on the Migrant Trail*. Berkeley: University of California Press, 2015.

Delévaux, Pierre. *Fortifications de Saint-Maurice, Suisse: La Galerie du Scex 1911–2011*. Saint-Maurice: Fondation Forteresse historique Saint-Maurice & Association Saint-Maurice d'Etudes Militaires, 2011.

DeLillo, Don. *Zero K*. New York: Scribner, 2016.

Derrida, Jacques. 'No Apocalypse, Not Now.' *Diacritics* 14.2 (1984): 20–31.

Díaz, Junot. 'Apocalypse: What Disasters Reveal.' *Boston Review* (May/June 2011): 46–52.

Di Cintio, Marcello. *Walls: Travels along the Barricades*. Berkeley: Soft Skull Press, 2013.

Dillman, Lisa. 'Translator's Note.' In *Signs Preceding the End of the World*, by Herrera (Kindle edition).

Dillon, Brian. 'Anna Lim's Vision of Nuclear Anxiety in South Korea.' *New Yorker* (1 Dec. 2019): www.newyorker.com/culture/photo-booth/anna-lims-vision-of-nuclear-anxiety-in-south-korea.

Dillon, Grace L. 'Introduction.' In *Walking the Clouds: An Anthology of Indigenous Science Fiction*, edited by Dillon. Tucson: University of Arizona Press, 2012. 1–12.

Dobraszczyk, Paul, Carlos López Galviz, and Bradley L. Garrett, ed. *Global Undergrounds: Exploring Cities Within*. London: Reaktion, 2016.

Druga, Jacqueline. *The Last Woman*. N.p.: Vulpine Press, 2018 [2014].

Duras, Marguerite. *Hiroshima mon amour*. Trans. Richard Seaver. New York: Grove, 1961 [1960].

Dürrenmatt, Friedrich. '"Ich kann mir eine Schweiz ohne Armee vorstellen": Eine Collage.' In *Unterwegs zu einer Schweiz ohne Armee: Der freie Gang aus der Festung*, edited by Roman Brodmann, Andreas Gross, and Marc Spescha. Basel: Z-Verlag, 1986. 28–47.

Dylan, Bob. *Chronicles: Volume 1*. New York: Simon & Schuster, 2004.

Egan, Timothy. 'Guru's Bomb Shelter Hits Legal Snag.' *New York Times* (24 April 1990): A16.

Elley, Derek. 'Review: Death & Taxes.' *Variety* (30 Nov. 1993): http://web.archive.org/web/20170916140717/http://variety.com/1993/film/reviews/death-taxes-1200435039/.

Endres, Danielle. 'The Rhetoric of Nuclear Colonialism: Rhetorical Exclusion of American Indian Arguments in the Yucca Mountain Nuclear Waste Siting Decision.' *Communication and Critical/Cultural Studies* 6.1 (2009): 39–60. DOI: 10.1080/14791420802632103.

Engelmann, Sascha, and Harriet Hawkins. 'Bunker Art: Christian and Karen Boros Collection, Berlin.' In *Global Undergrounds*, edited by Dobraszczyk et al. 91–5.

Erdrich, Louise. *Future Home of the Living God*. New York: HarperCollins, 2017.

Ernst, Alfred, Oberstkorpskomandant Z. D. *Die Konzeption der Schweizerischen Landesverteidigung 1815 bis 1966*. Frauenfeld: Verlag Huber, 1971.

Esquivel, Eric M. (story), Ramon Villalobos (art), Tamra Bonvillain (coloring). *Border Town* (four issues). Burbank, CA: DC Comics, 2018–19.

Evans, Joseph C. 'Berlin Tunnel Intelligence: A Bumbling KGB.' *International Journal of Intelligence and Counterintelligence* 9 (1996): 43–50.

'Explorer's Club Roundtable: "Rewilding" America.' *rewilding.org* (28 April 2018): http://web.archive.org/web/20221004031059/https://rewilding.org/explorers-club-roundtable-rewilding-america/.

Feifer, George. 'The Berlin Tunnel.' In *The Cold War: A Military History*, edited by Robert Cowley. New York: Random House, 2005. 189–208.

Finoki, Bryan. 'Tunnelizing Migration I: The Border Tunnel Capital of North America.' *Subtopia: A Field Guide to Military Urbanism* (5 March 2009): http://web.archive.org/web/20230307093832/http://subtopia.blogspot.com/2009/03/tunnelizing-migration-1-border-tunnel.html.

Finoki, Bryan. 'Tunnelling Borders.' *openDemocracy* (26 Nov. 2013): http://web.archive.org/web/20200422042150/https://www.opendemocracy.net/en/opensecurity/tunnelling-borders/.

Fleming, Peter. 'Has the New Dark Age Begun Yet?' *Literary Hub* (4 March 2019): http://web.archive.org/web/20221206080957/https://lithub.com/has-the-new-dark-age-begun-yet/.

Forsberg, Soren. 'Don't Believe Your Eyes.' *Transition* 109 (2012): 131–43.

Foster, Gwendolyn Audrey. 'Consuming the Apocalypse, Marketing Bunker Materiality.' *Quarterly Review of Film and Video* 33.4 (2016): 285–302.

Foster, Gwendolyn Audrey. *Hoarders, Doomsday Preppers, and the Culture of Apocalypse*. New York: Palgrave Macmillan, 2014.

Foster, Thomas. '"We Get to Live, and So Do They": Octavia Butler's Contact Zones.' In *Strange Matings: Science Fiction, Feminism, African American Voices, and Octavia E. Butler*, edited by Rebecca J. Holden and Nisi Shawl. Seattle: Aqueduct Press, 2013. Kindle edition.

Francis, Gavin. 'The Dream of Forgetfulness.' *New York Review of Books* (9 March 2023): 31–4.

Frisch, Max. '*From* Military Service Record.' In *Novels, Plays, Essays*, edited by Rolf Kaiser. New York: Continuum, 1989. 137–9.

Frisch, Max. *Man in the Holocene*. Trans. Geoffrey Skelton. New York: Farrar Straus Giroux, 1980 [1979].

Frisch, Max. 'Mehr Fragemut vor dem Ernstfall' [1966]. In *Unterwegs zu einer Schweiz ohne Armee: Der freie Gang aus der Festung*, edited by Roman Brodmann, Andreas Gross, and Marc Spescha. Basel: Z-Verlag, 1986. 13–27.

Gallanti, Fabrizio, Elian Stefa, and Gyler Mydyti. 'Concrete Mushrooms: Transformations of the Bunkers in Albania.' *Abitare* 502 (May 2010): www.abitare.it/en/architecture/2010/05/11/concrete-mushrooms-2/.

Galviz, Carlos López. 'Sheltered Lives: Shanghai Civil Defense Shelters.' In *Global Undergrounds*, edited by Dobraszczyk et al. 124–6.

Galviz, Carlos López. 'Time Underground: The Clock of the Long Now.' In *Global Undergrounds*, edited by Dobraszczyk et al. 245–7.

Garrett, Bradley L. *Bunker: Building for the End Times*. New York: Scribner, 2020.

Garrett, Bradley L. 'Burying Incomprehensible Horror: Yucca Mountain Nuclear Storage.' In *Global Undergrounds*, edited by Dobraszczyk et al. 85–7.

Bibliography

Geist, Edward. 'Was There a Real "Mineshaft Gap"? Bomb Shelters in the USSR, 1945–1962.' *Journal of Cold War Studies* 14.2 (2012): 3–28.

Gibas, Petr. 'Ideology and Fear: Prague Metro.' In *Global Undergrounds*, edited by Dobraszczyk et al. 161–3.

Gilman, Denise. 'Seeking Breaches in the Wall: An International Human Rights Law Challenge to the Texas-Mexico Border Wall.' *Texas International Law Journal* 46 (2011): 257–93.

Glasser, Susan. '#BunkerBoy's Photo-Op War.' *New Yorker* (3 June 2020): www.newyorker.com/news/letter-from-trumps-washington/bunkerboys-photo-op-war.

Goetz, Ingvild. 'Aschemünder.' In *Aschemünder: Sammlung Goetz im Haus der Kunst*, edited by Goetz, Suzanne Toew, and Stephan Urbaschek. Munich: Hatje Cantz Verlag, 2011. 6–8.

González, Betina. *American Delirium*. Trans. Heather Cleary. New York: Henry Holt, 2021 [2016].

Goodwater, W. L. *Breach*. New York: Ace, 2018.

Gouré, Leon. *Civil Defense in the Soviet Union*. Berkeley: University of California Press, 1962.

Govan, Sandra Y. 'Connections, Links, and Extended Networks: Patterns in Octavia Butler's Science Fiction' (1984). In *Luminescent Threads*, edited by Pierce and Mondal. Kindle edition.

Gowin, Emmet. *The Nevada Test Site*. Princeton: Princeton University Press, 2019.

Graham, Stephen. *Vertical: The City from Satellites to Bunkers*. London: Verso, 2016.

Grausam, Daniel. *On Endings: American Postmodern Fiction and the Cold War*. Charlottesville: University of Virginia Press, 2011.

'Great Green Wall Accelerator.' http://web.archive.org/web/20220913210522/https://www.greatgreenwall.org/great-green-wall-accelerator; accessed 22 April 2021.

Griggs, Mary Beth. 'Turns Out the Svalbard Seed Vault Is Probably Fine.' *Popular Science* (22 May 2017): http://web.archive.org/web/20221205012621/https://www.popsci.com/seed-vault-flooding/.

Hairston, Andrea. 'Octavia Butler – Praise Song to a Prophetic Artist' (2006). In *Luminescent Threads*, edited by Pierce and Mondal. Kindle edition.

Hamid, Mohsin. *Exit West*. New York: Riverhead, 2017.

Hammond, Andrew. 'From Rhetoric to Rollback: Introductory Thoughts on Cold War Writing.' In *Cold War Literature: Writing the Global Conflict*, edited by Hammond. New York: Routledge, 2005. 1–14.

Hampton, Gregory. *Changing Bodies in the Fiction of Octavia Butler: Slaves, Aliens, and Vampires*. Lanham, MD: Lexington, 2010.

Haraway, Donna. *Primate Visions: Gender, Race, and Nature in the World of Modern Science*. New York: Routledge, 1989.

Hare, David. *Berlin/Wall*. London: Faber and Faber, 2009.

Hassner, Ron E., and Jason Wittenberg. 'Barriers to Entry: Who Builds Fortified Boundaries and Why?' *International Security* 40.1 (2015): 157–90.

Heberle, Mark A. *A Trauma Artist: Tim O'Brien and the Fiction of Vietnam*. Iowa City: University of Iowa Press, 2001.

Hegland, Joan. *Into the Forest*. New York: Bantam, 1997 [1996].

Heller, Peter. *The Dog Stars*. New York: Knopf, 2012.

Herrera, Yuri. *Signs Preceding the End of the World*. Trans. Lisa Dillman. Sheffield: And Other Stories, 2015 [2009].

Higginbotham, Adam. 'The Narco Tunnels of Nogales.' *Bloomberg Businessweek* (6 Aug. 2012): http://web.archive.org/web/20221207185822/http://adamhigginbotham.com/Archive/Writing.html.

Higgins, Kyle (wr.), and Stephen Mooney (art). *The Dead Hand* (six issues). Portland, OR: Image Comics, 2018.

'History & Culture.' *Official Website of the Tohono O'odham Nation*: http://web.archive.org/web/20230203194144/http://www.tonation-nsn.gov/history-culture/; accessed 23 Feb. 2021.

Hoban, Alex. 'Chairman Mao's Underground City.' *Vice* (17 Nov. 2009): http://web.archive.org/web/20220323110923/https://www.vice.com/en/article/nnmk8b/chairman-maos-underground-city.

Hoberek, Andrew. 'Living with PASD.' *Contemporary Literature* 53.2 (2012): 406–13.

Hodge, Nathan, and Sharon Weinberger. *A Nuclear Family Vacation: Travels in the World of Atomic Weaponry*. New York: Bloomsbury, 2011.

Holden, Rebecca. '"Let's Dwell a Little": The Trickster within Octavia E. Butler.' In *Luminescent Threads*, edited by Pierce and Mondal. Kindle edition.

Holt, Jim. 'The Power of Catastrophic Thinking.' *New York Review of Books* (25 Feb. 2021): www.nybooks.com/articles/2021/02/25/power-catastrophic-thinking-toby-ord-precipice/.

Hopkinson, Nalo. *Brown Girl in the Ring*. New York: Warner, 1998.

Hughes, Langston. 'Bomb Shelters' (1965). In *The Collected Works of Langston Hughes, Vol. 8: The Later Simple Stories*, edited by Donna Akiba Sullivan Harper. Columbia, MO: University of Missouri Press, 2002. 175–7.

Hurley, Jessica. 'History Is What Bites: Zombies, Race, and the Limits of Biopower in Colson Whitehead's *Zone One*.' *Extrapolation* 56.3 (2015): 311–33.

Husien, Thaer. 'Beside the Sickle Moon.' Unpublished manuscript in the author's possession.

Ialenti, Vincent F. 'Adjudicating Deep Time: Revisiting the United States' High-Level Nuclear Waste Repository Project at Yucca Mountain.' *Science & Technology Studies* 27.2 (2014): 27–48.

Iglesias, Gabino. 'These "Wanderers" Are Heading for the End of the World.' *NPR.org* (6 July 2019): http://web.archive.org/web/20220714180421/https://www.npr.org/2019/07/06/738974776/these-wanderers-are-heading-for-the-end-of-the-world.

Ing, Dean. *Pulling Through*. New York: Ace, 1983.

Isto, Raino. '"An Itinerary of the Creative Imagination": Bunk'Art and the Politics of Art and Tourism in Remembering Albania's Socialist Past.' *Cultures of History Forum* (2017): www.cultures-of-history.uni-jena.de/politics/albania/an-itinerary; accessed 14 March 2023.

Isto, Raino. 'The Monument as Ruin: Natality, Spectrality, and the History of the Image in the Tirana Independence Monument.' *[sic]-A Journal of Literature, Culture, and Literary Translation* 2.6 (2016): http://web.archive.org/web/20220717065705/https://www.sic-journal.org/Article/Index/401.

Bibliography

Jameson, Fredric. *Archaeologies of the Future: The Desire Called Utopia and Other Science Fictions*. London: Verso, 2005.

Jelly-Shapiro, Joshua. 'What Are Borders For?' *New Yorker* (27 Nov. 2019): www.newyorker.com/books/under-review/what-are-borders-for.

Johnson, Giff. 'Exposing the US Nuclear Test Legacy in the Marshall Islands.' *Pacific Journalism Review* 12.2 (2006): 188–91.

Jones, Holly Goddard. *The Salt Line*. New York: G. P. Putnam's Sons, 2017.

Kadaré, Ismail. *The Pyramid*. New York: Vintage, 1996.

Kadaré, Ismail. *Spring Flowers, Spring Frost*. Trans. David Bellos. New York: Arcade, 2012.

Kahn, Lloyd. 'Refried Domes' (1989): http://web.archive.org/web/20230202231818/https://www.shelterpub.com/domes; accessed 31 Aug. 2023.

Kamysh, Markiyan. *Stalking the Atomic City*. Trans. Hanna Leliv and Reilly Costigan Humes. London: Pushkin Press, 2022 [2015].

Karber, Phillip. *Strategic Implications of China's Underground Great Wall*. Washington, DC: Georgetown University Asian Arms Control Project, 2011: www.fas.org/nuke/guide/china/Karber_UndergroundFacilities-Full_2011_reduced.pdf; accessed 2 May 2018.

Kearny, Cresson H. *Expedient Shelter Construction and Occupancy Experiments*. Oak Ridge, TN: Oak Ridge National Laboratory, 1976.

Kearny, Cresson H. *Nuclear War Survival Skills* (1979). Updated and expanded 1987 edition. Cave Junction, OR: Oregon Institute of Science and Medicine, 2004. http://web.archive.org/web/20221101062222/http://oism.org/nwss/nwss.pdf.

Kelly, Casey Ryan. 'The Man-pocalpyse: Doomsday Preppers and the Rituals of Apocalyptic Manhood.' *Text and Performance Quarterly* 36.2–3 (2016): 95–114.

Kelly, Walt. *We Have Met the Enemy and He Is Us*. New York: Simon and Schuster, 1972.

Kessel, Jonah M. 'In a Secret Bunker in the Andes, a Wall That Was Really a Window.' *New York Times* (26 April 2019): www.nytimes.com/2019/04/26/reader-center/ecuador-china-surveillance-spying.html.

King, Wayne. 'Link Seen among Heavily Armed Rightist Groups.' *New York Times* (11 June 1983): section 1, p. 1: www.nytimes.com/1983/06/11/us/link-seen-among-heavily-armed-rightist-groups.html.

Kirk, Andrew G. *Counterculture Green: The Whole Earth Catalog and American Environmentalism*. Lawrence: University Press of Kansas, 2007.

Kirk, Andrew G. *Doom Towns: The People and Landscapes of Atomic Testing*. New York: Oxford University Press, 2017.

Klein, Naomi. *The Shock Doctrine: The Rise of Disaster Capitalism*. New York: Knopf, 2007.

Knebel, Fletcher. *Crossing in Berlin*. Garden City, NY: Doubleday, 1981.

Koudelka, Josef. *Wall: Israeli & Palestinian Landscape 2008–2012*. New York: Aperture, 2013.

Kristensen, Hans M., and Matt Korda. 'Status of World Nuclear Forces.' *Federation of American Scientists* (Feb. 2022): https://fas.org/issues/nuclear-weapons/status-world-nuclear-forces/; accessed 22 Nov. 2022.

Lanchester, John. *The Wall: A Novel*. New York: W. W. Norton, 2019.

Lane, Anthony. 'Room.' New Yorker (24 Feb. 2016): http://web.archive.org/web/20190701093401/https://www.newyorker.com/goings-on-about-town/movies/room.

Lappé, Anna. 'The Battle for Biodiversity: Monsanto and Farmers Clash.' *Atlantic* (28 March 2011): www.theatlantic.com/health/archive/2011/03/the-battle-for-biodiversity-monsanto-and-farmers-clash/73117/.

Latour, Bruno. *Down to Earth: Politics in the New Climatic Regime*. Medford, MA: Polity, 2018.

Laxness, Halldór. *The Atom Station*. Sag Harbor, NY: Permanent Press, 1982 [1948].

Lee, Maggie. 'Busan Film Review: *Paradise in Service*.' *Variety* (1 Oct. 2014): http://web.archive.org/web/20221203092054/https://variety.com/2014/film/reviews/busan-film-review-paradise-in-service-1201318199/.

Lehmann-Haupt, Christopher. 'Cresson Kearny, Expert on Nuclear Survival, Dies at 89.' *New York Times* (12 Jan. 2004): www.nytimes.com/2004/01/12/us/cresson-kearny-expert-on-nuclear-survival-dies-at-89.html.

Lepucki, Edan. *California*. New York: Little, Brown, 2014.

Levi, Primo. *Survival in Auschwitz*. Trans. of *Se questo è un uomo*. New York: Collier, 1959 [1947].

Levine, Caroline. *Forms: Whole, Rhythm, Hierarchy, Network*. Princeton: Princeton University Press, 2015.

Lewis, Sean (wr.), and Caitlin Yarsky (art). *Coyotes* (eight issues). Portland, OR: Image Comics, 2018.

Longo, Matthew. *The Politics of Borders: Sovereignty, Security, and the Citizen after 9/11*. Cambridge: Cambridge University Press, 2017.

Lovay, Jean-Marc. 'Conférence de Stockholm.' In *Conférences aux antipodes*. Genève: Editions Zoé, 1987. 9–29.

Lowrey, Annie. 'The Bunker Magnates Hate to Say They Told You So.' *Atlantic* (15 Sept. 2020): www.theatlantic.com/technology/archive/2020/09/rising-s-vivos-and-the-booming-bunker-economy/616240/.

Luiselli, Valeria. *Lost Children Archive*. New York: Knopf, 2019.

Luiselli, Valeria. *Tell Me How It Ends: An Essay in 40 Questions*. Minneapolis: Coffee House Press, 2017.

Macdonald, Andrew [William Luther Pierce]. *The Turner Diaries*. [Washington, DC: National Alliance, 1978].

Macfarlane, Robert, *Underland: A Deep Time Journey*. New York: W. W. Norton, 2019.

Makkai, Rebecca. 'The World's on Fire. Can We Still Talk about Books?' *Electric Literature* (6 Dec. 2018): http://web.archive.org/web/20221128083532/https://electricliterature.com/the-worlds-on-fire-can-we-still-talk-about-books/.

Mandel, Emily St. John. *Station Eleven*. New York: Knopf, 2014.

Mandour, M. Alaa. 'Inside-Outside: The Making of the West Bank Security Wall.' In *Building Walls and Dissolving Borders: The Challenges of Alterity, Community and Securitizing Space*, edited by Max O. Stephenson, Jr, and Laura Zanotti. Burlington, VT: Ashgate, 2013. 99–113.

Bibliography

Mann, Don. 'Introduction.' In *Nuclear War Survival Skills: Lifesaving Nuclear Facts and Self-Help Instructions*, by Cresson H. Kearny. Expanded, updated edition. Skyhorse Publishing, 2016.

Mariani, Daniele. 'A chacun son bunker.' Swissinfo.ch (23 Oct. 2009): http://web.archive.org/web/20221115065308/https://www.swissinfo.ch/fre/a-chacun-son-bunker/7485678.

Martin, David C. *Wilderness of Mirrors*. New York: Harper and Row, 1980.

Masco, Joseph. *The Nuclear Borderlands: The Manhattan Project in Post–Cold War New Mexico*. Princeton: Princeton University Press, 2013.

Matsunaga, Kyoko. 'Leslie Marmon Silko and Nuclear Dissent in the American Southwest.' *Japanese Journal of American Studies* 25 (2014): 67–87.

Mbembe, Achille. *Necropolitics*. Trans. Steve Corcoran. Durham: Duke University Press, 2019 [2016].

McCarthy, Cormac. *The Road*. New York: Vintage, 2006.

McEwan, Ian. *The Innocent*. New York: Anchor, 1999 [1990].

McGirk, James. 'Remembering Life in Arcosanti, Paolo Soleri's Futuristic Desert Utopia.' *Wired* (11 April 2013): http://web.archive.org/web/20221226074258/http://www.wired.com/2013/04/arcosanti-paolo-soleri/.

McKittrick, Katherine. *Demonic Grounds: Black Women and the Cartographies of Struggle*. Minneapolis: University of Minnesota Press, 2006.

McPhee, John. *La Place de la Concorde Suisse*. New York: Farrar Straus Giroux, 1983.

McPhee, John. 'Structure.' *New Yorker* (6 Jan. 2013): www.newyorker.com/magazine/2013/01/14/structure.

Merrill, Samuel. 'Striving Underground: Stockholm's Atomic Bomb Defences.' In *Global Undergrounds: Exploring Cities Within*, edited by Dobraszczyk et al. 121–3.

Miéville, China. *The City & the City*. New York: Del Ray, 2009.

Miéville, China. 'Unsolving the City: An Interview with China Miéville,' by Geoff Manaugh, *BLDGBLOG* (1 March 2011): http://web.archive.org/web/20221203132229/https://bldgblog.com/2011/03/unsolving-the-city-an-interview-with-china-mieville/.

Morgan, J[ill] M[eredith]. *Beyond Eden*. New York: Pinnacle, 1992.

Morgan, J[ill] M[eredith]. *Desert Eden*. New York: Pinnacle, 1991.

Morgan, J[ill] M[eredith]. *Future Eden*. New York: Pinnacle, 1992.

Morrow, James. *This Is the Way the World Ends*. New York: Harcourt, Brace, 1986.

Moss, Alexander. 'After the End: Svalbard Global Seed Vault.' In *Global Undergrounds*, edited by Dobraszczyk et al. 247–9.

Murakami, Haruki. *IQ84*. Trans. Jay Rubin and Philip Gabriel. New York: Vintage, 2011 [2010].

Murphy, David E., Sergei A. Kondrashev, and George Bailey. *Battleground Berlin: CIA vs. KGB in the Cold War*. New Haven, CT: Yale University Press, 1997.

Myers, Edward. *The Chosen Few*. South Bend, IN: and books, 1982.

Nalewicki, Jennifer. 'Switzerland's Historic Bunkers Get a New Lease on Life.' *Smithsonian.com* (23 March 2016): http://web.archive.org/web/20221202134515/https://www.smithsonianmag.com/travel/switzerlands-bunkers-get-new-lease-life-180958233/.

304 *Bibliography*

Nevada Test Site Oral History Project. University of Nevada Las Vegas: http://digital.library.unlv.edu/ntsohp/; accessed 19 April 2018.

Newitz, Annalee. *Scatter, Adapt, and Remember: How Humans Will Survive a Mass Extinction.* New York: Doubleday, 2013.

Newman, Kim. *Apocalypse Movies: End of the World Cinema.* New York: St. Martin's Griffin, 2000 [1999].

O'Brien, Keith. 'How to Survive Societal Collapse in Suburbia.' *New York Times Magazine* (16 Nov. 2012): www.nytimes.com/2012/11/18/magazine/how-to-survive-societal-collapse-in-suburbia.html.

O'Brien, Tim. *The Nuclear Age.* New York: Knopf, 1985.

O'Connell, Mark. *Notes from an Apocalypse: A Personal Journey to the End of the World and Back.* New York: Doubleday, 2020.

O'Connor, Joe. 'How a Canadian Built a DIY Nuclear Bunker from 42 Buried Buses and Plenty of Concrete.' *National Post* [Toronto] (13 Oct. 2017; updated 17 Dec. 2018): https://nationalpost.com/news/canada/inside-ark-two-canadas-largest-diy-nuclear-shelter.

Ōe Kenzaburō. *Hiroshima Notes.* Trans. David L. Swain and Toshi Yonezawa. New York: Marion Boyars, 1995 [1981; original published 1965].

Okorafor, Nnedi. *Who Fears Death.* New York: DAW, 2010.

Olan, Susan Torian. *Earth Remembers.* Lake Geneva, WI: TSR, 1989.

Osnos, Evan. 'Doomsday Prep for the Super-Rich.' *New Yorker* (30 Jan. 2017): www.newyorker.com/magazine/2017/01/30/doomsday-prep-for-the-super-rich.

Ozeki, Ruth. *A Tale for the Time Being.* New York: Penguin, 2013.

Ozorak, Paul. *Underground Structures of the Cold War: The World Below.* Pen & Sword Books, 2012.

Parry, Nigel. 'Well-known UK Graffiti Artist Banksy Hacks the Wall.' *The Electronic Intifada* (2 Sept. 2005): https://web.archive.org/web/20221208194820/https://electronicintifada.net/content/well-known-uk-graffiti-artist-banksy-hacks-wall/5733.

Parry, William. *Against the Wall: The Art of Resistance in Palestine.* Chicago: Lawrence Hill, 2010.

Phillips, Jayne Anne. *Machine Dreams.* New York: Vintage, 1999 [1984].

Pierce, Alexandra, and Mimi Mondal, ed. *Luminescent Threads: Connections to Octavia E. Butler.* Yokine, WA: Twelfth Planet Press, 2017. Kindle edition.

Pike, David L. 'The Cinematic Sewer.' In *Dirt: New Geographies of Cleanliness and Contamination*, edited by Ben Campkin and Rosie Cox. London: I. B. Tauris, 2007. 138–50.

Pike, David L. 'Cold War Reduction: The Principle of the Swiss Bunker Fantasy.' *Space and Culture* 20.1 (2017): 94–106.

Pike, David L. *Cold War Space and Culture in the 1960s and 1980s: The Bunkered Decades.* New York: Oxford University Press, 2021.

Pike, David L. 'Future Slums: Problems of Urban Space in Science Fiction Cinema.' *The Apollonian* 5 (2018): 51–69.

Pike, David L. 'Haunted Mountains, Supershelters and the Afterlives of Cold War Infrastructure,' *Journal for the Study of Religion, Nature and Culture* 13.2 (2019): 208–29.

Bibliography

Pike, David L. 'Sewage Treatments: Vertical Space and the Discourse of Waste in 19th-Century Paris and London.' In *Filth: Dirt, Disgust, and Modern Life*, edited by William Cohen and Ryan Thompson. Minneapolis: University of Minnesota Press, 2004. 51–77.

Pike, David L. 'Wall and Tunnel: The Spatial Metaphorics of Cold War Berlin.' *New German Critique* 110 (2010): 73–94.

Powers, Thomas. 'The Nuclear Worrier: rev. of Daniel Ellsberg, *The Doomsday Machine: Confessions of a Nuclear War Planner*.' *New York Review of Books* (18 Jan. 2018): 13–15.

Preston, Julieanna. 'Subterra: Interior Economies of Underground Space. Conversations with Photographer Wayne Barrar.' *Idea Journal* (2011): 34–48.

Preston, Will. 'Apocalypse Burnout.' *Full Stop* (8 Feb. 2021): http://web.archive.org/web/20221002200933/https://www.full-stop.net/2021/02/09/reviews/will-preston/apocalypse-burnout/.

Ptacin, Mira. 'Could Doomsday Bunkers Become the New Normal?' *New York Times* (26 June 2020): www.nytimes.com/2020/06/26/realestate/could-doomsday-bunkers-become-the-new-normal.html.

Ptacin, Mira. 'I Am Not a Housewife. I'm a Prepper.' *New York Times* (24 Sept. 2020): www.nytimes.com/2020/09/24/opinion/sunday/i-am-not-a-housewife-im-a-prepper.html.

Pynchon, Thomas. *Bleeding Edge*. New York: Penguin, 2013.

Rama, Kejsi. 'Transforming a Former Military Island into an Eco-Resort: The Case of Sazan, Albania.' MA thesis, University of Strathclyde, 2016.

Rapin, Jean-Jacques. *L'Esprit des fortifications: Vaubin – Dufour – Les forts de Saint-Maurice*. Lausanne: Presses polytechniques et universitaire romandes, 2004.

Rhinehart, Luke. *The Long Voyage Back*. Permuted Press, 2014. Kindle edition.

Richter, Darmon. *Chernobyl: A Stalker's Guide*. London: FUEL, 2020.

Richter, Darmon. 'Futures Past: Pyongyang Metro.' In *Global Undergrounds*, edited by Dobraszczyk et al. 232–4.

Rivera, Alex (dir.). *Sleep Dealer*. Dist. Maya Entertainment. 2008.

Rose, Kenneth D. *One Nation Underground: The Fallout Shelter in American Culture*. New York: New York University Press, 2001.

Rosenfield, Karissa. 'The Dome in the Desert by Wendell Burnette.' *ArchDaily* (14 April 2013): http://web.archive.org/web/20220808193351/https://www.archdaily.com/359748/the-dome-in-the-desert-by-wendell-burnette.

Ross, Richard. *Waiting for the End of the World*. New York: Princeton Architectural Press, 2004.

Rotella, Sebastian. *Twilight on the Line*. New York: W. W. Norton, 1998.

Rowe, Josephine. 'Pattern and Forecast (Vol. 5).' *The Believer* (19 March 2019): http://web.archive.org/web/20190320104756/https://believermag.com/logger/pattern-and-forecast-vol-5/.

Ruthven, Malise. 'Physical Graffiti on the Border.' *New York Review of Books* (9 April 2018): www.nybooks.com/daily/2018/04/09/physical-graffiti-on-the-border/.

Sacco, Joe. 'The Underground War in Gaza.' *New York Times Magazine* (6 July 2003): 24–7.

Saint-Amour, Paul. *Tense Future: Modernism, Total War, Encyclopedic Form*. New York: Oxford University Press, 2015.

Sanders, William. *The Ballad of Billy Badass and the Rose of Turkestan*. Holicong, PA: Wildside Press, 1999.

Saxon, Kurt. *The Survivor* (1976–78). Rpt. 4 vols. (N.p.: n.p., 1987–88).

Saxon, Kurt. 'What Is a Survivalist?' (N.p.: n.p., 1980): http://web.archive.org/web/20230305220852/http://www.textfiles.com/survival/whatsurv; accessed 31 Aug. 2023.

Scarry, Elaine. *Thermonuclear Monarchy: Choosing between Democracy and Doom*. New York: W. W. Norton, 2014.

Scarry, Elaine. *Thinking in an Emergency*. New York: W. W. Norton, 2010.

Schäfer, Stefanie. 'From Geisha Girls to the Atomic Bomb Dome: Dark Tourism and the Formation of Hiroshima Memory.' *Tourist Studies* 16.4 (2016): 351–66.

Schirer, Ernst, Manfred Keune, and Philip Jenkins, ed. *The Berlin Wall: Representations and Perspectives*. New York: Lang, 1996.

Schnauber, Cornelius, Romey Sabalius, and Gene Stimpson. 'Introduction.' In *The Dream Never Becomes Reality: 24 Swiss Writers Challenge the United States*, edited by Schnauber, Sabalius, and Stimpson. Lanham, MD: University Press of America, 1995. vii–xiv.

Scholes Young, Melissa. *The Hive*. Nashville: Turner Publishing, 2020.

Schwartz, Alexandra. 'The Artist JR Lifts a Mexican Child over the Border Wall.' *New Yorker* (11 Sept. 2017): www.newyorker.com/news/as-told-to/the-artist-jr-lifts-a-mexican-child-over-the-border-wall.

Schwarz, Roberto. 'Misplaced Ideas.' In *Misplaced Ideas: Essays on Brazilian Culture*. New York: Verso, 2002 [1973]. 19–32.

Schweninger, Lee. 'Ecofeminism, Nuclearism, and O'Brien's *The Nuclear Age*.' In *The Nightmare Considered: Critical Essays on Nuclear Criticism*, edited by Nancy Anisfield. Bowling Green, OH: Bowling Green State University Popular Press, 1991. 177–85.

Schwenkel, Christina. 'The Current Never Stops: Intimacies of Energy Infrastructure in Vietnam.' In *The Promise of Infrastructure*, edited by Nikhil Anand, Akhil Gupta, and Hannah Appel. Durham: Duke University Press, 2018. 102–30.

Scott, A. O. 'Humans, Who Once Buried Their Treasures, Now Bury Their Dangers.' *New York Times* (1 Feb. 2011): www.nytimes.com/2011/02/02/movies/02into.html.

Seed, David. *Under the Shadow: The Atomic Bomb and Cold War Narratives*. Kent, OH: Kent State University Press, 2013.

Shang, Hui. 'How US Restraint Can Keep China's Nuclear Arsenal Small.' *Bulletin of the Atomic Scientists* 68.4 (2015): 73–82. DOI: 10.1177/0096340212451433.

Shelter. Ed. Lloyd Kahn, co-ed. and design Bob Easton. Bolenas, CA: Shelter Publications, 2000 [1973].

Sieff, Kevin. 'Under the U.S.-Mexico Border, Miles of Tunnels Worth Millions of Dollars – to Traffickers.' *Washington Post* (13 Oct. 2020): www.washingtonpost.com/world/the_americas/mexico-border-tunnels-drugs/2020/10/09/0f4dafe8-0438-11eb-897d-3a6201d6643f_story.html.

Silko, Leslie Marmon. *Almanac of the Dead: A Novel*. New York: Penguin, 1992 [1991].

Silko, Leslie Marmon. *Ceremony*. New York: Penguin, 2006 [1977].

Silverberg, Robert. *The Queen of Springtime*. Lincoln: University of Nebraska Press, 2005 [1990].

Smith, James, and Guy Woodward. 'Anglo-American Propaganda and the Transition from the Second World War to the Cultural Cold War.' In *The Bloomsbury Handbook to Cold War Literature Cultures*, edited by Greg Barnhisel. London: Bloomsbury Academic, 2022. 149–62.

Solzhenitsyn, Alexander. *In the First Circle*. New York: Harper, 2009 [1968].

Spiers, Miriam Brown. '"The Yellow Monster": Reanimating Nuclear Fears in Cherokee Science Fiction.' *Native South* 12 (2019): 52–73.

Stafford, David. *Spies beneath Berlin*. Woodstock, NY: Overlook, 2003.

Stefa, Elian, and Gyler Mydyti. *Concrete Mushrooms: Reusing Albania's 750,000 Abandoned Bunkers*. Barcelona: Actar, 2013.

Stocke, John Gregory. '"Suicide on the Installment Plan": Cold-War-Era Civil Defense and Consumerism in the United States.' In *The Writing on the Cloud: American Culture Confronts the Atomic Bomb*, edited by Alison M. Scott and Christopher D. Geist. Lanham: University Press of America, 1997. 46–60.

Strasser, Todd. *Fallout*. Somerville, MA: Candlewick, 2013.

Swanson, Carl Joseph. '"The Only Metaphor Left": Colson Whitehead's *Zone One* and Zombie Narrative Form.' *Genre* 47.3 (2014): 379–405.

Sweterlitsch, Tom. *The Gone World*. New York: G. P. Putnam's Sons, 2018.

Szonyi, Michael. *Cold War Island: Quemoy on the Front Line*. Cambridge, MA: Harvard University Press, 2008.

Taylor, Lawrence J., and Maeve Hickey. *Tunnel Kids*. Tucson: University of Arizona Press, 2001.

Teh, Yvonne. 'Film Review: *Paradise in Service* Is a Coming-of-Age Story in a Military Brothel.' *South China Morning Post* (8 Oct. 2014): http://web.archive.org/web/20180204072715/http://www.scmp.com/magazines/48hrs/article/1612043/film-review-paradise-service-coming-age-story-military-brothel.

Tree, Isabella. *Wilding: The Return of Nature to a British Farm*. London: Picador, 2018.

Tsing, Anna Lowenhaupt. *Friction: An Ethnography of Global Connection*. Princeton: Princeton University Press, 2005.

Tyler May, Elaine. *Homeward Bound: American Families in the Cold War Era*. Rev. ed. New York: Basic Books, 1999 [1988].

UNESCO. 'What are Biosphere Reserves?' (2021): http://web.archive.org/web/20230306184206/https://en.unesco.org/biosphere/about.

UNESCO. 'World Network of Biosphere Reserves' (2021): http://web.archive.org/web/20230314193028/https://en.unesco.org/biosphere/wnbr.

Vanderbilt, Tom. *Survival City: Adventures among the Ruins of Atomic America*. Chicago: University of Chicago Press, 2010 [2002].

van Gerven Oei, Vincent W. J. 'Bunk'Art 2: A Nuclear Attack on Meaning.' *Exit.al* (21 Nov. 2016): https://exit.al/en/bunkart-2-a-nuclear-attack-on-meaning/; accessed 14 March 2023.

Bibliography

van Gerven Oei, Vincent W. J. 'A Response to Carlo Bollino's "Defense" of Bunk'Art 2.' *Exit.al* (6 Dec. 2016): http://web.archive.org/web/20200421031448/https://exit.al/en/2016/12/06/a-response-to-carlo-bollinos-defense-of-bunkart-2/.

Vidal, John. 'Concrete: The Most Destructive Material on Earth.' *Guardian* (25 Feb. 2019): www.theguardian.com/cities/2019/feb/25/concrete-the-most-destructive-material-on-earth.

Villazana, Libia. 'Transnational Virtual Mobility as a Reification of Deployment of Power: Exploring Transnational Processes in the Film *Sleep Dealer*.' *Transnational Cinemas* 4.2 (2013): 217–30.

Virilio, Paul. *Bunker Archéologie*. Paris: Editions du Demi-Cercle, 1991.

Virilio, Paul. *Bunker Archeology*. Princeton: Princeton Architectural Press, 1997.

Vizenor, Gerald. *Hiroshima Bugi: Atomu 57*. Lincoln: University of Nebraska Press, 2003.

Vowel, Chelsea. 'Writing toward a Definition of Indigenous Futurism.' *Literary Hub* (10 June 2022): https://lithub.com/writing-toward-a-definition-of-indigenous-futurism/.

Vuong, Ocean. *On Earth We're Briefly Gorgeous*. New York: Penguin, 2021 [2019].

Wang Ting-chi. Email communication to the author (4 June 2018).

Wedge, Matt. 'The Cohen Case Files: Full Moon High (1981).' *Obsessive Movie Nerd* (8 March 2011): http://web.archive.org/web/20221128042642/https://obsessivemovienerd.com/2011/03/08/the-cohen-case-files-full-moon-high-1981/.

Weizman, Eyal. *Forensic Architecture: Violence at the Threshold of Detectability*. New York: Zone, 2017.

Weizman, Eyal. *Hollow Land: Israel's Architecture of Occupation*. London: Verso, 2017 [2007].

Wendig, Chuck. *Wanderers*. New York: Del Rey, 2019.

Whipple, Chris G. 'Can Nuclear Waste Be Stored Safely at Yucca Mountain?' *Scientific American* 274.6 (1996): 72–9.

White, Edmund. 'Round and Round the Eupcaccia Goes.' *New York Times Book Review* (10 April 1988): 9.

Whitehead, Colson. *The Underground Railroad*. New York: Doubleday, 2016.

Whitehead, Colson. *Zone One*. New York: Doubleday, 2011.

Wicht, Bernard. *L'Art de la guerre au XXIe siècle*. Lausanne: L'Age d'Homme, 1998.

Wikipedia contributors. 'Metro-2.' *Wikipedia*: https://en.wikipedia.org/w/index.php?title=Metro-2&oldid=832252615; accessed 13 April 2018.

Williams, Rosalind. *Notes on the Underground*. New edition. Cambridge, MA: MIT Press, 2008 [1990].

Winter, Lucas. 'Egypt and Israel: Tunnel Neutralization Efforts in Gaza.' *Engineer* (Sept.–Dec. 2017): 30–4.

Wong, Lily. 'Dwelling over China: Minor Transnationalisms in Karen Tei Yamashita's *I Hotel*.' *American Quarterly* 69.3 (2017): 719–39.

Yong, Ed. 'New Zealand's War on Rats Could Change the World.' *The Atlantic* (16 Nov. 2017): www.theatlantic.com/science/archive/2017/11/new-zealand-predator-free-2050-rats-gene-drive-ruh-roh/546011/.

Ypi, Lea. *Free: A Child and a Country at the End of History.* New York: W. W. Norton, 2022 [2021].

Zak, Dan. *Almighty: Courage, Resistance, and Existential Peril in the Nuclear Age.* New York: Blue Rider, 2016.

Ziauddin, Silvia Bergen. '(De)territorializing the Home. The Nuclear Bomb Shelter as a Malleable Site of Passage.' *Environment and Planning D: Society and Space* 35.4 (2017): 674–93.

Žižek, Slavoj. *Living in the End Times.* London: Verso, 2010.

Žižek, Slavoj. 'Preface: Bloch's Ontology of Not-Yet-Being.' In *The Privatization of Hope: Ernst Bloch and the Future of Utopia*, edited by Peter Thompson and Žižek. Durham: Duke University Press, 2013. SIC 8.

Žižek, Slavoj. 'Rolling in Underground Tunnels.' *Mondoweiss* (24 Aug. 2014): https://web.archive.org/web/20221206131132/https://mondoweiss.net/2014/08/rolling-underground-tunnels.

Zufferey, Jean-Gabriel. *Le Syndrome du hérisson: la Suisse et son armée.* Carouges-Genève, Switzerland: Editions Zoé, 1989.

Index

Note: **Bold type** indicates key discussions of terms; *italics* indicate illustrations.

Abbas, Basel 236, 268
Abbey, Edward 29
Abdurraqib, Hanif 5
Abe Kōbō: *The Ark Sakura* 146–7
Abrahamson, Lenny, *see Room*
Abrigo Nuclear (1981) 196, *196*
adaptive reuse, *see* shelter: adaptive reuse of
affect 4, 6, 10–11, 15–19, 130, 133, 189
affordances **8–9**; *see also under* bunker: as architecture; bunker: epistemological; bunker: ontological; bunker emergence narratives; bunker fantasy; comics; migration; neoliberalism; postapocalyptic fiction; science fiction/fantasy; tunnel; visual arts; wall
Afrofuturism 3–4, 6, 9, 193, 201–17, 253; *see also* Butler, Octavia
Afterland, see Beukes, Lauren
Ahern, Jerry: *The Survivalist* series 36, 103
Alas, Babylon, see Frank, Pat
Albania 20, 91–4, 104, 121–30, 168, 172, 175–82, 185, *127, Plates 1–11*
Almanac of the Dead, see Silko, Leslie Marmon
American Delirium, see González, Betina
Anderson, Poul: *Vault of the Ages* 210
Anishinaabe People 51, 83, 88
Anthropocene 5, 9–10, 111, 218, 292

antinuclear protest 5, 29, 62, 142, 151–4, 169
Anzaldúa, Gloria 251–2
apocalypse
  'A-B-C' warfare 6, 108
  alien invasion 62–4, 86, 88
  digital 199, 218, 278–9
  ecological xxi, 6, 7, 10, 110–11, 197–200, 229, 276, 279–83
  future 198–217
  nuclear xxi, 2, 6–7, 9–10, 14, 16–17, 31, 201, *13, 16*
  oppression and genocide 5–6, 201, 217, 265, 276, 278, 290
  pandemic 3–4, 6–7, 10, 78, 188, 197, 212, 218, 225, 281, 282
  religious 112–13
  zombie xxi, 191–8
Arizona 27, 86, 252, 253, 264
  Nogales 232, 250, 261–2, 265–6, *250*
  see also US–Mexico border
Ark Sakura, The, see Abe Kōbō
art, *see* visual arts
Asher, Marty: *Shelter* 65, 72–3
'Atomic', *see* Blondie
Atom Station, The, see Laxness, Halldór
At Winter's End, see Silverberg, Robert
Australia 15, 155, 275, *16*

Baldwin, James 4
Ballad of Billy Badass and the Rose of Turkestan, The, see Sanders, William

Index

Ballard, J. G.: 'The Terminal Beach' 15, 88, 182, 275, 278
Banksy 237, 244–6, 247, 277, *245*
Barrar, Wayne 176–7, 279–80, *Plates 1–14*
barrier, *see* wall
Barrier (2015–17) 266–7, *258*
Bartel, Paul, *see Shelf Life*
basement, *see* shelter: basement
Beach, Bruce 45–6, *45*
Beck, John 180, 185, 187
Begley, Josh, *see Best of Luck with the Wall*
Bell, Kirsty 185
Beneath the Planet of the Apes (1970) 215
Benjamin, Walter 14, 17–18
Berlant, Lauren 18–19
Berlin Wall 92, 125, 178, 181, 224, 226–8, 231–5, 256–7, *227, 231*
Berlin/Wall, *see* Hare, David
Beside the Sickle Moon, *see* Husien, Thaer
Best of Luck with the Wall (2016) 254, 270, *254, 255*
Beukes, Lauren: *Afterland* 78–9, 188
Bikini Atoll 154, 274
Bill Haley & the Comets 1, 21
biosecurity 273–5, 279–82, 286–8, *286*, *Plates 12–14*
Birch, Patricia, *see Grease 2*
Black people
  as creators 5–6, 81, 201, 206
  enslavement of 7, 130, 207
  in film and TV 59, 81–2, 195
  in literature 4, 5, 73, 195, 201, 207, 276, 278
  and sheltering 195
  see also Afrofuturism; inequity: racial; proper names; white nationalism
Black Rain, *see* Ibuse, Masuji
Blast from the Past (1999) 51, 61, 73–6, 78, 81, *74, 76*
Bleeding Edge, *see* Pynchon, Thomas
Bloch, Ernst 10, 17
Blomkamp, Neill, *see Chappie*; *District 9*
Blondie: 'Atomic' 71

Bong Joon-ho, *see Parasite*
Bonvillain, Tamra, *see Border Town*
border imaginary 259, 261–4, 270; *see also* migration; US–Mexico border; wall
border studies 251–2
Border Town (2018–19) 261, 262, 264, 266
Bradshaw, Peter 220
Brand, Stewart: *Whole Earth Catalog* 25–30, 33, 37, 44, 88, *28*
Breach, *see* Goodwater, W. L.
Brooks, Max: *World War Z* 196
Brown Girl in the Ring, *see* Hopkinson, Nalo
Brugués, Alejandro, *see Juan de los Muertos*
Buache, Freddy 113
Büchel, Christoph 270
Bunk'Art 179–81, 183
bunker
  as architecture 25, 91–2, 124–5, 137
    affordances of 11, 91, 224, 231, 238
  epistemological **15–19**, 49, 87, 133, 139, 182, 191–223, 290, *244, 245*
    affordances of 200–1, 209
  ontological 10, **14–16**, 18, 19, 49, 80, 88, 133, 135, 137–90, 193, 200, 217–18, 273, 288, 290, *271*
    affordances of 15, 51, 273
  as utopian space 9, 12, 129–36
  see also bunker fantasy; enclave; ruins, Cold War; shelter
bunker emergence narratives 51, 64–89, 202–3, 216, 281, *67, 68, 77, 78*
  affordances of 66–9, 79, 81
bunker fantasy xxi–xxii, *2*, 3–20, 35–41, 91, 129, 223, 224, 274–6
  affordances of 8–10, 17, 19, 111, 130, 139, 142, 276–7
  global 1, 90–4, 125, 133, 151, 159, 223; *see also* misplaced ideas: spatial
Burnette, Wendell 27

312   *Index*

Butler, Octavia 203–4, 206–8, 210–15,
     276
     Clay's Ark 3–4, 9, 14, 206, 212,
         280
     Dawn 213
     Kindred 201–2, 203, 206, 207
     Parable of the Sower 204–6, 208,
         225–6, 281
     Parable of the Talents 204–8
     Patternist series 203, 211–12
     Xenogenesis trilogy 203, 211
Byrne, Monica: *The Girl in the Road*
     278–9

California 42, 78, 277, 282, *43*
     Los Angeles 204, 278–9, *Plates 15*
         & 16
     northern 38, 206
     San Diego 253, 264, 268–9, 272,
         268, 269
     southern 76, *271*
     see also US–Mexico border
California, *see* Lepucki, Edan
Camper Van Beethoven: 'Good Guys
     and Bad Guys' 90
Canada 14, 45, 202–3, *45*
Canavan, Gerry 203, 210
Canticle for Leibowitz, *see* Miller,
     Walter M.
capitalism
     'disaster' 132
     inequity in 135, 194, 204–5, 276
     late 9, 20, 38, 79, 132, 182–90,
         272, 290
     post-communist 126, 176–7, 180
     'zombie' 197–8
     see also consumer culture
Captain Fantastic (2016) 37–9, *38*
Captive, The (2014) 78
Carrión, Jorge: *Los huérfanos* 147–8
Çashku, Kujtim 178, 180; *see also*
     Kolonel Bunker
cave 2, 19, 124, 205, 207–9, 238
Ceremony, *see* Silko, Leslie Marmon
Chaichian, Mohammed 254
Chandra, Vikram: *Sacred Games*
     12–14, 52, 148–50, 151, *13,*
     149
Chappie (2015) 199, 200, 202
Cherokee Nation 85

China 88, 94–101, 104, 123, 125,
     136, 148, 155, 159, 160,
     168–70, 183, 188, 211, 278,
     169, 170
Chornobyl 164–7, 283, *166, 167*
Christianity 13, 40, 112–13
Church Universal and Triumphant
     39–40, *37*
cinema, *see* movies
City & the City, The, *see* Miéville,
     China
civil defense
     American 24, 102–3
     Asian 91, 104, 168, 188
     European 91–4, 106, 111, 125,
         130, 143
     'self-help' 30
     Soviet 101–4, 183
Clare, Elizabeth *see* Church Universal
     and Triumphant
Clay's Ark, *see* Butler, Octavia
climate crisis xxi, 18, 111, 274–5,
     279–83, 290
     see also apocalypse: ecological;
         environmentalism; nature;
         seed banks
Cline, Ernest: *Ready Player One* 199,
     200
Cohen, Larry, *see Full Moon High*
Cold War
     counterdiscourse to 7–8, 151–3,
         276
     end of xx, 11, 146, 228
     espionage 148, 232–4
     legacies of xx, 11, 14, 17–18, 21,
         81–2, 91, 117–21, 131–3,
         139, 155–8
     nostalgia 4–6, 8, 9, 19, 66–9, 71
     see also civil defense; names of
         countries; ruins, Cold War;
         survival: Cold War;
         survivalism: Cold War;
         technology: Cold War;
         tourism: nuclear
Cole, Teju 249
Colorado 27, 34–5, 50, 86, 199, 283,
     288
comics 17, 27, 77, 88, 193–4, 261,
     273
     affordances of 155, 198n.24

see also titles of works
Connecticut 150
consumer culture 33, 35–7, 39, 42–9, 66, 126, 134, 235; *see also* capitalism
containment culture 67, 74–6, 183, 201, 224, 226, 228
counterculture 23, 25–33, 37
Coyotes (2017–18) 261, 262, 264, *263*
Crossing in Berlin, see Knebel, Fletcher
Cuban Missile Crisis 51, 53, 54, 74, 143

Dante, Joe, *see Matinee*
dark tourism, *see* tourism
Davis, Mike 276
Dawn, see Butler, Octavia
Day of the Dead (1985) xxi, 193
Dead Hand, The (2018) 155, *156*, *157*
deep-time speculation
in fiction 210–17, 219, 223
in history 5, 138, 217–23
Delarue, Claude: *Waiting for War* 109, 114–17, 285
De Léon, Jason 252–3, 265
DeLillo, Don
Underworld 92
Zero K 35–6, 190
del Toro, Guillermo, *see Shape of Water, The*
Demme, Jonathan, *see Silence of the Lambs, The*
DeMonaco, James *see Purge, The*
Derrida, Jacques 11
Díaz, Junot 197–8, 199, 276
Di Cintio, Marcello 226, 235–6, 264–5, 283–4
Dick, Philip K. 33, 148, 289
Dienstbüchlein, see Frisch, Max
Dillman, Lisa 260
Ding Shanxi, *see Kinmen Bombs*
dissident spatiality 19, 193, 201–9, 251, 276
dissident temporality **11**, 15, 19, 181, 193, 197, 201–9, 217, 222, 276
distant-future speculation, *see* deep-time speculation
District 9 (2009) 199, 200
Dog Stars, The, see Heller, Peter

dome 20, 25, 26–9, 88, 124, 164, 166–7, 226, 273, 280–1, 287, 28, *Plate 2*; *see also* Hiroshima: Atomic Bomb Dome; silo
Dong Zhenliang 99–100, 170
Doomsday Preppers (2012–14) 25, 42–7, *43*, *45*
Dreyer, Carl-Theodor, *see Vampyr*
Drop City 27, 60, *28*
Dr Strangelove (1963) 112
Druga, Jacqueline: *The Last Woman* 197
Duras, Marguerite, *see Hiroshima mon amour*
Dürrenmatt, Friedrich 105–6, 109, 111
dwelling 16–17, **18–19**, 261–72, 288–89

Earth Remembers, The, see Olan, Susan Torian
Eden trilogy, *see* Morgan, J. M.
Egan, Timothy 39n.58, 40
Egoyan, Atom, *see Captive, The*
Egypt 126, 235n.28, 238–40, 242
Ellsberg, Daniel 158–9
enclave
fictional 3, 35, 204–7, 212, 214, 225–6, 281
for nature 283n.24, 285, 287
as shelter 3, 40, 205, 225–6
utopian 9, 29, 199, 201, 204, 268, 281
Endres, Danielle 222
Enewetak Atoll 15, 88, 274
environmentalism 8, 29, 290–1; *see also* apocalypse: ecological; biosecurity; climate crisis; Great Green Wall; nature; seed banks; wall: sea
Erdrich, Louise: *Future Home of the Living God* 63
Esquivel, Eric M., *see Border Town*
Every Odd-Numbered Day 99–100
Exit West, see Hamid, Mohsin

Fallout, see Strasser, Todd
Farnham's Freehold, see Heinlein, Robert

feminism 6, 8, 27, 39, 55, 67, 189; *see also* gender; inequity: sexual
fiction *see* Black people: as creators; bunker emergence narratives; comics; deep-time speculation: in fiction; Indigenous Peoples: as creators; postapocalyptic fiction; postmodernist fiction; science fiction/fantasy; YA fiction
Finland 93, 104, 143, 220, *220*
Finoki, Bryan 230, 267
Flaningham, Jeff 42–3, 46
Foster, Thomas 203, 211
France 1, 105, 107, 122, 123, 137n.2, 145, 185, 266, 274, *186*
Frank, Pat: *Alas, Babylon* 34
Frisch, Max
  Dienstbüchlein 111–13
  Man in the Holocene 109–11
Fukiyama, Corey, *see Sin Nombre*
Fukushima Daiichi 139, 275
Fuller, Buckminster 26, 88
Full Moon High (1981) 65, 69–70, *70*
Future Home of the Living God, see Erdrich, Louise

Gainsbourg, Serge: *Rock around the Bunker* 1, 69
Galviz, Carlos López 187–8
Gaza tunnel 238–42, *239, 241, 242*; *see also* Palestine
Geist, Edward 101n.23, 102, 183
gender
  and the home shelter 44, 47–8, 74–6, 202
  norms 37–9, 58, 78–9, 81
  threat of captivity to women 42, 66–9, 75, 78–81
  violence against women 38, 78–81, 257, 262–3
  see also feminism; inequity: sexual; masculinity
genocide 6, 7, 130, 145, 207, 209, 234; *see also* apocalypse: oppression and genocide
Germany 47, 105, 111–12, 172, 183–4, 185, 188, 284, *184*; *see also* Berlin Wall
Get Out (2017) 59, 60, 66, 81–2, 88

Girl in the Road, The, see Byrne, Monica
global South 5, 138, 149, 151, 193, 274–80; *see also* names of countries
Gone World, The, see Sweterlitsch, Tom
González, Betina: *American Delirium* 277
'Good Guys and Bad Guys', *see* Camper Van Beethoven
Goodwater, W. L.: *Breach* 227
Gouré, Leon 102, 103
Gowin, Emmet *153*
Graham, Stephen 237–8
Grausam, Daniel 54–5
Grease 2 (1982) 65, 67–9, 71, *69*
Great Green Wall 279
Greenbrier, West Virginia 120, 131, 159–60, *161*
Greene, Graham 232

Haiti 197–8, 199, 209, 276
Hall, Larry 42–3, 46–7
Hamid, Mohsin: *Exit West* 261, 277
Hammad, Suheir 248
Haraway, Donna 203, 207
Hare, David: *Berlin/Wall* 234–5, 242, 243
Hawai'i 140, 141, 142, 143
Hegland, Joan: *Into the Forest* 38–9
Heinlein, Robert: *Farnham's Freehold* 34, 64
Heller, Peter: *The Dog Stars* 281
Herrera, Yuri: *Signs Preceding the End of the World* 259–61, 267
Hickey, Maeve 261–2, 266
Higgins, Kyle, *see Dead Hand, The*
Hillcoat, John, *see Road, The* (film)
Hiroshima 20, 143–6, 154, 160, 182
  Atomic Bomb Dome 83–5, 145, 146, 162, 167, 178, 181, *84, 163*
  see also Hiroshima mon amour; Ibuse, Masuji: *Black Rain*; Ōe Kenzaburō: *Hiroshima Notes*; Vizenor, Gerald: *Hiroshima Bugi*
Hiroshima Bugi: Atomu 57, see Vizenor, Gerald

Index

Hiroshima mon amour (1959) 145, 162, *163*
Hiroshima Notes, see Ōe Kenzaburō
Hive, The, see Scholes Young, Melissa
holocaust, *see* apocalypse: oppression and genocide; genocide; World War II
Honduras 266–7, *258*
Hopkinson, Nalo 201, 217, 276
    Brown Girl in the Ring 202–3
Howey, Hugh: *Wool* series 289
Hoxha, Enver 91, 92, 94, 121–9, 178–81
Huérfanos, Los, see Carrión, Jorge
Huffman, Doug 42, 46, *43*
Hughes, Langston 195
Hugo, Victor: *Les Misérables* 266
Hull, Charlie 36, 39, *37*
Hunger Games, The 44, 129, 199, 200
Hurley, Jessica 194–5, *196*
Husien, Thaer: *Beside the Sickle Moon* 247–8

I Am Legend (2007) xix, 197, *xx*
Ibuse, Masuji: *Black Rain* 85
Iceland 91
imaginaries, *see* border imaginary; bunker fantasy; tunnel: imaginary; wall: imaginary
India 12–14, 94, 148–51, 159, 277, 278, *13, 149*
Indigenous Peoples
    belief systems of 209, 221–2, 249–51, 261
    as creators 5–6, 51, 63, 83–9, 153, 193
    effects of nuclear age on 86–7, 143, 152–5, 221–2, 274–5
    in fiction 86–7, 153–5, 214–17, 251, 276
    genocide of 5–6, 7, 130
    land rights of 221–2, 249–51, 287
    see also names of Nations, Pueblos, and Tribes
inequity
    economic 82, 133–5, 204–5, 276
    of effects of climate crisis 274–5
    of effects of nuclear testing 154, 274–5

racial 48, 63, 81–2, 150–1, 194–5, 201, 205, 212
sexual 67, 74–6, 78, 81, 212
shelter 4–5, 35–6, 52, 198–201, 276
survival 16, 131–3, 140, 224–5, 282
see also prepping: privilege and; whiteness: privilege and
infrastructure
    civil defense 122, 125, 130
    conversion of 129, 180–1; *see also* shelter: adaptive reuse of
    post–Cold War 223, 275, 279, 284
    subterranean 101, 104, 138, 232, 272; *see also* underground
    tourism 160, 164, 177, 189
Ing, Dean: *Pulling Through* 29
Innocent, The, see McEwan, Ian
Into Eternity (2010) 219–20, *220*
Into the Forest, see Hegland, Joan
IQ84, see Murakami, Haruki
Iraq 85, 150, 205, 222
Iran 139, 205
Israel 94, 107–8, 130, 235–48, 256, 257, 284, *245, 247*
Isto, Raino 180–2

Jackson, Shirley: 'The Lottery' 59
Jameson, Fredric 9, 201
Japan 15, 51, 83, 86, 95–6, 140–5, 159; *see also* Fukushima Daiichi; Hiroshima
Jones, Holly Goddard: *The Salt Line* 282–3
JR 185–6, 268–70, *186, 268, 269*
Juan de los Muertos (2010) 197

Kadaré, Ismail 180
    The Pyramid 126
    Spring Flowers, Spring Frost 128
Kahl, Gordon 40–1
Kahn, Lloyd: *Shelter* 26–7, *33*
Kansas 42, 50, 288
Kazakhstan 36, 86, 155
Kearny, Cresson: *Nuclear War Survival Skills* 25, 29–33, *32*
Kelly, Walt: *We Have Met the Enemy and He Is Us* 290–1
Kelvedon Hatch 159, *160*

Index

Kennedy, John F. 24, 45, 53, 74, 76, 158
  Kennedy era 19, 34, 65, 67, 69, 70
Kindred, *see* Butler, Octavia
Kinmen Bombs (1986) 95–6
Kinmen Islands 94–101, 107, 159–61, 168–73, 181, 182, 185, *95, 96, 98, 99, 169, 170, 171*
Kirk, Andrew 26, 29, 154
Klein, Naomi 132
Knebel, Fletcher: *Crossing in Berlin* 226–7
Kolonel Bunker (1996) 126–8, 180–1, *127*
Kosovo War 121–1
Koudelka, Josef 246–7, *236, 247*
Kramer, Stanley, *see On the Beach*
Krasinski, John, *see A Quiet Place*
Kubrick, Stanley, *see Dr Strangelove*

Laguna Pueblo 85
Lanchester, John: *The Wall* 226, 229
Lang, Fritz, *see Metropolis*
Last Woman, The, *see* Druga, Jacqueline
Las Vegas, *see* Nevada
Latin American people 9, 196, 277; *see also* Cuban Missile Crisis; names of countries
Latino/a/x people 81, 254
Latour, Bruno 292
Lawrence, Francis, *see I Am Legend*
Laxness, Halldór: *The Atom Station* 91
Le Guin, Ursula K. 135
Lepucki, Edan: *California* 281–2
Levi, Primo 145
Levine, Caroline 8–9
Lewis, Sean, *see Coyotes*
Lim, Anna 142–3
Long Voyage Back, The, see Rhinehart, Luke
Lost Children Archive, *see* Luiselli, Valeria
'Lottery, The', *see* Jackson, Shirley
Lovay, Jean-Marc 109, 113n.59, 114
Love Story of Kinmen Island (1986) 95–6
Luiselli, Valeria 257
  Lost Children Archive 258–9

Macdonald, Andrew, *see* Pierce, William Luther
Macfarlane, Robert 10, 138; *see also* occulting
Machine Dreams, *see* Phillips, Jayne Anne
Madsen, Michael, *see Into Eternity*
Mandel, Emily St. John: *Station Eleven* 281
Man in the Holocene, *see* Frisch, Max
Marshall Islands 143; *see also* Bikini Atoll; Enewetak Atoll
Martín, Marcos, *see Barrier; Private Eye, The*
masculinity 24–5, 37–8, 44, 50–65, 74–6, 78–9, 207; *see also* gender
Matinee (1993) 59, 65, 71–2, *71*
Matrix trilogy (1999–2003) 129, 199, 200, 218, 289
Matsu archipelago 94–5, 97, 101–1, 107, 159, 168–9, 172–3, 185, *171*
Matsuo, Akinori, *see Love Story of Kinmen Island*
Mbembe, Achille 227
McCarthy, Cormac: *The Road* xx, 191–3
McEwan, Ian: *The Innocent* 232
McGirk, James 27
McKittrick, Katherine 17, 201, 211, 273
McPhee, John: *La Place de la Concorde Suisse* 105, 117–20, 131
Metropolis (1926) 289
Mexico 234, 237, 248–72, 284, *249, 254, 255, 268, 269, 271, 272*
  Nogales 232, 261–2, 265–6, *250*
Miéville, China: *The City & the City* 243
migration
  affordances of migration story 267
  anti-immigration measures xxi, 226, 229, 249, 253–6, 266–7, 276
  cultural traditions of 251
  fictional representations of 258–67, 270–2, 277, *258, 263, 271, 272*
  personal dangers of 217, 252–3, 256–9, 261

Index

reasons for 149–50, 251, 253, 257
support for immigrants 248,
268–70, 277, *250*
Miller, Walter M.: *Canticle for
Leibowitz* 211
Misérables, Les, see Hugo, Victor
misplaced ideas **9**, **14**, 17–18, 130,
133, 135, 227, 276, *Plate 10*
spatial 139–51, 200
temporal xxi, 3, 151–9
Montana 39, 288, *37*
Mooney, Stephen, *see Dead Hand, The*
Morgan, J. M.: Eden trilogy 200, 281
Morrow, James: *This Is the Way the
World Ends* 23
Mother Earth News 25, 30
movies
adaptations 199, 200, 234, *192*
audience responses to 15–16, 67–8
critical responses to 59, 70, 80
Disney 185
documentary 41, 88, 95, 99–100,
162n.82, 177–8, 185, 220,
186, 220
horror xxi, 58–60, 63, 81, 115, 288
monster 70–2, 81
postapocalyptic xix, 44, 63, 197,
199, 288, *xx*
zombie 196–7
see also titles of films
Murakami, Haruki: *IQ84* 15–16
music 1, 5, 34, 67, 69, 71, 72–3, 75–6,
90, 127–8, 146, 155, 189,
228, 273
Mydyti, Gyler 177, 181
Myers, Edward 47–8, *56*

National Geographic Channel 25, 42,
43, 60, *43, 45*
nature
in Christianity 13
return of 165, 275, 283–7, *167,
284*
survivalism and 37–9, 115, 138,
148
see also apocalypse: ecological;
biosecurity; cave; climate
crisis; Great Green Wall; ruins,
Cold War; seed banks; wall:
sea

Nava, Gregory, *see Norte, El*
neoliberalism 3, 20, 52, 135, 180–1,
200–1, 253
affordances of 181
Netflix 59n.28, *13, 67, 68, 149*
Nevada 71, 74; *see also* Nevada Test
Site; Yucca Mountain
Nevada Test Site 152–3, 155, 159,
160, 182, 185, 283, *153*
Newitz, Annalee 83, 217, 219
Newman, Kim 65
New York xix, 5, 35, 66, 82, 190,
195, 197, 215, 259, 274, 277,
xx
New Zealand 275, 280, 285–7, *286,
Plates 12–14*
Nichols, Jeff, *see Take Shelter*
Niddam, Igaal, *see Troisième Cri, Le*
Night of the Living Dead (1968) xxi,
81, 193
Nine Inch Nails: 'Survivalism' 34
Niu, Doze, *see Paradise in Service*
Norte, El (1983) 264
North Korea 104, 134, 139, 141,
283–4
Nuclear Age, The, see O'Brien, Tim
nuclear apocalypse, *see* apocalypse:
nuclear
nuclear colonialism 86–7, 153, 222,
274–5
nuclear disarmament, *see* antinuclear
protest
nuclear reactors 142; *see also*
Chornobyl; Fukushima
Daiichi
nuclear testing 139, 152, 154–5, 274;
see also Nevada Test Site
nuclear tourism, *see* tourism: nuclear
Nuclear War Survival Skills, see
Kearny, Cresson
nuclear waste 86, 138, 219–23, *220*
nuclear weapons
in fiction 35, 86, 91, 211, 279
in history xxi, 7, 94, 99, 116, 144,
158
missile silos 2, 10, 42, 45–7, 50,
116, 125, 288–9
see also Cuban Missile Crisis;
Hiroshima
Nusseibeh, Sari 247

318 *Index*

Oak Ridge, Tennessee 25, 29–31
O'Brien, Keith 34–5
O'Brien, Tim: *The Nuclear Age* 51, 52, 54–7
occulting **10–12**, 19, 259, 272
O'Connell, Mark 36, 45, 46, 164–7, 218, 290–1
Ōe Kenzaburō: *Hiroshima Notes* 143–6
Okorafor, Nnedi 201, 203, 217, 276
  Who Fears Death 208–9
Olan, Susan Torian: *The Earth Remembers* 214–16, 217, 261
On Earth We're Briefly Gorgeous, see Vuong, Ocean
On the Beach (1959) 4, 15, 16
ontology *see* bunker: ontological; open ontology
open ontology **10–11**, 17
Ord, Toby 218–19
Osnos, Evan 35, 46, 47
Ozeki, Ruth: *A Tale for the Time Being* 14
Ozorak, Paul 102n.30, 104

Palestine 108, 130–1, 235–48, 284; *see also* Gaza tunnel; West Bank Wall
pandemic, COVID-19 xxi, 7, 47, 48, 165, 253, 280; *see also* apocalypse: pandemic
Pan Lei, *see Love Story of Kinmen Island*
Parable of the Sower, see Butler, Octavia
Parable of the Talents, see Butler, Octavia
Paradise in Service (2014) 97, 170, *98*
Parasite (2019) 133–6, 202, *134*
Parfit, Derek 218–19
Patternist series, *see* Butler, Octavia
Peele, Jordan, *see Get Out*
Phillips, Jayne Anne: *Machine Dreams* 54
Pierce, William Luther: *The Turner Diaries* 31, 35, 40
Pink Floyd 224, 228
Pires, Roberto, *see Abrigo Nuclear*
Place de la Concorde Suisse, La, see McPhee, John

Planet of the Apes movies (1968–73) 199, 210–11, 215, *215*
Post, Ted, *see Beneath the Planet of the Apes*
postapocalyptic fiction xix, 5–6, 191–223, 253, 275–6
  affordances of 129, 147–8, 199, 202, 275, 283
  zombie 191–8
  see also Afrofuturism; deep-time speculation: in fiction; science fiction/fantasy
postmodernist fiction 51, 83–5, 87, 88
Powers, Thomas 158
prepping **34–5**
  consumerism and 33, 35–7, 39, 42–9
  mainstreaming of 24, 29, 34–5, 47–8, 142
  in popular culture 42–7, 52, 60–2, 78–9, 191–2, *43*, *45*, *57*
  privilege and 23, 35–6, 42, 50, 60, 63, 78–9, 132, 275
  see also survivalism
Prisoners (2013) 78
Private Eye, The (2013–15) 278–9, Plates 15 & 16
Ptacin, Mira 47, 63
Pulling Through, see Ing, Dean
Purge, The (2013) 52, 54, 59–60, 63, 64
Pynchon, Thomas: *Bleeding Edge* 189–90
Pyramid, The, see Kadaré, Ismail
Pyun, Albert, *see Radioactive Dreams*

Queen of Springtime, The, see Silverberg, Robert
Quiet Place, A (2018) 52, 63–5, 288

racism, *see* Black people; Indigenous Peoples; inequity: racial; Latina/o/x people; white nationalism; whiteness
Radioactive Dreams (1985) 51, 65, 70–1
'Radioactive Dreams' (song), *see* Sue Saad and the Next
Rama, Edi 178, 180–3
Ready Player One, see Cline, Ernest

Ready Player One (film, 2018) 199, 200
Reagan, Ronald 66, 67, 70, 73, 204
Reed, Carol, *see Third Man, The*
Resnais, Alain, *see Hiroshima mon amour*
Rhinehart, Luke: *The Long Voyage Back* 22
Richter, Roland Suso, *see Tunnel, Der*
River, The, see Springsteen, Bruce
Rivera, Alex, *see Sleep Dealer*
Road, The, see McCarthy, Cormac
Road, The (film, 2009) *192*
Roanhorse, Rebecca 5
Rock around the Bunker, see Gainsbourg, Serge
Romero, George, *see Day of the Dead*; *Night of the Living Dead*
Room (2015) 66, 79–81, 82, 88
Rose, Kenneth 103–4
Ross, Caroline 39
Ross, Matt, *see Captain Fantastic*
Ross, Richard 36, 120n.77, 187, *37*, *108*, *187*
ruins, Cold War
  fictional 85–9, 211, 215
  tourism 7, 83–5, 131, 137, 159–90, *84*, *163*, *171*, *173*, *174*
  see also shelter: adaptive reuse of
Russia 7, 90, 103–4, 139, 140, 275, *187*; *see also* Soviet Union
Ruthven, Malise 270

Sacco, Joe 238, *239*
Sacred Games, see Chandra, Vikram
Sacred Games (TV series, 2019) *13*, *149*
Saint-Amour, Paul 11
Salt Line, The, see Jones, Holly Goddard
Sanders, William: *The Ballad of Billy Badass and the Rose of Turkestan* 85–6, 154–5
Saxon, Kurt 25, 30, 34, 41, 44, 52
Scarry, Elaine 131–3, 140, 142, 175, 224
Scholes Young, Melissa: *The Hive* 48
Schwarz, Roberto 9, 14
science fiction/fantasy (SFF)
  affordances of 154, 205, 207, 210–17, 292

Black 5–6, 201, 206, 217; *see also* Afrofuturism
Canadian 14, 201–3, 217, 276
dystopian 3, 6, 63, 198–203
English 15, 88, 182, 275, 278
feminist 6, 27
future noir 198–203, 253
as genre 280–1, 292–3
from global South 193, 277
Indigenous 5–6, 63, 85–9, 193
Palestinian 247–8
survivalist 23, 24, 29, 52
see also deep-time speculation: in fiction; names of authors; postapocalyptic fiction
Scott, A. O. 220
security
  personal 55, 59, 134, 151
  state 55, 72, 92, 107–9, 121, 131–2, 224–8, 230–1
  see also civil defense; shelter
seed banks 222–3, 275
Shape of Water, The (2017) 66, 73, 81, 82, 88
Shelf Life (1994) 65, 76–8, *77*, *78*
shelter
  adaptive reuse of 76, 121, 124, 129–30, 135–6, 159–82, *76*, *169*, *173*, *174*, *184*, *187*, *Plates 4–7*, *9*, *11*
  backyard 5, 45, 57, 60, 67, 123, *32*, *57*, *61*, *62*, *69*
  basement 50, 52–4, 69, 71, 133–6, 141–2, 183, *70*, *72*, *74*, *108*, *184*, *192*
  city as 149–50
  collective 91, 93–4, 102, 104, 131, 139–40
  government super- 23, 102–4, 106, 120, 179, 184, 193
  group 36, 39–40, 45–6, 147, *37*
  home as 47–8, 58
  military 104–5
  open-air 20, 27, 50
  private super- 12–13, 23, 35–6, 42–3, 46–7, 74–5, 78–9, 190
  rejection of 195–7
  right to 129–36, 140, 142, 224, 253, 276
  society 109, 225, 273

violence in 54, 69, 79–81
see also bunker; cave; civil defense; dome; enclave; tunnel
Shelter (1973), *see* Kahn, Lloyd
Shelter (1986), *see* Asher, Marty
Shute, Nevil: *On the Beach* 4
Sicario (2015) 265, 267
Signs Preceding the End of the World, *see* Herrera, Yuri
Silence of the Lambs, The (1991) 75, 78
Silko, Leslie Marmon
   Almanac of the Dead 153, 251
   Ceremony 85–8, 153
silo 273–4, 287–93
   missile 2, 10, 42, 45–7, 50, 116, 125, 288–9
Silverberg, Robert
   At Winter's End 216–17
   The Queen of Springtime 216–17
Sin Nombre (2009) 257, 267, *258*
Sleep Dealer (2008) 270–2, *271, 272*
Soleri, Paolo 27, 29
Solzhenitsyn, Aleksandr 231
South Africa 78–9, 199, 200, 202
South Dakota 47, 48
South Korea 94, 133–5, 142, 283–4, *134, 284*
Soviet Union 14, 31, 101–3, 122, 125, 183, 232–3, *156, 157*; *see also* Chornobyl; Russia; Ukraine
Spielberg, Stephen, *see Ready Player One*
Spring Flowers, Spring Frost, see Kadaré, Ismail
Springsteen, Bruce: *The River* 5
Star Trek 59
Station Eleven, see Mandel, Emily St. John
Stefa, Elian 177, 181
Sting: 'Russians' 90
Strasser, Todd: *Fallout* 52–4
Sudan 209, 279
Sue Saad and the Next 71, 155
survival
   Cold War 22, 104, 111, 145
   equality of 131–2, 224–5
   post–Cold War 6, 23, 142, 145–6, 218–19, 237–8

survivalism **34–5**
   Cold War 22–36, 40–1, 191
   in popular culture 50–89, 103, 194, 203–8, 212–13, 216–17, 281–3
   post–Cold War 6–7, 22, 35–40, 42–9, 151, 275
   see also prepping
'Survivalism', *see* Nine Inch Nails
Survivalist series, *The, see* Ahern, Jerry
'Survival Mom' 47, 63
survivance **51**, 83–9, 146, 167, 217
Survivor, The (newsletter) 25, 30; *see also* Saxon, Kurt
Survivor, The (TV series) 44
Sweden 44, 93, 104, 139, 143, 188
Sweterlitsch, Tom: *The Gone World* 280
Switzerland 20, 91–3, 104–21, 125, 130–3, 139, 140, 142–3, 159, 168, 172–5, 285, *183, 107, 108, 118, 119, 173, 174*
Swoon 244–6

Taiwan *see* Kinmen Islands; Matsu archipelago
Take Shelter (2011) 51, 52, 54, 57–8, 150, *57*
Tale for the Time Being, A, see Ozeki, Ruth
Taylor, Lawrence 261–2, 266
technology
   Cold War 29n.26, 90, 103, 120, 152, 176, 189, 227
   post–Cold War 256
   speculative 115, 202, 209, 214–15, 217, 278–80, 289
television
   adaptations 88, *13, 149*
   news 265
   reality 42–7, 50, 60, *43, 45*
   TV movies 40, 43–4
   see also names of broadcasters and titles of shows
10 Cloverfield Lane (2016) 52, 60–2, 150, *61, 62*
'Terminal Beach, The', *see* Ballard, J. G.
Texas 250, 253–4, *254*; *see also* US–Mexico border

Third Man, The (1949) 232
This Is the Way the World Ends, see
    Morrow, James
Tohono O'odham Nation 249–51,
    255
tourism 117, 129, 283
    dark 224, 235, 237, *Plate 7*
    nuclear 7, 83–5, 92, 100, 131,
        159–90, 193, *84, 163, 171,
        173, 174*
Trachtenberg, Dan, *see 10 Cloverfield
    Lane*
Troisième Cri, Le (1974) 113–14
Trump, Donald xxi, 48, 139, 255–6,
    267, 270, 284
Tsing, Anna Lowenhaupt 252, 253,
    266
tunnel
    affordances of 231–3, 238, 240,
        242–3, 264, 267
    escape 233–4
    espionage 232–3
    imaginary 232–4, 237, 240–2, 264,
        267, 272
    in popular culture 233–4, 265
    smuggling 237–41, 261–2, 265,
        266, *242*
    use for resistance and subversion
        238, 240, 266–7, 272
    see also Gaza tunnel; Mexico:
        Nogales
Tunnel, Der (2001) 227, 230, *231*
Turner Diaries, The, see Pierce,
    William Luther
Turtle Mountain Band of Chippewa
    Indians 63
Twilight Zone: 'The Shelter' (1961) 52,
    59, 65

UK 43, 185, 226, 229, 232, 274, 286;
    see also Kelvedon Hatch
Ukraine xxi, 7, 140, 142, 188, 275;
    see also Chornobyl
Unbreakable Kimmy Schmidt (2015–
    19) xx, 51, 66–7, 73, 76, 81,
    82–3, 88, *67, 68*
underground
    hospital 168, *169*
    living 135, 147, 213
    metaphorics 242

military base 104, 122, 125; *see
    also* shelter: government super-
    railway 104, 190, 207
    storage 220–3, 288–9
    see also bunker; shelter; tunnel
Underground Railroad, The, see
    Whitehead, Colson
Underworld, see DeLillo, Don
US–Mexico border 248–72, *249,
    250, 254, 255, 268, 269,
    272*
USSR, *see* Soviet Union
utopianism
    affordances of 292–3
    art 268
    dome 27, 88, 226, 273, 287
    fictional 36, 134, 195–8, 281–2
    survivalism 31–3, 36, 110, 129–30,
        133, 195–6
    techno- 152, 217
    see also bunker: as utopian space;
        enclave: utopian

Vampyr (1932) 288
van Gerven Oei, Vincent W. J. 180–2
Varda, Agnès 185–6, *186*
Vaughan, Brian K., *see Barrier; Private
    Eye, The*
Vault of the Ages, see Anderson, Poul
Vicente, Muntsa, *see Barrier; Private
    Eye, The*
Vienna 232, 265
Vietnam 97, 107–8, 137, 148, 150,
    168, 219, 238
Villalobos, Ramon, *see Border Town*
Villeneuve, Denis, *see Prisoners;
    Sicario*
visual arts 128, 170–2, 179–87, 237,
    246–7, 248, 280, *186, Plates
    1–14*
    affordances of 268, 272
Vizenor, Gerald: *Hiroshima Bugi:
    Atomu 57* 51, 83–5, 86, 88,
    162n.82, 217
Vuong, Ocean 219
    On Earth We're Briefly Gorgeous
        148, 150–1

Wachowski Sisters, *see Matrix* trilogy
Waiting for War, see Delarue, Claude

322 *Index*

wall
affordances of 224–6, 231, 237, 243, 252–3, 267, 281
crossing 230, 248–9
friction 252–3
imaginary 230, 234, 249, 267–8, 272
in literature 225–6, 227, 229, 278–9, 281
Mauer im Kopf 257, 270
sea 274–5, 279
separation 224–30, 235, 243–4, 274
subverting of 266–70, 272, 287
see also Berlin Wall; US–Mexico border; West Bank Wall
Wall, The, see Lanchester, John
Wanderers, see Wendig, Chuck
Wang, Ting-chi 172
Wang Wen-Chih 172
We Have Met the Enemy and He Is Us, see Kelly, Walt
Weir, Peter, *see Witness*
Weizman, Eyal 238, 240, 243
Wendig, Chuck: *Wanderers* 50
West Bank Wall 226, 234–7, 240, 242–8, 253, 256, 268, 277, 284, *236, 244, 245, 247*
Whitehead, Colson
The Underground Railroad 190
Zone One 195–7
white nationalism 22–4, 35, 40–1, 50

whiteness 201
privilege and 4–5, 59–60, 62–3, 81–2, 214; *see also* inequity: racial
survivalism and 51–2, 65n.34, 66, 75–6, 89, 195, 207
Who Fears Death, see Okorafor, Nnedi
Whole Earth Catalog, see Brand, Stewart
Williams, Rosalind 200
Wilson, Hugh, *see Blast from the Past*
Witness (1985) 288
Wong, Lily 18, 288
World War II 1, 21, 105–6, 109, 111–13, 130, 137, 145, 185, 234
World War Z, see Brooks, Max

Xenogenesis trilogy, *see* Butler, Octavia

YA fiction 39, 52–4, 264
Yaqui Indian people 251
Yarsky, Caitlin, *see Coyotes*
Yucca Flat, *see* Nevada Test Site
Yucca Mountain 220–2

Zak, Dan 142
Zengali, Josef 122, 126
Zero K, see DeLillo, Don
Žižek, Slavoj 10, 123, 238, 240–1
zombies xxi, 60, 191–8, 253
Zone One, see Whitehead, Colson

EU authorised representative for GPSR:
Easy Access System Europe, Mustamäe tee 50,
10621 Tallinn, Estonia
gpsr.requests@easproject.com

www.ingramcontent.com/pod-product-compliance
Lightning Source LLC
LaVergne TN
LVHW062117190525
811683LV00009B/143